345,7302523
Arm

W9-AHF-595

Improper Submission

Records of a Wrongful Conviction

Erma Armstrong

Tanglewood Hill Press
PMB 410
170 W. Ellendale Suite 103
Dallas, OR 97338

ELMHURST PUBLIC LIBRARY
125 S. Prospect Avenue
Elmhurst, IL 60126-3298

Tanglewood Hill Press, Dallas, OR 97338
Copyright 2005 by Tanglewood Hill Press
All rights reserved. Published August 2005
Printed in the United States of America

14 13 12 11 10 09 08 07 06 05   5 4 3 2 1

Library of Congress Catalog Card Number: 2005926693

Publishers Cataloguing-In-Publication Data
(Prepared by The Donohue Group, Inc.)

Armstrong, Erma, 1929-
    Improper submission: records of a wrongful conviction/
            by Erma Armstrong.

    p.; com.
ISBN: 0-9654818-6-7

1. Eklof, Karlyn--Trials, litigation, etc. 2. Trials (Murder)
3. Criminal justice, Admistration of--United States, 4. Ritual abuse
    victims, I. Title.

KF224, E45 A76 2005
    345.75   2005926693

    381 pages

Cover design: Bruce DeRoos

Civil courage can grow only
out of the free responsibility
of free men.

— DIETRICH BONHOEFFER

CONTENTS

PART TWO

Preface

A killer, Jeffrey Tiner, was brought to justice in the year 2000 and given the death sentence, seven years after his senseless murder in Springfield, Oregon of an innocent man, James Salmu, who had given shelter to his new girlfriend and her children.

When this young woman, Karlyn Eklof, was finally free of his surveillance and subsequent ritual abuse and had come forward to testify, the prosecution twisted her eye witness account through coercion and a disregard of her basic rights, forcing her to enact portions of the killer's bragging following the murder. Because she would not plea bargain, they suborned witnesses to support the coerced testimony and released to the press and jury statements that misinterpreted forensic evidence that would have exonerated her. The defense acquiesced without access to that evidence, and the jury gave her all eight counts due the killer. She was held subject to possible capital punishment and sentenced to two life terms, since the killer, incarcerated in Nevada for other crimes, was not yet available for prosecution.

Here is the paper trail of that wrongful conviction. All that was covered up and withheld, which was subsequently considered unavailable in her appeals, is here for you, the reader, so you may be the judge. The *federal habeas corpus* will soon make its decision. What is yours?

—ERMA ARMSTRONG

Acknowledgments

I wish to acknowledge and thank the many who have assisted me and reacted to my writing of this book over the past eight years. First of all, I thank Cleta Brooks Lee for introducing me to Karlyn and asking me to type her story for a journal writing class. Primary credit is due, however, to Nancy (Paya) Gottfried, who called me and got me involved in Karlyn's case and eventually turned over all her journals, documents and research, with Karlyn's comments as she dealt with her lawyers. Without Paya's passion for Karlyn's innocence this book would never have been written.

I want to thank those who read my manuscript and assisted in its editing, esp. Elizabeth Lyons and Rae Alderman, and for their encouragement. I am also grateful to Pam Porter and Peggy Gasdorf, Karlyn's mother, for their reading and reactions to an earlier version of the book, which resulted in massive changes and many insights.

I want to thank an unknown person who was closely associated with Tiner's defense for forwarding discoveries that would exonerate her, along with supporting documents unknown to Karlyn's lawyers, to my attorney of inquiry which were inadvertently passed on to me. I also want to thank Mr. Tony Bornstein of the Federal Public Defenders office for receiving those discoveries and documents from me and beginning her *habeas corpus* defense.

Lastly, I want to thank Karlyn for her continuing help and encouragement in producing this book. Without her remarkable journals, comments on the documentation which Paya collected, and continuing input about her ongoing struggle for freedom, it would never have been possible.

PART ONE

Prologue: An Unlikely Trio

Deboarding a plane at the San Diego airport was an unlikely trio, a quick-moving girl in fringed black leather jacket, levis and black boots; her tall somewhat handsome companion likewise in western clothes; and a shorter, roughly dressed escort, a few steps ahead leading the way. Her laughter and excitement, her carry-on bag somewhat mixed up in her flying brown hair, registered with passersby as they made their way up the ramp from the plane and proceeded past the various arrival gates.

Potato, as their guide was called, seemed to know where he was going, and his eyes searched ahead for a certain bar. There would be a ride, he'd told them, but they didn't know what his connections were.

Karlyn was just glad to be in familiar territory and looked forward to seeing her mother and grandmother at some time during the few days frolic she and Dennis had planned. Maybe they'd get married. She sure liked her ring and the new clothes and the money Dennis wanted to spend on her

Potato's friends would probably be a good place to start. He was from San Diego too, but they had only met up in Springfield, Oregon where they'd both been living. It was nice of Dennis to include him in their spree, since he'd just received a disability settlement from a job injury.

Karlyn was usually ready for anything, but they were stopped at the bar by the cool gaze of a slight man resting against a high stool. There was no greeting of old friends, just a mesmerizing stare which drained her. She felt like a piece of merchandize as this stranger appraised her, turning to greet Potato just in time to avoid being completely rude. Then he was all smooth, welcoming them. "Good trip?" he asked. She guessed he was maybe okay.

"Karlyn Eklof, Dennis Heide: Willy Beard." He shook their hands and led the way. His arms were strong, his hair was tied with a string, and it hung down his back. He looked like he had just interrupted some work. Actually, Karlyn liked the way he moved and decided that he was no personal threat to her. He might even be someone she could count on.

They waited for their baggage and made their way to Willy's flashy car. No questions. Potato seemed to anticipate familiar surroundings. No need to part company. Better to be with friends than on their own. Dennis seemed more excited than she was. She sensed he was glad not to have to make decisions in a strange place so far from Oregon.

She knew some of the routes where they were going but not this area by the sea. God, it was really good to be back and smell that salty, burning air. The sounds, the attitudes! What fun to drive up to this hillside house in a cul-de-sac, share the parking drive with various vehicles, and be greeted by—this was—his wife, so nice they couldn't be more suburban. It was sort of a relief. There was another couple there, too, and before long they were just milling around, sharing drinks and small talk, and the guys it seemed were working on some bikes and car motors. Willy was a mechanic.

Karlyn was happy to be there. It had been a long flight. But Dennis, she wished he'd just sit down. She hadn't noticed on the trip—she sat by herself—that he and Potato hit it off so well. Now Dennis wanted to go with him to a topless bar, like that's a big thing, like it's something he should do without her. Ye Gods, how can I marry a guy like that, she thought.

Suddenly she forgot about Dennis. There he was, one she thought she'd never seen before, as though emerging out of a keyhole. But Jethro's eyes were there burning a hole in her. She already knew what they meant, that first glance. There was no way of taking her eyes away, of looking elsewhere. He offered her a drink, a fresh glass. She took a sip. She caught her breath.

She was embarrassed because she couldn't think of the usual things you say to a stranger. She didn't remember getting acquainted with him. But there was no leaving his eyes. His words were there, they talked. But they didn't need to. His eyes were saying things she couldn't deny. She thought perhaps they'd go away again, and she didn't like him very much.

But they didn't. As she sat talking she wondered why she couldn't exert her will. She knew how to handle herself in these kinds of situations. She didn't really want this, but she couldn't look away.

She was still talking, but then she thought she might be mumbling. He didn't seem to notice. His hand caught the back of her neck and he rocked her gently. She was so tired. It would be rather embarrassing to have to excuse herself for a nap… She forgot about everything…

It was a long time later that she found herself waking up. Had she passed out? She was embarrassed. Someone was joking with her, taunting her. But it was soothing. It was Jethro. He said, "Are you still doing that kooky cockroach lay?" leaning over and smiling.

Chap I: The Citadel

I t appears as a citadel, not high, nor remote, but wide, solid and sprawling, filling the space of a city block above a series of cascading steps and planted areas up from the sidewalks which encircle it. The three-story courthouse in Eugene, Oregon is sheathed in dark glass separated by structural elements and shrubbery and prefaced by a single-story entrance hall facing the south where visitors pass through a screening gate and are questioned before ascending wide steps leading up to the hallowed halls of justice. The hall also has an information desk and steps to the right leading down to a wide deep hall going north, which opens onto a cafeteria, a records department, evidence depositories, and various conference rooms and bureaus relating to the criminal justice system. Somewhere is an underground garage where an investigator or police officer might grandly arrive with an alleged criminal in tow.

Above the wide steps in the main structure is an island of desks where inquiries may be made of the court agenda and the time and location of each case being heard. Glass windows separate the public from the respondents. Respect for the law and for those who are assigned to enforce it are assumed everywhere. If there is any question in your mind that justice is being served, a tone of voice, not unlike that used for visitors to the country jail several blocks away, will remind you of that fact.

Here even your questions are suspect. If you should pose any during breaks to the officers who are orchestrating a trial in the court procedures, forget about a straight answer. You may know a case thoroughly, but they assume you don't and their responses are designed to mislead you and frighten you away.

Even the juries are misled. They learn that a judge's instructions to them may not hold, if he himself decides to make an exception. What was supposed to be an impartial court does not feel that way. And they are coerced into accepting a prosecution's statements that seem to be already prejudiced and hearsay "confessions" of the defendant no sane person would make. But there are pressures on them to accept these things—the defense attorney apparently does— as the fastest way of getting things done.

Perhaps I'm ahead of my story. It might be true that justice is being served for those whose resources compare with those available to the prosecution. But I'm speaking of a large majority of those being served who are indigent, and they don't stand a chance against the system once a case is brought against them. If they failed to accept a plea bargain in lieu of a plea of innocence, their alleged guilt is magnified with every means of treachery available.

Don't take my word for it, however. You will decide, after I take you through a sample case I know so thoroughly: that of Karlyn Eklof, now serving two life sentences for a crime she did not commit.

Oh, you know about her already? You already know she and her lover stabbed someone here in Springfield and threw his body on some rocks up the McKenzie? The one found by mushroom pickers a year-and-a-half later. Read on. Unless you know everything.

Meanwhile, consider that here is a citadel of justice, which has dealt with the laws of the constitution, its amendments and their application in a series of test cases over time, and has developed rules as a result of their outcome which are supposed to safeguard the rights of all, including those who are unable to pay for their own defense. There it sits, a reminder to the people that in this most democratic, most enlightened country in the world, where freedom triumphs over the evils of tyranny and oppression all around the world, justice is being served. It is there as an absolute guarantee of the full protection of human rights of its citizens under the laws of the land.

Don't be fooled. And don't be turned away, because the writer seems to be claiming things that you never dreamed could happen—who never expected to be involved in the intricacies of the prosecution of an alleged crime and who, until now, always supposed that the courts, the judges, and the criminal prosecution teams operated fairly, justly, and did not manufacture cases out of overdiligence to solve crimes.

Haven't you heard of public safety? The training of officers of the law is even called by that name, Public Safety Standards and Training academies. So how could any institute designed to ensure the public safety of the citizens fail to ensure their civil rights? Surely they would not do so by employing illegal means.

****

The "citadel" sits at the north of the grid of streets comprising the downtown area of Eugene, not far beneath Skinner's Butte, where the Willamette River edges the city. South of the citadel and to the west under giant firs is a small city park where the Saturday Market is held, which occasionally displays the wares of a subculture that has flourished in this university area since the 60s, in contrast to the more hightech culture just north of it. Beads, feathers, macrame, and soft metals predominate in the hand-wrought bracelets and earrings displayed in the booths. Also available are exotic foods, textile imports, paintings and pottery, perhaps with some distant connection to the art departments of the University of Oregon and Lane Community College. The sellers, however, in their prescribed denims, sandals, head scarves, and their own jewelry seem more closely identified with the fallout communities that perpetually inhabit the established camps for the homeless along the banks of the Willamette and McKenzie rivers, which converge and separate the communities of Eugene and Springfield.

What began as a beat culture, celebrated for its association with an unpopular war, has in many cases become submerged in drug addiction. Not far from the market are the downtown malls established to enhance and perpetuate certain kinds of homegrown businesses, not greatly removed from the booths at the market and attracting many of the same crowds. To wander, to lunch, or to browse there, if one is past a certain age, leads one in memory back to the 60s when the New World Coffee Shop on campus and Farrell's Ice Cream Shoppe on Patterson were the latest thing in terms of camp and Victorian nostalgia. Only now that culture seems passe again.

The market and downtown area to the south of the courthouse are like a dirty sandal to the area north, which includes the Hilton Hotel, rising above the citadel and viewing from its upper floors the Butte against the distant rises of the Coast Range, the most prominent of which is Mary's Peak. To the west of the Hilton is the Hult Center for the Performing Arts, a beautiful building with rising tent-like contours, its own conference center and various parking structures to accommodate the crowds. To the north of these are a number of upscale restaurants housed in incongruous settings of old mercantile and warehouse buildings. The past is not a part of these establishments, however. They may be housed in its remnants, but the mindset breathes of the arty, the hightech, and the bureaucracies. There is no nostalgia there.

Lane County Jail sits off to the west of these, better to serve the bureaucracies by being but a short drive to the basement entrances at the north side of the Courthouse. How handy, then, to pick up an indicted prisoner for a surprise polygraph or an arranged plea bargain, the first of which is supposedly not admitted into evidence, but is, and the second, not admitted at all or recorded, unless successful. Both are used as tactics to intimidate the defendant and to avoid an honest effort to look at his true defense, just two of the ways the state's 2% budget for criminal defense of indigent persons is whittled in comparison to the 50% allowed the prosecution.

****

Before the Oregon territory was explored or settled, an independent country came into being through a devastating war with its colonizing country, Great Britain. The Constitution of the United States of America, which our founders devised, though based on European precedence, was thought to be a first in guaranteeing that every man would be considered innocent until proven guilty, with all his rights protected. The previous pattern set in colonial times that led to the Salem witch trials had been based on the British system at that time, where prisoners were tortured in an attempt to gain a confession.

Never again would that be allowed to happen. It was soon determined that there were inadequacies in the Constitution to that end, and the Bill of Rights and other amendments were gradually added. Not until the twentieth century, however, was the problem of the defense of indigents addressed. As we shall see, even though it was addressed in principle, that principle has suffered great deterioration in that the funds for an effective defense have not been assured.

While those amendments were evolving, Eugene was being settled, first by a few immigrants who came over the Oregon Trail to the north and filtered down from the settlements in Oregon City and Salem to a few scattered homesteads. The principal homestead was that of Eugene F. Skinner, who established a cabin just south of Skinner's Butte, south and west of the present city, which was a boon to the straggling travelers who blazed a trail up from the south, expecting to make it an improved access into the area.

It came to be called the Scott-Applegate Trail. Its route departed from the Oregon and the California Trails in present Idaho and again at a point near the Humboldt River in Nevada. From that point it headed for the Oregon country up through Black Rock, down into California, then again into Oregon through the present Ashland and Grant's Pass. The steepest and most precarious part of the journey was in its approach to Eugene, known as Canyon Creek Canyon. Much effort was expended to make it passable, but it was only used for two large migrations, one in 1846, the same year as the Donner party fiasco in California, and the other in 1847.

Crime most associated with the Scott-Applegate migrations, however, was perpetrated by the hostile Indians, who targeted the pioneer's livestock and in one instance a fourteen-year-old girl who was silhouetted against a campfire as she attempted to bake bread over it. Her name was Hannah (Ann) Davis. She suffered an arrow through the calf of her leg and another through her arm and side before she fell into the fire. Removal of the arrows and treatment of her burns were a major trauma for the entire immigrant party. In addition they were beset with the task of carrying her on a makeshift stretcher by several men.

Though partly recovered by the time of the party's arrival in Eugene, she had to be put into a dugout canoe made of a burned out log to take her down the Willamette River to Jason Lee's settlement in Salem for medical treatment. She survived to marry and raise ten children and is buried in Mt. Vernon Cemetery at Eugene. The sacrifices, heroic rescues, and death by the diseases of tuberculosis and smallpox after their exhaustive trek far outweighed any concern for criminal activity for some time. Survival made friendship and mutual aid essential. Eventually the wheels of formal law enforcement became necessary, but there are tales of the populace taking the law in to its own hands in some hangings which took place in Springfield around the beginning of the twentieth century.

Springfield survived the episode but not the aura of being across the river and somewhat removed from the evolving structure of civil control over crime. It was a place to hide out or to blend into the wilderness of the upper McKenzie. If the police or a posse came looking, the residents didn't know anything. They didn't want any trouble, especially for their neighbors.

Interpreting the laws in their own way apparently carried forward after the arms of the law were established there. Who could know that in the next century the City of Springfield would be sued for two million dollars for violating the civil liberties and manufacturing evidence to convict two innocent persons after the guilty person came forward and confessed to the murder at a highway convenience store. That is one case where the police and district attorneys backing them in Eugene didn't get away with their crime, and it is a crime to hide evidence that would prove the innocence of someone convicted. Now there are judges who will not allow some of them in their courtrooms because of their lies and corruption.

Who knows what happened to create such corroboration on the Eugene side? It is not Denmark. It hasn't been rotten to the core, as they say from day one. Respect for law and order must have been earned in some measure by that city as it grew into a many-churched university town, an artistic issue-oriented center of intellectual activity.

Perhaps it has lately suffered an extra dose of corruption to accommodate laws, enacted to guarantee the right to counsel, but with little means to back them up. The *Gideon* and *Miranda* rules of the 60s, which we will review, have succumbed to economic pressures which nearly invalidate them, something which may have affected the whole country. It is frightening to realize that corruption at home, under cover of the law, might seem minor compared to the deterioration of international guarantees of human rights.

It comes as a revelation to me that these much-touted guarantees of equal access to the law were broken, ignored, and brashly explained away as the defendant's own error in this case that I have become familiar with, and those responsible were never charged with this violation of civil rights and their subsequent augmentation of a crime that never existed.

It is one thing to convict a person of a crime when no evidence exists except that which was manufactured by the prosecution. It is another when crimes exist but the punishment is manufactured. We have experienced a "three-strikes rule" as a means to avoid an accurate assessment of the seriousness of a crime. We have a populace so disturbed by the rate of crime that they support legislation to lock up those arrested according to predetermined formulas so that it is unnecessary to go to the expense of hearing their cases. To build and fund more and more prisons to house them, in numbers far exceeding those of any country in the world, in order to save the expense of dealing with their civil rights doesn't make sense.

We make rules to handle any offense, so that we do not have to deal with them on a personal level. We've lost our compassion, our helpfulness, our ability to rehabilitate and forgive. We've lost touch with our own humanity, our ability to imagine that but for our own good fortune the offense might be ours. Worst of all, we have closed our minds to demanding a fair trial for those accused.

****

The two most fundamental attempts to make possible a fair trial for everyone accused, no matter how slim their resources, were enacted by the Supreme Court under Chief Justice Earl Warren at a time when it was solidly liberal and committed to economic and racial justice. These were the *Gideon v. Wainwright* case in 1963, in which it was determined that indigent persons must be represented by counsel at state expense, and the *Miranda v. Arizona* rule three years later in 1967, by which any person must be made aware of his right to a lawyer to best represent his interests.

It seems unthinkable that any fairness could have existed before that time for indigent persons in defending themselves without both the right to counsel and the right not to be made to testify against themselves. As these measures were adopted, they must have greatly restored the hope that inequities which existed, in Eugene and elsewhere, would be addressed.

Unfortunately, that relief was promised, but it has not been fulfilled. While poor defendants are entitled to assistance of counsel at trial, the Supreme Court has failed to demand that the assistance be meaningful and has so diluted *Miranda* that it has had little effect on actual police interrogation practices. The message of *Gideon's Trumpet*, as in Anthony Lewis's book of 1964, which has been a must for students of jurisprudence, has not been heard.

When *Gideon* and *Miranda* were initiated, in the economic boom which followed World War II and enduring until approximately 1968, the gap between the rich and the poor was perhaps at its most favorable for the poor. The precedent for assistance at counsel was such that lawyers were expected to be effective and had not developed the many ways of avoiding that responsibility.

Very soon, however, as the economic gap steadily widened, the discrepancy between what would be done for a rich vs a poor client also widened. That gap increased until in 1989 1% of the population owned 40% of the nation's wealth and 20% owned 80% of it. Then a relatively prosperous decade for the average skilled wage earner occurred during the 90s. But now that trend has reversed and the gap has widened nightmarishly.

The terror of 911 has been real, but we confront it not only with a misguided war but also by awarding yet more contracts for corporations abroad and tax cuts for the wealthy. We cover this up by cancelling social and educational programs for the people. The gap in our national fiscal stability may now never be rectified.

The effects on jurisprudence for the poor accused of crimes are very real. In the year 2003, when this book was completed but not published, Oregon was experiencing a slash of $21.4 million from its former court budget, closing courts every Friday until the fiscal year had ended and eliminating public defenders for all but the most serious cases. The result, according to lawsuits filed in Portland and Eugene, was that the constitutional rights of defendants were being violated as part of a statewide reduction in court services, as cases kept piling up without attorneys for indigent defense. According to Lane County District Attorney Doug Harcleroad in 2003, there were 28,000 cases statewide whose arraignments and court hearings were postponed, trials delayed and reduced charges considered for defendants who could not afford an attorney.

Expecting that Karlyn's appeals might be expedited judiciously and favorably, I was obliged then to consider that publishing her story would have little appeal until a positive outcome might be anticipated. Moreover, in those appeals we were experiencing a complete lack of interest in establishing her innocence on the part of her defense attorneys. What was more disturbing than the delay of jurisprudence was the manner in which it was carried out when cases were addressed.

The Supreme Court, in requiring that a defense counsel provide effective assistance, has set the standard so low that even lawyers who are drunk or asleep have been deemed effective. It has been determined that in order to establish ineffective assistance of counsel, a defendant must show both deficient performance and prejudice; that is, deficient beyond the wide range of other professionally competent assistance, and also prejudiced; that is, showing a reasonable probability that the result would have been different if the counsel had been more effective.

Because these can seldom be established, the State will invariably find that any error examined in an appeal was "harmless" beyond a reasonable doubt. In other words, one's assistance at counsel can make gross errors and not be found deficient or prejudiced.

Moreover, in order to make these laws work throughout the pretrial, trial, appeals, and post conviction processes, the burden of error is placed upon the shoulders of the defendant, with no possibility of review or revisiting any aspect of the trial that had gone before. A defendant is effectively muzzled, unable to speak in his or her own defense, and completely dependant upon the effectiveness of counsel. Therefore, almost any deficiency can in hindsight be described as "tactical" in which the Supreme Court stresses counsel shall be given a wide leeway, and the defendant's rights are forfeited altogether. Because if a lawyer fails to raise an objection or argument in a timely fashion, the client is forever barred from having any court rule on it, a doctrine which is labeled "procedural default."

Procedural default rules penalize the indigent, since in this way the courts maintain and tolerate mistakes that are entirely foreseeable. The Supreme Court is unwilling to require that lawyers who would make fewer mistakes be assigned to indigents, and politicians and the public continue to get away with spending as little as possible on indigent defense. More than half of the $97.5 billion spent annually on criminal justice goes to the police and prosecution for criminal cases. In flagrant contrast, indigent defense receives only 2 percent of the total state and federal criminal justice expenditures.

In 2003 we allowed our president to overrule the UN and assault another country in order to create a "balance of power in favor of freedom," wherein our unparalleled military strength implied an unambiguous imbalance. Similarly, what chance would an indigent accused of a crime have against the above odds?

This is where corruption sets in. If lawyers were funded to be fair, perhaps they would be. As Justice Hugo Black said in the 1956 *Griffin v. Illinois* case, in which an indigent could not appeal his conviction because he could not pay the fee to obtain his trial transcript, "There can be no equal justice where the kind of trial a man gets depends on the amount of money he has." It goes without saying, while certain well-publicized trials go like clockwork, countless others are relegated to the trash heap of corruption.

Why? Well, how do you handle cases when you have 25 times as much money to prosecute as the defense has? How do you establish guilt when there are possibilities that could be explored to prove that the defendant might be innocent? You ignore the latter, of course. How do you establish a prosecution's effectiveness without discovering, and concealing, the fact that the defense might have a case too, if there were funds to develop it?

The answer is: You do it illegally. You use every trick in the book to violate the natural, inalienable rights of the indigent. You suborn witnesses. You withhold exculpatory evidence that would have proved their innocence. You lie, threaten, and belittle the witness who comes forward to testify against the real killer and deprive them even of the fundamental right to counsel and the *Miranda* warning. Then if the witness is instead indicted for the crime, there is no guarantee for an effective counsel.

And you do it gleefully, effectively, knowingly, and in counsel with others. The defendant's counsel may suspect, but he is not funded to thwart you. The defense will not be told of any impeaching evidence against witnesses.

And judges, likewise, evade their responsibility to make sure that information presented to the jury is real evidence, that it has a basis in fact, and that the jurors are not misled.

In Eugene there exists a citadel. It stands as a beacon of assurance to the populace that no man's rights will be violated as long as we have a Constitution in the United States of America. When we offer a plea bargain, in order to avoid a full defense of the accused's innocence, we are offering a torture such as that used in the Salem witch trials: if you confess you will be burned at the stake, but forgiven if you repent; if you do not, that proves your eternal soul will be damned.

In Rome there was a colosseum where the accused (gladiators) were fed to ravenous beasts. It is doubtful that trials were conducted in determining their guilt. As to their innocence, no trial was necessary. If they were innocent, they would redeem themselves by conquering their attackers, to the delight and thrill of the masses.

Without an effective *due process*, an indigent who is accused of a crime at the present time in the USA is quite likely to be convicted of it unless evidences of his innocence are easily obtained. Times and ideas change, and ways of determining guilt or innocence are framed into new laws according to the mores of the time. But when those laws are weakened to the point that they are almost entirely ineffective, we have, in effect, an original mindless intent, primitive and uncivilized in its affect, that is, to destroy that which we do not want to deal with fairly and compassionately.

****

Here at hand we have the story of Karlyn Eklof and the two life sentences she was given for someone else's crime when she came forward to testify. Now they have that someone on death row, and they know, in retrospect, the illegal ways that were used to convict her. But they are not going to correct those mistakes. It's called "procedural default." If she had had an angel, *i. e.*, someone to help her with money and influence, those illegalities might have been visited by effective counsel throughout her appeals. Such illegalities rarely are, however. Not for indigents.

Being aware of the ways this travesty on justice was accomplished makes us focus especially upon the corruption involved. Her story emerges, therefore, from her diaries, and from the court records and other documents we have gathered which would have been available to her defense counsel had they cared or been funded to search for them. Therefore we are inclined to proclaim here, emphatically, and to prove definitively in the pages to follow, this statement:

All the corruption that was "Rome" resides, if not elsewhere in America, certainly in the justice system of that citadel in Eugene, Oregon.

Chap II: A New Life

K arlyn Eklof and her three children came into Oregon some time in the spring of 1992 so she could go to a paralegal school in Salem. She had received a flyer about it, decided she wasn't getting anywhere among friends and family in the Imperial Valley near San Diego, and was ready to start a new life. Her friends, Kathy and Rob, had moved to Eugene just a few months before and encouraged her to come. She planned to stay with them briefly and then move on to Salem.

She said good-by to her mom, stepdad, and grandparents in San Diego, left her 70th St. apartment in La Mesa and took along a friend, Kevin, to help her drive her old '68 Dodge Dart and cope with her kids, TJ, in his early teens; Caroline, four or so; and David, two. It seemed a great plan. Karlyn, at age 29, could always attract friends to join her in a lark. It seems platonic relationships were her best forte. She could always handle them better than the heavy ones.

She could forgive herself for blasting her last two relationships that netted her Caroline and David. She was really still in love with Tomas, her first, fantastic lover from her early teens, who now served a prison sentence. She visited him for a long time, until he finally said it was enough; she must go on and make a life for herself without him.

What a fabulous family she had. They banded together to help her through her first early pregnancy, giving her a choice to end it and go back to school. The choice was wrong for her though, and she was soon pregnant again, wanting in the worst way to be forever with her lover. That baby, and the great happiness of being with Tomas became her ideal way of existence. When his petty crimes took him away, she still wanted to be there for her baby.

Her mom's success and great stability as a cashier in a high-priced restaurant for over twenty years did not appeal to her. There was, moveover, a wage gap that took place between her childhood when her mother first began to work, after her crazy father began to beat them all up, and the one she faced.

The income of the average family had been $37,800 in 1969, but barely crept up to $43,600 by 1989, and actually dropped to $43,200 by 1996 in real wages.

In addition, Karlyn's skills in no way prepared her for an average salary. Working full time at any time kept her far below the poverty level. She knew she was a disappointment to her mother, aunts, and grandparents, but there was no job worth being away from her children. Fortunately, her poverty in no way affected the love they showed her. There was always room for her at home and a special BBQ prepared by her loving stepdad Smokey. When public assistance wore her down, there was always the possibility that a new love would fulfill her, would make her feel more worthwhile.

In between, if she tried being creative in a restaurant, she aroused jealousy. If she took over as foreman for a set of vineyards, she found herself preyed upon by the manager. Nothing seemed to work, in and out of these jams. She really liked to be with people in her own situation. Raising kids was not something you could do alone. It was easier to do in a community.

She could always turn to her wonderful grandparents, who accepted her and helped fund her no matter what. But she dreamed sometimes of a really successful transformation, something she could be really good at. Hence, her trip to Oregon.

Kevin sort of lost his way. They ended up in Las Vegas, or was it a shared wish? She remembered staying in a cabin outside Reno before coming back into her home state, finding the route up to Klamath Falls, and coming across to the Interstate-Five (I-5) at Ashland. Finally, she wanted to ditch him at a truck stop outside Oak Grove but then thought better of it. They were both out of money, and she hadn't planned on that. It wasn't always easy to manage a platonic relation ship. But it turned out all right.

They drove through the steep Canyon Creek Canyon and approached the beautiful city of Eugene, alive with exotic blooms of spring in the serene and flat Willamette Valley. The river there flows north, as does the Nile in Africa, and there are not many that do. It proceeds up the flat green valley, dotted with low hills and buttes which orient one to the surroundings, to its confluence with the Columbia above Portland.

Kathy and Rob did not have room for them after all. It's not easy to be a welcoming friend to five exhausted people. Kevin soon found friends of friends and Karlyn, a cute little cottage provided by the Brethren House where they could stay for a month-and-a-half. Karlyn was used to all that. Nothing spoiled her optimism. The nicest thing about being down and out was that you soon found friends among the down and out. With no money to shelter you, you found others to help you. Pretty soon she had a community.

Then she found a little apartment at 53rd and Main. She felt great. Here she was dead center in a small town 1500 miles away from home on a new adventure.

Karlyn was always noticed. Well, she was beautiful, about 5'4", with glossy brown hair falling to her tiny waist. The curves above and below set the imagination on fire, and she knew; those grey eyes above high cheekbones always knew what fun it was to just be herself. She would always have friends, and she would do the choosing if she wanted to go beyond that.

She hoped, however, that she was wiser than before. She remembered the years she had tried so hard to be responsible, working as a cocktail waitress in three different bars, saving her money until she could buy a car. Then she met this gorgeous man who taught her so much about herself. But the certainty that she was loved, that she could be happy just like everyone else became just a memory; he was never even there when her baby girl was born.

She began to collect friends who had children so the security of their families would help her endure her loneliness. She bounced around. She brought a third child into the world alone. She began to make mistakes and unethical choices. It was time to go.

She felt a freedom here in Eugene. No one knew her who could draw her back into bad company. She wasn't working. She subsisted entirely on public assistance, and she felt a certain power to help other people because of having been down and out herself. She helped two different families who were homeless. She took in her son TJ's friends, gradually realizing that their evictions from their home situations were due to drugs. She had to kick them out, and she fought continuously to put her family's safety first. She would not tolerate drugs.

As a single parent, however, she was very vulnerable. After a stint as a card-dealer at the White Horse Tavern, where she was dismissed for breaking up a fight, her financial situation was not improving. She had not been able to get on with her set goals. She did register at Lane Community College, but that's as far as she got.

Then she was kicked out of her apartment after one of the boys she befriended broke a window. Fortunately, she was making new friends who could help her.

She met Corina Burch, who needed a car jump. After helping her they became good friends. She took Karlyn out to a couple of bars and showed her some places where she had worked. She then met Dennis Heide at the VFW. He lived in a little apartment around the corner from her and invited her to stop by. He was cooking chicken. Pretty soon they got to be pretty good friends. She helped him decorate with some furniture.

However, here she was being evicted from her apartment after too much ruckus and a broken window. She told Dennis what had happened. Though he was sure the landlord could not evict her legally, he was confident she might bring her further harm. Therefore he offered up his studio, stating he also had a surprise for them. His landlord had a house for rent and he had put a deposit down on it. In a short while they would have a three-bedroom house and a big yard.

The only condition was that they would have to do some yard work since the house was in the middle of a court surrounded by small duplexes. He was confident that soon they would be managing the complex. Karlyn piled her children and personal belongings into his small studio apartment and waited for this house to be theirs.

First Dennis told her the landlord had to fix the roof before they could receive the keys. Then one day she saw people looking at the house. She learned that Dennis had never even asked for the place. His landlord said that Dennis hadn't paid his own rent, let alone any deposit on the house she was waiting for.

Then she met his mom, who had taken her and the children to church. Now she realized Dennis lied to both of them. The trouble was he liked to make people happy in spite of reality. He took a lot of medication at certain times and blamed Vietnam for his unusual story. Karlyn had no choice at the time but to accept his disability and to take steps to avoid any future planning.

They were exceedingly cramped at Dennis' place. Corina offered Karlyn her spare room, but she knew that wouldn't work either. Then the two of them met James Salmu at the Driftwood. He walked them home to Corina's place. She realized she had already seen him a couple of weeks before at Amazon park with the children. She had been sitting in the sun in her swimsuit watching David in the wading pool when he walked by.

James Salmu did not come on to her like some other men. He was a kind of loner, drank too much, and kept to himself. But after she met him and he found out where she lived, he drifted toward her, in his somewhat drunken states, which would become a pattern. First he stopped by Dennis' apartment real late, at 2:00 A. M., a couple of nights in a row. This was a bit weird, and she didn't answer the door. She just spoke to him through a screen window, quietly so as not to wake the children or Dennis. She told him to come by at a decent hour after work when they could talk and have a few beers.

Finally James made it over at a decent hour, and they talked about what she was going through. He'd have never made it there except that he had a generous solution. He said, very humbly, "I've heard you're having problems. I'd like to help. Would you be interested in renting a room from me? It isn't much, but it's a home and a fenced yard."

James Salmu was 34 years of age, slight of build, 5' 6" tall, and weighing about 165 pounds with brown hair and green eyes. There is no doubt his was an offer with no strings attached. James was divorced, had no contact with his ex-wife and family, and very few contacts except for those at work and at the bar he frequented all too often.

Karlyn considered it a Godsend. Not only was she in an intolerable situation with Dennis, but she had been in a car accident caused by a drunk driver. Her right arm was swollen the size of a football and her lower back had sustained damage. She felt that she had been exceedingly blessed. It was Christmas Eve, and she agreed to move in. It was agreed that she would pay half the rent and buy the groceries.

The evidence established by the attorney at her defense, in a Motion to Suppress, showed that during January, February, and March of 1993, she and her three children were living with the victim as his guests, at 5282 Leota Street, Springfield, Oregon, and that he and the defendant, Karlyn Eklof, had a platonic relationship. Her story of the events of those months corroborate this.

Those months were exceedingly happy ones for Karlyn. First, they shared Christmas Eve together. She spoke on the phone to his mother for twenty-five minutes, thanking her for such a wonderful son. After the peace and quiet of an evening sharing food and small gifts for the children, James got away, finding the closeness too hard to bear. He spent the night out drinking and merrymaking most of the night.

The friendship hit snags from the very first, but they were not the kind of ones that weren't inevitable for two very different people sharing a household together. On Christmas morning, James and his dog Scooter got into it. They bit each other, according the Karlyn's story. The dog woke him up on the couch. Karlyn thought their behavior a bit rough. So she asked if Scooter could be put outside.

James didn't like it, because normally he would have given Scooter the run of the house where he kept a large bowl of dog food and water. It was the beginning of a bittersweet relationship. He would have to give up certain freedoms if Karlyn were to make her home there. It was a learning process and took a while.

On New Year's, which was his birthday, he had been out partying the evening before, came into Karlyn's room where she and the two little ones were sleeping, and climbed in on top of her. She socked him. He didn't belong in her room, and she didn't even know who it was at first. He scared her. They talked about it. He said he wouldn't do it again. After that, they resumed their platonic relationship and continued to enjoy a companionship for several weeks afterward.

They went to a party at his friends, Keith and Linda's. It was a nice, friendly party. Cards were played, and friendly jokes were told. Linda had worked and was tired. Karlyn cleaned up after the party. Linda said it was the first time she didn't have to clean up after everyone. Karlyn felt happy and accepted.

She made tacos one night and asked them over. Another night James had them over for a card game. One night TJ and Willy, his friend, had earned an all-night skating party. So Keith and Linda kept Karlyn's little ones while she and James took them.

James took TJ fishing, something TJ would never forget. Any guy would tell you how important that is. He was the first person she knew in Oregon whom she trusted TJ with.

But James was a workaholic and found his only release through drink. Sometimes that was not enough, and Karlyn would again find him stumbling into her room. There was tension between them because they each wanted a different outcome in their relationship.

At one time they discussed looking for another place for her and the children. She needed a room of her own and so did the children. James helped her write out a note to the Social Services that she would be needing a home-less resource check, because that's the only way she could line up help for the future.

She looked at a place in town, but no decisions were made. One reason was that James told her he had decided to go visit his family, also that he was thinking about quitting his job. He was bored living the same old way. Having Karlyn there sometimes just accentuated his loneliness and desire for a close companionship.

Meanwhile, Karlyn was falling into a strange involvement with two men she met at the White Horse Tavern. At first she enjoyed the fact that they were all from the same hometown, San Diego. Soon she was spending whole after-noons in their company, inviting them to her home so that she could look after and supervise the activities of her children while enjoying their company.

What began, however, was a kind of encroachment that would put her and her family in grave danger. Little did she know that their seemingly casual relationship was a testing ground for them, a search for possible victims, and that they had their own little area of business here which corresponded to other connections there in that hometown.

It is really difficult to understand Karlyn's antithesis to the drug culture. She seemed to know exactly what was going on around her, because these were the kinds of friends that were available to her because of the kind of vagabond life she led. But she always swore to protect herself, and particularly her children, from any exposure to it. Her self image denied any toleration of it, while in ways that perhaps she herself didn't even understand, she was easy prey. Not admitting, even to herself, that she could be prone to it, she perhaps allowed herself a vague kind of submission to those who would victimize her.

Spider and Potato could not have known the dire consequences for Karlyn, and especially for Salmu, of that subtle connection and the murder which transpired. But they were a minor part of a network of drug, pornography, and ritual abuse associates so pervasive, so hidden, and so well organized that their activities were seldom, if ever, perceived.

At the Grand Jury testimonies to indict Karlyn for the murder of James Salmu, Spider could only beg Karlyn in private, please, not to tell them anything that would indicate his real involvement that fateful night. And Potato, whom Tiner thanked profusely for delivering Karlyn into his hands, was never even questioned about it.

But the prosecution suspected Spider's involvement, because he failed his polygraphs and changed his testimony three times. Therefore they were able to suborn his testimony against her at her trial. The District Attorney at that time, Fred Hugi, had a transactional immunity deal with Spider's attorney, Robert Cole Tozer, that he would not be questioned about his proximity to the murder, in exchange for his suborned testimony. Spider was of no real use to them except as a key witness to convict her. A letter to confirm this (6-14-94) was hidden from Karlyn Eklof's counsel and from the jury, of course.

This kind of impeaching evidence is called a *"Brady"* violation. It occurs when information or evidence that is favorable to a criminal defendant's case is withheld by the prosecution The prosecutions' withholding of such information violates the defendant's *due process* rights, as in *Brady v. Maryland*, 373 U. S. 83, 83 S. Ct. 1194 (1963).

In the first place, it was Potato who delivered her into the hands of the killer, knowing what she would be subjected to and always keeping himself clear of any perceived connection. Together these two determined Karlyn's real susceptibility to the drug known as Rohyphenol, which renders the victim unaware of what is being done to her body, and also her gullibility in accepting their apparent innocence of what was happening.

Perhaps she didn't want to know at that time. There were things which happened to her in her childhood that traumatized her against revealing abuses she suffered at the hands of people she loved. Perhaps she felt safe in Eugene, and she liked the image she projected of a young single mother up from California with her children, making it on her own without attachments. These two amused her and helped her while away afternoons after TJ was home from school to watch the younger ones. She needed friends. But she had no idea what might be in store for her as she planned her next source of amusement.

To them she was a desirable commodity in their network. But they could not have known either where it would lead. Now the details of their acquaintance and of the operation will be told.

****

Karlyn met Spider (John Distabile) and Potato (Patrick Walsh) while she was working at the White Horse Tavern in January 1993. Upon learning they were from San Diego, her home town, she decided this was really neat; she would ask them over for a barbecue and some beers at James' house. She had two cars by this time that needed work, and these guys, being mechanics, were prepared to work on them for her. They began to come over quite regularly, working on the cars and just being really nice guys.

But something really strange was happening. When the children were totally occupied, asleep or off in the park with TJ, she began to notice a lapse of time, a couple of hours each time they came around. She also noticed bruises on her backside. Or did she imagine it? She must have dozed off. Maybe she bumped something. It seemed unusual to have one of them out walking her children when she woke up.

Or they would come over for a while and leave unnoticed, acting like some guardian angels. These were signs of major trouble, but they went unnoticed and unexplained, because Karlyn thought that in time she could pinpoint what was going on.

In the meantime she learned through Corina that Dennis wanted to know if she was still angry with him. When she got in touch she learned that he had received a settlement for a serious injury he had received at work, for which he had been receiving therapy when she was living with him. Now he wanted to make up for the lies and deceit that had caused her and the children so much grief at Christmas.

He also wanted to marry her. He wanted to spend some of his money to take her to visit her family in San Diego. And Karlyn, well, you know, she was always ready for a lark. You can imagine, being poor and strapped most of the time, what it would mean to her. But it was something that took a while to come together.

First Dennis wanted to go to Serenity Lane for recovery. It was a very hopeful sign that maybe they had something going for them. For all his problems, he was really a nice guy and didn't mind working! With much hope and commitment, he asked Karlyn to take care of his apartment while he was gone. She did. She went over a couple of times with Spider and Potato and hung some western things that Dennis liked so much. It also seemed a good place to hang out and leave the children on their own for a while. It was nearby so she could keep an eye on the house.

This one time she was the last one out of the apartment when she felt all of a sudden a hot spot on her butt. At first she thought something had bitten her, but in Spider's truck on the way to the store, it felt on fire and getting hotter. Arriving home she yanked her levis down to see what was burning. Spider and Potato took one look but evinced no great surprise or protest. They said instead, well, we gotta go. She had a perfect hand print on her butt.

There were times in Karlyn's childhood when she was misled or duped. She didn't protest or tell anyone. She kept thinking it must have been something she did. She must have earned it some way. Once when she was very young, she was punished severely by her parents for a petty theft and never revealed that a friend had threatened and traumatized her into doing it.

In her early teens when her father, who had been rolled down a hill wrapped in barb wire while a POW in Vietnam, started going crazy, saying, "You're not mine," kidnapping, beating, and raping her, she never told anyone. She never admitted it in any of her journals.

All she would say in them was that she was out of control, spent two weeks with her father, and returned home with a broken jaw. It was her older sister who wrote down what they knew of it for the police, when they were investigating her story.

She loved her father and had been his favorite. The years of an almost military discipline he had exercised over her, supervising her responsibilities and studies and causing her to wait upon him, had a numbing effect. She regularly woke him, laid out his clothes, and made his breakfast.

So after the trauma of his abuse, she probably accepted his rationale. If there was any improper submission, she blanked it out. Her mother was concerned only that she had returned home and was in control again. By that time she was in love with her highschool football hero, Tomas, which was the reason she was out of control. She probably didn't tell him either.

Years later, when she was twenty-one, she set out to find her real father, who was rumored to be a bigwig among the bikers. He had been the first husband of her "godmother" and was a very important figure in trying to create a liaison between the infamous Hell's Angels, of which he was briefly a member, and the metropolitan law enforcement.

All she received was a certain respect, a backing away, and her mother being made to sign a paper denying any connection. During her trial, the prosecution would use Karlyn's brief connection with the organization to belittle her and prejudice the jury, in flagrant disregard of her rights.

That hand print on her butt! She couldn't remember either Spider or Potato touching her, but they must have. Had she been drinking too much? Had she been drugged or hypnotized? She didn't want to think about it. She had lately been aware of strange, erotic feelings after she awoke, like after a wet dream. She wasn't quite sure what was going on, but she didn't want it to upset her life. She had been insecure for too long. Besides, now that she and Dennis were back together, she didn't need to depend upon her two drinking buddies so much for emotional support. She backed away from them and they didn't seem to notice.

This was when James was deciding to go visit his family, and she had been asking him, with Spider and Potato's urging, to allow her and the children to continue staying in the house while he was gone. He said he really didn't have any reason to come back to that house because of the memories and the divorce. His wife never called, never came by.

He was trying to work it out with the landlord that Karlyn would finish up some requested work on the house and keep up the payments. She was very excited about it. She told him she would stay in the house until summer, and he'd have the opportunity to keep the house if he decided to return. Meanwhile she'd have a two-bedroom house, a yard, and projects to keep busy.

It seemed certain now that she and Dennis were working things out. Then her friends, Dee and Rick, showed up, broke down and needing help. They stayed about a week. James was awfully nice about it. Keith and his wife continued to come by for dinner. So her friends were his, his were hers, and they were having a pretty good time of it.

People do indeed get caught up with Karlyn when there's a good time to be had. Suddenly Dennis invited Potato and her to go with him to San Diego. Well, besides getting married, Dennis wanted a native like Potato to show him what's worth doing in Imperial Beach; Potato was homesick; and Karlyn just wanted a short trip home and to have some money spent on her for a change.

James was fine with the idea. The children would be secure with three great sitters, plus four or five other people to check in on them. Corina and her roommate, Shawn, would take care of them. Shawn would prepare all of James' lunches and dinner, along with the children's. They would be her main job, and Corina would help as well as Kathy. Mike would also check on them, and so would Spider John.

It was a great opportunity for Karlyn to get a break from the children and to see her grandparents. At the time everything seemed secure to her.

Chap III: Knight in Shining Armor

I
t happened like clockwork. With the information and insights already revealed, one could almost predict the unfolding of her seduction and entrapment, not against her will, since she always saw herself in control, but in spite of it. Karlyn could be brash and sophisticated about her effect on people, and yet go unsuspecting. Because of her mindset on that day, the story is told as she observed it unfolding.

Flaunting her new fringed jacket, jeans and boots, she drew attention at the Portland Airport as Spider dropped them off. She didn't mind at all that Dennis and Potato sat together on the plane south, because she could be by herself to enjoy the eyes of strangers. When they arrived in San Diego, Potato's friend Willy, also known as "old Scooter Tramp," was waiting for them. He drove them to his house, his and Janette's. They entered from the garage where two motorcycles were on a ramp ready to have repairs, and there were a few people in the garage working on other ones. Like Spider and Potato, they seemed to be preoccupied with motor parts. They were rather attractive people, cordial and friendly. They greeted her and then seemed to forget about her.

Karlyn stood around watching, wanting to do something to help. There was keg of beer on tap, and they were invited to join in. As Karlyn says in her journals, eventually a mirror with lines on it was freely passed around. She never admits to her participation in all of this. She didn't even notice when Potato and Dennis left. She believes they were separated from her as soon as they got there. Some of the guys took Dennis to a strip place, which she didn't know about until much later.

Quite early on, she met Willy's wife and their two-year-old daughter. She recalled later that Jan was probably an outsider, not a party to the current of events, events that were about to ruin her life. This was similar to Spider's situation. He had a wife who was always complaining that he was gone so much. Jan and the child soon left, perhaps to relatives or friends.

Someone handed Karlyn a mixed drink. Eight hours passed, and she was awakened on a couch by a man who spoke directly as he leaned over her, "Are you going to lie there doing a dead cockie-roach lay?"

She blinked her eyes to focus and immediately arose. She didn't know this man. Without a word she left through the kitchen to the garage. There she saw Willy working at the workbench and asked him, "Where'd everybody go?" meaning Dennis and Potato. He said they'd be back in a little while.

She noticed that the man who had just awakened her was a well-built man with a goatee and shoulder-length hair wearing blue jeans, a shirt, and a baseball cap with the bill turned up. He looked so familiar: she felt very uncomfortable and thought maybe that's where an as yet unknown amount of time had gone. Just as in Springfield with Spider and Potato, she didn't trust herself that she hadn't just drunk too much and passed out. She did not want to look at him again.

A couple of riders, wearing leathers and full gear, pulled up on their motorcycles. Then she saw Dennis strolling up the driveway. She looked at the clock and realized that eight hours had gone by since she last saw him. She was very much offended that he'd left without a word. Her pride got in the way of her ignorance. She had to make a stand.

"Rule number one," she said, "is never to separate. You go together and you leave together." They had planned to stay a week just doing everything. They both knew they weren't ever going to get married. But it would have been nice to have fun running around together. Well, that didn't happen. She told him she would see him back in Oregon the next day.

She felt overchallenged. The man who woke her just stood there eyeing everything she did. She began to feel freaked out about this whole situation, but she couldn't lose her nerve.

Dennis began to argue, stating he wasn't leaving. She asked him where he'd been. He said quite boldly, "A titty bar!" That did it. She was embarrassed and angry. As they stood in the garage everybody was quiet, kind of waiting to see what would happen next.

Dennis was a handsome man, with a full beard, blue jeans, and a cowboy hat, belt and boots. She didn't want to lose his protection entirely but she sensed a terrible kind of challenge from across the room. Everyone seemed to be sizing her up to see how she would express her anger.

Another person she had met in Willy's garage that first night in Imperial Beach was Marney. She was there when Karlyn called a cab for Dennis. Karlyn didn't know their paths would cross again.

Karlyn told Dennis a cab was on its way. She held out her hand, palm up, and asked him for $200. For a second time he stated, "I'm not leaving."

She said, "Yes, you are," and asked Potato if he would make sure she saw her grandparents before she left. He shrugged his shoulders and said sure, I guess so.

The cab pulled up, and she said $200 please. In complete disgust he pulled out $1000 and handed her a $200 and a box with a set of pearl stud earrings and a diamond ring. She thanked him without a smile and said she'd see him back in Oregon.

Willy looked at her as Dennis drove off and said, "But he had $900 on him to spend with us this weekend."

She said, "So, and that was before he took off to the bar. If I wanted to come here alone I would have. But he feels he needs to take off on his own; well, now he has what he wanted." So Dennis took the cab, stayed at a motel, and made the next flight home.

She stayed around thinking she knew what she was doing. It was strange. In visiting with these people, she felt everybody was new and strange. But they all acted as if they knew her. No one tried to draw her out or get acquainted. Except for Potato being somewhere around, she felt she had cast herself off into an unknown world and was about to reap a whole new definition of her own words. She felt panic.

They didn't ignore her. For some reason she was the center of attention. All of a sudden she was treated like she was everybody's best friend. There were other people around she hadn't noticed before. She didn't know where Potato was either, so she just found something to do. She wiped some tools off and counted nuts and bolts.

The guy who woke her up, it turns out, was Jeff Tiner, otherwise known as Jethro. He had a beautiful Indian girl named Kathy with him, but he made a big show of dismissing her and approaching Karlyn as though she were his own property. He said, "There goes seven years of my life and you'd better be worth it!"

Karlyn had no idea what he was talking about. Everyone else seemed to understand him, but she was at a loss. She distanced herself from him, but that just seemed to amuse him. At that time she just wanted Potato to take her to her grandparents and then to the airport. But he bounced in and out so fast she couldn't get his attention. Not to make a big deal of it, she tried to wait it out and learn more.

Jethro asked her, finally, to go get something to eat. That seemed simple enough. She had to adjust to her surroundings some way, and Jethro was the one most interested in her. They walked up the street and crossed the boulevard to a bar.

She could hear a jukebox as they entered. The bartender came over and they ordered drinks. She looked around. There were pool tables at each end of the bar and various plaques on the wall from pool tournaments. There were just a few couples sitting around talking.

Willy joined them for a drink and then Patrick. They shot a game of pool and eventually all went back to Willy's and stood around the garage shuffling through motorcycle parts. Jethro worked on a VW bus motor all through the night with Leo, Cindy's boyfriend. Karlyn began to enjoy being around adults with no responsibilities, but she expected to be on a flight out the next day.

At early dawn Jethro asked if she wanted to go get breakfast. She telephoned her children. Dennis had made it back safely, though he left word that Karlyn was a b___! They got into a green VW bug. She thought Potato would be traveling with them, but upon departure he went in another direction.

After breakfast Jethro made several stops. He said that people owed him money. Karlyn waited in the car for what seemed like hours at a time. Since she was unfamiliar with the neighborhood they were in, she didn't know how to get back to Willy's, so she just sat waiting. This was more nonsense than she wanted to deal with. But at the moment she had no one else to turn to, so she decided to retain her good humor.

Then they stopped by a pawn shop. Jethro traded in a set of pearls for cash and purchased a set of earrings, Karlyn's birthstone, for her. There on the wall was a high mirror. He placed a black leather sombrero hat on her head, tilted it just above her eyes, and said, "Look, I'm your prince charming, the spirit you've been waiting for." She felt dazed and relaxed and just smiled, and he nodded his head in approval. Jethro could be very charming!

The car that they were in wasn't driving well. The motor was tired. This was a lot for Karlyn to put up with. So they were basically stuck there. Jethro gave Willy a call and described where they were. Willy recognized the area and told them about a little Mexican bar where they could wait for him to arrive.

The people inside were friendly to Karlyn, but a couple of guys who'd been drinking all day began to close in on Jethro. One took a poke at him, slurring his words, and then there were two others standing next to him. She couldn't tell if they were joining in or trying to talk the guy off. Either way she didn't like it. She wasn't used to just standing by. They were too close. She yelled, "Don't touch him. Back off!"

Jethro never changed his expression. He stood with his arms crossed. When Willy walked in Jethro was leaning against the pool table, but the three men were standing around him. Things had really heated up.

Willy said something to a couple of old hard-looking muchachos, and they called out to the three that surrounded Jethro. As they backed away, Willy walked over to them. He said, smugly, "I guess I forgot to mention. This place is strictly off limits to gringos. I've been coming here for years. I phoned the bartender and told her to watch out for you."

The bartender reached out her hand and said she was sorry, that her regular customers were territorial, and that they were welcome any time. They left the VW and drove back in Willy's vehicle. The day had zipped by, and it was evening. Karlyn couldn't believe it. At the time it seemed like a wasted day, but she was enjoying herself. She guessed that was the idea. At some point she cancelled her flight.

As night closed in they mostly hung out in the garage. Then the VW bug was towed in and was being torn down to exchange the motor. Leo was called in to accomplish the task. Potato was wandering around, drinking peppermint schnapps and handing out tools. Karlyn was looking at magazines and drinking beer.

The VW finally came together by morning, and it ran great. It seemed Leo and mechanics went hand in glove. Jan prepared breakfast, eggs and potatoes, and it was a beautiful day. Karlyn called her children. They were all in good spirits, so she cancelled her flight to stay another day. She still hadn't seen any of her family in San Diego and planned to do so.

Jethro continually spoke gently to Karlyn. That was new to her. He spoke as if she were the most important thing at that moment. And he kept telling her to look into his eyes. Then he'd nod his head, just a short jerk. She knew this was happening, but she was mesmerized by it. She became aware it had happened that first day, when she sent Dennis home.

Jethro drove her over to a restaurant where he was meeting a man named Louie. Now this Italian guy was fairly handsome, slender, and wore his hair real tall in the front puffed up like a girl's. To him, though, it must have been a statement of some sort.

Jethro said this Louie guy had been able to help him before with some kind of business. He hadn't specified what, but Karlyn felt a little in the way and wanted to go back to Willy's. After all, she had already asked Potato to help her get to her grandparents.

In the restaurant sitting close by was a guy about Karlyn's age, mid-thirties. What he was doing, she wasn't sure, but she thought he was watching them. He seemed very anxious to run up on Louie and Jethro. As they exited, Karlyn was the last one going out, and he asked her if she was all right. She just nodded. Louie said the guy was an instructor of martial arts. Louie gave Jethro some money and agreed to see him after a while, but Karlyn felt there was some kind of connection between them.

They went by a liquor store. Jethro knew the owner. They talked for a bit and then they went by Leo's. His house sat on a corner across from an elementary school. Leo had a boat in his back yard up on ramps. They drank a couple of beers, and Karlyn looked at his rock collection and talked to his girlfriend. She was a real nice gal. She took Karlyn into the house so the guys could talk.

Leo had been up for a couple of days and was exhausted so they didn't stay long. Karlyn was thinking, out of everyone she met through Potato, Leo and his brother were the only ones who hadn't looked at her as if she were the main course.

They arrived back at Willy's. She called her children. They were all getting along very well. She apologized for cancelling her flight, and Shawn said not to worry. She and James were getting along great. Karlyn told them she would fly home the next day.

Potato came in and out as he was accustomed to doing. Leo pulled up and stayed for a bit. Then everyone went to a bar for a drink and then took off to meet at another bar. Jethro stopped at a liquor store and there was Louie, the Italian they had met at the restaurant. The two of them spoke for a short time while Karlyn waited. This was a pattern she accepted from Jethro from the very first, and it is hard to understand why. Why did she need to be excluded?

Then Louie showed her a drawing and asked for her opinion. She liked it. It was a Universal Studios picture of the earth and a motorcycle rider riding away from the earth into another solar system. He quoted a price for it, at $200. It was strange how often that figure came up. When he said it she felt very relaxed. Both he and Jethro looked at her steadily. She and Jeff climbed into the VW bug and made a few more stops before going back to Willy's.

She needed to rest, so she got a room on the boulevard at the Silverado Motel. She remembered wanting to get home, and yet she couldn't pull away from this guy. If he needed something she had to be there. They both knew she had to get home. It was strange she let him set her up to stay the night.

He mixed them a couple of drinks and leaned over to kiss her. She shifted the pillows around and took a big sip from her glass. Well, she might have enjoyed the night, but the next thing she remembered was waking with no clothes on and mumbling at the end of the bed, and Jethro asking her about those drinks. It was morning, and the drinks were still there!

Startled, she blinked and looked over at Jethro. She saw he had tatoos all over his body, and his clothes were off too. She felt somewhat embarrassed, because she didn't remember getting to know him this way. She looked over at the night stand where the two drinks sat that Jethro had prepared the night before. There was water on top of the alcohol. The ice had melted. She knew something was wrong, because she would have finished hers shortly after he gave it to her.

He said she should get up and take a shower. She was exhausted and embarrassed. Again she thought she had just passed out on him and asked him where the night had gone. He sat up, grabbing a shirt, and said in a good humor, "I bounced you off the bedboard a few dozen times. You loved it. Come on get in the shower. It's time to go."

As her mind cleared, she had a strange terror. She remembered seeing someone with a camera leaving the room as she woke up. It came at her like a bad dream, so she dismissed it from her mind. She didn't put it all together until later, and she still didn't remember a thing about what happened during the night.

She got up, regretfully, and stepped into the shower behind him. The water felt great, but she looked at his chest, arms, and back. He had really hard-looking tatoos. She'd never been with anyone with tatoos like this. Nor did she remember seeing them throughout the bouncing he referred to.

He asked her, "What's wrong?" as she was drying off to get dressed. She looked over at the drinks, reached for a glass and drank it. It was the glass with his mixed drink in it. Then she answered, "Nothing." He drove to a bar on the beach. Again he said, "Look in my eye." She did, and he said, "I'm your prince charming, the spirit you've been waiting for." They left the bar and went to Willy's.

Potato was surprised to see her and asked if she had cancelled her flight. She told him not yet, and she hadn't planned to. Again she cleaned up and ate something. She had been ready to go home that day, but suddenly she cancelled her flight. Then she called her grandparents, and since Potato wasn't too interested in going, Jethro drove her over to their place. She would always regret that.

She hadn't seen them in a year and loved visiting with them. Her grandparents were everything to her. Their gentle influence throughout her life was restored.

In the conversations she had with Jethro over a period of a few days she sometimes felt Jethro had had advantages too. He seemed very knowledgable about law and about how to start a business. He said his father was a devout Christian and his brother was a state employee working hard checking property. She shared these things about Jethro with her grandparents, but they only stayed a short while. She learned that Jethro could be very impressive in the right settings.

They talked about Jethro coming up to Springfield, and Willy mapped out the area for him. Then they stayed the night in the trailer next to Willy's house.

She didn't like his tatoos, but everything he said was all right, or so she thought. He made a lot of plans with her: "Just stay in step, and we'll have a wonderful business in no time." He picked out her favorite colors as though he knew they liked the same things.

The next morning her flight was cancelled, and she was rerouted to another flight through San Francisco. They waited in the airport parking lot for about two hours talking. Again Jethro said, "Look here in my eye." And again he said, "I'm your prince charming, the spirit you've been waiting for." It was everything she wanted to hear, and again she fell for it. She had this amazing attraction to him. He would say just one or two words, and she would flush. That wasn't at all normal for her. She had been so much her own person before. Now she felt submerged in him.

She was excited that he was coming to Oregon and would be around to help her with her children, to get her started in classes, and to start a business. She told him she wondered why she had gone away, only to come back and find him here. When they said good-by Jethro handed her a $20 bill and said to get something to drink. He said to stay sweet and that he would call.

In San Francisco she had to transfer planes. She carried a large bag with her clothes and a couple of full-length leather coats that Jethro had given her, as well as some leather pants and a hat. Her luggage was so heavy it took her forty-five minutes to cross the airport. She barely made her next flight.

Here it was the eighth day when she finally did leave. She had lost track of time to the extent she could never tell exactly what happened, day by day. She was under some kind of spell. And really, she fell for this guy.

Nobody had ever affected her like Jethro. She didn't want to separate from him, and that wasn't at all like her. For some reason she just knew this was the guy who would be settling and fulfilling. She was convinced he was a knight in shining armor. Oh boy, was she wrong!

She was excited about introducing Jethro to all her friends. And she wanted to be sure he was away from Imperial Beach, where she couldn't see any future for him at all. Well, she was right about that!

The flight was a beautiful one. Karlyn saw the most beautiful cloud formations, like columns of counsel, she thought. And there was a splendid winged being holding out an open book. Behind the being was a circular cell holding a bearded man. Something special was being broadcast that day from the heavens. Karlyn truly believed she saw this.

Spider picked her up at the airport. He said he knew what she had seen and called it something in Italian, meaning a biblical revelation. When she asked him to explain or just repeat what he had said his face went glum, his mind preoccupied.

He told her that Potato had called, and they talked about her visit. When she asked what they talked about, he just said that it sounded like she had a good time. He said he had been over to check on the sitter and James, and they didn't expect to see her yet.

She was so glad to be home. She had missed her children. She had never left them before. They were doing so well. And they weren't looking for her for another day or two.

But Shawn, the sitter, was tired and ready to go. James said she did an excellent job. Karlyn told everybody that she met somebody who would be a friend for all of them for always.

Two weeks went by, and she and Jethro phoned back and forth. She had no memory of what was said, just plans for him to come up.

What is interesting, though, is that during those two weeks before Jethro arrived, John was nervous and tried to talk Karlyn into stopping his visit. As he stood rapidly speaking about what he thought were relevant issues and not having this guest coming up, Karlyn finally agreed that the timing was all wrong.

He started coming over almost daily and showing his affection more than just as a friend. Potato also phoned John and told him he needed to tell her that. Her friends' concerns finally got through to her. She had begun to wonder how she could have been so much controlled by Jethro.

Spider was asking her every question imaginable about how she felt about Jethro. It was apparent to him, as Karlyn later perceived, that she had been infatuated and subject to subliminal messages. The danger signs were there, which they understood so well, since he and Potato already knew how sensitive she was and had themselves covered up their intentions with the same kind of facade.

She finally agreed with him and called Jethro's father, where Jethro was, and asked him not to come. The spell was over. But he insisted. He said he had too much paper work wrapped up in coming. And he must come, and he would come.

Spider and Karlyn picked him up at the airport. He was the last one off the plane. When Karlyn saw him she stood back. He did not look the same. She finally saw him as he was. And Spider had never wanted him to arrive at all.

Chap IV: The Celebration

Jethro was the very last one off the plane. Karlyn was excited. He did arrive. But he didn't look as handsome. Something was different. But she ignored it; she just wanted to get him home and show him off to the children and everybody else.

She introduced him to Spider, and they drove from Portland to Springfield. She wasn't sure what it was, but he had changed. Something was different about him. His features seemed changed. During the previous two weeks she had told everybody what a wonderful man she had met. He was knowledgeable about law; he was gentle speaking; he was big and strong! Unfortunately, her prior responses to him were due to his brainwashing tactics, which he used from the beginning. Over the phone, those key words continued to influence her emotions and thinking. During the ride home she was seeing him through Spider's eyes.

When they arrived back at the house, she couldn't help feeling that something was wrong. In different surroundings and with friends and family present, it was difficult for Jethro to reestablish a mental control over her. She had no time to hover over his every word. She began to remember what had happened at the Silverado Motel. It was a helpless, faded, embarrassing thought.

She introduced Jethro to her "roommate," as she called James, with some misgivings. Soon afterward, James and Jethro went into her room where they did a line of "meth." Jethro spoke to him about climbing in on me, told him that was to stop, although he didn't blame him, and they both laughed. James assured him it wouldn't happen again. Jethro spoke about wanting to start a life up here, and James encouraged him. Opportunities were great. They talked over some ideas for a business.

Everyone went out back to the weight set, drank beers, and smoked cigarettes. Then Spider took off to his place. James went to the bars.

Karlyn camped the children out on the living room floor and started a candlelight bath with mixed drinks. At 2:00 A. M., while in the tub, Jethro called Potato in Imperial Beach and told him, "Thanks, man. You did me right. I owe you." Karlyn felt honored. He was comfortable and had accepted her and her family. At this point she thought he was truly the man she'd always wanted and that all her dreams were coming true. Was she wrong!

She introduced him to everyone around. After all, that's all she talked about from when she got home until he got here. It seemed someone special walked into her life and was strong enough to keep up with her and her children, their schools, their ball games, their friends, her friends, the terrible twos. He would be someone who could help her get through her college classes, which she still wanted to do; and provide the kind of teamwork a single parent longs for.

The next day they went and looked at a tow truck, a motorcycle, and parts to run a business. Karlyn really thought, this is it! We're going to make it. He threw figures together and talked a lot about what Willy had. Jethro had to have whatever Willy had, a house, a wife, several vehicles, cycles, a tow truck, etc. She figured he was going to settle for nothing less.

He took off a lot over the next few days. Soon Karlyn rarely saw him. He was in and out. She thought he was going to town to locate a place to open a business. But what he was really doing was business all right, but it wasn't the kind to make for a happy home.

Karlyn wasn't sure what was going on, but he ordered a small delivery of "meth" to Spider's house and some cash from his cousin in Arkansas to start this transaction. The money was delivered Western Union. Unfortunately, he made it known to a couple of people he was introduced to just what business he was capable of, and they responded.

When "Karlyn got wind of this, she wasn't very happy. He didn't do any business at James' house. He knew how she would feel about it, so he and Spider did their thing in that direction. Spider was uneasy about it too, but he still wanted to participate in it for the money.

She saw less of Jethro during his stay, but figured at first that he knew what he was doing and what it took to start a wonderful "tow" business. She stayed busy at the house. James had her doing some projects that he told the landlord he had already done. So she enjoyed painting and fixing up the wood trim. The living room soaked up the paint, and she moved on to the bathroom, the kitchen, and then the laundry room shelves. She felt very productive, and it seemed to make her happy.

Karlyn thought she had made a great impression on this guy, whom she thought was here to answer all her dreams. She could just visualize their business and watching it expand. She would be going to TJ's ball games and enjoying a community of activities and a beautiful future. But that all changed drastically that next weekend.

James mentioned again wanting to go to see his family in Fresno before it was too late. He was lonely. Tina, since their divorce a year before, had never even stepped back into the house. The overnighter card games he held were the only activities the house had known since his wife left. He liked his privacy also, however, and he didn't realize how much he missed his family until Karlyn moved in with her children. But he wanted something she couldn't give him.

After Jethro had been in town a few days, however, James must have sensed something else about him and Spider. Then he said, quite openly, that the possibility of going south occurred to him, and that he felt it was time to go home. Karlyn thought it sounded pretty sudden to her and asked if everything was all right. He said, "Yes, I just think I need to go see my family."

He told Jethro something of this and agreed to talk to him later. He spoke to Karlyn again about the landlord and said if she kept doing the little repairs that were expected the landlord would probably agree on her extended rental. In hindsight, Karlyn came to believe he was at that time uneasy, but was being very generous without knowing the true facts. But neither did she.

She asked him to let her know what was decided. If he was truly going, she wanted to meet with the landlord and confirm this new plan. He continued by stating that all he would be taking was his personal belongings, stereo, and what would fit in his car.

Later Karlyn thought perhaps James knew there was something else afoot, something he had challenged her about previously. He said she hadn't done anything wrong, but it was just a couple of people who had come to see her. She asked him what he meant by that. He said it wasn't important, not to worry, and that he needed to go see his family anyway. He was unable to tell her.

Well, everything seemed to be falling into place for Karlyn, however, and she gathered some people together for a party. She was quite oblivious to any trouble that might be stirring.

Spider offered to make pizza. Jethro bought a few things, a tub to put the ice, beer, and sodas in and a set of bathroom towels, because Karlyn liked them. She later thought he did these little things for her to show he could. Because the big stuff she thought they had set as goals weren't ever in the picture yet.

During Karlyn's stay at James' they had had much fun. In retrospect, Karlyn would remember the times TJ and his friend would watch the children, and James and she would run up the street to dance and have a couple of beers. Sometimes they'd get in the car and go further down the boulevard to another place he liked to go. He had several places.

He took her and the children to do laundry and grocery shopping. He talked to TJ a lot. When Dee's bus had broken down, he let her stay a couple of days while Spider worked on it. He enjoyed being helpful, and he liked the company. Dee didn't just hang out. She was truly grateful for the help and made herself useful around the house before she went on her way. And it was through her that Karlyn met Al Hope.

So now it seemed Jethro, Spider and Al were doing business. Jethro got Al's address and he and Karlyn drove out one day. They told her to go into the trailer while they stood outside and talked. She had some chains and gold necklaces that needed fixing. Al was making jewelry and offered to fix them.

While she was looking at all the things he'd made Jethro showed her a little silver gun Al had. She hated it, but said it was cute and handed it back. She didn't think anything of it at that time. She wasn't interested. It was not an issue for her. She went back to looking at the jewelry, and it wasn't long afterward that they left. Al was suppose to bring her necklaces out to her sometime during the next week.

Only a couple of days later Al was invited to the party and asked to bring his daughter. His daughter and Caroline, Karlyn's daughter, had played together a couple of times and got along real well.

Karlyn had no idea the gun was brought home. No mention of it was made traveling home. Everybody knew how she felt about guns. At least she thought they did.

A day or two went by. Jethro was in and out. Karlyn was working on projects in the yard and in the house. They were preparing for the party, planning so much in such a short amount of time. Everyone seemed to be giving them their blessing Karlyn was overjoyed that her friends didn't find anything wrong with their togetherness. Well, if they did, they certainly didn't say anything. She was very happy and loved the respect everyone seemed to have for each other.

It must have been less than a week into Jethro's stay that they planned the pizza party. So much had happened since he had arrived already. He didn't always look like the person Karlyn had been looking for, but he sure did have some answers. He clicked right into her needs, she thought. And he made her feel like she was serving him well. He would be returning to San Diego for business and was also planning a trip to Arkansas before he returned.

The party started during the afternoon. The guys, James, Keith and a few others, were throwing horseshoes in the backyard. A dart game was on the opposite side, basketball in the driveway, and the children were all playing with bubbles and balloons in or next to the patio for safety reasons and in order to be in sight. Linda's little sister was a great help to Karlyn at the party. Karlyn gave her one of her blouses too.

A couch, a long table, and chairs were set on the patio, and the table was laden with chips, dips, candy, fruit, and vegie strips. And there would be pizza, and tubs full of beer and soda. Spider was in the kitchen preparing the pizza sauce. The whole house and back yard were full of good spirits and togetherness, friends coming, going, and coming back again.

The party couldn't have been any better. James invited Keith and Linda; Spider invited a couple of his friends; Karlyn invited Kathy and Rob and James and Kathleen; and some of James' friends from the bar showed up. But they didn't stick around because it was a family atmosphere.

The weather was beautiful. Karlyn enjoyed so much all the people gathering and also welcoming Jethro. So, well, they decided to call it an engagement. They had Spider's great pizza and then took pictures. After that people started to leave, a few at a time. By about 9:30 to 10:00 P. M. the remaining guests were preparing to leave. It was a Sunday night, and people worked the next day. Jethro said he wanted for them to be alone that night, so Karlyn asked Dave and Tracy to take the two little ones with them as a last-minute request. They didn't seem to mind too much.

When all the guests had departed, Debbie, Spider's wife, was still there, in tears, crying on the patio.

Chap V: Jethro's Agenda

A t ten o'clock Karlyn had just about everyone out the door or on their way. The last ones left were James, herself, Spider, Jethro, and Debbie. She asked Debbie why she was crying. She said she wanted to stay. She said, "Why does Spider always get to stay. He doesn't come home from here until 2:00 A. M."

Karlyn assured her Spider had never stayed there at the house, even up to the dinner hour. She asked him what Debbie was talking about, but he directed her to leave, that he would see her at home. Karlyn comforted her and explained that he would be home soon, that Jethro wanted for them to be alone that night, and that James was going to the bar soon. Francis, his friend there, was looking for him. He'd been hiding from her all day. Deb left.

Jethro said he wanted for them to be alone, but he wanted to be sure they were alone for the whole night. He offered James money for a motel. He took cash out of his pocket and offered it to him, but James said he did not want it. He said he had his own money.

Jethro and Spider went out to the back patio together, to talk apparently, but they came right back in. Karlyn was in the kitchen for a while and didn't quite know what was going on. TJ and his friend Steven were out wandering around in front of the house. Something happened after that Karlyn didn't see. TJ later said he saw Jethro hit James, either then or later.

When Karlyn became aware of the situation Spider was standing with his foot settled on top of the heater trying to intimidate James. He told James he'd better do what's good for him. "Take the money," he said. "You'd better do as you're asked. Take off for the night!" She saw Jethro standing at the end of the couch in the far end of the living room. He was smoking a cigarette and holding an ash tray in one hand.

James paced back and forth from his room to the living room stopping by the bathroom door looking at himself in the mirror. Karlyn guessed he was deciding whether to shave or not before he left for the bar. It was obvious he didn't want to go.

"James," she said, "call Keith." James called Keith and asked him to meet him at the bar. It would have been great if Keith wanted to join him.

After he hung up James said, "He doesn't want to drink any more tonight." As he said that, Karlyn became aware that John was a big part of this. He was standing there with Jethro. She knew Jethro wanted to be alone but couldn't figure out why John wasn't leaving also.

She bit her bottom lip and said, "Ask Keith if you can come down there for a while."

James said, "Do what?"

She said, "Stay the night." So James called and asked Keith, who was conferring with Linda.

James said, over his shoulder, "They said no."

"Well, that's bizarre. Why not?" Karlyn asked. James said something about Linda's little sister being there and with that he hung up. He explained he made her uncomfortable and there wasn't room for him anyway.

After he got off the phone Jethro made some kind of remark, she couldn't remember what, because she was becoming very upset. She called Linda back and said, "What's going on?" Linda said her little sister was sleeping on the couch and while she was visiting, there was no place for James.

By this time Jethro asked James, "Explain exactly what did you do, James?" James should have left it right there. He didn't have to explain.

James stated, "I kissed the girl's mouth with my tongue and it made her uncomfortable." John said something to Jethro, Karlyn couldn't hear what it was, but indicating his concern. Then James, watching them closely, now stated he was going to the bar! There was a gap now in the conversation because of his change of motivation.

Karlyn asked James, "Did you ever apologize to her?" And James said no. She asked him, "Don't you think you should?"

James said, "I'll handle it in my own time."

But Jethro said, "No. Let's you and me take a walk to the bar. You can call Keith to come meet us, and we'll all go together and apologize to that little girl." Suddenly an ugly, insane scenario reared its head. No one could understand where it was coming from.

Jethro knew the girl from the party but showed no respect for what James had honestly and openly admitted. With a diabolical thrust, Jethro started in on him, asking question after question. And James answered him, each time hoping it was the last question. He moved around the house attempting to leave, then holding his ground. Karlyn hoped desperately that Linda would call back.

But Jethro made it clear to James that he was going to apologize to that girl. He asked Karlyn, "What kind of friends do you have here?" She felt there was an ugly wall between them. None of her natural defense mechanisms would work here. For all her friends' quirks, she knew them to be pretty decent people. She was as frightened as James.

But she felt it more dangerous not to go along with Jethro's inquiry. She asked James, "What, can't you get a woman?" shrugging her shoulders and trying to make a joke of it. But, as she learned, it didn't matter what kind of friends she had. Jethro was there to cause trouble. She didn't know at that time what she was dealing with.

James went for the door but paced back to his room. Karlyn wanted to assuage Jethro in any way she could. She said, "Hey, James! Women aren't good enough for you! Come on, go take care of the matter now!" Karlyn liked the little girl and didn't want her afraid of him. She thought the best that could happen was a little talk between them there so they'd know, too, what a creep she was dealing with. She was very upset and embarrassed.

James went to his room and put his jacket on but was stopped by Jethro in the living room. Karlyn left the house to bring in the plates of leftovers and came back in. She thought if she got busy, it would lessen the pressure building up.

She came in to the kitchen. James passed her. He went to his room and came back out. He left his light on, so it was obvious he wasn't leaving right then. Karlyn sat down casually on the heater. She figured things were finally calm and was relieved. John and Jethro seemed preoccupied with other things and occasionally exchanged remarks on the patio. James went to the bathroom and looked ready to go. She sat on the heater cleaning her nails with the tip of a buck knife. She thought they worked well because the tip was curved just right for cuticles.

Anyway, James came out of the bathroom, but just stood around. So she asked him, "Well, what are you going to do?" She said it with a hands-up gesture, forgetting in her nervousness about the buck knife, and it flew out of her hand and bounced off the wall.

She told James she didn't mean to do that, and he said, "I know," picked it up, and handed it back to her. She folded it up, set it on the table, and went back to the dishes.

After that she watched the guys to see where things were by this time. They seemed okay. James was drinking a beer and preparing to leave. He and Jethro exchanged words. Karlyn couldn't understand what was said.

Then James walked over to Karlyn, who was away from the others and, suddenly, just "head-butted" her. This was an obvious gesture of desperation. Surprised by the sudden blow, her automatic reaction was to pelt him one with her fist, which landed on his right cheek. She socked him! Then she asked, in defense, "Why did you do that?"

He straightened up and mumbled something. She suddenly in that quick second saw something in James' eyes she had never seen before, but the urgency didn't register quite yet. He said he didn't know. He said he deserved the punch. His eyes darted back and forth across her face. Later she believed that he was trying to tell her something.

He went to his room, grabbed his cigarettes, and was going to the bar. She told him he needed to clean his eye where she had pelted him. She told him she was sorry, but she still didn't understand why he had "head-butted" her. He could have used a stitch but didn't want any help. Jethro was moving around them, moving his body like a wrestler about to spar. Karlyn wasn't too concerned about him. She was trying to help James. But the tension between James and Jethro brought her efforts to a standstill.

James went to his room and shut the door. He came right back out with his jacket on, but he wasn't leaving. He went back and forth from his room, doing absolutely nothing except going in circles. Karlyn decided he might have been drunker or hurt worse than she thought.

His cheek was bleeding. He went and wiped off his face with a towel. But at that moment Jethro came alive, in total control again. He told him to get ready; he'd walk him to the bar and call Keith. He, Jethro, would help him take care of the problem!

Somehow James and Jethro tumbled. When Karlyn came back in, all she saw was Spider standing between the kitchen and living room watching. Jethro popped him or slapped him, she wasn't sure which. James was on one knee saying, "What the hell is this?" Then whatever had happened was over, and James regained his stability. He sat down, totally weary.

When Karlyn went in to see, James was sitting up on the couch. Jethro was standing next to him. Jethro made a motion with his hand. It was cupped, and he held a gun in it. Karlyn just kept walking as if to ignore it. But she shook her head, "No! No!" She finally reestablished communication with him. He put it away and she didn't see it again. She was choking back tears of relief.

Spider headed out with the two boys following him. She followed them and approached the truck just as both truck doors were closing. As she reached the truck window, she told him to get the boys out of there. She said, tearfully, she had thought he was going to kill James.

John gave her a strange look, reached for the ignition and started the truck rolling back out of the driveway. At the time she didn't realize her remark would be a reality statement. She thought it was just an overstated figure of speech. She didn't believe it anymore.

They agreed earlier that TJ would go to work with Spider the next day to be trained in auto tune-ups. She later learned that Steve was taken home. The idea was for the boys to go together and learn. The truck backed out, and she reentered the house.

James moved toward the kitchen. To separate them and to avoid any more confrontation between them, Karlyn took control and walked James into the bathroom. His cheek was bleeding from where she had hit him. She said for him to come and get it cleaned up. Besides she didn't want Jethro to see what she'd done. She was embarrassed that they had disputed so suddenly and that her diamond ring had placed a cut just below his eye, but she was also afraid of what she'd seen. Would his response to her terror hold?

James started arguing and just creating noise. Karlyn grabbed him, turned the water on in the tub, and told him to get his face cleaned up! She thought they might have to take him to get a couple of stitches. But James was just running off at his mouth, enraged and out of control. She was trying to help him, but she was just making things worse. He was pissed, and he didn't realize the danger he was in. She was shaking.

Then he was shaking his head and mumbling. But he was shouldering her to go. As she looked behind her, she realized that Jethro was standing over them. Jethro said something low. She prayed that he was finally concerned and was just going to look at the cut her ring had made. She tried to shut the water off but instead pulled the shower on. She thought, well, that ought to cool James off. Believing that Jethro was there to help, she left the room, trying to busy herself in the kitchen, hoping they'd all leave soon for the bar.

James stood up, then stepped into the shower to shut the water off. Or maybe he was just shaking off the water. But she heard Jethro say, "Place yourself over there." Standing at the sink with soapsuds on her hands, she heard a "Pop, pop."

And she heard a moan. She stopped the running dishwater and looked over her shoulder at the bathroom door, shook her hands free from the suds, and started towards the bathroom. She stood there terrified for a moment, then went in. Jethro was standing over James. James was sitting at the end of the tub with his legs crossed, snoring. She couldn't see all of him; Jethro was blocking her view.

Jethro looked so coy. He stepped around the door and said, "Reach out your hand." As she slowly did, palm up, he placed there a wrinkled piece of metal. Her body stiffened. He said, "This one bounced!" She let it drop to the floor. He picked it up and placed it in his pocket.

He stepped back into the bathroom and said, "Come here. Stand there."

She went in, petrified, numb! James was sitting up, head bowed down, legs out in front of him. Blood was bubbling from his mouth, and a straight, thick drop of blood was coming from his temple.

James never lifted his head as he tried to ask Jethro, "Am I dying?"

Jethro said, "Yep, you're out of here, son."

James said, "I'm Christian."

Jethro said, "That's what they all say." Those were James' last words, as Jethro wrapped a towel around his hand and shot James in the chest. Then he unwrapped his hand and shot him again. Same area. He said, "This guy won't die!"

Karlyn's knees buckled. She ran to the kitchen sink. She felt helpless. Tears streamed down her cheeks. She panicked! She grabbed the only thing she saw. It was a flimsy steak knife. She returned to the bathroom and pointed it at Jethro, but as he just looked at her, she felt so foolish.

The look in his eyes penetrated her. Did she think she could stop him!? Terrified, she waved the knife over James out of confusion. She didn't want to be next. No words were spoken. But James was gone!

She saw the smug look on his face, with James lying there. He wondered about the knife. She got so scared. She went back to the sink, put the steak knife back in the rack. How could she imagine using it to stop Jethro? She hoped she didn't piss him off or she'd definitely be next. But he was just puzzled by her motive.

Then Jethro yelled at her. "Get something to clean this up, because there is blood on the wall," he said. She was so afraid; she did exactly what he said. She ran to James' room to get his blanket, not to help Jethro, but to try to comfort James. It was the only way she knew to let him know she was there. The fear and urgency left her dumbfounded. As she placed the blanket over his legs she tried to tuck it under his hands so he'd know she was there somehow. In the face of death, the spirit is still there. Karlyn felt a strong sense of communication.

Jethro's head turned to light a cigarette, and Karlyn felt to see if James was still alive. He was gone.

Karlyn remembered how painfully struck she was to look at Jethro, the animal, who had just killed her friend. She loathed him. Her jaw tightened. She stepped back from him. Her eyes said it all. There would never again be any understanding between them.

Then he said, "You'd better get it together." He looked down at his prey and said, "That's a sleeping bag. Help me zip him up in it."

Her legs wouldn't unlock. At that he started zipping up the sleeping bag and sliding James' body into it. First his feet and legs, and then he leaned the body forward to pull the sleeping bag up to his chest. He continued until she saw James' body disappear into the bag. She was frozen in horror.

The towel he once used to cover the shots, just minutes before, was once again in his hand, and the gun. Karlyn thought she was next, but instead he reached behind the body and wiped a portion of the wall where there was a smear of blood. The towel went into the sleeping bag. She never saw the gun after that, but she knew he had it and would use it at any time.

He ordered her from room to room. There was no question about helping voluntarily. The disappointment of knowing the truth of just who Jethro was and of losing a dear friend were only the beginnings of her hell. Then he closed the living room curtains and went out to back the car up to the house. Her mind was completely blank. All she could do was stand there.

As he lifted the corpse up, supporting it against his chest, he said, "Grab the end." He swung around to back out of the bathroom, expecting her to accompany him. As he continued to back out, he was struggling alone to carry the dead weight. He shifted the weight to his advantage and then said, "Grab the other end." She knew he couldn't cope with another confrontation, so she pinched the very ends of the sleeping bag in hesitation, reluctantly obeying the letter of law which could destroy her.

Jethro opened the front door, laboring. The trunk of the car was wide open as he wrenched James' body, wrapped in the sleeping bag, through the door and toward the vehicle, allowing it to fall into the trunk. James' legs and feet slid in behind. Then he closed the trunk.

Jethro was like a mental maze walking around. He calculated any moves of an inevitable investigation. He took a towel to the wall where James had leaned, to a spot on the floor, and also to a smudge on the edge of the tub. He told Karlyn to get her clothes off and while he was gone to paint the wall.

He took every stitch she wore and left her standing there naked. It was the same technique used to strip the humanity from all those debased by the Nazis. He knew just what he was doing. He took the towel, her clothes, a map, and his cigarettes with him and told her to get a grip on herself. Before he left he put something in the back seat, walked around the car, checked it, and left. He waved and said he'd be back.

She stood there frozen, naked, unable to think or reason. She felt as if he were still watching. She saw the phone sitting on the back of the couch, but she was too petrified to touch it. If he were watching, she'd never make it through the dial tone. She thought of her children. How could they ever escape from him now?

She went to James' room and put on a pair of his levis and a tee shirt. She then just sat there and rocked herself. Then she opened his drawers, and got a couple of pairs of his sox and a couple of tee shirts. She just wanted to touch them, to believe somehow that he'd be back. She was sure she saw James spirit there by the door. She could hear him asking her, "Why, Karlyn? Why?"

She finally realized she'd been told to clean things up, but she couldn't move. But if he came back and saw her just sitting there, well, she didn't know what would happen. So she painted the small area on the wall where James had leaned.

She went into her room, got up, looked around, and went back to her room again. She laid down, and then moved around again. She just didn't know what to do. But one thing for sure: She wasn't going to let Jethro see her in any way look weak or confused. She knew he would kill her at a moment's notice. Thoughts of her father's discipline and the friends she protected from his violence flooded her mind.

The house was completely silent. She could hear absolutely nothing. She just wanted help, but there was none. She was afraid to cry or show any emotions. She didn't know what would happen. If he suddenly came back, she had better be doing what she was told. But she realized, finally, that Jethro did not have to have a reason to react. This scenario sprang entirely from the evil in his mind.

Her fear, disappointment, and shame finally took control. A couple of hours went by. At two or three, maybe, Jethro returned. She had hoped he'd just leave. But that's not at all what he had in mind. He spoke boldly of his disposal of the body, bragging about his demented torture. He was nervous, in an excited kind of way, like an obvious psychotic. He said he cut off James' fingers and bounced him down some rocks. His gleeful rationale didn't make any sense.

He said something about going two steps forward and then three steps backward. He didn't seem aware of whether he had a sympathetic audience or not. He lit a cigarette and monologued that once he got the corpse out of the trunk of the car, he rolled it over an embankment and it got stuck. So he climbed down to get it unwedged and then decided to just cover it up with rocks. He said he prayed to Odin to send a bear to eat the flesh, leaving no remains.

Before she could allow herself to pass out in horror, she separated herself from him and went to her room. She just couldn't believe it! She lay in bed, not knowing what to say or how to go on living. She didn't want to be next. Her children and herself! She was so afraid she couldn't imagine how they'd all survive.

He followed her in and laid down beside her. He didn't really seem to be aware of her. Her reactions to him were the last thing on his mind. He lit another cigarette. Their backs were to each other. He smoked a while and said, "We'll have to remodel or the ballistics will show up." He knew he was going to prison for what he did, but he was going to make it as hard as possible for them to figure it out. After a long while, Karlyn finally fell asleep from exhaustion.

Then it was morning. She was awakened by the phone. TJ was home already. John already knew what happened. Why else wouldn't he have taken TJ and Stephen to work with him that day as they had planned. Dave was calling that he wanted to bring the children right home, which he did, He dropped them off and left.

Karlyn saw the car pulling into the driveway. It was Jethro. She didn't even know he'd gone. He'd gone out to get a cup of coffee.

Response to Public Record
Jethro's Record

The actual records leading to the wrongful conviction of Karlyn Eklof are presented at the end of this and succeeding chapters, as well as in the direct context of the narration, in order that the reader may decide for himself the extent of misrepresentation which the prosecution employed. Also given are the comments, *in italics*, which Karlyn has written on the actual documents.

Although these records had not yet been investigated, the crimes of Jethro are here quoted and summarized to provide more background for the characters in the story:

"On May 12, 1987 he entered an Alpha Beta store in Chula Vista and placed six packages of meat in the front of his pants. When confronted, he attacked the owner with an 8" blade knife puncturing and lacerating his right arm and biceps. When he was intercepted on June 5th, it became evident that he had been on parole for four years and had been stealing meat from Alpha Beta and other stores to sell to friends for cash to pay for rent. His attempts to change his appearance and his name when arrested indicate a pattern of petty theft of long standing."

I am serving two life sentences for the crimes of Jethro Tiner. Here is an arrest record of one of his previous lesser crimes, which is worded as though it were a crime I, myself, had committed:

"The defendant (myself) on or about the 21st day of March, 1993, in Lane County, Oregon, acting in pursuance of a common intent with Jeffrey Dale Tiner, did unlawfully and knowingly possess and have under his custody and control a .25 caliber firearm, Jeffrey Dale Tiner having previously been convicted of the felonies of Possession of Counterfeit Money in 1981 in California, Conspiracy to Defraud in 1981 in California, Burglary in 1985 in California, and Assault With a Deadly Weapon With Great Bodily Injury in 1987 in California; contrary to statute and against the peace and dignity of the State of Oregon."

Strangely, these are given as actual crimes for which I was charged, having been handed all of Jethro's charges because I would not plea bargain.

He allegedly killed a man while in Folsom whom he considered to be a child molester, but it was never proven. He also fled the scene of an accident, some time after the murder in Oregon, which left his girlfriend at that time permanently paralyzed, for which he did time in Nevada, before being brought to Oregon to await trial.

Karlyn, herself, had never been charged with a crime. though every effort was made during her trial to make it appear that she had. She was once arrested on May 21, 1990 and charged with assault. Although the assault was described by others and there was an attempt to elude arrest, it was determined on May 23rd that elements of a crime were not present and she was released. Her statements about the assault at that time were: *"As far as I'm concerned I had every right to defend myself. I was only looking for my car to be coming down the street, I was holding my 15-month-old daughter in my arms, I was not looking for any problems, and it was a beautiful day.*

As a witness stated, I stopped the other two girls from continuing a fight they were having, and then Mr. Scott socked me! I was definitely having a very bad day.

It was determined we were both to blame. This is also when Craig stole $500 from me so my children didn't have a place to move into. This Craig also wrecked the car.

The pattern of misrepresentation evident here becomes more egregious as other public records accumulate.

Chap VI: A Most Unprofessional Job

T hat next morning her son TJ was in the living room asking where James was. Karlyn told him she didn't know. TJ saw James' glasses and baseball hat on the living room floor and set them on the TV. She felt so helpless. The children were dropped off in the driveway by Dave.

Jethro told her to tell TJ to watch the children. Then he told her to follow him. He was going to move James' car to the airport. She spoke up and told him to park it at the bar. She was playing for time, hoping to get attention somehow. Jethro was supposed to be going back to San Diego. She didn't want him changing anything. Then he decided she should say that James left the party and went to the bar.

But he grabbed James' shaving kit and put it in James' car, deciding that it was better to say James must have left town. He handed Karlyn the keys to her car, the title of which he had recently put in both their names. This was the last time she had the keys, ever. He drove James' car to the market and parked it. The dog was in the car, so he took him with them, taking the wheel, and dropping him off several miles away. He also instructed her to toss James' keys, one at a time, out the window. After that he pulled into the Safeway parking lot next to the carpet store. He said he wanted carpet to throw forensics off.

He drew a diagram for the owner and purchased carpet and linoleum. Karlyn started getting antsy in the store. She wanted to cry. She wanted to run, but she just got rude.

It turned out Jethro put her in a position of responding to a choice of linoleum. She snapped, "Whatever! Just do whatever you are going to do!" He was so calm and cool. She couldn't handle all this. She just wanted to be with her children. She wanted to know if they were safe. She didn't know who might be at the house.

But she had no way out of this. and Jethro made that very clear. He told her she had better get control. She hated him for what he did, and for the helpless feelings she had. She tried to regain her balance but she couldn't. She was just learning to suppress her emotions and wait until he would leave.

The carpet was brought to the house, and he casually started his master plan of altering the house. Al Hope stopped by and helped him remove the carpet. Keith came by at lunch time, asking about James. Jethro spoke up and told him he left with some woman to the bar. Then he suggested they meet at 5:00 P. M. and go look for him.

Karlyn was told to wash the car and hose down the trunk. Without saying anything, she did what she was told. She thought, by her not saying anything to Al, he would realize there had been trouble. But she didn't want to get caught looking at him too long. There was rust in the trunk. She thought it was blood, but it wasn't. The metal moved when she sprayed it with water.

It was a nightmarish week. Karlyn learned to respond to inquiries in a way that satisfied Jethro . She must appear to be going along. But she was watching hopelessly while Jethro covered his tracks. She realized she was having to lie all the time and to fake a certain role expected of her by all those who had congratulated them on that fateful evening. She just hoped she could get by until he was gone.

Jethro contacted Spider a couple of times, once to prime the car at Kathy and Rob's house, and again to have him take it to his shop to work on the brakes. Karlyn wasn't told about this until later, so she didn't know which day it was.

Later Jethro had Spider also change the tires. While he was doing these things, he reminded her that the police would take her children. They really did not have any conversations. It was a tacit understanding. If she could escape him she would. But while he made preparations to leave town, she knew that she would have to do whatever he said. It was something they both understood perfectly.

How Jethro managed to cover his butt is difficult to determine. Days went by when he wouldn't come near the house. But he checked to be sure she was there and to give her instructions, until the day she was asked to leave. She could not say anything to anyone which would alarm them and cause them to take steps to protect her. Her terror was real. She had to survive, and her children had to survive. At any time he could come with her car and destroy any one of them.

She had a check coming. That was also on her list as a way of survival. She didn't want to leave. She knew once Jethro left to go to San Diego she could clear this up. But no! Jethro had no intention of leaving her there, but sometimes it seemed he had no intention of taking her! He deliberately created an ambiguity about her status so that she would have to delay any action.

He took all of them to a motel once. He was afraid that Keith, the police, and the media were closing in. He predicted every step of what was happening. All of this was just too crazy for Karlyn. She just wanted him to go. The next day as they arrived back, they saw a detective car outside the house, so he took them all to Kathy and Rob's and told Karlyn to go back and handle it. She took a deep breath, looked at her precious children under his control, and started out walking.

When she arrived back at the house, the detectives were there with the landlord. They were there in order to check on a missing person's report. It was obvious who the landlord was. She and her daughter were throwing accusations and dirty looks at Karlyn. They would have evicted her on the spot, but Karlyn begged the detectives not to allow it. It was a matter of life and death to Karlyn. If only she could just gain a little time!

One of the detectives seemed sure he had talked the landlord into allowing her to stay. But the other detective, a Captain Smith, sided with the landlord. They also wanted her to go to the department for questioning. When she was returned they told her to remove her things from the house.

They said she didn't belong at the house any longer and that she should find shelter at that time. But she knew she could not secure her children or gain protection of any kind in order to move. Therefore, she was forced by the detectives to continue the charade and agree to leave, who used the landlord to enforce their decision. She was evicted on the theory that she was not a tenant, only a guest of James Salmu.

As she pulled her belongings together, the landlord's daughter stood by screaming profanities and accusations at her. Karlyn spoke to her briefly, reasonably, hoping she might understand the dilemma she was in, at least until she could gain time. But instead the daughter got on the phone to James' family, filling them full of fears and anger toward her. She tried to keep calm and cooperate with everybody, because wherever Jethro was, he was watching her, and her children's lives depended on her every move. As they left the house, she pressed on to gather her belongings, as she was instructed to do.

Jethro drove up and said, "Well, I guess you're coming with me!" There was no chance for her to escape from him now. He went to tell Jimmy to bring the truck.

She asked Kathy if she and the children could stay there. But Kathy said she could not afford to lose her place because of overcrowding, though Karlyn's trunks were okay to stay. Karlyn left five army trunks behind. While they were there, Kathy allowed the police to go through her things, something she had agreed not to let anyone do.

Losing her belongings, her friends, and the beautiful life she had built up for herself wrenched Karlyn's heart, destroying her self respect completely. For the moment she couldn't even think of James and what he had lost.

All she wanted now was safety for her children. Jethro instructed her to pack the car with just enough clothes for the children and a few things for herself. Then they headed south. He seemed to sense for a while the shock she was undergoing. He told her he was sorry that he caused her so much trouble. In his soft voice, he said he drank too much and got carried away. He could always strike a pose to assuage the minds and hearts of her children.

He also said he would return them to her family and then turn himself in. He said it was the most unprofessional job he'd ever done, and he'd be the laughing stalk of the yard. He deserved to be caught, and it would just be a matter of time.

The shame and disappointment to even think of bringing him to her family widened her awareness of pain and devastation. Traveling south, he kept looking through his phone numbers. He said that there would be friends he could leave her and the children with. But Karlyn would not have that. In spite of the pain she would cause them, he had promised to take her home to her family.

As Karlyn and the children were forced to accompany him, he was able to produce associates through various phone calls, who were set up along the route to assist him in destroying them. How the children could endure it, we'll never know, but for the moment the abuse didn't involve them. Through the fear he could induce, with the incessant phrasing of his rationale, through hypnosis and brainwashing, sometimes induced by some type of drug (Rohyphenol), she began to suffer many abuses.

He wouldn't let Karlyn use her ID for any hotels coming down. He wanted to be able to say he never saw her after leaving Oregon. He mentioned dumping them off, herself and the three children, at a couple of his prison friends' homes, promising to return. But then he never stopped. He was always thinking. And Karlyn kept saying, "Oh no, we're going all the way south. I have family."

They stopped at his brother's place in Fresno and stayed a few days or perhaps a week. He almost convinced her to stay there. He would build himself up as a mountain of a man in his own eyes and for the children's benefit, but in her eyes he was less than a snake. She struggled to understand, but everything he said had nothing to do with what he did.

He and Dave, his brother, coated the trunk. They looked at rentals. Dave tried talking to Karlyn. He said this wasn't the first time his brother had been in trouble or the last. Karlyn tried to laugh like she knew what she was doing, but they both could see clearly how dumb this guy's life-style was. He said, "Well, maybe you do care enough about him to change him. Good luck!"

There was only one role for Karlyn. That was a supportive one. Beneath that was a fear for her life. But gone was her sparkle, her joy, and her personality. With Jethro she became haggard, jumpy, scared, and withdrawn. And he despised her for it.

Typically, she would be asked to dress up; they were going out. As they consulted street maps, shady districts, alleys, and byways, there would be a bobbing of cars, a pulling alongside. If necessary, there would be a loaded drink forced upon her for her hideous role. In the morning, she would smell herself, would hope for her turn in the bathroom of the crowded apartment. There was no way of feeling whole again. She describes this episode in her own words at the end of this chapter in response to a police report and again in one of the last chapters.

So the ride with Jethro didn't end in Fresno as he would have it. The veneer was too thin for both of them. But when he did get them all the way to San Diego and, of course, to his neck of the woods, Imperial Beach, he wouldn't let them go. He had plans for them. The first couple of days there were spent in a motel. She really didn't have any idea where they were. She did know they were in San Diego, but she had no idea that they were right next to the border.

Karlyn finally called her mom and grandmother and told them she thought they were all right. They told her about flyers and phone calls they had received about James. She kept reading her Bible as she had done on the way down. Never once did Jethro give her the keys or leave them where she could get to them.

She had a candle in the bathroom, the one thing she had taken from James' room to help her adjust to the loss of him. It was a blue pyramid. While sitting in the tub reading her Bible, she noticed a gold flicker. How unusual. It did it again. The candle burned down enough so that she could see it had an ornament hid in it. She pulled it out and got excited. It was something special: an old-fashioned phone locket.

A little while later she noticed another flicker. She thought, no, what's this? And again it burned down enough to be pulled out. It was a 1913 gold Indian-head coin. And no kidding, there was a third piece, a triangle shape. It was like a good omen. She felt very lucky and thought that even though so much had happened, things were going to work out. There were so few things to keep her going.

She wanted to see her family in the worst way. But how could she ever do that without endangering them? It would never happen as long as she was in Jethro's control. He did, however, know where her grandparents lived and had met them, from before. This caused her much fear.

But no, the good omen was but a grasp at straws. Daily her condition got worse, no matter how hard she tried. Jethro lied or tried to hide whatever he was doing. No progress was made in placing them in their own place. That's when the bouncing began again and the missing hours. Bruises! No hope for any sort of viable relationship with her captor.

At one time she had liked him so much. But now he disappointed her no end. She really believed, when he moved the children and her to avoid the media for their own safety, he would put them in a safe place and go back to explain what he did and what happened. At least, since she couldn't escape from him, she tried to believe that. She kept trying to believe that once the children were settled, he would come forward, gather the proper people together and clean this matter up. But he squirmed and wormed his way deeper and deeper. She'd never been so far into corruption.

He kept saying he knew he was going down for this one. Understanding that, you'd think he'd know the right thing to do for Karlyn and the children. It was just a ploy, a bid for her acceptance of his crumby life-style. She'd never been scared of anyone a day in her life that she couldn't walk away from. But this, she had been scared every day since she learned his true colors, and would probably always be afraid.

She thought often of James' mother's pain. When she could still hope to get away, she prayed just for her comfort and solace. She prayed his mother would get over this, be comforted by the Holy Spirit, and would always remember the love they shared in this life. With much time to herself, hoping for an escape of her own, she prayed that his spirit was safe and free. And guarded by the angels of the Lord continually.

Jethro always kept the car keys and one of the children with him. From motel rooms to his friends' houses, Karlyn never really knew where she was. The freeway she knew was south, and sometimes she could smell the beach. After a while, a couple of girls helped her get her direction. It took a while, but she finally figured out the area he was operating in. After that, little by little, she could figure the direction she needed to go to get some help.

He took them to people who allowed her to clean the children, prepare some meals, and rest for a day or two or three. Then he'd say, "Say, it's getting too crowded. These people need a break—not used to kids." And he'd move them again. Then he'd tell her he had to check on this job or that. Always excuses to go in and out, to leave them, and to make them stay, stop and go, packing and unpacking the car. Hurry up and wait! Empty promises filled with fear and confusion, not to mention the embarrassment and confusion of unaccounted-for time lapses and damages.

She made the suggestion to him to let her go for help from the welfare. He would state that she couldn't go to welfare because detectives would take her children.

Paranoia set in. He didn't want anybody to know exactly where they were. For a while he had her convinced that he just couldn't get two and two together. She thought, well, a woman, three children, and no place or money; She guessed he was trying to make do.

But the truth is he had a heroin habit. As she became aware of it, she guessed that he had gradually acquired a dislike for her in general, unless he could use her in his scheme to sell her services. She didn't know at the time that all the moving around was senseless. But because of the trouble he had put her in, he was looking for any way out and was getting quite reckless about it. He was past the point of saying the honorable things that kept her stupid to his ways. His patience was very thin. She was very scared.

At the time she first talked to Steve Walker in response to learning from her family that they were looking for her, she was coping by trying to fulfill Jethro's expectations of her and realizing that, finally, it was she who was rejected.

****

There were a number of police reports which relate to the period just covered above in Karlyn's last days in Springfield, her sojourn in Fresno and her first month or so in San Diego. It is important to know what was learned by the police during this time, and especially, how many things were transformed over time. Sometimes her own reactions to the reports are included in italics, or the transformations are added in elite type to distinguish them from the report.

Sometimes, however, the reports are analyzed in detail according to recent information the writer has acquired from the findings of Tiner's lawyers when he finally went to trial. Comments on these late discoveries by the writer are in brackets. When the findings are included, they are in elite type.

Detective Alan Warthen contacts Glen Dent

On April 2, 1993 Glen Dent, owner of East Side Floors, in this first interview, confirms that Eklof and Tiner had purchased new floor coverings at his business.

He said the male was a tall, tattooed, "biker looking," rough guy. The female had dark hair... did most of the talking... and talked loud and rough.

She kept referring to the guy as her "old man." He remembers that the guy took cash out of his pocket and paid for the carpet. [At her Grand Jury a year later, he changes this and says he thought she did.]

Terry J. Bekkedahl of the Forensic Laboratory

This reports refers to Captain Richard Golden, Acting Chief, and Steve Walker concerning the missing person investigation of James Salmu, that he had gone to the scene where Salmu was last seen and had located blood spatter on a wall and bathroom door. He also noted a brownish/red stain on a clothes dryer in the utility room. He stated that bloodstains on the hallway wall and bathroom door were removed and tested. He returned to the residence on April 7th and failed to locate any other evidence of blood stains.

When Karlyn examined this report, she stated:

The bathroom failed to show any residue of blood. The blood spatter on the wall was consistent with his going by it to clean the scratch made by my ring after he "head-butted" me. The dryer was noted to have had a stain the size of a hand, but was not tested! I declare the rust stain on the dryer was just that, a rust stain.

You wouldn't believe, however, what was made of the above report at Karlyn's trial. This information has been made available by attorneys for Tiner's trial:

A. OSP Forensic Report of 4/29/94 Exhibit 4 - "blood" from hallway wall tested "positive presumptive as "blood." What the hell is "positive presumptive?

B. OSP Forensic DNA Test 6/29/95 Exhibit 4 "no comparison can be made."

C. OSP Forensic DNA Test 8/17/95 Exhibit 4 "no conclusions can be drawn."

Yet, this forensic guy lied under oath, at DA Fred Hugi's prompting:

Q: That blood [from Exh 3, the utility room dryer] was ultimately sent to the Portland Crime Lab and the DNA from Mr. Salmu's bones was compared to that?

A: That's correct.

Q: And matched that; is that correct.

A: That's correct.

Q: And they gave you some figure as to the...

A: The figure that was provided by the DNA unit was one in fifty-one million, two-hundred thousand... [probability of matching Salmu's DNA].

The key to the above is that Eklof's trial was in September of 1995. The final OSP Report "inconclusive" DNA test on Exhibits 3 & 4 was only written on 8/17/95 and stamped DA "received" on 8/24/95 three weeks before her opening arguments. Bet money that the DNA "inconclusive" report was not provided to trial counsel for Eklof, or they would have called Bekkedahl for his perjury. It is also gross prosecutorial misconduct for Hugi to solicit Bekkedahl's perjury, while concealing the exculpatory DNA test results.

Once Bekkedahl lied about Exhibits 3 & 4, he tried to bootstrap them from the positive Salmu blood on the wall to match that inside the bathroom (Exh 2) to give a big description of blood spatter directional humbug to solidify his perjury. Hugi solicited it.

The same type of forensic blood spatter scam was used by the same Springfield cops/OSP lab to falsely convict Boots and Proctor on a bogus homicide indictment resulting in their $2M lawsuit [and, if you can remember that far back, by Bekkedahl's predecessor in the OSP lab, to establish that Diane Downe's daughter was pulled back into the car after being shot].

Newly discovered document, Exhibit C, hidden from Eklof Trial, dated April 1, 1993

This hidden parole office document, not available but known to the writer through discovery by Tiner's lawyers, shows that Eklof was a primary homicide suspect as early as April 1, 1993, before she even left Oregon for San Diego, within days of alleged crimes. Exhibit C states:

The police repeatedly claimed she wasn't initially a suspect, in order to clean up lack of *Miranda* warning in all of the initial conversations with Eklof. Hugi and the cops also made that claim in her pretrial admittance hearings, lying to gain admittance of the *un-Mirandized* Eklof statements from April 1993 to May 1994, which include: **every tape the state used at Eklof's trial.** Hugi deliberately, willfully, and knowingly concealed this evidence at the time of Eklof's statement suppression arguments in her pretrial proceedings. The state, *i. e.*, cops and prosecutor, repeated told Eklof's court, counsel, and jury that Eklof was not a homicide suspect until the Salt Lake City conversations, at the earliest, that she was a "missing person" only. This blows any claim of "voluntariness,' where police documentation shows Eklof as a focal suspect in a homicide investigation from ten days after alleged crimes.

The above information will be repeated later in the book when its availability to her appeals counsel for Post Conviction Relief is discussed in detail.

Taped phone call between Jethro Tiner and Steve Walker

When Jethro reported to his parole officer on April 5, 1993, after arriving in San Diego, he was handcuffed and a call was put through to the Springfield Police Department. Jethro is talking as though he didn't know where Karlyn was and hadn't seen her since Springfield. Steve tells Jethro, "Okay, now Karlyn has called here… And she's ah she's ready to talk to us… I just want to give you every opportunity to tell me everything you know about this man (James, and his disappearance) before I talk to Karlyn again…"

This of course is a lie. It is at the root of the abuse Karlyn would suffer

more and more, first from Tiner and later from those he charges with using
and keeping track of her.

In his phone call to Steve, he admits his former addiction. But as Karlyn
reacts to this phone record later on she states:

*I did not know of his usage at this time, but I knew he had access to
meth—who doesn't? But heroin addicts are a very risky bunch. They have no
mercy for their victims They sell whom or whatever to get their fix. If I had
only known the system he was pulling or pushing me into. But how could I
have known? I was waiting desperately for him to get us settled and then
leave!*

Taped phone call between David Tiner and Steve Walker May 6, 1993.

Dave states that he called Springfield the day after Karlyn was evicted…
He refers to a night Jethro took Karlyn out for the evening while they were at
Dave's house. Dave asks his wife what she thought of Karlyn. She says that
Karlyn seems to be a hard woman.

Karlyn's reaction to this report at a much later date brings back her
recollection of just how Jethro's abuse was accomplished. In her own words:

*This must have been the night Jeff took me to a bar. I remember we
parked the car on the street. It was still midafternoon, and the place had just
opened up. I think the bartender, however, was there just for us. I didn't think
so at the time, but I look back now and see a pattern.*

*The place was next to a termite place. I remember the old "bug" sign.
We had a few drinks. I listened to the juke box. Some people came in and got
rather friendly, and we left a short time after that. He did do some talking to
the owner quite a bit of the time. The next thing I remember is that Jethro's
walking me out the **back** door and our car is [now] parked there.*

*Then we were driving down an alley and he put the car into a rocking
motion. The car coming toward us does the same thing. They stopped and
talked. I was disappointed that he didn't have more to say. And they took real
good looks at me! It was still daylight, but we didn't get back to Dave's until
long after dark. I don't remember anything in between. But something happened to me. I think he sold me for his drug habit, but they'd done something
to me so I don't remember. It has been like this ever since I met Spider, Potato,
and Jeff. It seems there's a system out there, a real clever system. Sell women
and hypnotize them so they don't remember! I'm not sure how to explain it.*

Dave essentially covers for his brother. He tells Steve Walker that Jethro
didn't tell him anything about what had happened in Springfield, that he didn't
know what had happened to James. At this time he does not tell Walker about
Jeff and him going in the car to coat the trunk, and that Jeff told him what had

happened.

Then he mentions he didn't want Jethro and Karlyn around after "all that crap at my house, you know," when Karlyn elbowed his neighbor. Steve asked if the police were called or if it was a mutual fight kind of thing?

Karlyn is the best one to tell it:

I overreacted to a move Jethro had made. Jeff was standing over me, and he made a move and I jerked back. The neighbor was standing next to me and I elbowed her. She and I made amends immediately afterwards. Even the neighbor's girls, who were her friends standing by the pool, saw and understood it was an accident.

We all sat out by the pool and talked the next day too. I was so nervous around Jethro; I tried not to show it. Jethro had me on an emotional roller coaster. From the murder to the traveling to the silent body language he used, he scared me. He had full control. And this monkey business of selling me and erasing my memory had me full of anxiety and wondering what would happen next.

In his call to Dave, Steve Walker mentions they have some information about Karlyn's connection to Hell's Angels. [Karlyn at one time was told Bob Dahle, who was her godmother's husband, was her real father, and she sought him out.] Dave talks of a certain class she has. Karlyn responds:

Bob Dawley (Dahle) rode with them for one year in the sixties, and that's it. He also passed away in 1981. A man who I have never met, to speak of. Dave mentioned my decent upbringing and high quality taste. The dress I took I apologized for. I had permission to wear it. Dave told me, don't worry about it.

Taped phone call between Karlyn and Jerry Smith

April 26, 1993, Smith asks Karlyn what's going on… you ah suddenly disappeared. She replies, "Well I wasn't trying to. I have had one hell of a month… no place to go… about drove me nuts…" While asking her routine questions, Smith says, "Well, you see, you're talking to somebody who doesn't know as much about it as Walker and Walker is not here today… What are you so upset about today?" Her reply:

As I explain, Smith cut me off when expressing the need for help. I had plenty of fear. Anybody can read this report and see it. He accused me of making excuses. My priority was to secure my children. I took the time to connect out of respect. I did lie to him out of fear. And I begged to be let go, so I could be settled.

She tells him, "This isn't an excuse. This is my life. You threw me out on the street, you and that landlord… I had every right to be there. My rent was paid... you guys threw me on the street with my babies... promised me that my name was not going to be in the newspaper and it was, two-page article... You guys told me to go, find some shelter. I asked you do I have these rights?... I've tried and I've been moving ever since... It took me a month to get here, but I finally made it to my mom's and you know what: I can't stay there because my mom sold her home; it's empty. Are you happy now?"

I was kicked out and tossed right back into Jethro. Smith is saying why didn't I call when I did have a chance. I'm begging him to let me help but to let me get to a secure situation. I have never run from their questions, but I couldn't survive one day without my own key to a door of safety. Smith disregards my cry for help. As much as I wanted to tell Jerry outright, I couldn't, because the more he spoke uncaringly, the more I tensed up. I was already as tight as a rope. Smith continues, "Well, we still have some unanswered questions." [Dialogue continues from transcribed phone call:]

KE Well, I will answer them, but I would like to get my babies into a (garbled) established situation.
JS Do you have a... an appointment today?... So you don't?...
KE (garbled) skip over to the next town just to have some peace and quiet from this shit. It's just all over down here. Do you know this isn't...
JE It's all over down there? *Smith's sarcasm was gut-wrenching.*

Karlyn says, "Okay, you questioned everybody several times. Everybody gave you as much as they could. I (garbled) I'm doing what I can, people. I would like to get into a motel quietly with my children, you know a little kitchenette and then I'll be fine, and I will be able to discuss this with you or you can send somebody to talk to me. I don't care but **I'm going to have an attorney present.** I'm going to have my mother present. I want it recorded. I want to know exactly what everybody up there's been saying. I want to read your report." Later she observes:

The more I beg this guy the more he denies me. How could I have known that he would continue to hound me, taunt me, and that, in the end, an attorney is what he would always deny me.

Smith asks what happened to her boyfriend, Jethro. She responds, "Well, he just has his way of living and I have my way of living... down here... the guy will not have anything to do with me. He will not talk to me. He thinks that it's all, you know, like putting him back into prison type situation, like it's a setup or something. I don't know what he thinks. He won't talk to me...

Then Smith asks her about her association with the Hell's Angels, and also with Dennis. She replies, "I do not know any Hell's Angels. I did meet one or two a few years back, and I collected a couple of pictures and things, but, outside that, I have no idea what you're talking about..."

Regarding Dennis, she says they should get his paperwork from the Veterans first before they start messing into him. "That's why I got away from the weirdo..."

Asked if she kicked the crap out of him at a place called Swingers, she replied, "As a matter of fact, I slapped Dennis because he grabbed me in a way I should not have been grabbed... in front of people. What else was I supposed to do?..." Shortly the conversation ended. She later explained:

I was certainly glad to hang up. I remember very well how shattered and scared I was. It seemed every time I got on my feet one of those Imperial Beach people would be there to sidetrack me or get me going in another direction. I was trying so hard to get into a safe, predictable situation, but I was being suffocated.

Chap VII: Under Surveillance

When they first arrived in Imperial Beach, Karlyn literally fell out of the car from exhaustion, having no memory of what had occurred to cause so much fatigue. From one place to another, Tiner kept control of Karlyn, nearly starving her and the children at times.

Once not long after they arrived Jethro pulled up to the High Tide Tavern, yanked her out of the car, and slapped her face several times. All of the children saw it. TJ told the police about it later. It was his way of keeping her in line. The tension between them was building. His acquaintances observed his behavior and remarked that he'd better do something.

During the first ten days of being bounced around Imperial Beach, Jethro allowed Karlyn a visit to her grandparents. He wanted somebody to see her alive. She found out that detectives were calling everybody trying to locate them. Even Salmu's family was calling claiming to be Springfield police. People were in an uproar. Therefore Karlyn made a phone call to detectives requesting help from her grandparent's phone. That call was summarized at the end of the previous chapter.

Then Jethro visited his parole officer. He was handcuffed while a call was placed to the Eugene-Springfield detectives. In that phone call the police told Jethro that Karlyn had been talking to them. It was their way of applying pressure. Then the officer inexplicably released him. You can imagine what that did to Karlyn's security. As explained in the chapter before, a document well-hidden during Karlyn's trial established that Karlyn was a co-suspect in the crime from April 1, 1993 onward. The police's lies to Jethro were a way of getting to both of them, and they were not interested in her security.

But to Karlyn at the time, she considered that Jethro was the obvious suspect and that telling him that his hostage was sneaking calls to the police about the murder was pretty stupid. It was her son, TJ, who was the first to recognize and alert her of the danger that Jethro was planning. The tone in his voice shook her, but she didn't know how to avoid his vengeance. Whether or not Jethro believed what they were telling him, he would use it to intensify his abuse.

Karlyn couldn't tell whether she was coming or going. Her main objective was to keep the children clean, clothed, fed, and together. Since they were under his control, or the watchful eye of one of his friends, they paid dearly.

Then he would relent. He would go back to trying to control her with reassurances and promises. He would speak to her in a low voice, repeatedly telling her he was going to turn himself in and suggesting over and over again in a hypnotic tone that he was her prince charming. He kept one or both of her youngest children next to him and one eye on her constantly. He never allowed her near the car keys.

He continued to place them in different settings with people who said they would help them. Usually there was no phone and no car. She thought at the time these people were the poorest people she had ever seen. Later she came to know their true meaning, that some of these places had been set up as dropping-off places for victims of the ritual abuse, which they would gradually be sold into. Who could ever describe such overwhelming poverty, barren apartments, or their location?

Karlyn is sure that Jethro promised money to people if they would watch them. That way he could get them out of the car and have the freedom to move around. Sometimes she hardly saw him. His friend, Leo, the mechanical genius, did his very best to help her and the children, letting them stay around his yard and being sure she kept her sights on getting the children in school. He always had logical things to say and was concerned. It was so reassuring to have one person among Jethro's acquaintances who didn't seem like a predator.

She didn't know if he understood what they were doing to her. Because she didn't understand it herself! She'd never been so lost or confused in her life. She just kept trying to get out of people's way in their homes and into her own. But somehow Jethro kept right onto her, turning things upside down. And, of course, she couldn't turn to her family without endangering them, nor to welfare without fear of losing her children. Therefore, she was drinking and that certainly didn't help.

For such a poor town she sure got handed a lot of beer and excuses. She couldn't even find a ride across town because any acquaintances she made were Jethro's too. No money. No gas for the car even if he would take her. Jethro was back in his neighborhood and doing whatever it was he does. He sold her car tools and pawned her diamonds several times. And then the car.

Her clothes were stolen. He kept her against the curb, as they say. But she held on, hoping things would get better and she could see her way out.

They did manage to keep the children fed, but they were always being moved in this square he had her in. If only she could have gotten a grip on all this. But she kept hoping he would clear up this mess. She believes they both knew he never would turn himself in, and the logical next step for him was to get rid of her. He no longer said he was sorry or even gave her a hug to keep her believing.

She got to her stepbrother Jeff's in Lakeside. They were okay there, sort of, with Jethro's acceptance. But then he was going to jail for a stolen car! He gave himself up. So everywhere they stopped, someone was in jeopardy of some kind. The pressure was definitely on. But her little brother Jeff did try to make the best of things. He was truly interested in her safety. He thought that she truly cared about Jethro and was completely heartbroken. Letting him know the truth was not something she could do.

She even took Jethro to a friend's work ranch and got him great work, towing and grooming avocado trees. But of course he had to be in Imperial Beach. He had to go. Nothing she did was good enough. Then her Cutlass was traded for a Cadillac, but not in her name. She didn't have any say or knowledge of this transaction.

At some time during those first six weeks after the murder, Karlyn had some trouble with her son TJ, which is not hard to understand. TJ had always to keep his mouth shut and not cross Jethro for any reason. Karlyn and her son argued, and TJ suddenly disappeared. To ease the pressure, Willy told Marney, the girl she had met in Willy's garage her first night in Imperial Beach, to take TJ to her house out in Tecate.

Pretty soon her son TJ's father came around. Well, this was her great love, Tomas! He heard she'd had some trouble. They had spent eight years together, but he got bored. They were very young. She remembered now some of the bad times, when he took off for the bars and the girls and ended up in Soledad for a few years.

He said, "Karlyn, do you have any idea what you're with? This guy, Jethro, he's the type that when let out of the hole, everybody finds another part of the yard to go to or something to do! He's dangerous." She was finding that out, thank you. Rather she had found that out. But she told him she kept hoping he'd do what's right.

Tomas was pissed, but because of their long love and bond, he just stood aside and watched and let her know he was there. He and his girl just had a baby whose heart needed surgery. He had appointments and told Tammy and Jeff to keep an eye on things. They did go to Willy's with Karlyn once and with Jethro a couple of times. But that ended real quick. Everybody had different friends. She felt after a while that the need to keep moving was the only thing Jethro and she had in common.

Karlyn's mom gave Sparky, her brother, her mobile home, the only way, at twenty-eight years old, he'd leave. There's a nut by itself. Therefore her home needed to be packed. So Karlyn spent a week helping her move and stayed with Diane and Raymond's for a couple of days. Then Jethro went to jail with Tony Acosta for breaking and entering but got released. Jethro said that anybody who released him from jail was the lesser of fools, whatever that means. Wherever she was, Jethro, often with his Kathy, whom he was seeing again, came and went. At least they were drifting apart, she thought.

Then he showed up again after she was finally getting herself together at Mom's. Since she couldn't put her mom in danger, she pretended to be glad to see him. It was because of her family's safety, and her ultimate dependence on them, that she could never send him on his way.

Her family had tried to accept him at first, until they came to know who he was and what he had done to her. But they were in the same kind of double bind that she was. As long as he knew where she was, at any time he could come around or bring her to them. And where they had once accepted him into their lives, there had better not be any betrayal or their lives would be in danger also.

So when he came around, there was nothing Karlyn could do except to go along. She even thought she might marry him, if the abuse would stop. Nor could she actually tell them in detail what was happening to her. Their outrage would put them in danger.

Once under surveillance by the police, she had no choices. There would be many times, in her contacts with them, that they would fail to understand this. She was required to keep in touch with them, but it was impossible to furnish them with the information they wanted while she was still under Jethro's control. And when she finally did escape and was willing to bring the truth home to them, they would nail her to the cross. They would make her their victim.

So when Jethro showed up again, she asked him if he wanted to go to Nevada, maybe see his mom, and get married. Maybe if complete devotion was mentioned, they might get some direction. He said, "Yes."

She thought, "Oh shit, now I'm really gonna get it!" Then she asked Val, her sister, and Tony if they wanted to go with them. Val and Tony had been fighting. She thought, "What's going on? Is there nowhere without turbulence? Just a few minutes of peace!" Nothing was right. She couldn't figure out why. But Jethro convinced her sister and brother-in-law that he was going to marry her.

Well, they got all the children settled at Val's and took off. Karlyn thought maybe this guy was gonna pull through after all. Nope! He knew where he was headed, what tables to hit, and the game he was going for. Val and Tony fought the whole way!

But it had been the weekend of the Don Laughlin Run. She'd never seen so many bikers, and neither had anyone else. They stayed overnight, and Val and Karlyn had fun shopping the windows of stores while Jethro and Tony slept.

Jethro won a few hundred dollars on a table, he said. Putting things together afterward, however, she knew he had probably sold her again, but she had no memory of it.

Then Jethro put a fork in Karlyn's neck because she smart-mouthed him. And he pulled over in the Arizona desert and was going to shoot her. His attempt to be rid of her was causing him a lot of frustration. He obviously was not committed. She arrived home ill.

Home again, well, again there was no place to stay because her mom's property had rules about visitors. Val and Tony had no room. Robert couldn't have them because the children were too small, which Karlyn found to be just about everybody's excuse. Samantha did help for a week; and Chris Dickens, Yollanda, Tina, and Willy. They all took them in briefly.

Yollanda cleared out a room in her house to provide shelter for Karlyn and her children. While she was there Karlyn made a phone call to John Distabile and Dave Wilson in Oregon to get help. They were sympathetic but acted with caution. She suspected that John was involved, and time would tell how right she was.

Tony, Marny's son, took the children out to his house for two days. Then Popeye stepped in and gave Karlyn a big direction that Sparky was going to sell her his car. But that folded on her: Sparky would always set her up to believe in him and then yank the carpet out, just to see her fall. So he could laugh. He even tried to take her children away by using her grandparents, a story with exasperating details.

Finally, Karlyn's grandparents loaned Jethro $714 for an apartment, with her diamonds as collateral. It was extremely generous of them but not atypical. Karlyn's and Jethro's immediate plan then was to get her safe into an apartment and he would turn himself in. So that they could look for an apartment and settle in, the grandparents took TJ and Caroline but not Immanuel, because he was too young.

As soon as the grandparents left with the children, Karlyn had only to remind him of that plan, and he socked her so hard she thought her eye had come out. The baby saw everything. Jethro himself was in shock that it didn't knock her out. But she was too scared for the baby to be left with him to allow herself to pass out. She lost her equilibrium for nearly a week and the whole side of her face was burgundy.

He moved her three different times, spending her grandparent's money on hotels, each time closer toward his dad's place, which was north of Imperial Beach.

Once he told her he was taking Immanuel to see his father. It was during this time that he raped Immanuel, her two-year-old son. As she passed in and out of consciousness, she awoke to see that he had never left, but had molested her baby. He said, in great pain and bewilderment, "That bad man hurt me in my butt, Mama."

For a long while after that the baby never did seem the same. He acted strange to her. This whole thing was out of control and getting worse. She couldn't get out of bed without blacking out. His hitting threw her way out of balance. She wanted to hang on long enough to get the keys. Once when she had strength to try it, he caught her.

He didn't get pissed. He understood, and she thought for a moment he wanted her to get away. He knew what damage he had done to her life and to the children's. But she found she just couldn't see well enough to drive. He got in and drove. They went up by his dad's "vista" but then they came back, of course, to Imperial Beach. She was in no shape to see people. His friends did see her face and thought with shame for her situation.

They stopped to get groceries and to go to Leo's, but then Jethro got arrested for stealing toothbrushes. She never knew quite what that was all about. At least, at that time, she finally had the car. She went to Willy's and told him what happened. He said it was normal for Jethro to do stupid stuff like that. That's just the way he was. She never saw the stolen toothbrushes.

Her grandparents had expected her back the next day to pick up TJ and Caroline. A whole week later they saw her and her face was still a wreck. They saw her eye and wanted to know what happened to the money. She told them Jethro had what was left of it and was in jail.

Since he had $350 of her grandparent's money still on him, Karlyn set about trying to get him out in order to get the money back. She felt free for a little while, but the pressure was still on. Then, after all, she didn't have a car, because it broke down on the freeway. Leo and Willy towed it and sold it to Tony for bail money for Jethro.

Being on her own finally while Jethro was in jail, Karlyn had the courage to apply for welfare assistance. It created just enough distance between her and Jethro to cause her to reach out to people outside the circle of his surveillance.

While gathering herself together and beginning to feel a bit more whole again, she met Donny by the store out by her grandmother's when she went for a walk late one night. In retrospect, she thought she shouldn't have been out walking at all.

Donny understood what kind of trouble she had been in and wanted to help. He was also from Imperial Beach. It ended up that she and the children stayed with him for about a week until her check came through. Her grandparents were helping her get back and forth at that time. When Jethro realized she was on her own at last, he began fighting it and also anyone who was trying to help her.

Since the trip to Las Vegas, she had been subject to his intermittently arranged drug-induced abuse sessions, in which there were also filmed sexual assaults. She only knew of this because of the arrangements he made to have her alone with him and the hours lost and damage to her body. Now that she felt able to regain her freedom through the help of Jethro's own friends, her new acquaintance, and her grandparents, she was ready, if necessary, to put in a call for help.

Jethro was seeing Liz now. However, when he again tried to corner Karlyn, in order to lure her into an abuse session, Liz got beat up pretty badly by him for helping to keep him busy while Popeye got her away from him. She heard Popeye got shot for it, too. Throughout all of this, Jethro remained calm and cool, using whatever fear and intimidation tactics he could to control anyone who would help Karlyn. But he was planning an even greater revenge.

Karlyn could hardly believe she could still function, but she was beginning to get her courage back. She asked Willy to give her back the Cutlass, but he said no. Then he gave her an old station wagon with a flat and starting problems, but she got those fixed and began rolling.

Beginning to feel much better, she asked Donny to take the children and her to the Sportsmen Club for dinner. He stayed with the children in the restaurant while she went for a swim on the beach. But as she crossed the street she saw Jeanette, Willy's X. They always got along really well.

They went in to the High Tide where Karlyn was thinking to say thank you to some people she felt had helped her. She thought they'd have enough time to have a beer before the children and Donny were finished eating. She was excited that she had finally got on her feet and that she even had Jethro's friends looking out for her. She had made up her mind that she and her children would be saying good-bye to Imperial Beach. She had a car, money, and a friend. After all that had happened, she couldn't ask for more.

Well, Gary had been bartending and there was only one other couple there when Jeanette and Karlyn left. They were strange, watching her in the mirror and smiling. She was also aware that everything seemed so quiet at what should have been the 6:00 P. M. happy hour. Anyway, they left together, and Jeanette went home. Karlyn went back to the restaurant, but Donny and the children had left for the beach.

She decided to put a note on the car to tell them she had gone back to the bar to talk with Gary and to pick her up there. Well, he didn't see her note and took the kids back to his place. She didn't even remember getting back to the bar or even halfway up the street. She couldn't remember how she got messed up.

Chap VIII: Ritual Abuse

She did remember, much later, that a man named Mark had appeared at the tavern door, and the bartender signaled for him to back way, stating, "Not yet, not yet!" Karlyn had been drugged. Ten years later, on June 12, 2003, she wrote she was having what felt like a nervous breakdown, suddenly remembering again that episode. After going back to the White Tide she had a drink, went unconscious, and woke up naked in a house. The first thing she saw was Tiner with painted eyes streaked black. Her letter continues:

He held a leash in one hand, wore no shirt, and had pulled on the leash. There was a young woman attached to it. My struggles today come from the shock of witnessing the captive woman's neck snap as Tiner tugged on the leash.

My screams of her falling caused Tiner to stomp on me. He broke my leg and fractured my face. Patrick Walsh stepped out from behind the man who was videotaping. He then wrapped me up in his coat and carried me out to a vehicle.

Next came the young woman who never woke up. A very chilling realization knowing that I was not to have a future. I lay in a shallow grave begging Tiner not to hurt my children. Next to me was the silent young woman. Tiner shushed me and shot twice, hoping to hit his mark, one in me and one in her. Someone standing behind Tiner began shoveling dirt on top of us...

I am absolutely clueless as to who pulled me from the grave and dumped me off behind the Tavern for somebody to find me in that broken state.

The writer includes the above remembrance to emphasize that the nightmare never goes away. There must have been a lot of other women being tortured and victimized at the same time. For a long time she wasn't able to remember much of it.

What she remembers most is that one of the other girls fell on her. That's what woke her out of the trance they put her into. It had never happened to her before that she had been awakened during her trance. That's why she resisted. She thought the girl was dead and realized what was going on around her. She saw the camera registering the event, the naked girls, and some grotesque-looking man carrying out orders to everyone.

She jumped up to attack the beast, but she only ended up getting beat worse than the girl had been. They carried Karlyn out to a truck, a gold-colored one with bars, on a dirt yard.

Someone was saying we would have gotten away with all this but for that one! She'll remember. You shouldn't have beat her or touched her. You blew it for all of us. Snuff her! But someone grabbed her up off the floor.

Long afterward she remembered that it was Potato. At that time, however, she knew she was seeing for the first time a ceremony so staged, so evil, so banal—that was the word, banal, because it was also so brutal, mindless, and stupid—far beyond those episodes Jethro had sedated her for previously. Those had been probably for the porn market. This was ritual abuse. But it was so gross, so sickening. It wasn't like a ceremony at all. It was like animal torture. Only these were people.

After someone rescued her from what was to have been a grave, her remembrances vary. At one point she believes Jeff Malley and two guys had her in a white van. Pete was the driver. They put her in their van and took her to some hospital. They said she wouldn't go in, so they took her back to the bar to find Willy.

Well, the next thing she remembered was being against a wall behind the High Tide. There they dumped her on the ground and took off, probably to go find Willy.

Much later Karlyn did remember more of what happened. But her mind was so damaged when she first began to tell it that she couldn't remember much. Having once been wakened so traumatically, however, she had many flashbacks as her mind healed. She also wondered how many more times she had been a victim when she didn't wake up!

Tina was there in KC's apartment, which was just across the parking lot, and she didn't help. Tina was scared and KC had told her not to let anyone in.

But when KC found out who it was, she got pissed at Tina and helped Karlyn. Tina said that being from Arizona, she had been in a club with her husband and very often they would gather two hundred or so people and do girls like this, and she had to clean up and bed them (the girls) often. But in Karlyn's case, she didn't know what to do.

When Willy arrived, he first asked Karlyn why she was crying. She tried to get up and couldn't, because her right leg was broken. Then he took one look at her and said, "Oh, shit!" Willy was pissed. He told Tina to leave and get some ice in a hurry. And he told her, "You should have helped her. She's your friend. She'd have helped you!"

Karlyn was scared! She knew these people! What did they think they were doing?

So they all knew about it! Willy went to get help. He got Karlyn to the back door where Cindy and Leo were shooting pool. Karlyn stumbled and fell on Cindy. Leo put her in his car and took her to his house where all the guys came around to find out what had happened. Then they all went in different directions. Well yes! It is unbelievable that this went on right under their noses, and several of them were involved. Did they just reserve the High Tide and reel in the victims?

Donny was called. Karlyn was so crazed she couldn't tell who anybody was. Tony said, "She's faking it." Everybody else said, "No way! Look at her. She's been beat bad. Who did this?"

Kathy and Cindy said it was more than one person. This girl can hold her own. Karlyn at that point had no idea what had happened. Eleven weeks went by before she could even touch her face.

Jethro showed up with Kathy at Leo's later that night. Their story was that they went to a bar where Potato overheard some guy bragging about doing some girl and doing her good. Kathy said she took a pool stick to him and chased him down the street. It was a cover, and they all knew it. It was Jethro who staged it.

So who do you think carried her out to her station wagon when Donny showed up? Jethro! For two days she lay around at Donny's, until the third day. Then she finally could stand up long enough to get to the car and to the Grossmont Hospital where they cast her leg.

While she was treated at the hospital, her children were kept by a friend. When she was released from the hospital and lay on the living room floor with her children surrounding her, it was then that her grandparents showed up at Donny's with the detectives from Oregon she had called to come down and help her.

But she just couldn't talk. Not that day. She couldn't remember anything. But she knew that she would one day get all the truth out. Fractured face, leg broken in two places, she looked and felt awful, pissed off and humbled at the same time. The obvious condition she was in was a sure indication that she and her children had been in danger and that the detectives should have responded to her call for help, which she had made several weeks earlier.

She felt such a failure to herself, her children, and her family. Her grandparents were so hurt at the sight of her. Chris Dickens came over and said,

"You know this and you know that, but most of all, we love you. Get better."

She felt so stupid. She got over to Willy's after the detectives left. He rode her on his motorcycle two blocks to the High Tide. The place was packed this time. Everyone gave her a hug for pulling herself together. But she was there just to find out what happened to her. Where was everybody when she needed them? Wasn't anybody going to do anything!? She only knew that at one point she had wakened and had seen other women being tortured. And other things were falling into place. It was really hard to sort out friends from foe.

That was when Willy told her that John Distabile and Jethro had been friends ten years ago. Jethro was scarcely to be seen by anybody that night, which she thought was very strange. When she did see him, he was with Liz. But she knew he'd had a big payoff. To support his addiction and get even!

Silently, Karlyn thanked Liz for taking him off her hands. Evidently she thought of him as Karlyn had, that he'd be a great worrier type, honorable and disciplined. Were they wrong! Anyway she and the children stayed at Chris Dicken's after that. He picked them up at Donny's. Before that the children were at Nana's.

Karlyn's letter of June 12, 2003 sheds some more light on what she now believes was happening on that fateful night ten years ago:

A third man involved that night I suspect has a very long history with these types of life-threatening incidences. It's possible this one named Louie taught Tiner, Walsh, and Distabile how to drug women and videotape killings.

When Tiner was eighteen years old he stood on the Imperial Beach pier with Louie while Louie shot two men. Tiner told me that was his first job.

The night that my drink was drugged and I woke in that situation I described, I believe the incident which snapped the young woman's neck wasn't suppose to happen. Louie's anger at that moment and yelling, "Snuff the bitch!" meant that Tiner was a slob and had just ruined months of work getting things in order to videotape girls getting killed.

The cameras were turned off because of the accident and because of my waking in distress. Tiner's stomping on me, probably meaning to kill me that way, and my rescue, by someone behind the camera, meant that the tape was useless and had to be destroyed so that there wouldn't be any connections.

It is strange, but [afterwards] Tiner wanted me gone and so did Louie.

One cannot know what truth lies in her revisits to the traumatic night when she was almost killed. There are still huge gaps in what she was able to put together, especially after her experiences of the next six weeks while she was in her little apartment in La Mesa. Her flashbacks will be continued as she encounters several more people who were actually involved in the abuse ritual.

She suffered so much because she was afraid to tell anyone. After the abuse ritual, she was still as destitute for help as before, except that now there was trauma in her waking consciousness. She knew what they were capable of doing. Friends weren't friends anymore. She started going inward and not talking to people she used to trust.

Sparky pulled some crap, as was mentioned previously. It is almost too much to tell, that her own brother could also be so treacherous and deceitful. He was saying the police were there taking her children, that TJ was going with him, and that Karlyn was a useless mother and had it coming. He said that whatever he could do to make things worse, he would ride it out.

The details are beyond comprehension. If Karlyn really has a brother like that, she is to be pitied for it. For nine dense paragraphs in her original journal she outlines his treachery. In any case, it is really too much to burden the reader with. She does make reference to it in response to a police report, however, which will be included later.

Then in August her cast was ready to come off. They said they were going to put pins into her leg. No way, she said. She healed just fine, and Bob, her stepdad, along with her mother, helped her get into an adorable apartment in La Mesa. She just wanted a place of her own. So she got one. Everything would be better now, she thought.

A portion of the following document sums up Karlyn's contacts with the police during the above period:

H. Thomas Evans, Att. [from] Law Memorandum to Suppress No. 10-94-04750: In May, 1993, the police learned Defendant had left the area and they began to try to contact Defendant via telephone by calling numbers they found on the victim's old phone bills. Police contacted Defendant's mother and grandmother by telephone and told them they had a missing person and suspected Defendant of involvement in the victim's disappearance.

The Defendant called the police and denied involvement and repeatedly requested that the police stop calling her family and also requested that an attorney be provided if and when she came to Springfield to talk to the police. The police continued to call anyway and advised Defendant that "they were not going to go away." This contact continued for several months. [Either this is in error, or the reports were destroyed.]

The police also began contacting the Defendant's family and Defendant in person. The police also contacted Jethro Tiner and told him that Defendant was giving them information about the victim's disappearance. This was a lie designed to cause conflict between the two suspects. The police told the Defendant they were telling Jethro Tiner this false statement to frighten Defendant into going to the police to escape the wrath of the co-suspect, Jethro Tiner.

During the period from March 21, 1993, through June 14, 1993, the Defendant was suffering mentally and emotionally from the shock of having been present when Jethro Tiner killed the victim and from fear of Jethro Tiner for her own safety and for the safety of her children. Her stress level was worsened by the continuous contact by the police and her fear of co-suspect

Jethro Tiner.

On June 14, 1993 [the date was actually June 12, 1993, the detectives from Oregon visiting her two days later], certain unknown individuals, whom Defendant believed were acting on behalf of Jethro Tiner, beat and bruised Defendant, blacking both eyes and causing contusions to her face and broke her right leg in two places. This was preceded by a period of virtual enslavement where the Defendant was repeatedly drugged, sold into prostitution, filmed while being raped, abused, and threatened with death. All of these activities caused the Defendant to have a terrible fear of Jethro Tiner and to suffer mental and emotional trauma and partial amnesia of facts of the death of James Salmu.

Report of interview between TJ, Karlyn's son, and Steve Walker

June 14, 1993: "On 6/14/93 Detective Lewis and I located Karlyn Eklof and her children at 395 Brightwood St., Chula Vista, CA. Karlyn was asleep on the sofa after being at a local hospital all day. She had been treated for injuries suffered from a fight with an individual that she would not identify. Her son Tommy came to the window and talked with me for several minutes."

Here I am brutally beaten, and they know I can't talk, so they drill my child. We are very scared. I had lied about the events which happened before. I did what I was told, because I wanted to stay alive. But now the police knew I had called and was trying to reach for help, but they offered me no protection.

Taped phone call between Carl Eklof and police

August 26, 1993: The actual call is missing. It is important to note, however, that Carl was talking to the police. Though the actual dialogue is missing, Karlyn's reactions to it in her journal are important. They tell so much more about the totality of her dilemma in regard to the police, other details about her continued surveillance by the white slavery gang, and her out and out despair:

...conversation with Sparky [Carl]; my so-called brother. I came to him asking for a car so I could leave with my children to find safety. Several times during my struggles of trying to survive he caused me great harm. At one point, after leaving Donny and going to Chris Dickens, I stayed with my mother, but before I was brutally beaten, nobody would help me or believe what was going on. So my baby, Immanuel, and I would get tossed back out on the street. My grandmother could handle Caroline and my mother would take TJ, but I was told to fend for myself.

I was scared, brokenhearted, and being abused. I had a station wagon for a very short time, which Willy gave me, but that soon was taken. Like everything else, I was a wreck, confused, scared, upset, lonely, and disappointed. My stepdad finally said I want you to stay with us. Well, figure this out! I didn't know how to thank him, because I didn't know how to explain. I

was loving my children and yet losing my mind. Every day I would get sarcasm from my family. Your trouble is you're worthless. I was begging for help,
but they just didn't understand.

The final blows had already been dealt. And now they were just sitting
back waiting to see if I remembered!

Terry Daws took me to Imperial Beach to show Willy I had taken care of
the car paperwork. Louie showed up with another guy. I asked, "Does anybody care what happened to me? Doesn't anybody want to do anything?"

He said, "Sure honey. What do you remember?" I said, "Nothing." He
said, "Can you remember my number? Call me the minute you remember and
I'll be right there to take care of it." I thanked him; finally somebody wanted
to help me.

It was four months later I realized he was the other guy behind the
camera, the man who said "Thirteen, what's fourteen? Snuff the bitch!" Also
Herbert offered me his number and said the same thing, "I'll take care of it
the minute you remember." Both men practiced martial arts on a regular schedule for years and were the two men behind the camera.

Now about Sparky's conversations with police. I had no idea he was
speaking with them and giving them false information. I was drowning in pain
and trouble, and he added much confusion and threatened my grandparents
not to help me. He called police and gave false complaints that I was holding
my family at gunpoint...

Police arrived and kicked him off the property. My stepdad has tried to
love Sparky and my mother, but there is no going between them. Sparky is a
dangerous troublemaker!

Mother has recently put a restraining order on him. So did his girlfriend. Sparky made a police report I stole things from his motorhome. Mother
had to give him her motorhome so he'd move out. He also decided to move TJ
with him. I found out and was upset.

I picked up TJ, brought him back to my mother's. The neighbor saw the
things I took were just my son's and told my mom just that. My mother has
allowed Sparky to do much damage to her life as well as the people around
him. We think if we ignore it, he'll grow up. Well, that hasn't happened. I asked
for help, and he played me and then kicked me! I needed somebody to trust...

The people I turned to for help—I wasn't choosey—I'd ask for what I
needed and would barely get that most of the time. I was listened to and then
told lies, which kept me going no further than where I was. It's a real gut-
wrenching feeling being manipulated or lied to when only basic, simple ne-
cessities are requested.

My grandparents and my stepdad were silently trying to help me. Sparky *was creating calamity and showing hysterics, causing a scene at both places when I could barely get through the door. Both live in small mobile home parks and can't afford any disturbance...*

In the phone call, Sparky... *clearly states my cry for help from Jeff and the fear that he's going to kill me and the children.* Sparky comments to the police about Karlyn's situation. *I finally found a spot to sit still for a minute. Nobody to pressure me about park rules: only so many people can visit for so long. Children are annoying, etc. They're messy; they eat too much. I did my very best to be on the heels of my children, trying very hard not to get into anybody's way.*

Some of those people, like Sparky, actually enjoyed my distraughtness. My effort to show appreciation, in trying to keep things organized, was driving me to emotional wreck. Being moved around and disgraced was more than I could handle. Not mentioning the damages that were done to me that I was unaware of.

I got to the point where I felt if I sat still long enough, Jeff or one of his copartners would catch up. In the beginning I thought I knew all that was going on and could handle it long enough to get help. But then the wickedness started being too much. And slowly, it got even worse; I'm still struggling with the awful truth of what some people are capable of.

Interview of Scott Tiner by Richard Lewis, detective, in Escondido

January 22, 1994: Lewis states that he and DA Fred Hugi contacted Scott Tiner, who is Jeff Tiner's younger brother. Scott explained that back in May of 1993, or sometime around Labor Day, he talked with his other brother, David Tiner. He indicated that David told him that Jeff had admitted to him that he killed the missing guy up in Oregon. The next time he saw David and Jeff together was at his father's house in Vista. At that time, David told him to just keep cool and not mention anything.

Scott Tiner advised that a few months ago he received a call around 0300 hours in the morning from his brother David. According to Scott, David was bothered very much by what Jeff had done and asked Scott if he thought he should call the police. Scott indicated that he told Dave to go ahead and he would support him even though his brother (Jeff) and Jeff's friends scared him.

Please note Karlyn's reaction to the above report. Her comment is very important.

Yes, they were scared too, and so was I. Notice no one ever suggested that I did it!

It would take some time before Fred Hugi would decide that indicting Tiner would take too long. With him incarcerated in a Nevada prison, Karlyn Eklof would be the easier bait.

Chap IX: The Apartment from Hell

Karlyn's experiences of ritual torture, described in the previous chapter, from which she thought she had finally extracted herself, only intensified after she established herself in her little apartment.

Most of the descriptions are from an edit of her first two "tablets" which she brought with her from Salt Lake City, her very first writings. Some of it is rambling and almost incoherent, like the worst kind of nightmare, as she tries to remember and piece together what had happened to her as the abuse and mind-altering tactics continued. Besides this mental confusion she also lacked the skill to describe and organize the events verbally and in the right sequence.

The style of the narrative is chaotic and disjointed, because her mind was being abused and sometimes did not make logical connections. Recall at a later time, after her mind had healed and the police betrayal had forced her to look deeply into the motives of those who were always trying to help her, will be important, because it adds things she remembered which were not in her first writings.

She starts out with a great show of control and independence. Be prepared, however, to be drawn into the quagmire of her memory. The garbled sequences only confirm the devastation visited upon her mind.

****

With the help of her grandparents and public assistance, Karlyn was able to get a little apartment. She began to feel secure at last. This was in September of 1993.

Her daughter, now five years old, started kindergarten. Her oldest son was provided school out at her mother's. And she and the little one spent their days together in the apartment. But it didn't take long before she noticed strange and unusual things happening again: a noise late at night, an aroma on herself as though somebody had been touching her, and her pictures disappearing.

She became very frightened. She was still struggling, sometimes in a fog, trying to remember how her leg and face got fractured. The pieces just weren't fitting together. She couldn't control the shadowed flashes that were trying to surface.

However, she was still not aware of the damage that had been done to her through programing and suggestion. As it continued, however, she came to perceive it was an abuse ring, not entirely connected to Jethro, but with many people getting payoffs.

Although she had chosen an apartment with schools nearby, the school three blocks away wouldn't accept TJ because they were on the north side of the boulevard. So TJ went to her mother's instead of just down the boulevard, and he rode a bus to a school ten miles away everyday. Then the same thing happened with Caroline. Caroline was picked up at 7:45 A. M. a half block away, then taken to La Mesa Elementary on 70th Street and Tower Avenue about three miles away, and brought back at 2:00 P. M. Karlyn didn't like it a bit. After everything they'd been through, she wanted to keep her children close.

She got school lunches started for Caroline through welfare. Caroline never did remember what she had for lunch. She also developed a radical bad attitude and was very disrespectful and disobedient. Nickelodeon was what she demanded every minute. Where had her precious little girl gone, and what was happening now?

The strangeness started at the apartment. She would find her doors standing open. She never had locked her doors, but at the risk of Jethro finding her, she locked everything. Once he did drive into the parking lot and sat with a girl in the car with him for a while, and she was terrified.

The children couldn't open the door, however, without a key, but she was always there to open it for them and to stay with them. When they wanted to go out she made sure it was locked again. Therefore, she was a nervous wreck when she would find it standing open. All she wanted was to have her family safe, and that just wasn't happening.

Then a man came to the door, actually to the front yard, saying it was unusual for him to ask, but he really needed something to eat. So she welcomed him in and fed him: ham, eggs, potatoes, beans, tortillas and a couple of beers. Karlyn's nature was to be extremely generous and concerned. She gave him a set of clean clothes and a leather jacket Jethro had given her.

He seemed so pleased. He overstayed his welcome, however, and she told him she'd been through a horrible nightmare, and, in reality, he'd have to excuse her. She couldn't help him any more.

He wanted to know if he could help any, and if she could remember anything. She thought, "What! That's strange. I never told him I couldn't remember. Time to go." Out he went. Until 10:00 P. M. that night, when he returned and said he didn't have a place to stay.

She tried so hard not to place him at Imperial Beach, but the more he talked the more he revealed himself. Then Terry Daws came over to see if she was all right, kind of wondering if she was getting to the bottom of why this guy was around.

Then it slipped out of Terry's mouth that maybe this stranger was a runner for a peckerwood named Jethro and needed help from a woman to move some heroin across to Arizona. Well, that wasn't her! But she told him it was just one of those idiots creeping and crawling around, listening and watching. Terry was surprised.

She said, "That's it. Whatever he's about, he can get out! Now!" She threw the jacket he had left over the back fence. Then, from time to time, she saw where someone had been using it as a pillow. It did blend in with the colors of the tall grass back there. Also there was a real tall pine tree where some sort of people were climbing and watching, signaling to others in different areas of the neighborhood. She could see it, smell it, feel it and hear it, but she couldn't stop it.

She was hoping her resistance was helping the situation. Wrong! Her mail was being tampered with; her phone also. The locks on her door, which she had repaired, turned out to be no good. Then a square piece of glass was removed to unlock a window. Every way possible was used to get in.

Caroline went to school one day, this was the week before Halloween, and she had her hand burnt, her right hand. And then a week later her left hand was burned, and she came home with a different dress.

Gradually she remembered who this guy she had helped was. He was there the night she had got beaten at the High Tide. Gary, the bartender, kicked him out just before her ordeal. He and a girl he was with looked at her really strange. It was the same guy. She saw them in the mirror, but when she looked at them they'd smile. They were some of the last people to leave before it began, and she was pretty sure the girl was one of those in the ritual that night.

Then her neighbor, Mike, introduced himself and a few other neighbors and friends. Karlyn liked to have people over. The first night she met them they were up all night, partying and exchanging biblical information. It was an interesting event, but comfortable. She still had all her marbles, she thought.

Mike told her of his involvement with people in the past who had had her experience. Then he apologized to her that she had been so abused and handed her a fullsize drawing of a man with great features. Then all at once, it came to her. He had said if she had any questions to let him know. But he was also there the night of the ritual. He saw her being attacked! He was the doorman, one of them She couldn't believe it! Everything was unfolding right before her eyes!

In showing her the picture, he wanted to help her remember the man who was responsible. It turns out he greatly regretted his involvement in what happened. He had been asked to testify on similar events, and when called to testify was told they didn't need him. It would seem they didn't want to convict anybody anyway, and they didn't want any precise witnesses. The police regularly raided joints like that just to clear the air.

He said he couldn't stand hearing the pain those girls were being put through. He wanted his head cleared of all the noise. If he could help pull her through and help her clear her thoughts, then he would feel somewhat in the right direction.

She looked at the picture and knew for a certainty what was being revealed to her. It was Jethro! It was full, clear, and complete. She remembered. If Mike thought he was helping her remember, he was merely confirming what had been her gut reaction all along. It was enough to scare the feathers off a bird. She felt sick. She was only getting flashes—bits and pieces, but still only fleeting moments—and she knew there was more.

She got hold of Tony and Val. They came over. She showed them the fullsize drawing. Tony saw it right away. He was pissed. She finally had a few answers. They recalled the trip to Las Vegas and how they had all tried to like Jethro.

She was gaining enough perspective to realize that these people who were visiting her apartment were fishing to see if she had begun to remember anything. She thought that to be strange. She realized it would not be in her best interests to reveal the bits and pieces she did remember. On her knees again, she asked God to provide the strength she would need to withstand the attacks. The enemy had her under surveillance. Getting in and out to observe her seemed to be easy for them.

A guy named Paul Hoyte called. He said he had heard about the occult people tormenting her. She thought, "Who is this guy?" He sounded sincere, and he said he knew he could help.

Help all right! He was another plant to occupy her time. More than that, he was the "occult" himself. He told her a story about a 17th century guillotine sword he was the holder of. On Halloween there would be a gathering, and she would have a white dress on, a wedding gown-type dress, and she would be beheaded! And it would save everybody a lot of trouble if she would just go with it. It was going to happen!

She interrupted, "Look, my head comes off! Well, just put it back on,

and I'll sing so loud the whole world will wake up." He was going to tell her
how to avoid the inevitable, but she told him to get out. He left, but unfortunately he took the drawing. She didn't realize it until the next day.

But first, after he left, he came running right back into her apartment.
He was scared. Somebody had chased him back in. Well, she chased him back
out. The police came. A neighbor called them. She told the officer that this
guy was bothering her about some sword they had planned to use on her on
Halloween. They took him away. She decided that all of the occult happenings
didn't necessarily have anything to do with controlling her. Paul just thought
she would be a great sacrifice.

She turned to three former acquaintances who had recently been released from prison, probably from years back through her little brother Jeff
and Tomas. But she knew she could trust them because of past connections.
Pete came and checked on her. Robbie had been on the phone earlier when
Paul was there. Robbie had told Paul, "Don't you even come around here
again! Don't you threaten her!"

Soon Robbie showed up. He was in a full body sweat. He had come
from quite a distance to protect her. The last thing anyone wanted, especially
Karlyn, was another Oregon incident. The guys knew what they were there
for, which is more than Karlyn ever did. She was confused, but she kept her
faith in the fact that the right people were taking steps to stop all this crazy
stuff.

The next day, also, another person called, this one saying he was a friend
of her father's and could help. His name was Bruce Lampbert. "Doesn't it
ever end?" she thought. At this point, however, she didn't cut him off. Somebody had to be right. She needed someone who was not a part of all this.

At the time, however, she decided that as long as she was in her present
location, only her friends could control the abuse that came her way. Only her
friends knew who the perpetrators were and how to reach them. She did call
upon Bruce Lampbert, however, quite soon afterward.

Her upstairs next door neighbor had a couple, Debra and Tim Shaw,
staying with him and sleeping in their car, so Karlyn asked Debra to come in
and get something to eat, to rest and to shower. Karlyn trusted her, and she did
need somebody to be there on Halloween. She had told them all she could
remember about what happened to her in the ritual abuse and what this new
guy, Paul, was threatening her with.

Then she saw other people coming in and out and recognized trouble.
The girl, Debra, had brought some clothes from her Imperial Beach storage.
There, in a large box, was Immanuel's Snoopy sweatshirt. Karlyn's blood
went cold. A lot of things were stolen while she was with Jethro. They were,

yes, from Imperial Beach, all three of them, including the neighbor and the visitors.

But it turned out that she did, after all, need them very badly. Since Halloween was approaching, she called her father's friend, Bruce Lampbert, and told him all the crazy stuff that had been happening. He came, and, along with Deb Shaw and Tim, stayed with her on Halloween.

People in the neighborhood, who neither heard nor heeded whispers of occult events, went about their celebrations, while the victims awaited the enemy. But Paul Hoyte didn't raise his head. He had no victim who would simply go along with the ritual agenda while he plotted a way for her to escape. That Halloween was a nightmare for Karlyn.

Her friendship with Deb and Tim might have gone on, because Karlyn needed protection, but a man from the Chula Vista welfare office came to call on her, and became her friend . He had heard that some very sick people were on her, so he came to see if he could help. He seemed to be sincere, but there was something strange about him. She liked him though. He and his daughter stayed over one night.

But what was strange was that he had what appeared to be a red contusion over his ear near his temple, like someone she was remembering from the ritual. Deb saw it; Tim saw it. Karlyn thought they knew when she saw it, because they came close to her to keep her from showing fear. They knew too!

By morning the man took his daughter down to the trolley, and Karlyn kicked everyone out. Enough was enough. How did she ever come to this spot? If she was there just so Jethro could be sure she never went to the detectives with her story, it was time she took the risk and got out of there.

She started packing up the apartment. She told the landlord that the people coming around weren't what she had planned on. But what she told her was being passed on to her son, and whatever they learned was being passed on to others.

These people were using sodium pentothal, hypnosis, and other mind-altering drugs. The landlord and her son, the neighbor and his friends, all the people who dropped in from nowhere to make her acquaintance, were entering her apartment, slipping these into her food, her drinks, and into her unconscious self.

They were using these ways to learn more about their victim. Posing as friends, they could question her after she was drugged in order to have a complete history of any friends, relatives, or secrets Karlyn might have. They would use this information then to get in close and cover their moves. And there was no end to the moves they were capable of planning in order to damage her family.

If necessary, they would call on others who were aware of her situation through a vicious network of persons who covered each other's butts. These people might also have been school bus drivers, teachers, volunteers, and the list goes on. Karlyn eventually learned more of the connections. It seems everyone knew who she was and who the culprits were, but no one would stick their necks out to protect her.

Going to her landlord was but a signal to others to step up the intrusions. Any show of strength or resolve was to be thwarted. Gradually, when she tried to read she couldn't make out the words. Her eyes felt like two magnets pushing away from each other. She tried to concentrate on writing. When her thoughts would try to reconstruct the events of James' death, her ears would harden, and she felt great pain in them. She would change her thoughts, and the pain would go away.

Sometimes these torments drove her to strange nightmares. She imagined that her family were all imposters, complete lookalikes, and placed here by another country taking over, and her real family was being held under water in submarines, where bombs were going off, causing them great fear and anguish.

She imagined that her grandmother was holding people's faith together. There were contaminated water signs posted on the beach. She tried to keep people out so they wouldn't find the submarines. She imagined that all mechanical objects were breaking down: sink faucets, vehicles, everything she touched. Radio stations were having conversations with her conversations and were tuned right into her apartment.

Most of the time, however, the strange things that happened were very real. They were set up to cause her terror. Her phone had to be reconnected once a week. The phone lines in the laundry room were also cut. She found a pair of little bitty ears on her stereo table. She flushed them down the toilet.

Her window blinds were old and bent, until one day they were brand new. The flowers on the shelves above the windows next to her Bible were wrapped in cellophane. When she touched them, the skin on her finger split and little cuts and burns formed. She ate a chicken breast dinner from the restaurant across the street and had severe chest pains for hours. She never could figure out the many ways her body was being contaminated.

Tanisha, the girl upstairs, came one morning and was standing over her asking for $2 for bus money, stating that her grandmother was waiting for her. But Karlyn awoke to find herself sleeping on the apartment living room floor with a portable TV on top of her. As she was trying to collect her thoughts and figure out how Tanisha got in and why her TV was bouncing off her, Tanisha took the money and left. So she had a key too! That hurt!

She found, mixed in with Caroline's dolls, one she'd never seen before with strange markings on it. Her screen doors were turned around and upside down. The bottom of the front one was forced inward. The doorbell was removed. Altogether she went through six phones in six weeks. Robert, when he came, saw that her phone lines were indeed cut.

Before most of these happenings, Tanisha and Karlyn would talk daily. Then a friend came by to ask Karlyn to help her clean up an apartment she was moving out of, some vacuuming mostly. She decided that Tanisha could watch Immanuel at her apartment and wait for Caroline's bus to come. Karlyn was gone only an hour and made it back just as the bus arrived.

Tanisha was just coming down the stairs. She said she had to give Immanuel a bath. Karlyn asked her why. She said, "He pooped all over himself." She knew something was wrong because he was completely potty-trained. Tanisha also had a friend there by this time, a guy named TK. But there was also the girl who had just brought Karlyn home. Karlyn was not happy but she said she'd take care of it.

Immanuel wanted a bath. TJ had just come home for the weekend. Immanuel was showing hard splashing and kicking like she'd never seen before in the bath. She asked TJ, "Did you teach him to swim?" Just then Immanuel rolled over in the water and lay still. "Oh, my God, TJ. They hurt him!"

Then, as she grabbed him, he said, "I died, Mom." And he pointed upstairs. Karlyn was scared and pissed. She got him dried and dressed. They walked out into the hall and toward the stairs. Immanuel wouldn't go. He pulled away and grabbed a big stick. Then he was ready! Karlyn picked him up and took him back to their apartment. She was so scared, so sorry, so helpless. Why was this happening? Why were so many people doing them wrong?

She called Tanisha and told her she was very angry and wanted to know what had happened. She denied TK being there. Karlyn knew better because she saw him herself. The next day she asked her again. The more she tried going over what had happened, the more Tanisha tripped over lie after lie. Finally Karlyn heard her talking to TK: "She knows. Don't come over any more." Then she shrugged it off and acted as if she were Karlyn's friend and could handle her gripes.

The landlord's son was watering the lawns from time to time. He always avoided Karlyn's area, and only her area. Also, when he would blow leaves or grass, he would blow them towards her apartment, leaving paper wrappers and such for her to pick up.

But the worst experience hadn't happened yet. That was the day Karlyn's children were separated from her for twelve-and-a-half hours with grave consequences. First she had a scare that turned out all right. But later it seemed to be just a rehearsal of the big whammy!

First, Robbie and Doug whom she thought were her friends dropped her off, stating that they would return with the children soon and to stay put. When they didn't show up for a long time she could hardly stand it.

The landlord's son, Jim, was air-blowing the parking lot. He stopped long enough to say, "Does it hurt?" and made a sarcastic face and laughed. He turned the blower back on. She called the hospital to see if anyone had brought children in. Nobody had an answer. They just kept asking Karlyn questions that were going nowhere.

She called anyone, everyone. Finally Randy, Terry and Mike showed up, bringing Mike's friends, Michael and Michelle, who lived at Alabama Street, in San Diego. Karlyn had met Mike through Robbie, whom she considered a much-loved brother, except, by his ignorance, it was easy for these people to parade upon him and, consequently, her life. So Michael and Michelle were no different! It seems they came to get in on the action.

When the children were finally returned that day, by Robbie and Doug, with no unfortunate consequence, she then had some new acquaintances to prey upon her and her children. Mike didn't know his friends very well. He had brought them over, stating they understood she was having problems from a strange direction. So now Michael and Michelle said they were having the same problems suggested that they should help each other and stop these people, or at least recognize who they were.

So it turned out that on another occasion, Mike took Karlyn and the children to Michael and Michelle's house on Alabama Street, where she met "Pit Bull" Mike and Lori, who also had experienced these fears about their children. Karlyn felt pretty puny and weak, but so much that was ugly had happened to them that she was glad that another family understood and would listen to her complaints. They seemed so sincere. They had spaghetti dinner. The children played together, but once it started getting dark and Karlyn wanted to go home, there was some excuse or another tossed at her.

She tried to stay polite, but then the weirdness started. People were coming and going, arguing, and fighting outside. The police came and took "Pit Bull" Mike, and then released him in a couple of hours. Mike loaned the car to a guy named Stewart to go get him. Immediately Karlyn saw how she was being set up and thought that Mike and Michelle were too. The children fell asleep while they were waiting for the car to return.

The car didn't come back. Karlyn tried to stay calm. She went to a pay phone throughout the night and the next morning, trying to get a car. She was definitely getting her children out of San Diego. After all, they had just wanted to be in Oregon before all this damage was done. But she and Michelle sat up all night, doing art projects and talking, because she sincerely thought Michelle was a friend.

Mike left, in seeming frustration, and Karlyn got fed up trying to get a ride home. So she asked Michelle to please watch the children. She would go to her apartment, get the other phone numbers to call, and get a car. They were leaving. She had just had enough. She could clearly see that things weren't going to stop.

Before she went for a car, she felt relief that the day would bring safety, and that she should walk with the children on the boulevard. It was several miles from the apartment, and she didn't even have bus money. But about then a helicopter was going in circles and there was a roadblock of police. Who knows, maybe there was a film being shot or maybe a real fugitive. So she decided she felt secure leaving the children with this couple and their three-year-old son.

Tim, a friend, saw her walking. She explained to him how she felt, and he gave her a ride. His car broke down, however, but she got home, and she changed into a dress. She was so desperate, she wanted to steal a new truck off the Ford dealership. She called Terry and Herbert, who talked her out of that. Oh, yeah, she told Tim, don't leave me, and he did. He left with the neighbor's camera.

When nothing came together, hour after hour, trying to connect with friends to help and everyone saying don't leave your apartment, we'll take care of it, she just couldn't stand it. Finally Randy drove her over to Alabama Street. But it was all wrong. Nothing looked right. Then two blocks over they found another Alabama Street. So were anyone and everyone who tried to help her was on the wrong street?

When they finally found the house, Randy was nervous. He wanted to go. The children were both asleep. She picked up Caroline, put her in the car, and then Immanuel. "Pit Bull" Mike was at the kitchen table with Lori, Michelle, and some guy named Ken. Another man was there. She didn't remember his name. He was going fishing.

Michael pulled up in his car. Karlyn said, "How long have you had your car?"

He said, "All day."

"Why didn't you come and get me?" she said. "You knew I was looking for a ride."

Michael said he had to clean up his garage, with a real coy face. Karlyn was feeling sick. Her biggest fear had happened, and she was not even sure what it was, but a mother can feel it.

As the car with them in it pulled down the road to the second Alabama Street, some guys pulled up to the street sign and pulled off the top layer like a bumper sticker revealing a different name to the street.

As Randy delivered them to her apartment, he stayed pretty quiet. Then he said he was scared to death for them., that somebody had covered up the perfect crime. Karlyn asked him, "Why us?" He said why not. She had a predictable schedule and it was easy for them.

Caroline did sort of talk and seemed to be okay, but Immanuel was just limp and pale. Karlyn had tears rolling down. Randy dropped them off. Terry was waiting and stayed with her all night, as did her neighbor, Larry, from upstairs.

They examined the children and found several scars that had never been there before. There were bright red wounds in various places on their bodies from head to toes, which were covered with a white salve. At her request Larry got his Polaroid camera and took a picture of their wounds for Karlyn.

David had a bright half moon on his belly button and on his back. Something had shot through him. He was brutally traumatized. Caroline was just groggy. She had a faraway stare. But the baby was so weak and scared that he woke up again about 3:30 A.M.

After examining the children, Larry said, "That's reconstructive surgery, high technology of the best kind." She had never heard of anything like that, but he and Terry confirmed that the children had been damaged and put back together. After being with her all night, Terry was exhausted and went home to sleep. Larry went to get ready for work. Karlyn called Robbie and asked him where the hell he had been. One wonders how these friends could just stand by and know these things were happening.

There were big bucks involved for capturing on film the pain and agony Karlyn and her children endured, but the perpetrators were also having an ultimate high in getting away with it. When she and her children started to show signs of fear, confusion, and loss of appetite, recently acquired friends begin sealing the gaps for any unexpected intruders such as relatives. They were learning their phone numbers and addresses, which were later used as subliminal key words to induce confusion and fear and to convince them they were not who they were.

Soon they were believing that their own family members and oldtime friends were enemies or spies. Then they had no one to turn to, to tell that strange and unusual things were happening. Hours were missing from a day. Foods were tasting funny. People were in the apartment when they woke up. The children were walking around in a daze. Clothes were missing. Strange aromas were in their underclothes and on their bodies. Someone had been touching them. That's the first thing that one tells to the new friends, hoping for protection.

Karlyn turned to her children as they awakened. Immanuel was absolutely stiff and scared to move. Then when he saw it was Karlyn and heard her voice, he cried in slow motion. Her body wanted to fall apart. Her heart was shattered. She picked him up gently. But he didn't want her to see him. She took him to the bathroom and showed him the mirror and said, "You're gorgeous, look."

He said, barely moving, "No, Mama," and he tried to hide in her hair. She gently turned him, and he looked so surprised that his face looked familiar to him. Then he ducked and said, "My teeth!" barely moving his lips.

She said again, "Look, you're gorgeous!"

He hesitated. Then he said, "No teeth, Mama," and slowly cried. When he finally looked in the mirror, he took a double blink and couldn't believe he was fine.

After that happened to David, he tried so hard to act out what had happened. He'd kick his boot off high in the air, rip his jacket off, point his fingers like a gun at his stomach and say, "The bad man shoot me, mama!"

She knew something had to have happened to Immanuel. He lost his speech except for a couple of words, his teeth were chipped, and his back and belly button showed a bright red half moon. For the next three years of his life, his older sister interpreted his words. Nobody else could understand him.

It was two weeks after this happening that she and the children walked into Von's Super Market and heard, "Management, management, your films just walked in the door!" TJ was with them and asked why everyone was staring at them. But Karlyn was never able to get anything out of the clerk, not even to admit he'd said it. The same thing happened in Salt Lake City. An acquaintance's son recognized her from films he brought back from a trip to Arizona. She was not able to get them. No one knows where the porn films come from, or cares.

When Karlyn insisted that these things happened to her after she came forward to testify, she got an awfully cold shoulder from the cops, and even from her own attorneys in Springfield. They didn't believe her. But they could have supported a compassionate concern. The police, however, would rather carve a case to their own satisfaction and familiarity than to have to deal with any unusual problems.

Perpetrators in the marketing business who offer a small line of pornography and ritual and sexual abuse items, as in the above supermarket, love cops who don't believe. It makes their job a whole lot easier.

Karlyn still didn't know who was to blame for the damage to her children. She didn't know who had been thwarting her rescue of them. But she wanted desperately to find help and to stop these people who feel it's okay to destroy human beings, who are the children of God. She decided then and there she would not stop or rest until the proper people were informed, those who were in a position to find them and to bring justice and destruction to them!

A few weeks after this trouble, on November 11th, TJ's birthday they left the apartment and the town of La Mesa and stayed two days at Val's. Karlyn and the children and their luggage were picked up by Bruce Lampbert.

They threw their luggage in the back of his VW cropped bus. It had a back end like a truck. They pulled into a gas station on the corner of La Mesa Boulevard and University Avenue.

There Caroline pointed to a building behind the bank where a mini schoolbus was parked and a driver was sitting. She said, "Mommy, that's where the bus takes me for recess, and I have to sit at a red table where people yell and scream at me!" Karlyn looked at Bruce and they both looked at Caroline and TJ.

Bruce said, "Well, let's stop and get help. I've got a friend, Don Brinkley, who might know something about this." They were cut off on Spring Street by a sheriff's road block, so they had to go around Lemon Grove to Spring Valley on the back side of El Cajon and 2nd Street, where they saw storage places that seemed to be closed down because of the graffiti on the buildings. The windows were painted black. The mini schoolbuses were sitting outside these old places.

Bruce stopped outside a blue and gray house on Sacramento Street. It reminded Karlyn of a dungeon.

Immanuel and Karlyn both felt very ill. He started passing out. She got upset and told Bruce, "You get us out of here now!" TJ couldn't see why she was upset. He was confused. But something had happened. Somehow the baby and she had been there before, and it wasn't right. She just couldn't remember. Perhaps it's best she didn't.

Karlyn's parents went camping with their VFW friends and had a gift exchange thing the day they arrived back home. That was on Friday, November 13, 1993.

Before Paul Hoyte told Karlyn about the guillotine thing, he first told her that homeless people, families with mental handicaps, and outpatients were the most vulnerable to being pressured by persons involved in satanic damages. These were professional people, including teachers, therapists, and health workers, who supposedly conferred with each other about the welfare of their students and clients.

First, by withholding medications from sick persons requiring them and introducing them to a circle of persons with the same disorder, these people can work their mischief on innocent victims as a way of showing their power to help them get better! Because of their professions, they are able to acquire drugs and are paid high dollars to serve them on demand. With these unbalanced people in control, there is a clear path of destruction.

They are then able to gain control of the unwary and supply them to those profiting from satanic abuse. They can prescribe for children also, supposedly for attention deficit disorders, and lure them into situations where they can be abused.

Karlyn learned that the very people she went to for help were the ones who insisted on her agony. They never sought evidence to convict perpetrators within the ring. The detectives who visited her, the Chula Vista welfare officer, Caroline's teachers, her landlord, and her friends and neighbors were all involved, if not in the process, at least in the process of not disturbing the process.

The area where this activity of ritual abuse is being carried out is in San Diego, Arizona, and Nevada, in a five-mile standoff point like a devil's triangle, called "Tecate." It allows for a jumpingoff point from one place to another, in case of trouble or chase. It is terribly easy to dispose of bodies there. When they are discovered or uncovered, as they say, at some isolated ranch, it is easy to blame the illegal immigration traffic, the "coyotes," so to speak or a drug deal gone awry.

There are always many people missing, especially women. Their disappearance is usually attributed to "trafficking," that is, they are among the hundreds of thousands who are abducted into prostitution and even domestic service in countries where they have no contacts or language skills to defend them. They are even more available for ritual abuse than persons like Karlyn who are known to others. That there are hundreds of them who wind up in pits and mass graves does not seem to disturb the police on either side of the border between California and Mexico.

A euphemism for seeking to observe ritual abuse in the Tecate area is called "football bets," and there are many sources of information about where to go. Frequent locations of the rituals are empty mobile homes on lonely properties and old wooden rectangular houses. Karlyn's ritual beating began at the High Tide, vacated for the evening by watchdogs paid for by Jethro and perpetrated by his paid cohorts. She believes they took her elsewhere, where they had accumulated other victims and the participants. Nobody wanted Karlyn to get permanently injured, and they thought she'd never know.

The abuse that Karlyn and her children experienced appears to be connected with the making of porn and ritual abuse films, the selling of her "services" to support the drug habits of Jethro and others, and to control her so that she would not go to the police about her knowledge of the Salmu murder. Her susceptibility to certain drugs, her special attractiveness, and her feeling of being trapped made her especially gullible and a great asset.

Chap X: Witness Tampering

Except for the minor street skirmish outlined at the end of chapter five which was dismissed, Karlyn was never charged with any crime. The only criminal tendencies that could be attributed to her thereafter were due to the expanding and exploding imaginations of others. First there was Tiner, as he suggested them braggingly to his brother Dave. Then there was Dave, first denying any knowledge of the murder, and then producing his gradual revelations and embellishments as he found himself the center of attention as a witness. But, finally, there was the prosecution team in Springfield, who would extrapolate the vilest behaviors of every murdering accomplice they'd ever dealt with, in order to attach them to Karlyn. Eventually they knew it would be a long time before they could bring Tiner in, and their reputations were at stake for solving the disappearance and reported murder of James Salmu.

Perhaps it is a masculine thing, but Karlyn's degradation during the ritual abuse and white slavery episode was but fuel for the fire of their imaginations. Sympathy for her ordeal never entered their minds. Therefore, I am wondering whether the reader also might have difficulty in imagining it and sympathizing with it.

When I read her journals about what happened to her after that point in her story, I wondered why she wasn't more careful. One can imagine the terror she was under while "allowing" the cooperation that had to take place while she was still with Tiner.

She "allowed" him to sell her, even though we know what he would have done if she refused. For example, she and the children sipped a Coke laced with a drug that would sedate them on the trip down. And she remembered hearing what Tiner ought to do with the children if the contact failed to bring her back. This was the pattern which occurred over and over. She was in control, but she was not in control.

One has to believe what fear she was under to cooperate thus with her own degradation. The control was transferred also to others, who likewise sedated her and terrorized her.

Therefore, it is a big stretch of the reader's imagination what she would do when she had moved on, when she could not have expected any of them to turn up ever again. Would she become so destitute that she would allow this to happen with strangers? She had allowed herself to be sold out of fear and trauma in order for Tiner to survive and support his habit. And she might find herself also drugged and used by those in his network who took over his control, but she must not do so for her own survival.

I, the writer, have met people I thought I could trust with Karlyn's story. Occasionally I have revealed my concern and involvement in trying to help her. But even old, very liberal friends have turned a very cold shoulder to her story, admittedly a much earlier version than this. Most of those approached, even with momentary concern for her, turned away. A social worker who often visited the prison where she was for a while told me, "Those girls who run with criminals get what they deserve."

Well, yes, she has gotten what she deserves by this time, and ten times more, but she is no murderer. I have been told several times, "You mustn't get involved. She says she is innocent, but that's what they all say." These reactions are, however, just extensions of the system which convicted her in the first place. A person who could be brought so low, not only to associate with such persons, but to sink into such degradation, must be guilty.

At this moment, to continue her story using my own interpretations and descriptions, I am not able to do. I cannot prejudice the reader with my own reading between the lines of the story she tells here. What she doesn't say is the worst part of it. You have to imagine what actually happened.

She will be given one more chance to explain what happened between the lines in a later retelling of this episode, which I will include in the chapter on She Came Forward. Either way, it seems she had no choice but to be preyed upon, this time by strangers.

I must first allow the reader the privilege, or the remorse perhaps, to interpret and to read between the lines. To me it is heartbreaking to read her words and to imagine her state of mind as she experienced these things:

Bruce Lampbert removed us from my apartment and my stepdad then took us to the airport. We stayed three days in the San Francisco airport upstairs nursery, wondering how to get back to Oregon. I was frightened and demoralized.

A black maintenance man on his lunch break allowed me to be walked away by two men who gave me a bloody vaginal infection. When I complained about my treatment, a security guard with a strawberry birthmark gave me something that took the infection away and referred me to the security P. D. They provided us with bus tickets back to the place of origin.

She arrived on Monday morning, November 15, 1993, in Eugene. Dave Wilson picked them up and took them to John Distabile's where Patrick's mouth dropped open. John, of course, would not allow her to alert detectives that she was there in Oregon to testify. She and her two children, Caroline and Immanuel, stayed with John and Debbie, then went to Minnie's for the next day, and saw Babs, who was a very good friend. Spider disconnected the phone, so therefore she couldn't spend any time with Babs, nor could she, of course, make any contact with Springfield police. But she spent the evening of her birthday again with John and Debbie.

Somehow they managed to get together more Greyhound tickets to get Karlyn and her children on their way out of state. So much for Spider and Potato! They wanted her to be as far away as possible so as not draw any attention to the case.

Although the ticket purchased was to Denver, Karlyn stopped and got off in Salt Lake City where she had breakfast. She couldn't take the bus ride any longer. Her neck and shoulders from the ride were very weak. She made some phone calls to get the children and her a place to sleep and eat. She had no money. They needed so much help.

She first went to the YWCA. Since they were from out-of-state, they referred them to a bishop who placed them in a shelter. They walked miles in the snow for a Thanksgiving dinner that was offered to them. Then the Catholics sheltered them and found them a family who took them in for four months.

On January 29, 1994, Steve Walker and Rick Lewis called Karlyn in Salt Lake, bringing forth many elements of James' disappearance. She felt she had lost touch completely. She just couldn't believe so much had happened. Then the detectives visited her and the children for three days, promoting other people's versions of the homicide.

That is when Karlyn wrote the two tablets which would be her defense, as though her life depended on it. These tablets were taken from her when she arrived in Eugene, but they were never used. They were hidden so that they would not be compared with the version of her story the police forced upon her.

Although they were finally returned after her trial, they then took six months of her journals, which she wrote after her arrest, when they were setting her up with all of Jethro's charges. These have never been returned. First they had no intention of using the story they had asked her to write down in Salt Lake, and they didn't want her to have a record of all the lies, plea bargains, and treachery visited upon her during the time after her arrest.

The writer at one point tried to track them down, through an investigator she had entrusted them with and her defense attorney during her trial, John

Kolego. Finally he said to me over the phone, "Look! That's been a long time ago!"

The above period of time while she was in Salt Lake City is described from her journals. A precise analysis of police tactics was written by one of her earlier defense lawyers who was later dismissed. It gives a cogent picture of that time period:

H. Thomas Evans, Att. at Law, [from] Memorandum to Suppress No. 10-94-04750: ... The police began a new and devious path to get Defendant to confess to facts that implicated her in criminal acts that were related to the victim's death. They began to tell her that they knew Jethro Tiner did the murder and that they only needed the Defendant as a witness. They alternatively (sic) claimed to be her friend and that they wanted to help her, then that she would go to prison and lose her children, always dependant on whether she talked to them and told them everything she knew about the victim's disappearance.

Finally, mentally and emotionally exhausted, the Defendant began to give in to police pressure on January 26, 1994, ten months after the police first questioned her about the victim's disappearance. On this date she spoke to the Springfield police detectives in Salt Lake City, Utah, and told them about an argument between her and the victim and Jethro Tiner, and that she was in the house when Jethro Tiner shot the victim several times.

The next day they obtained more incriminating facts and then they advised Defendant of her *Miranda* rights. The Defendant invoked her rights, but signed no document, saying she wished to have an attorney before she spoke further with the police. The police, realizing Defendant was not going to talk to them if they said they'd use her words against her rather than their supposed target, co-suspect Jethro Tiner, stopped mentioning Defendant's rights and went back to the old tactic of alternating claims of friendship, promises of "a plane ticket anywhere you want to go," threats, bullying, and long exhausting days of questioning.

The police lured Defendant back to Eugene on the pretext that they merely wanted her to testify before the Grand Jury as a witness against Jethro Tiner. They told her to just pack stuff for a couple of days and then she was to be flown wherever she wanted to go, subject only to telling them everything.

Karlyn's phone contacts with Police Captain Jerry Smith and the two detectives Steve Walker and Rick Lewis while she was in Salt Lake were frequent and often unrecorded. Some of those which were recorded are excerpted here.

They give some sense of how she is rallying in her ability to handle herself, but you can see how brutally she is led along and set up for the trap they are preparing for her.

One of her phone calls was taped, and that audiotape was played at her trial. It was said to be inculpatory, as were the last two videotapes she was coerced to make. The question exists, however, were these played to her Grand Jury? If they were, they were not listed on her indictment and were not admissible at her trial. If they played only her inculpatory tapes and not her exculpatory audiotapes, it is *reversible error.*

As before, Karlyn's written responses to police record are given in italics.

Taped phone call between Karlyn and Jerry Smith

March 21, 1994: The tape begins in the middle of a conversation.

S Steve said you were writing things down...

K I've got about 350 pages of that whole encounter...

S What, uh, anything enlightening you could share with me at this point?

K Well, they told me that I needed an attorney to speak with anybody...

S Who told you you needed an attorney?

K Rick did... Yeah. He said, he read me my rights in the back of the car.

S Well, yeah, but that's just telling you to look, you know, you don't have to talk to us... And if you wanted an attorney before you talked to us, you can have one... that's just a rule we have to play by. **But we got, we got to tell people that.**

Of course this never happened, no matter how many times I protested about answering their questions or wanting an attorney. If I didn't answer they would start harassing me, threatening to arrest me and take away my children on the spot.

Taped phone call between Karlyn and Rick Lewis

March 22, 1994: Rick and Karlyn discuss the message left for her to call Steve. It is clear that she had called Jerry Smith the day before, but Rick's interpretation of it is different. It appears that Jerry has said Jethro has accused her of participation in the crime, by stabbing James, but she didn't respond...

They inform her this has come about because Rick and Steve have visited Jethro where he is incarcerated in Nevada for fleeing the scene of an accident in which his companion is badly injured and paralyzed. It seems that he has now decided to let Karlyn take the rap for the murder since he will not be tried for it for some time. She is angry and defensive, therefore, in her remarks to Rick.

KE Well, did you visit Jethro?

RL Have I visited Jethro?... Yeah...

KE Okay, does he have a statement or what... okay, well, does that put me in there or not?

RL Well, I can't really discuss that with you. It probably wouldn't be, ah, prudent for me to discuss that I don't think right now.

KE It's my ass, Rick...

Karlyn goes on, "You know, talking to Jerry yesterday was kind of upsetting to me cuz he told me I was crazy and that I was full of hot air. Sure, in the beginning, yeah, because I was scared, but you know what? There's just some things that you gotta draw the line somewhere, and when I can start to remember things and put 'em on paper, which I've done—and by the way, it's not three hundred and fifty pages, there's a hundred and seventeen pages that I've written from just knowing that man… "

Rick, "Have you remembered anything else besides what you told us when we were down there the last time?"

Karlyn, "I wrote everything down and then I got baptized. I have everything written down that I could possibly remember, even if… okay, now the knife that was brought into it… the knife, that was a steak knife in my hand when I went from the kitchen. When I heard the second pop, and James was on the bathroom floor, that steak knife was in my hand. That never penetrated James. That never touched him like Jethro said…

When Jerry asked me about it, **I didn't wanna say anything, because you told me I needed an attorney…**

Taped phone call between Karlyn and Steve Walker

March 30, 1994: *I was on a street corner, trying to watch after my children, and could barely hear Steve over the phone. After Jeff and his damages, the police were setting their traps. They belittled and taunted me, because I was full of fear and humility. Since the brutal beatings, the rape and hypnotic sex acts that were filmed, I was a wreck and told them so over and over again, but they didn't care. I was treated like a hunted animal with no place to run or hide.…*

I keep reminding them I wrote everything down. In other words, now I needed my attorney.

I had tried for two weeks to speak with Steve personally. I was told by police to call a certain day every week and I did. I never hid from them or denied any contact. I state I chose to be on one team. This is the second or third time I clearly state I'm on their team.

Karlyn states she wants people's heads to turn over the stuff that those guys pulled and how they pulled it, the whole strategy, their game plan. She wanted it all exposed, every bit of it. Steve asks if she is saying there was more than just Jethro? She says "Yeah. They had that whole thing planned, the whole trip going down to San Diego, the whole thing, and I had no idea that they were even friends. I did not know that Spider had known Jethro long before I had ever introduced them…"

She is asked what kind of things Jethro told her on the way back down to Fresno? She replies, "We didn't really have a whole lot to say to each other. The drive down is really vague to me. I don't really know that we even talked too much… I couldn't remember the ride too much. Somehow he kept me in a sleepy state of mind…"

Karlyn gives a description of the way Jeff introduced himself to her and that she wants to nail him in court for what he did. Walker reminds her that in order to nail him she'd have to remember things that happened. *I complain of the state I had come out of, the distraughtness, that my nerves were gone, and that I could hardly read or write. I was a wreck. I had literally to fight for my stability.*

Karlyn mentions the drugs that were used on her, the brainwashing and hypnotism, or whatever, and now she is putting it all on paper. She has it all in the little backpack she walks around with "waiting for you guys to come get or **waiting to have an attorney** present while you know… I don't know what direction to take it in, but I know there's a lot of things in there that people are gonna say, "Oh, she's crazy." Tough shit!...

She is asked about the night when Jethro was trying to get rid of James' body, did he talk to her about going up the river? She says, "No, no, no, he never said anything to me. I don't think he trusted me too much. That's why he abused me so bad. He tossed me around to other people when we got home." She is asked if he said anything about throwing the body out over an embankment. She has no real answers. *I get emotional. I get frustrated. I didn't like trying to remember. I wanted to go at my own pace to remember. The pressure was too much.*

It was like being on a roller coaster, asking for help, needing help, and nobody knew where to push the stop button. Since that time I have, on my own, regained my balance, no thanks to all the professionals who were ignoring me and saying I'm crazy. Yes, it is crazy what happened to me, and it's even crazier that professionals, who have solved many greater mysteries, still deny the damages that I went through! Who do you turn to for help? It seems that only the church people are trying. Through the power of prayer and biblical reading I have got my balance back and my strength and desire to get this story told....

Steve asks only for details that Jethro may have told her. He and Karlyn at times seem to be on different wave lengths. *However, Steve and sometimes Rick I felt really wanted to get to the bottom of all the abuse, but were stopped by Smith. Slowly almost everything has come back to me. I was scared of Jeff and those people. I have tried to write everything down. It is easier than talking about it...*

I state my willingness to open my eyes to the whole circumstance. Anybody else would have quit. I also say I once believed Jeff to be different, and I had no control over him. I complain about the beatings and filmings of the children and me too. Those are being held over my head. I clearly complained about all these things long before interrogation...

He asks what Jethro said to her when he came in the bathroom. She said, "I don't, I think I just froze. I don't know. I don't think he said anything, he just looked... and he looked so strange. I mean, it was just like all puffed up, but yet he was calm. It was strange. It was just like, God, dude, get a grip. He just wasn't the knight in shining armor and the glorious dude I thought was gonna be in my family tree, you know. He just..."

Regarding that night, Steve asks her to try to remember some of those blank times the night of the murder about what was going on. She replies, "You know at the time I m not sure if I was mesmerized, hypnotized, drugized... I don't know because I normally would have gone to the phone and got help." Steve suggests that there was probably quite a mess to clean up when he left. "Just from the party," she replies...

In the pages which follow, many details of the party and its aftermath are gone over, repeating what she has told them so many times...

Potato is discussed. Karlyn states that all three of them were very close. "Yeah, Spider and Willie, Jethro and Potato were all very close, except for Potato isn't like Jethro. He, you know, he's the one that helped get me away from 'em along with Liz, and Liz got herself-you saw how I looked? Liz looked worse." *Liz was beat. KC wouldn't let me see her and Willy said he would watch over her. He said some black dude did it?? Right! Is there a black dude involved in the films?*

Steve asked her if she ever called the bar to talk to Jethro. She explains that for a while she had liked Jeff, thought he was somebody different, and sometimes he was really sorry for what he put me through. *I was still under his control. I tried to think it was just a big dream and that he would do as he said and come forward. He still used the words he said to draw me to him: I'm the one you've been looking for. Then he would look directly into my eyes. I could feel a change over me. I could explain it if anybody was listening—hypnotic programing, if anyone wants to know. Those people were a part of an occult ring. I was trying to survive.*

She said, "They still beat me up. They still attacked me. They put me through what they call their coming out party for somebody that he owed a debt to. Tossed me right in the middle of a bunch of guys and they passed me clear across town… He taught me one thing. He scared my ass straight…"

*Steve tells me to get rest. I know he understands. He knows what I have been through. He knows how I've been worked over by Jeff **and** the police!*

Taped phone call between Karlyn and Steve Walker

April 8, 1994: When the transcription begins, this conversation is already in progress. Karlyn and Steve are discussing Jethro.

KE …I have a question. Hasn't he even come up with any kind of an apology…

SW He's not even apologizing for what he did to Jamie… you know, broke her neck…

KE Yeah, that's not the only girl he hurt. I'll visit her, and I'll help her through her life with things she's gonna need. You know I've always been able to get by on very little. I'll be there for that one…

SW No… his (Jethro's) only thing is that this guy was a pervert, child molester and he deserved everything he got.

KE How does he explain… the things my children… and I went through, so what makes him any better? *Jeff is so much worse than the things he killed James over.*

Steve is asking Karlyn when it was that she heard about Jeff cutting James' fingers off. She says it does sound familiar. *It only sounded familiar. I was still putting things together. I wasn't sure where I heard it, but it was that night when he returned. Then Dave told Smith and Smith asked me. At the time I didn't know anything, I thought, because my emotions and memory were shot.*

Steve asks if Jethro said it.

Karlyn says, "Yeah, he did. I just thought he was bullshitting me. I don't know. I still don't know. He still… it could be bullshit…"

I mention seeing Jeff and some girl in my apartment parking lot in a white car. I was so scared I locked all my windows and door for days. I feared he'd kick in my door. I almost lost my mind from the damages that were being done to me and my children. Fear, so much fear!

She tells Steve that Leo, Potato, and those guys wanted to turn Jethro in for the reward, but then she states: "Right, and, ah, oh God, I missed it. I lost it, I lost my thought. It occurred to me that they were all very scared and very worried for me, because I guess Jethro might have mentioned that he was gonna snuff me anyways. Because just because I knew, and that he was gonna have to end up taking the fault for it because he knew I would talk sooner or later, that somehow, sooner or later I'd remember everything."

Taped phone call between Karlyn and Steve Walker

April 19, 1994: *There were a couple of phone calls missing in between this one and the last one I have a record of, which was on April 8, 1994. The point is, they told me a lot of things they didn't want in the record.* There are preparations underway already for her trip to Portland, which are confirmed in the opening remarks.

Karlyn states, "The closer it gets, the longer it gets, but it also tells me that nobody's messing with me, too. Cuz I can account for all my time... that means a lot to me... And I did talk to the father of one of the kids that had the tape that was bought off the market; and he denies any part of it. His dad just says you know he's got a lot of growing up to do..." *This was a kid who went to Arizona, saw the tapes, and recognized me when he saw me in Salt Lake.*

This call is rather upbeat. For the most part details of the killing are reviewed. Then they review the arrangements made for them to pick her up at the airport. Steve says they'll grab a bite to eat if she hasn't been fed on the airplane, and asks if she has any other questions. She said, "Well, I'm all set. I just wanna get this over with..."

*In the other phone calls that were made between this one and the one on April 8th, they had told me I could have a flight anywhere I wanted after this was over, **I would have an attorney present**, and I would only be there a couple of days. One thing they kept asking me was to pick a place for my return flight. I told them, well, I needed to go to Arizona, I needed to get back to TJ, and conversations like that.*

At first I had thought I would be in Salt Lake a while, but I knew they were reeling me in. That's why I didn't prepare better for departure. I just wish they had been more honest with me, so my children didn't have to go through foster care after the emotional upsets we had already been through.

There were other calls, which were held back and not recorded for a long time. There is no way that the DA Fred Hugi could say at the pretrial and trial hearings that she hadn't been a suspect all along, but he did. These calls provide important clues as to how they were building their case against her. Karlyn's comments are given.

Taped phone call between Dave Tiner and Jerry Smith

September 7, 1993: As stated, this report from the previous fall was entered into the record belatedly, which indicates that Smith didn't want it known that they were trying to pin the crime on her.

Dave, Jeff's brother, like Sparky, is saying things to be on a band wagon. Dave gives his opinion and secondhand stories to chalk up points. He lies about the dog being hurt. He also admits Jeff had no remorse. He talks about a stabbing I never did. Dave's bullshit story, like Sparky's, pisses me off.

To be noted is the fact that Dave tells an enormous tale, compared with his first interview on May 6, 1993 with Steve Walker. In four months' time he has gone from knowing nothing about the crime to an elaboration and interpretation of what he thought happened.

Bullshit here! Dave is telling a pack of lies. But just watch where it goes! Although he tries to soft pedal it in his testimony to the Grand Jury, just wait until Jerry Smith forces it on me in the interrogations which are video-taped!

And wait until the time when the State gives me my final chance through the Court of Appeals! My own appointed defense attorney quotes "me" as confessing it, at my trial, and cites the page number in the trial transcript where Jerry Smith is quoting Dave Tiner's elaboration **at this time,** *which he backs down from during my trial, saying, "I can't honestly tell you... [how many times she stabbed him]!"*

Is there anything hearsay about this?

Jerry asks Dave if Karlyn ever acknowledged to him that she had stabbed James. "Yeah, she did," he replies. What, specifically, he is asked, and he tells how she had to throw away this "bitchin" knife she had. Then he tells about a piece of pottery she left, which he swears has dried blood on it. *All of this is bull! Anything else, Dave?...*

Dave gets carried away. He is asked which room of the house did this assault occur in and where'd she stab him at (sic)? Dave says, "I thought it was maybe in the kitchen or living room or back and forth between the two... All over the torso, I assume. That's an assumption."

Jerry Smith asks, "Did **she say**... did she say how many times she stabbed him?"

Dave, "Oh, **I, I think** about forty or fifty."

Right here we have the whole story of my life, right out of Dave's lying mouth. I never spoke to Dave or anybody about any details of what happened. Jeff would have killed me. I'd never have said that! Look how the police go for anything illogical!

Dave goes on to call his brother psychopathic...

Dave expresses fear of his brother, tells of an actual threat on Jethro's part if he said anything. *Well, so if I had so much involvement, why doesn't he mention his fear of me!*

Dave confirms some details he had heard about the carpet. *Jethro took it out to throw forensics off from the bathroom.*

Dave relates what he had heard about Karlyn suggesting James go to Keith's. *I suggested Keith because I thought it was a normal suggestion. Whatever Jethro's intentions were* **I was under the impression it was romantic.** *I don't care who's around when I care for a person. I'm not ashamed to show it. Besides, we had our own rooms. So when Spider started in on James, I got confused. Just being friendly, I suggested Keith's, not knowing that push would come to shove.*

During these transcripts and throughout all the conversation—what happened is referred to as "they." I would like it to be more specific: "he" or "she." I am not a "they."

Dave says "They said..." *but I never spoke to him about this thing, although we did speak about a few other things..."*

Smith tries misleading Dave into saying, "But she admitted..." Dave says a couple of times, "She only nodded her head." Again the officer says, "They drove....' *Correction: "He drove." Besides, "they" cannot drive a vehicle. It only requires one person, which I am not the one! He never gave me the keys to the car!*

Dave repeats what Jerry tells him to. Jerry says, "But **she says** she stuck him forty, forty or fifty times, huh?"

Dave says, "Yeah, or thirty or forty, or something like that, **stabbed him quite a few times.** She's all bummed out because she had to throw the knife away. She liked the knife, you know." *He's backing down, but he's given Smith just what he wants, which he'll hold onto no matter how much he discounts the rest of Dave's bull.*

Smith asks Dave about the location of James. He states a river. Then when asked about water, he says there was none. *I believe Dave was telling part of Jeff's story and part of what Smith wanted to hear.*

Dave, through these pages was real gung-ho to help police, and when we were at his house he was real gung-ho to help his brother and even told me a few things for my protection. Smith told Dave about my leg being broken and my body being bruised. Both of these men confirm Jeff and I were not together at that time. He was with somebody else.

Smith talks about the victim's family being in contact with Karlyn's family, their hearts being in the right place, and for Dave not to speak to anyone. *Sure, Smith, this is a story just for you! So you can begin to make it stick! What about Dave's other lies?*

Smith does correct Dave on his exaggerating about the dog being killed, which never happened. *So I don't know whose stories were worse: Jethro's or Dave's.*

This report also is not signed.

Taped phone call between Dave Tiner and Steve Walker

September 7, 1993: This call took place just after the above call, the same day. Steve refers to that call. It also was not entered into the record until much later.

Dave confirms Jeff's way of making innuendos and confirms James' family contacting anybody and everybody, stirring things up. Again he refers to Jethro's veiled threat, "Well, not really threatening. Um, I mean, you know, not I'm gonna kill you or whatever, but he said, well, you know, **maybe I'll come up in a month or two and we'll take a ride out in the country again, you know,** bring one of my buddies with me, and I inferred it to mean, you know, like the last ride." *Was that so Dave would go along and implicate me? What else could be added, the way he had blabbed to everybody?*

It is again suggested that Dave should not contact the Salmu family at all. Dave is asked did Karlyn speak to you? He says, "No, no, she didn't." And then confirms what a surprise it would be if I heard from him at all. *I notice that through the transcript the police were doing the explaining. I thought this was supposed to be an investigation.*

Dave says they were making jokes. *I have never joked about this ever, and I wish the people asking these questions would state directly, "he" said, and not "they." I am not a "they" and I did not have a say in this whole thing. Nor did I go with him when "he" left with James in the trunk of the car.*

Dave was asked if Karlyn was shocked when Jeff told him what happened. He says, "No, not really, I think she felt that he trusted me. You know, at the time I'm nodding my head and saying yeah, yeah, yeah.." *That's a lie, because I remember wondering why he would say anything at all after detailing so much cover-up. And how can Dave answer for me? If we were both nodding our heads, I would think we were both shocked. Besides, I left the table. I wanted no part of this conversation. I went outside with my children.*

Again the piece of pottery Karlyn left behind was brought up. Dave extends his deep concern for a possible blood print on it and the possibility it was stolen from James. *Neither are true. There was no blood stain, and it was a gift to me from a dear friend some time ago.*

People keep adding more false details to emphasize their perspective. Can we get back to the facts? Please!

Dave says TJ is antisocial. *Well, you stupid son-of-a-bitch, if you just got dragged from your home under those circumstances you'd be a little withdrawn too.*

Steve refers to the "fight" between Karlyn and Dave's neighbor. Dave said it was about "speed." *I don't do drugs. Just about anybody who knows me knows that. Jeff had been using her phone. He gave me $10 to go pay the phone bill. I gave it to her. Then he says he already paid her. I thought he was angry with me for not checking with her before giving her the money. He came closer. I flinched to cover my head and elbowed her. I was a nervous wreck. She knew it was an accident. So did the neighbors watching by the pool.*

...confirms how fast people were stirring things up, with James' mother calling Dave's mother, when he had just heard about it. *This not only created confusion, but Jeff was getting strange ideas about what to do with me.*

The whole bit about the Hell's Angels is discussed. Dave is avidly confirming that it was true. He remembered it, that is, when Karlyn's dad died in a motorcycle wreck in '82. Walker calms him down with what Karlyn's mom had said to him, that, supposedly, Karlyn had just made that stuff up. *Well, I have had some other information, but I had very little contact with those who knew him.*

Dave is concerned about testifying for the death penalty. So he tells his story, the scrapes he's been in, for the record. Dave and Steve speculate about how long it took us to drive to Fresno. *I slept on the ride down, but Jeff, as far as I know, drove straight through. He mentioned to me a couple of stops he was going to make to some ex-con friends, but changed his mind. He did that a lot.*

He was going to leave me in Sacramento with an old inmate, but he got there and I guess didn't stop, unless he sold me there too and I don't remember. I thought at the time that he called someone and tried real hard to get close to the area of the number. Then the next thing I knew he said, "Nah, I won't stop here."

He tried to dispose of me and the children, and then kept us right with him. That's a real eerie feeling. I kissed his ass! I lit his cigarettes, dumped the ash tray, kept the children quiet, and stayed quiet myself.

It's very possible those places he mentioned would be stops. Very well could have been, and with his system of drugging and selling me, I would not remember.

This same Dave, who sold me to both Jerry Smith and Steve Walker at this time, told me in the interrogation room, "My brother is going to kill both of us!"

This report is also not signed nor entered into the record until much later. Jerry wanted Steve to keep Dave's testimony quiet until they could pin it on me!

Taped phone call between Rick Tiner and Steve Walker

February 8, 1994: Rick Tiner is Jethro's cousin who lives in Arkansas.

In the same class as the above calls is this, another smoking gun held back from public record until Jerry Smith could work me over. It was made later, but the police knew they were closing in.

Right away Steve mentions that Jerry Smith had also called. *There is no record of that call. He was preparing Rick, making suggestions, putting words in his mouth. Rick Tiner sounds nervous, says he had talked with Mr....Mr. Smith up there.*

Rick Tiner answers a question with, "And ah he ah you know we talked about what kind of protection he thought that I'd be able to get. Um... If I... he asked me if I'd be willing to come up there for Grand Jury."

Walker explains what a Grand Jury is, and Rick is concerned about getting enough time off. Steve says it's not a trial... "And the defendant, or in this case, Jeff, is not there, and there's no defense attorney or anything like that..." *Seems to me they're only after Jeff at this point.* "But not everything that you heard, I guess, from other people but what you know to be ah facts yourself you know what was told you and those kind of things by Jeff." *Those are not facts. That's where you're all wrong, Steve. What Jethro may have said is hearsay, not facts.*

Rick told Steve about his cousin Jethro's telephone calls just after the murder, that people might be looking for him and not to say anything, then to keep him posted on what people were saying. It seems that Jethro had called him from Roseburg and that Rick had sent him three hundred dollars by Western Union. *I didn't know about this at the time.*

Later when Jeff began to tell him more about what happened, he explained that "this guy was molesting her (Karlyn's) kids and that… they'd never… never find him again…"

"And he had misled me, ah, believin' that when he was up in Oregon that Karlyn had a fifteen-year-old daughter that was his daughter from when they knew each other a long time ago… and he was saying that this guy had molested her kids." Rick goes into more details, also erroneous, about the disposal of the body.

Steve asks, "What did he say about Karlyn, her involvement in it?"

Rick answers, "He, he didn't. More or less, you know, we took care of that who… whoever was there with him, or whoever was you know… we went back to the house (when Jeff was visiting Rick) and ah Jamie had… was packing the car up and they ended up ah I went down to the bank and cashed another check for three hundred dollars and gave him three hundred dollars to head back to California." *In Grand Jury Rick said he kicked them out. His story changed.*

Steve asks if Jeff told Rick that nobody would ever find the guy again? The answer was yeah…

There was a letter to Rick from James' sister. This was in September…

Jeff was in Fresno but was gonna head towards Reno, then it seems that Jeff called Dave and wanted to come to Fresno, but Dave didn't want him around. Dave was on the phone with Rick then, telling him what he knew…

On this page Steve asks Rick, "Um, did he, did he mention anything about how **he**, ah, **they**, killed James?" *Wow! Steve is going right along with Jerry's plan, but here he slipped.*

Here Rick says, "I asked him if he was involved in it, and he said… Jeb, don't worry, cuz we took care of it… That's why, you know, I kind of speculated that he had done something with the body to where… they'd never find it…" *When Rick talks on his own, he says "he" did it. Not "they."*

I have been very sensitive about statements where it is said "they" killed him, or "we" took care of it. Now that I stop and think about it, Jeff may be giving up the fact that we means "he and Spider" took care of it. We does not mean me. I did what I was told, helped lift the body, and painted the wall.

Rick says, "I knew that he was involved, but I didn't want to think that he could do something so brutally… that way…" and he mentions some details of the murder. Steve asks him where he heard them. His answer is, from David. Jeff didn't tell him any of that stuff. He said he had to sit down and write on paper, step by step, what was said and how things went to get a better perspective. *Yes, Rick, you and me too.*

Chap XI: Grand Jury

The Grand Jury process, for which Karlyn was being groomed at this time but was never privy to, was explained to her in a phone call from Jerry Smith on March 21, 1994. Here are her mumbling words, and his:

S Do you know what a Grand Jury is?

K Excuse me?

S Do you know what a Grand Jury is?

K I don't have a clue.

S Well, in Oregon a Grand Jury is a body of seven citizens who hear testimony offered by witnesses in particular cases.

K Uhuh.

S And Grand Jury is a secret proceeding which there is no... nobody else besides the witness, the seven Grand Jurors and the... and the prosecutor...

K Right.

S Can be in the room. Nobody else is there and the prosecutor and the Grand Jurors can't uh tell anybody else what the testimony was. And what their job is, they have a couple of responsibilities: 1: They are an investigative body and the other 2: is that they make a decision of whether there is sufficient cause to move forward on the prosecution of whoever the subject matter is and uh in a particular case. So all they are doing is a check and a balance. What they do is they assess what the police is presenting to them uh in a case against somebody, and they make a decision whether there is enough information there to put the case into a trial. The defendant has no right to be in there nor does he have any right to know who or what was said. How do you feel about testifying before that group of people.

K Well, I never thought I wouldn't be. You know?

S I don't understand.

K I've been looking very forward to meeting everybody who has had a little bit to say about my life and (mumbled)...

S Well, the Grand Jury doesn't have anything to do with that.

My comments at that time, as well as the conversation itself, show that I still don't understand. Still I'm thinking it's something like the trial itself and write "reeling me in" and "misleading" on the transcript, even when reading it some time later.

The most important point is this, however: the detectives were always leading me to think they were taking me to Grand Jury in order to testify against Jethro. I thought my tablets, my story, were for that purpose.

The prosecution was accumulating witnesses for the Grand Jury in order to indict her. Here we can see how they began to groom the testimony of Spider John Distabile. Her later responses to his transcribed testimony tell many things which cannot be otherwise included in the story.

John "Spider" Distabile testimony for Grand Jury

January 24, 1994: Mr. Kosydar asks Spider, "Mr. Distabile, do you know a Karlyn Eklof?" *This confirms the reason for the Grand Jury....*

He is asked, "Had you met Jethro before that (at the party)?" The answer is no...

John is asked several questions to which he gives negative responses: "...before you left or any time that night at James's house, you didn't see any fight?... You didn't hear any argument?... You didn't hear a raised voice?... You didn't hear Karlyn and Jethro ask James to leave the house?" *Because Karlyn didn't ask James to leave. Karlyn asked why couldn't he go to Keith's.* "Are you scared of this Jethro Tiner?" To all of these questions, John's response is in the negative.

Spider confirms I did not ask James to leave. I did suggest Keith's. Spider went to Kathy's and removed my things and took them to Dave Wilson's. When I found out, I got a wishy-washy big-brother-type answer. But when I got my things that were left at Dave's, it was a bunch of junk and dirty laundry. Spider dumped all my things out and took my camera and God-only-knows what. I didn't get any of my children's pictures or mine. I had five trunks of stuff. Kathy allowed officers, and Spider, to go through my things. I never gave Spider permission to do any of this...

Spider is asked, "When was the last time you talked to Karlyn?" He answers, "She came up just before Thanksgiving and I told her to leave." *I couldn't get my stuff, I couldn't get any help from anyone...*

Spider confirms there were no bikers. *But what he fails to realize is, if I'm not mistaken, the statement is referring to him. He and Potato were the only ones that came around...*

Spider says, "I don't appreciate being jousted around."

Grand Jury testimony of Deborah Marie Distabile

January 24, 1994: The testimony of Spider's wife takes place approximately the same time as Spider's. In his testimony statements are made which indicate they have already questioned her, yet his begins before hers...

Deb, Spider's wife, praises the atmosphere of the party... She again states how impressed she was with the people. Nobody was drunk. It was mellow and fun.

She says my children are good, which is agreed upon by all who know me. My relationship with my children is very loving, caring and sharing...

Deborah said she was surprised when Spider all of a sudden shows up with a kid at the front door.

She reacts the same way I did. Why did Spider and Jeff act so eager to get the house empty? And she makes a good point. Once this got out, things were going through her head as well as other people's, I'm sure. That's how a blown-out story got started. That's where Smith spent too much official money chasing down rumors and couldn't face the fact it happened as simple as I told him. So he worked me over, in sheer desperation, to have his gory conviction.

After Spider failed his polygraph on February 10th, detectives interviewed both him and Potato to find out if any of the things I had been telling them were true. The day of the polygraph he was interviewed by Steve Walker.

John "Spider" Distabile Polygraph Interrogation

February 10, 1994: Here is a summary of Steve Walker's report and Karlyn's comments: Distabile told Steve that he was frightened of Jethro and that Karlyn was crazy. He felt that the only way to stay safe was to remain out of the investigation...

He said that both Jethro and Karlyn tried to get Salmu to leave the house because they wanted to be alone... they were shoving him around... At one point, Karlyn, Jethro and he were standing in the kitchen. Salmu came walking from his bedroom towards the living room As he walked down the hall area, Distabile said that either Karlyn or Jethro threw a butcher type knife towards Salmu. Distabile said the knife came by him and bounced off the wall several feet away from Salmu. He said that he also saw Jethro slug Salmu in the face, knocking Salmu to the floor. He hit him hard enough to knock his glasses off and cause instant swelling in Salmu's eye. *I didn't see Jeff hit James. I was probably at the sink. I was waiting by the phone for Linda to call, facing the bathroom. I stopped there, cleaning my nails, kind of watching. When James came out of the bathroom I asked, "So what are you going to do?" And the buck knife flew out of my hand and bounced off the wall to the side and behind James. I apologized, and he handed it back. I set it on the table. He said that's all right. Things were still friendly, I thought.*

He said that Jethro produced a small handgun and was holding it in a threatening manner towards Salmu. He told Salmu that he ought to shoot his "dick" off. He said that at one point, Salmu was moving towards the door when Karlyn stepped in front of him blocking his exit. Karlyn said something like, "What's wrong, can't you handle a woman?" Distabile said that he was becoming frightened and concentrated on getting out of the house. He told me that he was concerned about his welfare because he thought that Jethro was upset with Salmu because he had tried to sleep with Karlyn. Distabile said that he himself had slept with Karlyn in the past and thought that Jethro might react the same way towards him. *Changing his story trying to be a victim. He was the one who started on James to leave. I never slept with Spider. We did grab ass, necked once.*

He told me that as he was going out the door to leave, he thought that Salmu was going to follow him out. He said that as he went through the door, it slammed shut behind him preventing Salmu from leaving. He got TJ and Steve Chase into his pickup truck to leave and then Karlyn came out. She told him to hurry up and get the kids out of there because she thought that Jethro was going to kill Salmu. *Spider acts innocent and protective, but he's the one who marched back in the house from the patio, telling James to take the money and get out.*

Steve asked Distabile what he thought was going to happen after he left. He said that he was hoping that Salmu would leave, but that in reality he knew something terrible was going to happen to him. Steve asked why he didn't phone the police after he got home to report what was going on. He said that it "wasn't any of his concern." When Steve suggested that he might have prevented Salmu's death, he became upset and said that he didn't have anything to do with it. Whatever happened was caused by Jethro and Karlyn.

The actual polygraph examination report summary states that "This examiner talked to Mr. Distabile about his being deceptive to seeing someone do something to James that would have resulted in his death." He was asked if he saw anything that could have resulted in James' death. John said, "Yes, I saw several things that could have killed him." The report, by Fredrick E. Ackom, Detective also states that when Distabile left he knew they were going to kill James. Also that Karlyn told him after that, that James was gone, and implied he was up the Willamette River somewhere. *Both of these statements are grossly untrue. I came out to the truck to tell him what I feared. And later I did not discuss this incident with John. These are lies. I had not discussed this with anyone. Jethro would have killed me. But he was working on the car for Jethro which I didn't even know.*

Grand Jury Testimony of Willis Albert Morris

April 29, 1994: This is the date of one of the actual Grand Jury hearings to which Karlyn was not privy.

I do not know this person. Jeff and Jamie met this person in Nevada and told him his story. Every time Jeff tells his story to somebody it gets uglier...

Morris says that Linda Louise Little, whom he had been living with in Reno for four years, had met Jeff (Jethro) and Jamie through drug dealing while he was in jail for shoplifting. When he got out in January 1994, Jethro and Jamie came over, and Jeff told him he was wanted in connection with a murder in Oregon...

A few days later Jeff got in an accident and Jamie was seriously injured, and he left the scene and was in the hospital with a punctured lung and a broken collar bone under the alias of John Williams. Shortly afterward he ended up on their couch, having fled the hospital. Later Jeff told him how "him and this... this girl Karly Ann... had killed and cut up... a so-called child molester, you know, cut his arms and legs off and bagged him up and took him to... he told me an Indian reservation close around, and put an arm here and a leg there and scattered it all over..."

Then it turned out this "Karly Ann had the guy in the bathroom, beating him up, and he was all bloody and everything and screaming... and Jeff told her, 'Hey, look, man, I'm here on a traveler's pass... we are just going to have to kill him because I can't have him talking.'" *Either Morris is talking bull or Jeff gave one hell of a horror story.*

Grand Jury Testimony of Linda Louise Little

April 29, 1994: *I do not know this person nor have I ever met these two. She states she copped heroin for Jeff five times a day. Is this a habit or a business? She also describes the way their operations were conducted.*

Little says she was strung out on heroin and met Jeff through a black guy named James... Jeff came the next day to her apartment and she started copping for him four or five times a day because she knew where to go, who to buy from. She met Jamie...

She said he started bringing Jamie with him all the time and they became very close. "He would go to the stores, he was cashing checks, fraudulent checks, and I would sit in the car... he would get the money and then we would go cop... I mean, we did that seven, eight, nine times a day. We were spending thousands of dollars a day on dope..."

He finally told her about the incident in Oregon... "He said him and a girl killed a baby raper... a creep." While beginning to tell this the witness is sobbing...

He continues the story, telling her essentially the same one he told Morris. "He didn't go into the details then. It was later on as we became closer that I became more aware of the crimes that he was committing. You know, like I realized that the reason he had me in the car was to drive, you know, while he was in the... I didn't realize that at first." *And where did he leave Jamie while this was going on? Hustling, if he hustled them and used these other women to cop for him, why did he hide it from Jamie, and me? I didn't understand about this addiction or what was going on.*

She states she didn't realize the person he was. He came off so honest and honorable, and then the nightmare began. That's the way he moves in on people. He'll have you innocently sitting right in the smack middle of something, and you not even know it. And later on when he tells his tall tale, he'll have you being the great lookout driver to a caper.

When asked if he ever mentioned Karlyn or how... what he thought of her, she answered, "She was a wacky broad. I mean, from what he described... he called her an Angel baby. She was supposed... I guess her dad was supposed to be a Hell's Angel and she was crazy... he would give her a wide birth, you know."

These people had a pretty ugly impression put onto them. But when they refer to the events, even in repeated statements, "he" is described as the killer throughout. My point is, police say "they" and these people and even his brother Dave say "he", not "they" killed him.

This person would have been a great witness at the trial. The prosecution would have called her in to corroborate my participation in the crime, but the cross-examination would have revealed just exactly what Jethro was doing to Jamie, to her, and what he had done to me. That's why they didn't call her.

Grand Jury Testimony of David Lee Wilson

April 29, 1994: Dave Wilson was the person who had the two little ones and returned them the next morning.

He states he returned my little ones the next day at 12-1 P. M. I believe it was closer to 9 A. M. Perhaps the carpet man can verify that we were in the store about 11 A. M. ...

He also tells about picking Karlyn up after she came in on the bus in November. She stayed that day and night with him and his wife. "The next day she wanted to go over and see Potato and John." *I didn't even know Potato was there!* She came after her suitcases, but Wilson says that they had company coming and couldn't have her stay. Neither did Spider want her to stay.

Grand Jury Interrogation between Fred Hugi and John "Spider" Distabile

May 2, 1994: In this third interview Spider states Jeff and I approached James to offer him $40 for a motel. *This is false. Jethro offered James some money and Spider told James: do what you are told, take the money and go. It's a good offer. Spider had his foot up on the heater. I remember James looking at me and me looking at everybody. I do remember James and I did not know what was going on...*

Spider says that Jethro was asking who's been messing around with Karlyn. "He wanted to know who had a loose zipper. I just kept my mouth shut." Again Spider talks about Karlyn and him having sex. *Well, we grabbed ass naked at my girlfriend's apartment. And that was the only time. It wasn't long after that Potato told him to tell me he had a wife. Well, I finally was told and felt pretty stupid. But I wanted to be friends with both of them, and within a week or so I was introduced to her and became friends. We all went to a child's birthday party in the neighborhood and enjoyed it very much...*

Spider describes a butcher knife going past him and bouncing off the wall. *It did not fly past him, and it was not a butcher knife. My buck knife I was cleaning my nails with flew past James and bounced. It was only an accident. No butcher knife, and nobody got hurt...*

Spider states Jethro produced a lighter he thought looked like a gun. *And it was a gun. I wasn't aware of this happening, and Spider sure as damn well knows a gun if he sees it. Why didn't he get help?*

Spider states clearly it looked to him like Jeff was going to leave James alone after that. He thought it would be done with. But then Jeff shoved James again. *I did not see this. But their argument was on and off...*

When I went out to the truck the boys were in it. Spider was just getting in it. I said, "Get these boys out of here." *Spider says I said it in the house. That is false. Both the boys have verified that also. The statement, "I think he is going to kill him" was not stated in front of the boys, though I believe I said it out by the truck. Spider says I said it in the house...*

Spider confirms that James had every opportunity to leave the house, just as he did. At one point he says Karlyn was standing near the door. *No, I was behind James. Spider went around him out to the truck. James could have gone but just stood there. Then I went to the truck shortly, about a minute later, I missed what happened then.* Spider says he did not see Karlyn hit James. It was Jethro...

Spider answers a question: He hoped "they" wouldn't kill him, but they did. *Excuse me, I did not!*

Spider says they told him about a week later that they were leaving, and "he told me that Karlyn had kicked him and that he had put him in the dirt." Asked what did Karlyn know about that, he answered, "She didn't know anything, really. She just... she was standing alongside, yes." *Thank you, but I never heard this conversation. I do remember, however, Spider pulling up and just standing there. I have never spoken about this to*

Spider or anybody else. And on Line 13 he states that I didn't...

Spider is asked why he didn't call the police. He said, "I was afraid. The guy was still on the loose. I had no idea what he was going to do. He knew where I lived and everything." *I know the feeling. That's exactly why I couldn't.*

Spider says he came into the back the next day and picked up his cooler looked inside and saw new carpet. He was on his way to work, about 7 o'clock in the morning, didn't see Salmu, but hoped he had made it to work. *This wasn't true, although the back door was open, unless he was there twice that day. The carpet came in later and was in the hall for three days.*

Grand Jury Testimony of Patrick "Potato" Walsh

The following interview and testimony of "Potato" fills in many gaps in the story, many details that Karlyn had forgotten or had neglected to write into her journals:

May 2, 1994: Potato describes meeting Karlyn at the White Horse Saloon in Springfield sometime in 1992. She had said, "Maybe you heard of my dad, his name was Bob Dolly (phonetic)." Potato explains he had heard of him... "He worked with the legal metropolitan law thing with the bikers and stuff. He was one of the good guys..."

What Potato describes about the meeting of Jethro and Karlyn is pretty general. He says he himself also met Jethro at Willie Brand's house and that Willie had been in prison with Jethro. *Although Potato is unconcerned about these connections, Willie was the one who was waiting in the airport when we arrived down there and it was at his house that I met Jethro. It was to Potato that Jeff called after he arrived in Springfield to thank him for getting us together.*

So they all knew what Jethro's operation was about and what they were getting me into. He also knew how susceptible I was to whatever mind control he and Spider had tried out on me. Seeing that bright red fresh handprint on my left rear buttocks, they had been able to dismiss my concern by simply just saying a word (hypnosis).

My state of being unaware was only the beginning. By the time I met Willy in the San Diego Airport I was fully encroached upon by Patrick and John, who had already set in motion their rancorous intentions.

As we walked through the San Diego airport, passing an open bar, a man sitting at the bar turned toward Patrick, Dennis and me. The man was Willy. He looked right through me as if he knew me. I felt like a lamb chop in a lion's den. He raised himself slowly off the bar seat and began to walk with us in formation as we exited the airport lobby. Patrick began the introductions on the way out to the parking lot. Willy's Cadillac, the color of burnt orange, was the chariot that awaited us.

Willy escorted the three of us back to his house in Imperial Beach, a place I was once warned never to go into, before I ever left San Diego [La Mesa] the first time. As a matter of fact, we were separated immediately, and Dennis returned eight hours later. I believe it was set up, because when he returned something about me was different. I snapped at him to leave and he left. I know now that somebody had taken me off and put subliminal or hypnotic suggestions into me. It was at this point I noticed my life change dramatically—a sleepy state of mind.

When I woke up there was Jethro, standing over me. I remember he had a pretty Indian woman, Kathy, with him and told her to leave. Four years down the tube, he said, and I remember him looking at me and saying, "Yeah, this one will do." ??? Kathy, the Indian girl, was taken to the trolley and Jeff and I went to have a drink. Later we went to the Silverado Motel.

I also realize something. Potato wasn't there the night we met, but, as I said, Jethro thanked him for putting us together. He called him at 2:00 A. M. after he arrived up here.

About Karlyn's trip to Springfield before Thanksgiving, Potato says, "It surprised the hell out of me. 'Cause I hadn't talked to her for two and a half, three months before I came up here… I didn't even know where she was. I assumed she was out in Lakeside. That's where she told me her mom or somebody lived out there…"

Potato tells the Grand Jury he first met Salmu with Karlyn at the White Horse, but about the disappearance, all he knew was what he read in the papers.

Grand Jury Testimony of Ricky Lee Tiner

May 2, 1994: Ricky, who lives in Centerton, Arkansas, identifies himself as the cousin of Jethro Tiner. He said he last saw Jethro in July 1993 when he brought Jamie to stay for five days. He said that during that stay they had a talk about some things that had happened here in Oregon…

To start with, he received calls from Jethro on March 17, March 18, and then on the 22nd, stating that "he was getting ready to return to southern California, and that there may be some people looking for him. He said he couldn't go into detail on anything… he would tell me more… face to face what had happened, what it was that **he** was, you might say, hiding from…"

Later "he said that he was involved in a murder. This guy was molesting this Karlyn's kids, and that **they** had disposed of the body and they would never find it."

Here Ricky says that "He said **he** got… **they** got rid of the body and that it would never be found." *Ricky starts to say "he" and then he stops and says "they!" He knew what Hugi wanted to hear. After all, this Grand Jury was for her.*

A little play on words, I'm sure. Also, where are the tapes from all these people, conversations about their agreeing to come in and testify.

Grand Jury Testimony David Wayne Tiner

May 2, 1994: Dave says Jeff and Karlyn were talking about what happened. "I thought they were pretty cavalier about the whole thing… the way they talked to each other. Kind of a… kind of a game of one-upmanship, you know. Well, yeah, I'm bad, I did this. Well, yeah, I'm badder, I did this, you know." *No, we were not. Jeff might have told his brother and I was there for part or the first of the conversation, but I was not discussing it. I have always been too scared. Jethro told me "Look! Your sparkle is gone. Pull yourself together. Can't you hang?" I was so depressed and disappointed.*

I was trying not to show it. If I ever pulled myself together at all, it was to keep from making Jethro angry at me...

Dave clearly states Jeff said **he** took the body and **he** drove the car and **he** snipped fingers and **he** dumped the body off. *In all this conversation, he says "he", and that's the way it was.*

The question is asked, "How did she indicate she is upset to you?" He answers, "I don't know. She said something like, you know, 'I had to throw the knife away,' you know, kind of..." *He stammered and stumbled. See, he couldn't even answer this, cuz it never got said. Bull!*

I didn't understand how a man would go to such depths to cover a crime up and then tell people what he did. I remember at that time feeling humiliated and disappointed. So much damage. I have never been so afraid for my life and my family's. My children are precious to me...

Dave, who in January quoted his brother saying Karlyn stabbed Salmu 30 to 50 times, is backing down or at least showing that he didn't believe it much in the first place:

Question by Hugi: Either of them indicate how many times the guy was stabbed?

Answer: **I honestly couldn't tell you.** I know that after that, at some point in this whole ordeal, I guess Jeff had shot him in the chest...

That was all he would say about it at the time. He knew he would be called again to testify in the trial and is beginning to wonder if he should have passed on his brother's mad ravings. Yet, that would be the basis for Jerry Smith's final testimony, where he will quote Dave's **previous phone call** and make it stick. Even Karlyn's own defense counsel, in writing a brief for her appeals, will refer to it erroneously in the transcript and say, "At other times *defendant* told police she stabbed the victim 30-50 times (Trial transcript p. 472, which is *not* the defendant, but Captain Jerry Smith quoting David Tiner's previous phone call)." Of course, there was little, if any, blood and no forensic evidence to back up any of this.

After the interrogation the police brought Dave in to sit with Karlyn *"for about three cigarettes worth."* This must have been during her second day of incarceration after she was indicted.

He "smokes!" And tells me how bizarre all this is and says, "You know, Karlyn, he's gonna kill us both." "Yeah, Dave, I know."

The police at the trial said that Karlyn confessed to the stabbing when placed alone in an interrogation room to talk to Dave Tiner and John Distabile.

****

In my correspondence with Karlyn while writing the first draft (her ghost-written account) for this book, two critical issues were introduced: the reason her polygraph went haywire on the question about the gun, and the tactics used to pressure her to plea bargain: ...

"Referring to your question, 'Did I ever say to Dave Tiner or John Distabile during the interrogation visit that I stabbed James?' Of course not. There was never a statement of that sort. If you refer to a phone call I made from Salt Lake, I admitted to pointing a steak knife as I told you. I also clearly stated that at no point was the steak knife ever used as a weapon. At no point

did I cause harm. No wound was ever inflicted. I even stated the same thing in my two tablets...

"Even in the videotapes I do not admit to any stabbing, though Jerry Smith has me skating on the edge of a false confession each hour we spoke. I repeated a little more of what he rehearsed through coercion. By the time he got his fill I talked myself right into rinsing a knife that was never used. I tried to say it didn't need rinsing because there was never any damage done.

"I can't help what happened in that horrible interrogation, and I can't help the mental trauma that I suffered from. Though I do know what happened and what I have tried to do is to tell what every character has done in evolving the story.

"I was very careful not to talk to Dave or John. I mostly listened. Dave told me his brother was going to kill both of us. Dave neglected to tell me that he had altered his version to promote team support for the police. Pretty much the same tactics they told me: either get on one side or the other, it's this team or that. Since I was the only one on my team with three children it was an easy choice to believe the police.

"As for John, he was shifting in his chair, repeating, 'Say I didn't do anything. Tell them, Karlyn. You tell them.' He wrung his hands over and over again saying, 'Tell them to let me go.'

"I said, 'I don't need you here, John. Just go, get!' He jumped up and left in a whirlwind behind where he was standing. So, I'm quite confident no statement was made about a stabbing. Had that been true, don't you think it would have been used as evidence? Fred Hugi would have eaten that up. But he didn't have it.

"That's why Jerry Smith spent so much time working it into the videos. The whole idea of it came from Jeff Tiner who told his brother a grotesquely exaggerated story to thrill his brother, which it did, until the police kept bugging him to weigh his options. It's funny how people fear exposure of their own life experiences and will do plenty to avoid it. Dave does have skeletons in his closet. Well, I didn't stab James and this is so frustrating trying to prove it, though it can be done.

"When a wound is inflicted, medically speaking, a rush of bodily fluids flood the glands and overload the area opened. The coroner never found any such opening. As a matter of fact, Steve Walker said he observed the coroner on several exams. They found no evidence of wounds suffered other than a temple gunshot wound, which was the cause of death.

"My polygraph was also clear on that particular question. The only one that tripped the test was the bullet that was dropped in my hand. The question was, 'Did I ever hold the gun?' No! But a piece of the gun did touch me. That *bounced bullet Jethro dropped into my hand, and I dropped it to the floor. The polygraph agent said, 'Had he known that, he would have redirected the question.' Jerry Smith was proud of what he had done. And the poly agent wasn't allowed to retest me. Jerry Smith was trying to pump this case up to something called a 'Bruno' case. But when James remains were found, it didn't even resemble the Bruno case nor did it match the video 'confessions.'*

"I saw grown men in their scandalous attempts to cover their butts. I was told at one point that this case was being thrown out. The next thing I know I was being handed nine new charges and was told to take an eight-year plea bargain or I would be guaranteed life. That was said by Thomas Evans and Judge Ann Aiken who told me her job was to convince me to bargain and that it wasn't her problem that those ol' boys fudged with cases. She told me it was better to do eight years and get out and finish raising my children than never to have raised them at all."

This concludes Karlyn's written response to my questions after I began to study the documents and her journals.

Grand Jury Testimony of A. G. Hope

What went before in the interviews with this monstrous person is not available. But this writer has uncovered a huge bonanza of evidence that prosecutor Fred Hugi suborned Hope's perjury against Eklof by delaying his indictment for child molestation charges for two years. This was the key witness who finally swayed the jury by stating that Karlyn had procured the gun for Tiner before she ever went to San Diego, or ever met him, for that matter.

In the Grand Jury testimony Hugi is conducting at this time, one can see him grooming Hope for the double whammy he will deliver at her trial:

May 12, 1994: Al states Karlyn mentioned something about a gun to him before Jethro came up. *I'm sure I didn't do that, because I've never liked guns. This is a lie. I've never needed a gun nor would I ask him for one. He was a friend of Dee's and our girls played together...*

First Al says he thought James was Karlyn's husband. But then she started talking about her old man getting out of prison down south... and she was going down to, you know, meet him when he gets out or something like that. And it was not too much longer that they... she returned ... with Jethro and stuff. And had asked me about the gun before she left.

Karlyn's response to the above tells only about what was known about Al Hope at the time of her trial and thereafter. It was Tiner's lawyers, when he finally came to trial, who uncovered the truth about his perjury.

Al really lies a lot. **When I went down to San Diego I didn't know Jethro at all.** *This is a good example of witness tampering too, because Al was in trouble for furnishing a handgun to a felon. And I've never referred to anybody as my old man. They were careful not to ask him this during the trial,* *because Kolego would have cross examined him about it, proving I didn't ask him about a gun before I went to San Diego. Kolego could have asked him anyway, but he wasn't there to defend me.*

Al says Karlyn started talking about her roommate raping her and stuff. *All lies. I didn't ask for a gun, and I didn't have any money, and I did not hear Jeff request one. I do remember, as I walked into Al's trailer, the two of them stood outside and spoke directly to each other. I did see a little handgun at Al's. Jeff showed it to me. I said, "It's cute" and handed it back. I was interested in getting my neck-laces. Al said he'd fix them.*

Asked who paid the money, Al says, "I can't… I think Karlyn handed me the money. I'm pretty sure she did." *I had no money. He has to help the police establish that I am responsible for getting a gun for Jethro, a felon, not him.* He mentions going to our pizza party and going over four or five days later looking for a baby-sitter for his daughter.

He describes helping **them** with the carpet, furnishing tools, and taking the carpet away for **them**. *I did not assist in the removal or replacement. I was washing the car, as I was told to do.*

In a letter Karlyn wrote me while I was first trying to get her story together, she referred to the above:

I reread Al Hope's Grand Jury statements. He's such a liar. He makes me sick. I never never inquired about a gun, and I never accused James of rape. That's all bull. The police must have said, "How sweet he sings to our tune!"

Al Hope is extremely knowledgable about guns. He did boast about his use of them during Vietnam and carried a collection even afterwards. He used to wire his yard for land mines, as I was told by Sherri, a woman who used to rent from him and his mother. The interesting thing is how dumb he played about the caliber when questioned in the court. Plus his line of questions at grand jury prove even more that detectives had planned to arrest me from the beginning, even though day by day at the interrogation they told me it was Grand Jury for Jethro.

Grand Jury Testimony of Kathleen Leslie Miller

May 12, 1994: Longtime friend of Karlyn's from San Diego, Kathleen states that Jethro asked her for bullets in the days preceding the murder, but she knew he had been in prison and didn't want anything to do with it… She states that Karlyn wouldn't ride in a green car, was obsessed with green, and that was why Jethro was painting it gray. Her interview was brief. *I joked with her about the car. I had to play a role at that time.*

Grand Jury Testimony of James Benjamin Davis

May 12, 1994: James Benjamin Davis, who knew Kathleen Miller and her boyfriend, Rob, met Karlyn when he came to the pizza party. He states Jeff paid him money, $80, to tape and primer the car. *This was done while I was being interrogated [at the police sta-*

tion] and then thrown out of the house. I was surprised when I saw it. Jethro is fast at everything he does.

Grand Jury Interview of Glen Odell Dent

May 12, 1994: Glen Dent was owner of the Eastside Floors carpet store where Jethro and Karlyn went the day after the murder. An interview with him shortly after the disappearance, included in an earlier chapter, can be compared significantly with the one he gives now. At this time he recalls that "she was real pushy. She needed material right then." The time was around 11 o'clock.

He said, "She was loud and she just kept pushing that she didn't care what it was, she wanted it cheap and she wanted it right now and she had to have it." *I never actually spoke to him. I wanted to be back with my children. I was very distraught and upset with Jeff. Dent says I wanted carpet cheap and now. I know that's a lie, because I didn't even know Jeff was thinking about changing anything until we pulled up in front of the place.*

Of Jethro he said, "He seemed to be a fairly nice fellow." *Yes, I guess so. He was very pleasant when he gets what he wants. He drew a diagram for Mr. Dent, a bathroom layout, and he paid Mr. Dent. So, of course, Dent thinks or remembers him as being nice.* **That was probably the only time I got smart mouth with Jeff. I paid dearly for it later. His looks and body language kept me from doing it again.** *That's why by the time we made it to Dave's I was so jumpy. I wished I could have told Kathy and Rob before we left, but I didn't want anybody else getting hurt or involved.*

Chap XII: The First Interrogation

Ignoring all rules of *due process*, Karlyn's prosecutors proceeded in their drive to frame her for the murder of James Salmu. Eventually her defense would stand by completely ineffective in preventing this. Her prosecutors pursued her relentlessly until her conviction was an accomplished fact.

Hugi even stated at the end of her trial that Eklof's statements were "lies from beginning to end," although he was presenting her "confession" as the evidence needed for her conviction. Why did Hugi knowingly present "evidence" he knew to be false? It has been stated that he brought in all the evidence to overwhelm the jury, and then waited for the closing argument to discount its validity. Well, her counsel failed her completely. John Kolego didn't even give a closing argument.

It has been left for Tiner's lawyers, when he was finally brought to justice, to prove that her statements were involuntary. In fact, the State pee'd. After Tiner filed an Appeal to Dismiss motion the state was on the verge of having Eklof's statements declared "involuntary." They truly ran that danger. Then the State moved to dismiss, never having filed an opening brief. They were not required to give a specific reason.

While leaving these developments to be brought into the story when they were discovered by the writer, it is important to state what has been the precedent for establishing voluntariness: "The bottom line in Oregon for over 100 years has been that before a confession or admission can be received into evidence, the state must prove its voluntariness." *State v. Smith*, 301 Or. 681, 700, 725 P.2d 894, 906 (1986).

A confession is initially deemed to be involuntary, with the burden being on the State to prove it was voluntarily given, that the police made no promises. A confession or admission cannot be received into evidence unless the State proves it was made without inducement of fear or promises.

The police denied Eklof's requests for counsel. She was grilled for nine days, including one where they drove her around the area trying to improve her memory. *Due process* is violated by use in a State trial of a confession where the declarant's will was overborne by prolonged interrogation by numerous law enforcement officers after repeated requests for counsel were denied. The length and location of the interrogation are also relevant surrounding circumstances in determining voluntariness.

Her early counsel attorney Evans gives his account of her treatment:

H. Thomas Evans, Att. at Law, [from] Memorandum to Suppress No. 10-94-04750: Defendant agreed to go to Eugene to testify before the Grand Jury against Tiner. Once Defendant arrived in Eugene, she was constantly under the control of the police. They selected and paid for a motel, gave her a daily food allowance, drove her wherever she went, provided child care all day every day, and closely monitored her at the motel. The police alternated interrogators, usually two or more at a time and questioned her all day and every day for eight straight days. Over the eight days of interrogation they continued to foster the false belief in Defendant that they only wanted her statements to use against co-suspect Tiner. They grilled her all day every day to force her into changing her statement to conform to what the police believed occurred.

During this period the police used various interrogation techniques to get Defendant to change her statement to fit what they believed the facts to be. Sometimes they pretended they were just helping her so she would be a good witness. Sometimes they made crude sexual references and jokes as a technique to gain power over Defendant. They suggested facts and bullied her into "admitting" facts that were not true. Defendant periodically requested or inquired about an attorney. These inquiries were put off or argued with. They said variously that it (the attorney) was all taken care of, that Defendant was mistaken or misunderstood if she thought they said she needed an attorney, and, finally, why did she need an attorney; was she lying?

Karlyn's account of her arrival in Eugene, the onset of the interrogations, and a summary of her feelings at that time she wrote in her journals. The following is taken from those:

We flew in to Portland on April 27, 1994. Detectives escorted us back to a motel in Eugene where we stayed ten days through horrific interrogations, producing four videotapes enacting the crime. Many times I asked for legal counsel but these requests were either ignored or I was told they were simply preparing me for Grand Jury testimony in order to indict Jethro Tiner. I was there to help them...

But in the end, my story was distorted to fit what Jethro told Dave and others so I would be afraid to come forward when he wouldn't and didn't. And many of those who testified against me were under threat by the police because of initial perjury or their own criminal activity. Why wouldn't they give the police the version they wanted? The more I could be implicated, the less likely they would be.

So finally we have the police detectives, who couldn't indict Jethro when he was serving time for another crime. Even when he was brought to Grand Jury to give testimony against me, they counseled him to take the Fifth in order to complete their prosecution of me without complications. They had invested much time and energy in distorting my testimony, and they didn't want their "evidence" refuted in any way. Their reputations as master crime solvers were at stake.

While my testimony was being brutally distorted to fit Captain Smith's brilliant deductions of how the crime was committed, four videotapes were made, under threat and pressure, in which I am made to reenact their sequence of events. Each time it was done, I didn't get it quite right according to what they had in mind. Until the last time.

I trusted Steve and Rick and always checked with them if they thought I was making a mistake. If for any reason Steve saw during interrogation that my story was getting worse, after Smith was sitting alone interrogating me, why didn't he tell Rick or stop Smith? I didn't know that for them police work meant practicing and carrying out the law and solving cases by any deceitful means whatsoever, if they were asked to. That came before protecting my rights, my life, my freedom, and my need to be with my children.

I was brutalized and degraded, especially before the last video. Under threats I was made to say, in essence, "Absolutely, absolutely, I am here of my own free will and what I have to say is true to the best of my knowledge." Even when I was finally allowed to file a complaint about their tactics of sexual harassment and threats to take my children away, I was made to say that, even so, what I said on the tapes was true and unaffected by this. But I hadn't seen them yet.

The day the officers Smith and Walker showed up at the motel to take me to go before Grand Jury, I thought we were finished after that. That's what Smith told me, and that's why my children were brought there with us to Grand Jury. The officer asked two ladies to watch the children. We were here for Grand Jury. One lady says, "Oh, but Grand Jury isn't meeting here today." And Smith says, "Please just watch the children," and we walked down the hall. I went to the restroom, put some lip gloss on, came out, and Smith says, "That's a nice touch. Make yourself pretty."

****

The version given here, a more or less complete transcript, consists of transcripts of the first video verbatim, with Karlyn's comments in *italics*. Their constant and suggestive questioning caused her to make misstatements continually and to mix up the sequence of events that happened. This version, therefore, is also *their* version, with her comments.

State v. Karlyn Eklof, Transcript 4/29/94 Reenactment

K: Karlyn Eklof
S: Steve Walker
L: Rick Lewis

S: My name is Steve Walker. I am a detective with the Springfield Police. I'm at the address of 5282 Leota Street in Springfield, Oregon. Standing next to me is Karlyn Eklof on my right. On my left is Detective Rick Lewis, Detective John Umenhofer, and Detective Don Myers who will be in this video. We will be assuming roles throughout it. Karlyn, are you aware that the video camera's going? *They didn't ask me if they had my permission to video. I was trying so very hard to be cooperative, and they just kept taking advantage. And what I mean by this is they made me feel like if I didn't cooperate I would be charged for murder which eventually I was.*

K: Yes I am Yes I am. *I was so nervous I almost relieved myself the second we walked in the door.*

S: And, that this is the house on Leota Street where you used to live?

K: Yes it is.

S: Okay. And the filming of this video was voluntary on your part?

K: Absolutely.

S: Okay. What we would like you to do, why don't we move into the next room. Let me document this, today's date is April 29th, the time on my watch is 6:42 P. M. What I'd like for you to do Karlyn, is just in your own words, explain what took place on the evening of March 21, 1993. Tell what was taking place in your home, who was present, and then just move through the events of that evening. When you get to a point where we're talking about particular persons, who is going to be a role player, we'll move that person into position and you just move them to where you want them to stand,

K: Sure.

S: And you move to where you want to stand and go through the events of the evening. Okay?

K: Okay. Okay, we had a pizza party and it went really well and I had a guest up from San Diego, his name was Jethro, Jeff Tiner. And *we* wanted to be alone that night. *Somehow throughout all this they, the police, have me stating we wanted to be alone. When actually I didn't know why Spider and Jethro wanted to clear the house out. Spider even had Deb crying in the patio. She said something about why are you allowed to stay, John? You never take me anywhere. You're always over here and come home after 2:00 A. M. Spider has never stayed at this house past my children's bedtime because I usually go lay down with them. So whatever has he been pulling?*

He asked my roommate to leave and offered him some money to go to a motel, and suggested that he should go. And James said he had enough money and he didn't need Jethro's money, he wasn't going to go. He was going, James was getting ready to go to a bar to meet Francis, and Jethro wanted to be sure that James was not going to be home that evening so that we could be alone. As a matter of fact, he said, "I want to be with my wife." We're not married. I had just met him just a week or two before that. Well, I had requested that he ask Keith if he could spend the night there, why spend money on a motel when you have a best friend that lives down the road. And overnighters were very casual between all of us. We spent a lot of time together. I was on the phone with Linda, Keith's wife, yea, and uh, asking her, asking her to you know talk to James. James got on the phone,

S: Can you uh, whose going to be James.

K: Okay, you be James, and the phone stretched in from here. Okay, so James is on the phone with Linda asking if he could stay the night with Keith because we wanted to be alone. Spider came in and was uh, standing right, basically with all of us here and he put the phone down. Linda did not want him to stay the night. He said he wasn't allowed to go over there and spend the evening.

S: Where was Jethro at this point?

K: Jethro was in the living room smoking a cigarette listening. He, 'cause, he had just left from this area talking to James and wanted the house to ourselves. And because, um, James wouldn't take the money. I think Jethro walked to the kitchen and probably flicked an ash off his cigarette and then went into the living room. Let's see, Spider had his foot up here and was talking to James telling him to just take the money. You know, just go to the motel, relax, go have fun, somebody else's paying for it, why not? And James, he just didn't want to party, he couldn't be convinced. He was going to go to the bar and come back. So he's off the phone and I'm upset with him because he'd made a remark, "I'm not allowed to go there because of Linda's sister." *I wasn't upset yet—another Smith input•.* "What's wrong, why?" "Well, because I kissed her sister good night one night and I went a little bit too far and I made her uncomfortable." "Well, what did you do, what happened?" And he says, "Well, I stuck my tongue in her mouth and I went too far and I made her uncomfortable and I'm not allowed to be in the house at the same time as her."

Well, during the party, I'd never noticed that there was any uncomfortableness. Spider, I believe, went to the back and I don't see him for a few minutes. I don't remember where he was but I believe he went to the patio and I think Jethro and he both went to the patio so I could talk to Spider, I mean to James. I wanted to find out a little bit more about what was going on and why he wasn't allowed there. I have a little girl and a son. I had two little children and I thought, "If you're not welcome at that house with that little girl, what about my little girl?" And so James, he didn't let me think. James, is off the phone and he's trying to talk to me and he started for the door, James started for the door and uh, to the front door.

And I like went, "Hey wait, what do you think you're doing? Whoa, whoa, well, a woman isn't good enough for you, hey wait, there's one there. woman's not good enough for you, what are you going to do, gonna handle the situation. For one thing, the little girl's twelve years old and you're 34. That's not acceptable to me. I think you should go apologize. This is what I think you should do. Not go to the bar, not hang around, go take care of it. Apologize to the young woman. Now." *I only suggested to him to go to Keith's. Jeff and Spider were the ones who bullied him.* He said, "I'll take care of it in my own time." And he walked to his room and I stopped, I was tired of going, "Hey, hey, whoa, whoa, that's not going towards Keith what you did." And he kind of pushed me off. And I went, "Bam, bam, bam, well do it, take care of it. Okay? Now would be a good time."

These things are not in the right order. It happened later when he "head-butted" me, after a scuffle with Jethro, and not because of going to Keith's. But they have me saying, as though I had started all of this: And I split his cheek open and he probably should have had stitches, at least one or two. And there was blood on his cheek and going down his shirt and I'm like, "Well, I mean now, you need to take care of it now." And he's like going, "Hey, I deserved that, okay, look, I deserved it." And he kind of wiped his shirt and he had a little bit on his shirt, and I said, "That's ridiculous, clean yourself up."

Now, Jethro is still over in the corner smoking. And he's like real coy, now James is going either back to his room and he went inside, James went into his room to put his jacket on like he was going to leave. And he didn't leave because he left the door open and the light on. And he came back up the hallway, and I'm over here wondering, okay, I'm going to get Linda back on the phone, I want to know what's going on. And I'm sure that's when I saw, no it could have been right then, but anyway he started going back. James goes towards the living room and he's like talking to Jethro and I'm still wondering on the phone, I think I've got Linda back on the phone. And I want to know more about what's the deal here. Can you guys come down here, as a matter of fact I was talking to Linda because I asked her to come on down. You guys get back over here, let's get this thing straightened out, cause it seems a little unusual for me. And uh, she was considering it, she didn't have a problem with that, she was considering getting this thing dealt with. I said, "Wait, whoa, whoa,"

Okay, James and Jethro are arguing and he popped him and I came out of the kitchen and James was on one knee. *In these statements I have rushed into events. I was so distraught and under so much pressure. Even with all that had happened and all that I was going through I tried. The police made me feel filthy, guilty and damned-if-I-do and damned-if-I-don't. I did what I thought best by trying to expose this, and all this was going to be used against me. So they would believe what parts were convenient for conviction and deny the rest.*

S: What are they arguing about?

K: Well, Jethro had asked me, "What kind of friends have you got? What kind of house am I in? I'll show you how this thing is handled." This is what he's saying to me or at least to both of us. Now, I'm wondering if the boys, you, what's up, I go out this way because I heard a "pop." And I came in to see what was up. James was on one knee and Jethro was standing over next to him like this. And like, James was saying, "What the hell's going on here?" And I went out the door and I went out to Spider's truck and I saw the boys and Spider were still there and Spider was just getting into the truck and I said, "I think he's going to kill him, get the boys out of here, for God's sake, get out of here now." And of course Spider did. He left.

This is the first time it was mentioned like that, because TJ and Steve said I say it differently. Also the previous page happened after this one. This is all screwed up. Because I wasn't a part of any of his and Jethro's falling out, and I wasn't aware it was that dramatic. I missed it. But as James walked freely through the house he at one point shoulder butted me and I socked him. So these pages need to be reversed and not so compacted. It is worse because there was room for movement.

I came back in the house and everything seemed fine. James was just getting up and I felt like an idiot because I'd gotten so dramatic out there in front of the boys. And uh, it was pretty heated in here, obviously, the uh, James was getting up, I walked over here to the kitchen and I looked over my shoulder to see if everything was all right and James was just getting up and Jethro had something like a pistol in his hand, a little silver, and he had it kind of like, like it was kind of hidden but not. Like that. He was standing way over here cause there was a couch there but he had it more like this. And he was looking at me to consent and I just shook my head, "No, no."

And I walked back in the kitchen and James came back towards me, like in the dining area, cause I was trying to keep an eye on things. James was coming over this way and I said, "Get, come here buddy" and he said, "I'm going to the bar." And I said, "Get cleaned up, come on, come on, get cleaned up, god, get your face cleaned up." I brought him in here, I said, "Come on, come on, get your face cleaned up." I turned the water on and I'm splashing him, getting him cleaned up and he was trying to help, he was cleaning himself too. And there wasn't anymore blood coming and he was pretty much staying there and he was turning and arguing with Jethro about whether to go to Keith's.

S: Jethro was in here?

K: Right, Jethro was right over here behind me and they were arguing over going to Keith's or getting it straightened up and I was like, "Come on, come on," I wanted to pull him with me but he just stopped. And I just got out from between him because I got in between them in the kitchen and I got in between them in the living room. I got out from between them. There was, nobody was stopping. I mean, the argument just went on. It wasn't loud and aggressive, it was just simply going between them. So I came out of the bathroom and Jethro said, "Here, have a seat over here."

I'm over close to the kitchen, I'm going to get things cleaned up and picked up. I figured I was doing nothing but making things worse in there. *I wasn't making this worse, they were. I just thought it was me.* So I came into the kitchen and I was getting some things done. I think I stopped and went out in the back yard to see if food was still left out there and came back in. *This was earlier. I was at the sink when I heard the pops.* And they're still in the bathroom, okay, I thought everything was fine, it seemed to be okay. I thought maybe we should take him to get a stitch. And, like, that never did get brought up. The two guys were in there and I came to the counter and I was trying to do things, I didn't know whether to call Linda back on the phone and get Keith over here 'cause things were getting really out of hand and I didn't have control of the situation any further.

Neither one of them would listen to me. Well, I think James knew what Jethro was going to do by the way they were looking at each other. Now that I think about it. I didn't catch it before. I just never had been through anything like this. And I was over here and then I heard a "pop" 'cause I had water on. I heard a "pop" and I looked and I thought, "Oh god," and I stopped and then I thought, I think I heard another "pop" cause I stood right here. I wanted to see, I didn't want Jethro to see me. And I looked, and I heard snoring. I could see James' feet and I stepped back and I didn't know what to do and I said, "Oh god, oh god."

Okay, so then I had this steak knife in my hand. Let's see, from here I couldn't really, I didn't want Jethro to see. But I couldn't really see James other than his feet and I heard snoring. He was, I stepped back and I thought, "Oh god, what am I going to do?" And then, there was Jethro, and he goes, "Come here, I want you to see this, come here." And I stepped in here and as I, right, I was standing here like well, I see, and he was moaning and gurgling. Jethro said to get something.

L: Can you see the gun with Jethro now or not?

K: No, I don't believe I did see it. I'm not sure, I don't believe I did 'cause I was so devastated that James was there and there was blood on the wall behind his head. It was all smudged. It wasn't very much but it was there and I could tell that he was hurt. It wasn't like Jethro was sitting here talking to him threatening to shoot him off, bing, bing, bing, no, he was shot somewhere. Um, he had blood on the wall and then he told me to get something, and I went and got, I went into James' room. I went up the hall and I grabbed a sleeping bag off of his bed.

Okay, I didn't know what I was doing. I just wanted to help. I wanted to comfort him so bad, I came in here and I tossed it over him. I stepped back, and Jethro was just standing right there. I thought, "What am I gonna do?" And uh, I went back out. I still had the steak knife in my hand and went back out and, I don't know, I just couldn't believe I didn't know what to do. It was like, god, and I thought I wonder if anybody heard. I wonder what's going on here. Um, Jethro came out and he dropped a metal piece. Jethro came out and he dropped a metal piece in my hand. It was a little wrinkled. He said, "Oh, it bounced." I went, "Yuck." And he stuck it in his pocket. He picked it up and he stuck it in his pocket. He picked it up and stuck it in his pocket 'cause I dropped it on the floor right here. *I just dropped it. I didn't want to touch anything, and I didn't say 'yuck.' I never said, 'yuck.' Captain Smith was creating little cute notations during the interrogation, and they were coming out in my statements.*

S: Do you know what that little metal piece looked like?

K: It was, it looked like, it was a bullet. It was wrinkled up. It was a cap or something. It was, he said it "bounced." He went back inside and, you know, went over here just to, I can't believe, I just couldn't believe I walked in here, I couldn't believe, I went, "Oh god," and James said, I could hear James say, "Am I dying?" And Jethro said, "Yep son, you're out of here." And uh, he said, "Well, I'm Christian." And Jethro said, "Well that's what you all say." and there was another "pop" and I don't even know where I was right then, I heard the third "pop" and it was so amplified I thought the whole neighborhood could hear. And I just, I didn't know, it was over with.

Jethro wanted some help putting him in the sleeping bag. He said, "Come in here, I want you to see this." And uh, I didn't say anything. He started zipping up the bag and he wanted, he was zipping it up and I was behind it and Jethro was over there and he said, "Help me get him in here and put him in the car." *These statements are not in the correct order. I was pressured so much just to get the information out I was confused. If you had your head beat like I did you'd be slow to remember too. All those emotions are mixed up.*

The sequence was more like this: I bolted from the bathroom, went to the sink and held on for a second. He said something to James. I returned with a table steak knife. I waved it but didn't touch anybody or anything as I realized the mistake I could have made. I turned to leave to go back to the counter and Jeff wrapped a towel around his hand and placed it against James' chest. Out of the corner of my eye I saw this, because I had got back to the sink. He said, "Get something." I was confused. I went to James room and got his blanket, his "sleeping bag." I wanted to comfort him.

Oh yea, I put my steak knife back in the sink. I didn't have this in my hand or anything, here, thanks. I was looking for any kind of movement. He didn't have any kind, there was nothing. He was gone. Okay, so basically,

S: I didn't hear what you said, you said you were looking for movement?

K: Yea, I was looking to see if, you know, I was trying to see any kind of breath, and I was sure I didn't see anything.

L: _____ *Where's this question?*

K: No, no I didn't, I didn't check him or anything because Jethro had covered him. He had him, he was already wrapping him up. And it was,

L: Like this?

K: Yea, he was putting him over.

L: Now, is he still up like this against the wall?

K: Yes he was. And uh, then the blood was on the wall and, oh god. (Transcript: sounds of whining, snorting, etc.) And then _____, and um, and he went and backed the car up, um, then he grabbed a towel and wiped it all up and I think he was,

S : Were you here when he did that?

K: I think so.

S: Where'd he get the towel.

K: Well, I had a little table sitting here in the corner. A little metal table.

S: What did you do when Jethro went out?

K: I just stood back.

S: You stayed inside?

K: I just stood back. I was hoping James [Jethro] would say something so I could figure out what to do 'cause if he had said something I would have tried to lock the door or something. I didn't know what to do. *I followed him. I didn't know what to do. And I stood next to the heater. He closed the curtain, shut off the lights, opened the back door, and backed the car up. I was so dumbfounded. My spirit was gone. I tried not to look scared. I didn't want to make Jethro nervous.* It, he, he came back in and he continued to put the sleeping bag...

S: Jethro came in,

K: Right, Jethro came back in and he continued to put the sleeping bag around, zipped him up...

L: Where's he at here?

K: Well, as he slid the body this way there was blood down the wall and he had taken one of the towels and wiped it off and he was trying to wipe his hands off. I don't know, maybe he had touched James when he tried to put the blanket over him, the sleeping bag over him, and his hand, I didn't see any blood on his hands. He had slid him out just a little bit and moved him over to get the bag on and he told me to pick up the end. He said, "Pick up the end." So...

L: We're going to just take the bag off Detective Umenhofer to simulate the, so I've got his shoulders up here...

K: Right. Right.

S: And you're holding the feet end? *The feet end of the sleeping bag. I never touched his feet.*

K: Right. This, none of this was here. Let's see, you're ahead of me. Okay, so he's got, he's having a real hard time holding on to him too. So I, so he backs all the way up to the door and you know, I don't even, I, he didn't sit him down or anything. I think he left the door open.

L: The door was open already.

K: Yea I think so because he had backed the car up and he was moving. He wanted to move this real quick. Um, we all went out and he was looking at the neighbor's house over there and he goes, "I think there's somebody in the window." And I didn't, I didn't look. I was just holding on, and then he set, he had set James down and I still had a hold of the sleeping bag...

L: Set him down like this?

K: Yea, and he got the keys out and he opened the trunk. And he set him in there. And I took his feet *I never touched his feet—it was the corner of the bag* and then I remember, I just, I just walked away and he shut the door and he came inside and he said, "You got to clean this up and I'll be back." *There was no mess. He just wanted me to go over the area.* And he said, "Give me all your clothes." I said, "What?" He said, "Give me all your clothes." So I gave him my boots, my socks, and my levis and my shirt and my panties and he took them. He grabbed his cigarettes and he took off. *He had to open the door. He took my clothes for a power of discipline. After we arrived in San Diego my clothes were taken from me several times. All my personal belongings were stolen.*

S: Did he take anything else with him?

K: Um. he had a map with him. He was outside, I was standing in the kitchen window
_____ and I went into my room and I put something on, I think it was a tee-shirt and some
panties and a pair of socks. I don't think I put any levis on. He um, he walked around the corner
of the car,

S: Where were you standing then?

K: I was standing right at the table because I didn't know whether to call Keith or call the
police or just call God for one thing. And he was walking around the car and uh,

S: What was he doing walking around the car?

K: He was bent over checking the front end. He was like this. He was checking the front
end lights and I just, maybe he was thinking about what direction to go and I don't know. He
didn't talk to me about that. He uh, he laid something in the back seat. He opened the car and he
laid something in the back seat. I don't know what it was and he didn't say. He came back in and
he had a, he got his clothes, he got a bundle of extra clothes himself and off he went. From there
I went in, I got paint and I scrubbed the tub and I did the carpet cleaner across the carpet

S: How did you scrub the tub, what did you use?

K: I think I probably used, like GM, let me think. It was probably one of the little metal
scrubber pads. You know, the SOS pads. *No SOS pads were there at all.*

S: What was in the tub?

K: Well there was a little bit of residue from his blood, washed. helping him wash his face.
There was some from the water. It wasn't much but it was, I was told to clean up so I did.

S: Did you clean the wall?

K: Yes I did. I wiped it down. That was already wiped down. That was just, that barely
needed anything. I think there was a sponge in there at the time that we used regularly to clean the
tub and I reached for that and I wiped whatever was there, there wasn't really anything 'cause
Jethro had wiped it off. But, I took a sponge across that and then um,

L: What did you do with the sponge?

K: I had, I had the sponge and the scrubber for the tub and the roller for the paint right
there on the tub, and Jethro, when he got back, he took them. I don't know what he did with them
but he took all that.

S: When he got back. When did he get back:

K: A couple hours later.

S: What time did he leave with James' body?

K: There used to be a clock on this wall and I'm so sure that I saw five minutes to eleven.
I'm not sure if that's when Spider left or when Jethro left but I know that I saw five minutes to
eleven on the clock and I don't remember seeing the clock when he arrived 'cause when he did
arrive I was really amazed that he wasn't gone all night... I wish he never would have come back.
But he was, I was in the kitchen wondering if there was anything else I should clean up 'cause I
don't want him to come back and be angry at me. I didn't know what to expect. *He knew I was too
weak for all this.* He pulled back in and I thought, "whoa," and I tried to make sure I had something on and he said that he had, he said that he, "Put him where nobody could ever find him," and
he was hoping for a bear from Odin, to send a bear and he said he had clipped his fingers and
stuck a penny in his mouth, his lucky penny, an 1881 penny or something. 1909 penny, I don't
know. But it was an old penny that he had.

S: Why would he put a penny in his mouth?

K: I don't have a clue. It's a whole thing, I don't know. I never asked him. I didn't want to
know. I,

S: You said he clipped his fingers off?

K: He said he clipped his, three of his fingers off.

S: Three of them?

K: Uh huh. And then stuck a penny in his mouth. And in fact when I was asked to leave by the landlord a couple days later, um, I found the penny under the bed in the bedroom. That night when he returned, I'd gone and laid down, he laid down and smoked a cigarette. I had my back to him and he had his back to me. I had nothing to say and I didn't know if I should say anything.

S: You found the penny that he had stuck in his mouth?

K: The one he said he'd stuck in his mouth. I handed it to him and he goes, "Well, I can't even do this right. I blew the whole thing. I did this whole thing wrong. I mean, I'm going to be the laughing stock of the yard." I don't know what all that means either.

S: Okay, then what happened?

K: The next morning came, I answered the phone, Dave was calling and I woke up because David had the children and he called. It was about 9:00, 8:30 or 9:00, and he said, "Well, I've had enough of the children, I'm bringing them back." Okay, that'd be great. And I walked out here and TJ was sitting in the living room, the television was against that wall, he asked about James, and I said, "I really don't know." And Jethro was just pulling in the driveway. I guess he went to get coffee and cigarettes, I'm not sure. I believe he had coffee, a 7-ll cup in his hand, I'm not sure. I was just surprised because I thought he was in the house and there he was pulling up.

S: Could you back up just a little bit? When he arrived home from getting rid of James, and you guys had a conversation for a little while, what happened after the conversation?

K: I went to sleep. I didn't know what, I just was in my room. I wanted to stay in one place at peace. I didn't want to stir him up cause he seemed really anxious when he returned. He was really apprehensive over everything that wasn't in place. I mean, everything had to be right, he really didn't check the bathroom too much but he was checking everything like, seeing if you know, the phone was where it was supposed to be and the, seeing, just seeing, I don't know what he was looking for but he was just looking. He never really did check the bathroom. I suppose he figured I did a good job.

S: Okay, so you went to bed. Did he go to bed with you?

K: He laid next to me but he didn't cover up. He laid next to me and I kind of looked over my shoulder to see what he was doing and he was just laying there smoking a cigarette.

S: Did he make any comments to you, say anything to you?

K: No, he didn't say anything to me. *I'm trying to get them to see the silence between us. I didn't have anything to say. I was at a loss for words. I was trying very hard to understand why.*

S. So you fell asleep?

K: Yes I did, 'cause I woke up to Dave's phone call telling me he was going to bring the kids back.

S: Why don't you continue on then from when you got up and,

K: He wanted James' car moved. He wanted it to go to the airport and I told him I didn't think that was a good idea, and to park it at the bar where he usually goes. And he insisted on the airport. He wanted it to appear that he was out of town and wasn't... you know. Just...

S: When did you go and park it at the bar?

K: I was trying to bring attention. Because that's where he goes. If he's not there and his car's there, well, someone's going to start, you know, looking, finding, come on. I don't want to get caught up in this situation anymore than it was. I needed something to be noticed, something that I didn't have me say that or he would see me do. Know what I'm saying? I didn't want to register his temper. *The next day I was pissed at him and couldn't show it. He broke all rules of loving humanity.*

S: Okay, so you had the discussion about moving the car and then what happened?

K: He got into James' car and he turned it around and he pulled up, it was pretty close to the mail time because I was looking for the mailman. And he said, "Follow me in the Cutlass, and he tossed me the keys and he said, "Tell TJ to watch the kids." I said, "TJ, we'll be back." TJ again wanted to know where James was at. "I don't know, I don't have a clue." And I followed him and he went over, down the street, up around the corner, around the next corner and he went to the market. He pulled in behind the market and,

S: Where's that market located?

K: And the puppy was with us. The dog was in the car. *I was remembering things and not hearing. I was struggling and, damn it, trying very hard.*

S: Which car?

K: In the Cutlass. He was in the Cutlass. I think he was in James' car to begin with, he was in the Corvair. He was, he was in the Corvair, that's why I didn't remember the dog. He was in the Corvair, and uh, *I even stunned myself when my memory fell into place. This is no bull. I struggled to put this into perfect focus and I still didn't get it right. Thanks to Smith. Since I am thinking so cautiously about Jethro's emotions towards me I had to be so mellow, so well-behaved, which means I wasn't at all involved, especially to any stabbing like Smith has me admitting in the last interrogation and as Jeff wanted people to believe. But I didn't, and that's the truth.*

S: He was in the Corvair when Jethro drove it down to the market?

K: Yea.

S: Where's this market at again?

K: It's, if you come up from Leota, you take a left and you go to the next corner, the boulevard, and you take a right. About a block down is a bar that we regularly that we went to.

S: Which bar is that?

K: I don't remember the name of it. I just know, he had a birthday party there. Francis and I decorated a table for him there and, I've only been in there a couple of times and its,

S: Okay, there's a store parked across from the bar?

K: Right. A little mini-market.

S: That's where he parked the car?

K: Right. And then, excuse me, he brought the pup and put him in the car. He drove down the street and up around and came back out on the boulevard.

S: Which way did you drive? Are you referring to Main Street? Boulevard I mean?

K: He went down behind the market, he drove out behind the market going south and then he came back up around the streets and came out on Main Street again wherever it loops back around and comes in. He came out there and he handed me James' keys and he says, "Toss these out one at a time. Take them off the ring and toss them out one at a time." So that's what I did. He turned on to Main Street and went west. And I took the keys off one at a time and tossed them.

S: How many keys were there?

K: I don't think, maybe seven or eight, maybe not even that many. I'm not too sure. I didn't even count. It could have been five or six, I'm not sure. He turned at the railroad tracks.

S: What street is that?

K: 28th.

S: Which way did he turn?

K: He took a right turn down 28th. I don't really remember much of that ride from there.

He found a side road and he said, "Let the dog out." I opened the car door and I let the puppy out. *I was so sad. I tried not to let Jethro see.*

S: What was around that location?

K: It was a really nice, it is a green grass very large location. A very large area of green grass and there was a little house that sat off in the distance, not very far.

K: 500 feet, maybe less. Probably less.

S: Was that on 28th Street?

K: No.

S: So you left 28th Street somewhere.

K: Yea, and I'm not even too sure because I'm not familiar with the streets but I know it was a real nice location and,

S: How far did you drive, how long did you drive?

K: A few minutes.

S: You stopped the car and he said, "You let the dog out." *He says how far did I drive. I didn't drive that car after going to the market. I wasn't allowed to have the keys again ever.*

K: Yes he did.

S: And did you do that?

K: Yes I did.

S: Then what happened?

K: Then the only thing I remember from that morning was being right inside the carpet place he had taken me over to, on 54th Street next to the Safeway, there's a carpet place and he had purchased linoleum for the bathroom and a can of glue. He was in there for quite a while and uh, talking to the owner describing the bathroom. He had drawn out a, you know, a diagram of the bathroom and he knew his inches. I mean, he knew, he did everything precise. The owner was kind of confused when he described it but when he drew it out, excellent dimensions, he knew exactly what he was doing. And he purchased it.

S: How was it paid for?

K: Cash out of his pocket. I didn't have any money. Uh, I didn't have any money. I was, a matter of fact, it would be like a couple days, a week, before I would receive a check from social services that time. The carpet man, he had purchased carpet for this area out here too. The living area. And he got that right.

S: Why did he want to get these things, what was the discussion about that?

K: Well, he really didn't have to do that. That really wasn't necessary but he said he didn't want forensics to get directed to the bathroom. He wanted to cover up and make it seem, put it out there where there was nothing going on and kind of keep things turned around where nobody could figure out what he'd been doing or what had happened that night. He wanted nobody at all in the bathroom.

S: So you *(he!)* made the purchase at the carpet store and then what happened?

K: Brought it home and laid it in here and I made lunch. Keith and other friends showed up asking for James. I was making a sandwich and I told them I would call as soon as I saw, as soon as I knew anything.

S: Keith come into the house?

K: No he did not. Um, Jethro had the door with, he was pulling the carpet and a friend of ours, Al Hope, had stopped by and he had jumped in to help Jethro start slicing it into fourths so that he could uh, that might even have been Tuesday, that might have not been that Monday. And he was, I'm not sure.

S: Let's focus on Monday, what happened after you,

K: Well, I remember coming back and uh, making sandwiches and Keith showed up with a friend and he said, "I'm scared, I'm really scared." I knew exactly what he meant. And he wanted to know where James was at and come in the house but the carpet or something was still in the way. I don't think that he started the carpet for a day or so. Anyway, but the other carpet was laying out. Matter of fact, I think Jethro had been doing the bathroom, doing the linoleum in there cutting that down to its specifics. Getting that cleaned up. And I put some western things in there and decorated it and I put those back into place and made the house look nice cause I didn't want the children upset.

S: Okay, what happened after that?

K: Well, the day went by and he did a lot of running around out there and I don't even know what he was doing or who he was running with but he was in and out quite a bit. He didn't want to be here obviously. And uh, he had made a lot of plans with me to. I'm very encouraged by corporations in putting things like that enterprises together, you know it takes a lot of paperwork and strategy to do that and I've been encouraged by that. So he kept my mind on that you know, talking about my plans and what little conversations we had it was something that I wanted to hear. And he, like I said, was in and out, the car, he had taken my Cutlass over to a friend of ours, Kathy and Ron, and sort of priming on that. *But I knew nothing about it until I arrived over there.*

S: On the priming where?

K: The outside of the car. Changing the color of it.

S: Is there a, is there any time when you did anything to the car?

K: Yes. That day as a matter of fact, when Al showed up, just before that he had told me, right after I'd made the sandwiches and before Keith had showed up, he told me to clean the car and do a good job.

S: Who told you that?

K: Jethro. He said clean the car. I started hosing the outside and he opened the trunk and he said, "And in here too." I looked in there and it looked like there was blood in the trunk but there wasn't. It was rust from the trunk of the car. But I hosed off the outside and Al had seen the look on my face and he looked at me and he just, like real subtly, said..

S: Was Al there when you were hosing the trunk?

K: Yes he was.

S: You've _____ Al Hope.

K: Yes. He was very deeply concerned and he knew I was too. We both didn't want Jethro to see us looking at each other. You know, we didn't want to throw him into a frenzy 'cause he's a big guy.

S: Did he talk with Jethro?

K: Sure. I don't know about that. I don't think so. I'm imagining, I don't know, I can't speak for Jethro. Um, he continued to do the carpet and he split it up into squares and,

S: What happened to the carpet?

K: It went into Al's truck. In the back of Al's truck. I'm not too sure what he did with it from there. But there really wasn't anything wrong with the carpet other than it was kind of stinky and old and green.

S: Okay, go ahead and continue.

K: Oh, where was I? I'll figure it out, hold on. I washed the car and then uh, I never did have the car keys after he arrived here. I never had any part of that. Let's see. A couple days had gone by and he'd got the carpet laid and they swept and they cleaned it, got that laid down. Um, of course, Keith showed up again at lunch hour. He showed up three days in a row at lunch hour. And finally, I guess, the third day he'd had enough.

S: What did you tell Keith when he came over?

K: I didn't really get a chance to talk to him because Jethro jumped in to visit as soon as Keith, _____ pulling up he was right out to talk to him. And I remember, the second or third day I guess, the first day it wasn't, I was able to at least hear what he had to say and tell him I would let him know and all when James came home. I'd tell James to call. Uh, the last days I guess when he finally made the police report and I thanked God he did. But it still didn't get the direction that it needed, that I could do anything about at that point. The um, that third day, I guess it was, Jethro had told me, well, we'll go down the Boulevard, _____ and we checked the bars, we'll look for James and he, pretty well, tried to play off to be Keith's friend and James' friend. And he said,

"Well, I'll meet you at the bar at 5:00 and we'll just go out looking for him" And every time Keith had come by, at two other times, he had told Keith, "Well, I'm out looking for him too."

S: Keith phoned the police to file a...

K: A missing person.

S: Did a police officer come out here?

K: ... um, the fourth day I believe it was, yourself and Officer Jerry Smith.

S: Was there ever any uniformed police officer?

K: No there wasn't. *I hadn't remembered the uniformed officer, but there was one.* There was a landlord in the house when I, Jethro had taken me to a Motel 6. He said, "Look, I'll get this straightened out one way or another." And the children were at Kathy and Rob's and then out with us in a hotel. He goes, "Look, I'll get you guys away from the situation and the media and I'll get it all cleared up. I'll take care of it. I'll take care of everything."

S: What day was that?

K: I believe it was like Wednesday or Thursday 'cause I was out of here Thursday if I'm not mistaken.

S: Where did you go?

K: Well, I took my things over to Kathy and Rob's and down the road with Jethro. We stopped at a couple of hotels. He didn't allow me to use my identification for any of the hotels. He didn't want to be seen with me. He didn't want to say that we were together traveling. He wanted to dump me off in San Francisco, Sacramento, San Francisco, Fresno, wherever he had an inmate friend that he knew was out. He had planned to drop us off there and I insisted on being with my family. I wanted to come straight to San Diego. If I had to be in a trauma, then I wanted to be there.

S: Was there a point where you did make a stop in California?

K: Between the motel and his brother Dave's.

S: Where is his brother Dave?

K: In Fresno.

S: Did you stop and visit?

K: We stayed there a couple of days.

S: What happened there in Fresno?

K: Well, they were very gracious, very kind. They took into consideration of, I guess Jethro told Dave what he had done, or what "we" had done. I, you know,

S: How do you know that?

K: Well, I don't, I didn't really know that at the time. I know that while we were there Jethro and Dave took off and they came back and the trunk, it was coated with a really neat coating. It was like a Teflon coating. And I thought, maybe they should have just done the whole car cause it looked really neat. And um, he had, he had told me that he had told Dave what he had done. And I was like, "Oh good, great, just wonderful" And we stayed a couple days.

I watched his children while I cleaned their house and his wife was really neat to let us stay there. *I did their laundry.* Dave had tried to tell me that his brother wasn't what I thought and I didn't understand. What he was getting at obviously, he knew kind of that he (Jethro) was very disappointing to me, but I thought he was going to straighten this out and clean this up as he had told me he would.

S: Do you remember the point that Jethro told you that he had told his brother?

K: Right.

S: Where were you at when that happened?

K: I think they were coming in the door after doing the trunk and I was in the living room.

S: What kind of conversation took place around that?

K: Not much.

S: Was there anything more than that?

K: Not really. They were talking about a lawsuit that Jethro was trying to put through the State for an injury that he sustained being incarcerated.

S: I mean regarding the incident up here in Springfield.

K: I was never really a part of that conversation. I don't recall that Jethro and Dave and I were talking about that, 'cause I never discussed this with anybody except for you guys.

S: ... do you remember Jethro saying something to Dave?

K: Dave and Jethro said they had been talking about it.

S: Were you present?

K: No, had they been talking about it in my presence I probably would have had a fit but I don't remember anything, I know that they were talking but I wasn't aware that this is what they were talking about. Part of the conversation had to do with getting relocated up here and getting me out of trouble. As a matter of fact, Dave said he'd be more than happy to help relocate me there and he was looking for a larger place and that it would be great to be roommates, all of us until Jethro got back up there. *Dave took us to a place that was being renovated. It had a huge yard and had been a cement company or yard for cement trucks. The place was for rent.*

S: Do you remember Jethro complaining about losing anything.

K: I don't remember anything of that nature at all.

L: Do you remember laughing about anything?

K: None of it's funny. I know, scared, _____you know um, I, an attitude for me with him sitting there and if he was boastful and bragging about a situation, I'm not going to laugh about it because I don't think its funny one bit. And I don't see where Dave has any right saying that I did because it wasn't funny and I had a lot of fear there and he should have saw that the children and I needed help. And he did, otherwise he wouldn't have offered us a place to stay. And if he thought I was that sick and that funny then he would never have offered that. So, if he wants to pull me in with, you know, any deeper, that's fine.

S: How long did you stay in Fresno then?

K: Um, I'm not even sure. Three or four days maybe.

S: Where did you go from there?

K: Jethro's little neck of the woods at Imperial Beach. I didn't even know that I was in Imperial Beach when he took us to a hotel. I didn't know I was that close to the Tijuana border. I had no idea.

S: Once you arrived down in Imperial Beach, did you ever have occasion to meet Jethro's friends or,

K: Oh, absolutely.

S: Do you remember one of their names?

K: Absolutely. I've... that place is a nightmare. It's wicked. um, a neat couple, Leo and Cindy, who tried to help and wanted the children to stay but um, that wasn't quite acceptable at first because they weren't really, they didn't know who we were, they didn't know what kind of trouble we'd been. Although, they, Jethro had opened his mouth to several of his friends and so they pretty well knew. *Soon enough.*

S: What did he say?

K: I wasn't there when he said what he said. I don't really know. But they knew what he had done. He had told them. He just never said anything in front of me.

S: Was there any conversation about some kind of reward or something?

K: As a matter of fact, Leo wanted to turn Jethro in for the reward because he was really upset about what he had done towards me and the children _____. And it didn't stop there because they did some pretty awful things to me.

Chap: XIII The Polygraph

Police Report by Steve Walker

April 30, 1994: "Karlyn agreed to a polygraph to confirm that she was telling the truth about her involvement in the murder of James Salmu. At 4/30/94 at 1000 hrs I transported her to the Lane County sheriff's office where she met with Detective Bill Kennedy, a licensed polygraph operator. During the next three hours Karlyn participated in the polygraph. Detective Kennedy prepared a report following the polygraph which outlined his questions and Karlyn's answers. *I didn't even know I was going to do a polygraph until Steve pulled into the underground. I told him I knew I could pass it, but I told him my nerves and emotions had been put through so much I wasn't sure what the poly would be picking up. "If anything," he said, "don't worry. It's not admissable." So I tried. Kennedy and Smith made me feel so very uncomfortable and filthy.*

We returned to the Springfield police station at approximately 1330 hrs. During that time Karlyn discussed the polygraph and what information the test provided. I told her that Detective Kennedy said the polygraph showed that she was deceptive when asked if she had stabbed or cut Salmu in any manner. She told me that she did have a knife in her hand, but she didn't stab Salmu. Karlyn indicated that she was tired and wanted to be reunited with her children. At 1700 hrs. I drove her and her children back to their motel."

As the officer pulled into the underground garage he told me we were there to do a poly and not to worry; it wasn't admissible in court. I told him I'd been through so much I have mixed emotions. I don't think it's fair at all the way they pushed me. I was completely exhausted. I'd been through so much damage, and the police gave me no space at all. I tried to cooperate on everything I knew. They knew **I needed an attorney, and continually gave me somebody to talk with, other officers, not an attorney.** *Not one of them was a lawyer. I'd also like to indicate the time of pick up to the time of delivery. Seven hours for days of continuous threats and insulting remarks. All I wanted was help and somebody to stand by me.*

Polygraph of Karlyn Eklof conducted by Bill Kennedy

April 30, 1994: Eklof was present in the Lane County Sheriff's Office, read the prepared statement of consent and signed same. Investigators from the Springfield Police Department were present and talked with Karlyn subsequent to the conclusion of the examination.

At issue was whether or not Eklof in anyway cut James Salmu at the time he was killed, and if she had any idea of the location of the body. The questions asked were:

1. Did you in any way cut James Salmu on purpose with a knife? Ans. No

2. Did you kill Salmu? Ans. No

3. Do you know where James Salmu's body is? Ans. No

4. On purpose are you holding back any information from the police about the murder of James Salmu? Ans. No

It is stated by the examiner that she did not answer the questions truthfully. The following discrepancies are given:

Although she had not told the police she actually saw Tiner fire one of the shots into Salmu, she showed how Salmu's body jerked when the bullet hit him in the chest. *I may have jerked my body when describing this from fear.*

Also I made the same jumpy motion every time Kennedy spoke out a question. His voice was going right through me and I told him so. I asked him to stop making me jump.

Kennedy informed Eklof that he felt she was not being truthful regarding cutting Salmu with a knife. She maintained that she did not cut or stab James Salmu with a knife. *I tried to tell them what happened, and they, **he and Smith**, kept telling me it was different. They weren't there, I was. They kept telling me I was a liar, that I stabbed James. I told them over and over again I did not. Then Smith would turn it around.*

It was noted that Eklof was talked to several times about controlling her breathing and movement during the test. *When Steve brought me in I was fine, but then Kennedy and Smith were rude. I was scared the way he was throwing his voice at me. He also pressured me by his position—legs spread real wide—and the belittling little statements he'd say. He'd say, "I'm counting your breathing. You're holding back. See, you're doing it again," and he kept taunting me. "Put your feet flat. Look forward. Keep still." When I asked him to please loosen the finger grips he refused. Then, noticing my fingers were turning purple, he loosened them. It was also very cold in that room.*

In addition to the first questions, a mixed zone of comparison was also given, consisting of relevant and irrelevant questions. The relevant questions follow:

1. Did you shoot Salmu? Ans. No

2. Did you hold the gun in your hand when the shot was fired that hit James Salmu? Ans. No

3. Did you fire any of the shots that hit James Salmu? Ans. No

Though considered relevant, the above were actually irrelevant, since she had nothing to do with the gun. She did react to question two. *Walker and Kennedy later agreed that Kennedy, not knowing a bullet was dropped in my hand, would register one of the questions and the fact that I saw and held the gun at Al's house a week before. I did not know Jeff brought the gun home, nor did I hold it after the murder.*

When he was told about it he said, "Oh well, had I known of those

things," and that's all he said.

Smith and Walker still had me believing the polygraph was just one more thing I had to do to prepare for Grand Jury. Smith would say, "Let's go over it again. I don't want you getting impeached." Then he'd tell me what he believed happened. It got too exhausting trying to correct him. He just wouldn't let me tell it the way it happened. He told me his way was the way it happened and that the sooner I said it that way, the sooner all this would be over with and I could go.

****

Since the illegalities in the use of the above information in the trial and the various appeals of Karlyn Eklof never came to light, they will be dealt with here. Tiner's lawyers gave a step-by-step delineation of how the State used hearsay/polygraph-related evidence at Eklof's trial. The device used at her trial was to present the actual evidence, but not to say the word "polygraph," being an example of a notable application of Oregon case law in regard to the use of polygraph evidence.

Eklof's counsel could have been ruled "ineffective" at trial, since they did not object to the admittance on these grounds. It also did not matter that Eklof signed a polygraph waiver form. Two statements were made during her trial: that Eklof "was not being truthful" and also that key State's witness John Distabile lied to the police in an interview. Both of these statements were based directly on what was revealed in their polygraph evidence.

My source states that this is *reversible error*, with a question mark. Why, because the police cannot vouch for the truthfulness of other witnesses.

"We expressly hold that in Oregon a witness, expert or otherwise, may not give an opinion on whether he believes a witness is telling the truth. We reject testimony from a witness about the credibility of another witness..." *State v. Middleton*, 294 Or. 427, 657 P. 2d 1215 (1983).

In Karlyn's trial, her defense counsel, John Kolego, made no objection.

****

District Attorney Fred Hugi and Captain Jerry Smith were frustrated when they had found little that was inconsistent in Karlyn's testimony in her first interrogation and nothing, essentially, to convict her on. They weren't satisfied.

The first video was what she had come forward to say, though she was pressured and frustrated because events didn't come out in the order that she remembered them. She spent so many hours being hassled by the officers to confess to their version that it was difficult to hold her own against them.

Especially after the polygraph, which they said showed she was lying.

She was afraid and confused. They had never said she was under suspicion though it always seemed like she was. But she was always told, whenever she would ask about a lawyer, that she didn't need one. She was there to give Grand Jury testimony against Jethro and didn't have to worry as long as she told them the truth.

She was frightened because of the way they were treating her, but she had no one to talk to about them. They had promised to be her friends and had said they believed in her. How could they let this happen?

The first interrogation was actually traumatizing to Karlyn. You can imagine what it was like to be filmed after being questioned all day long. Each day she was told she would soon be ready to go before the Grand Jury. Later she was sure they must have had great fun lying to her, telling her she was a liar, and making her do it again.

The second videotaped interrogation took place on May 2, 1993 and it lasted over an hour. It was conducted by Jerry Smith, Steve Walker and Tom Yates. Only those questions which were different from the first interrogation, questions to which Karlyn has written comments on, are given here.

After the opening statements and questions, the transcript contains only those excerpts. Again, Karlyn's comments upon the transcript are in *italics*:

The Second Interrogation
Tape of Audio
Karlyn Eklof
Case #93-2024

I'm Steve Walker. I'm a detective with the Springfield Police and today's date is May 2, 1994 and the time on the watch is 3:13 P.M. Also present in the room is Karlyn Eklof and Jerry Smith and Tom Yates and we're talking with Karlyn at the Springfield Police Station regarding the incident with James Salmu that occurred on March 21, 1993.

S: Karlyn, you are aware that the video recorder is going and the conversation is being recorded?

K: Absolutely.

S. Okay, what I'd like for you to do is just in your own words, I know we've talked a lot this morning, but just in your own words kind of reflect back over that evening and as best as you can recall, the incidents of that evening to tell them to us again, if you would.

K: Thank you. (Mumbled) The evening was going very well. Jethro and I *(Jethro!)* wanted to be alone. Jethro asked James to go to a motel and he offered him some money to go. We were standing in the kitchen talking and uh Spider tried to convince James to go ..

K: [later in the tape]... and I said that's well that's not really the issue, I think you need to go apologize to that young woman. He said, well, it's a past issue. I slapped him. I slapped him a couple of times. And I hit him pretty hard. I was angry at his attitude. *I never slapped James. Again these are Captain Smith's words coming out of my mouth. When James head-shoulder-butted me, that's when I punched him. I never wanted*

James to leave. It was Spider and Jethro who wanted James out of the house.
I just suggested Keith's as a way to resolve the discomfort that was starting
up, until his best friend didn't want him down there. And I asked him to go take
care of it....

K: [later]… and Jethro said come here I want you to see this. And then that's when he did
that and uh I told him to take him out of his misery. God what are you doing? And I went in the
kitchen, I stood next to the refrigerator for a few minutes or less. And I looked around and didn't
know what to do. And uh (mumbled) I was unable to stay there very long. There was a steak knife
sitting up on he counter (mumbled). And I grabbed it, went to the bathroom and told Jethro if you
don't take him out of his misery I will. *These were Smith's words again, coming out of*
my mouth.

And uh I stuck it to his chest and I would have forced it in. But he was already gone. And
it was at the point to where I wanted to see this stop 'cause he had been moaning and he was
gasping for air and there wasn't anything I could do. I couldn't stop Jethro and I couldn't help
James. And uh just before that he had told Jethro that he was Christian. And then Jethro said that's
what you all say. This was about 20 minutes altogether. I would say it was so long, he was
suffering. He was, Jethro was playing cat and mouse with him, it was awful, uh Jeth… Jethro was
playing with this guy. Is he too stubborn to die or what? And uh about this time I told him, I'll…
I'll take, I'll take… take him out of his misery or I will. And uh Jethro thought that was like funny,
'cause I couldn't do it. And uh he reached over and popped off another round into his chest.

These three pages are a perfect example of the nonstop rambling statements I
was making. I'd been through so much. All I tried to do was assist the police in
reenacting the event. I couldn't even do that right.

*Again, **I never said anything**. I was speechless. I did bolt from the bath-*
room and go to the sink. Out of fear and confusion I picked up the little steak
knife. I did wave it over James. I stopped. I realized that I would have made
the same mistake Jethro was making if I had touched him, and so I backed out
of there. So I told the police I made a foolish reaction, but I caught myself
before any damages were done. Knowing full well my innocence, I expressed
this to the police. Smith turned it around and twisted me. He filled in the blanks.
And those are the statements that are coming out of my mouth. And, by the
way, did I even take a breath during these statements?

K: [the questions backtrack] …I do believe I saw TJ and Steve coming in the back door at
one point and I asked them not to get involved. And uh I just barely remember them being there
because I wanted to concentrate on it. *I was doing dishes and trying to figure why this*
argument even existed. It went off and on. Too much going on, I didn't want any bad
things to happen and everybody knows it got from bad to worse (mumbled). *It was at that*
moment that I realized there was ongoing activity, because it was stop 'n go!
Stop 'n go! But I just barely remember, they could have even been at the front door when I was
telling them to (mumbled). 'Cause I think I remember telling them to get off the porch, I'm not
sure…

S: What kind of things were going on between the gun shots?

K: James was dying.

S: What was Jethro doing?

K: Standing over him.

S: Saying things?

K: We were talking to him. We were talking. It was… James was fading in and out. And like I say James, Jethro was playing cat and mouse with him… *We were not saying a word. Jethro was speaking to him. I did not talk at all. Again Captain Smith's filling in the blanks of my memory. Those words were coming out of my mouth…*

S: Now earlier where… You also talked about, you had a knife in your hand and you were cleaning your fingernails or something. What kind of knife was that?

K: That was a buck knife that Jethro had bought and gave to me.

S: Okay, and James had (mumbled) by or something and was walking towards you and you confronted him something about getting squared away with this girl.

K: I said I did take care of it, it flung out of my hand. *I asked him so what are you going to do? The buck flung and bounced. I apologized. He handed it back. I set it on the table. Later on in San Diego I found it in a bag at the motel room.*

S: Was the blade open?

K: No it wasn't. *Yes it was. I had just closed it.*

S: It wasn't open.

K: No it wasn't.

S: What happened to the knife then?

K: He gave it back to us, I'm sorry I didn't mean to do that and he said, I understand and he handed it back to me and I sat it on the table by the phone…

S: You referred several times today about Jethro was just playing cat and mouse with James.

K: He was.

S: And enjoying the torturing.

K: It seemed like it to me. He was really proud of himself and I lost all respect for him.

S: When you picked up a knife out there, what kind of knife was it?

K: it was a regular table steak knife, with a wooden handle, you know, about so long with a little tiny edge.

S: When you went back into the bathroom then, what happened?

K: I told Jethro to take him out of misery or I would. *I never said a word. As Jethro was telling me to come here, I want you to see this, James was going in and out. Jethro said two or three statements. James nodded in and out, then died.* Oh God is what's going on here… I approached James as to stop his pain for him and I did start to stick that into him. But there was no reason to, 'cause he wasn't there and it was already a mess so I didn't want to be part of the same mess that Jethro was making so, as quick as I was there, I backed up and then I did go into his, right here and it didn't… I didn't…

Just before that I bolted from the bathroom, scared and confused. I went to the kitchen, held onto the sink, then picked up a steak knife, returned to bathroom, motioned it over James. I realized it wouldn't be a good move, no matter what my intentions were. I bolted back from the bathroom to the kitchen. I realized I almost made a tremendous mistake. I put the steak knife right back in the drainer with the rest of the dishes and then did what Jeff told me to do, "Go get something." I went to James' room. I grabbed his sleeping bag to comfort him if he could comprehend. I just wanted to comfort him, but he was gone.

S: Right here on the breast plate?

K: Yeah, It was right right there. And I took it back to the... I'm at the bathroom, I took it to the sink.

S: Your intent was to do what at that point? Were you trying to ease his suffering?

K: All I wanted is James not to suffer anymore. 'Cause Jethro had just creamed *(I want to hear this word. I believe it's a misprint in the transcript)* him so much.

S: So you were just trying to be compassionate at that point. *Yes.*

K: I wanted James' pain to stop. I didn't want him to hear Jethro's voice anymore, I didn't want him to feel what Jethro was doing. *Yes.*

S: You weren't successful at doing that though were you?

K: No, there was no point in it.

S: Yeah, how far did the blade actually go into him?

K: It really... The T-shirt that he was wearing and I uh I would say it wasn't much even to the nail the point of the nail... the tip of the thing. Because as quick as I went to him, it stopped, I stopped and my whole body backed up and my hand came with it. *There are Jerry Smith's words coming out of my mouth.* Because Jethro thrust for him like he was going to put a bullet and I (mumbled) He was over fidgeting with the gun. And then he was going to plant another one in him. He looked dissatisfied that he did have another one, is what he was checking. And I wasn't going to be a part of (mumbled) people in there, and there wasn't anything I could do 'cause he wasn't, his chest, he wasn't moving. And he planted another one in him.

S: Did you leave then after he fired that fourth round?

K: I backed up, I got out of there. And I went to the sink to to rinse out the knife, it wasn't dirty. Seemed like I needed to do that I just set it back on the counter. I think, I think I stuck it in the sink and then just stuck it up on the counter 'cause it wasn't dirty. I could, I did rinse but it didn't seem to need that it was just, it was just a reason to get out of the bathroom...

I never put any knife under water. Jerry Smith told me I did. Hours I told him I didn't and finally he convinced me I did. But it did not happen that way. See how Jerry jumps in right where he has his mark, right at the point of me saying the tip of the knife, I remember the hours of harassment over me just stating I made the motion. He took advantage of my honest statement and twisted me into a convicting statement. If this really happened to the effect that Jerry has me stating why not more detail, like everything else? What did I feel like and did the shirt rip, and how much blood spilt? None of this is asked. Such details are omitted because he knew none of this ever happened...

Steve: Did he do anything else to James' mouth besides putting a penny in there?

K: I don't know. He could have put boots to him, like he did me.

Smith: Did what?

K: He could have put boots to him, you know stomped all over him like he did me. After he got me down south. I still have a boot print from him right here. I keep my mouth shut (mumbled). I wouldn't put it past him. I never thought about it until now but yeah he probably stomped all over him, I don't know.

Steve: Did he mention something like that?

K: No. No. He really didn't want me to know where he took him. So I didn't, I wasn't going to carry this as far as I have with you guys.

Smith: Well did you guys ever go for drives out in the country?

K: I didn't get a chance to do that with him.

S: (Mumbled) out of town?

K: No, I wanted to. One of the nights we went to a motel that to me is out of town. And uh he wanted to think he'd get me and the children out of the way of the media, so I wouldn't get nervous and uh crazed and bring attention to us before he had us ready to go. I was like this, I was upset.

S: What day was that?

K: Well, it was just the day before we left. It was after he'd done the car. He was moving so fast and moving me around so fast like it was two to three days later.

S: Have you ever shared this information with other folks?

K: No. No. Nobody else has any business, nobody (mumbled) I couldn't talk about this with anybody else or he would have killed me if I did. He tried. I guess I'm just too stubborn to die. I guess he's finding that out, when people don't want to go they just don't go. I did ask Potato how come he went so far, after Potato and Popeye got together and said we gotta get you out of here, this guy's just taking you...

End of Tape. *How convenient. I'm not even able to complete my sentence, so there would be no follow up of my statements.*

Chap XIV: Captain Smith's Agenda

After producing the first two videotaped "confessions" of Karlyn Eklof, the police realized that they were still exculpatory. They would not reinforce the image they wanted to project to the jury, that Karlyn had participated in the killing of James Salmu by stabbing him with the kitchen knife. Allowing her one day of rest to recuperate, they proceeded again with their grilling, in order to produce the evidence they wanted.

There are several considerations here, any one of which could have invalidated the evidence they expected to produce. First, they are obviously adding to a prolonged interrogation rendering her confession "involuntary." Secondly, the first two exculpatory tapes would invalidate the later inculpatory videos proving that pressure had been applied.

Third, were any of the videos or the inculpatory audiotape made in Salt Lake played for the Grand Jury? If so, they are not listed on the indictment. Fourth, if Hugi played audio and/or videotapes to the Grand Jury in lieu of live testimony by Eklof herself, fraud occurred. She was in town, being interviewed by police on two dates the Grand Jury met, April 29 and May 2, 1994. She had come into Eugene from Salt Lake under the State ruse that she was there to testify before the Grand Jury.

In Tiner's Motion to Compel Production of Grand Jury-Related Evidence, the State refused to respond to certain charges of prosecutorial misconduct, including the above issues. Answers to this motion might well have exposed a wholly fraudulent indictment for Karlyn at a time she was still undergoing her appeals. This writer had no access at that time to his trial documents, however, since they were unavailable at the Supreme Court records offices because of pretrial processes that were ongoing.

It is known that the State had provided many Grand Jury transcripts, but that there were other mysteriously missing police testimonies. If cops played only inculpatory videotapes to the Grand Jury, but not her prior exculpatory audiotapes, it is *reversible error*. In order to satisfy *due process* during Grand Jury proceedings, State is required to present any evidence which objectively refutes facts as they appear from the State's evidence which is presented to the Grand Jury.

There are many questions in the writer's mind about the formality of the Grand Jury itself. How many rules were broken? Karlyn evidently was at hand on two of those occasions in order for them to secrete her in a room with Distabile and also Dave Tiner to see what they would say to each other. The fact that the interview with various witnesses took places on widely spaced occasions from January on indicates that April 29, May 2, and May 12, 1994 may have been the only formal occasions.

The real double whammy though is what they were doing to the key witnesses, John Distabile and, especially, Al Hope, in order to suborn their testimonies. With incredible disregard for the safety of the community, they let a child molester who had violated his own daughter in order to produce and sell pornography over the internet walk the streets for two more years in order to get him to say that Karlyn had arranged to procure the gun which killed James Salmu.

This fact just blows my mind! It is impossible not to mention it at this time, though the details must proceed in the narrative at the time they are discovered. The reader deserves to know where this is going. All the way through the prosecution and persecution of this young woman who was there to bring forward the truth of what happened to Salmu, they withheld this information, which constituted *"Brady"* violations of the most egregious kind. A *Brady* violation occurs when the prosecution suborns witnesses and otherwise withholds exculpatory evidence from the defense counsel. So much for the citadel of justice.

The Third Interrogation

Since the prosecution quoted extensively from these videos and presented them as exhibits of her "confession", those that have been underlined in the exhibits are here underlined so that they can be carefully studied in the context in which they appear and alongside the comments which she makes concerning what was happening to her at that time:

The third video was taken on May 3, 1994 at 7:17 P.M. The interrogation is taking place at the Springfield Police Station, this time with only Karlyn and Steve Walker. Again, the taped interview takes place after a full day of brainwashing, by teams of experts, in which she is made to say over and over again what she might have been thinking, which she is then made to state as though she were speaking to Jethro, which is why, even in the preceding videos, one is astonished to hear her saying things you know she never said.

When she argues with them about their suppositions, they threaten her that if she doesn't get it right they might be there forever. Therefore, she is saying things that Captain Smith has told her she must say and trying, like some stupid person, to fill in the story to their satisfaction so what she has come forward to testify will be completed.

Again, the excerpts that are recorded here from the complete transcript are only those which are different from the previous videos, or ones that she has written additional comments about, which are presented in *italics*:

S: Where were you standing when that happened?

K: Well, behind the toilet tree and closest to the door of the bathroom. Between the door and the sink. I was, devastated, um, James was in misery. He had taken enough of Jethro, they'd been going at it for about 15, 20 minutes (*it was really about 7 or 8 minutes*) and uh, I couldn't stand it. So I went out of the room, I went to the kitchen, and I looked for something and I picked up the steak knife and I took it in the bathroom and I put it up to James' chest. I wanted to take him out of his misery because I couldn't stand the moaning and the suffering. And Jethro didn't seem to care because he was trying to hold on a conversation with James and it was just repulsive. And I closed my eyes and I thrust it forward and I did not believe that I had put it, penetration, but I now believe, without wanting to believe, *these are Smith's words* that I did penetrate James and that when I jerked back, I realized what I was doing and I backed up and I took it back to the sink, rinsed it off, and set it on the counter. Later on I put it with some things that I had cleaned the bathroom with... *Not true. I did not rinse it off. It was put in the dish drainer.*

I did not penetrate James. I tried to tell officers all day long that it didn't happen that way. But Smith told me I did and to apologize to Steve for standing by me. He said Steve believed me and he wouldn't have any of that. Smith said he knew what happened and my cock-and bull-story wouldn't fly. To quit wasting department time. He again told me to apologize to Steve. So Steve came in and I told Steve the Captain says I have to apologize to you. He says by his years of experience, his logic, I stabbed James. But that's not the way it happened..

S: So you came back in the bathroom with the knife, and went up to James... Did you say that you had felt your hand touch his shirt or his skin? I guess he had a tee-shirt on.

K: And his jacket. *My point here is a steak knife would not have gone through the suede jacket he had on. Smith must have forgot to realize that.*

S: So when you pushed the knife forward, you felt your hand touch his skin and then you pulled back, or his shirt? *This never happened. When I did touch James it was after*

Jethro had the sleeping bag over his upper body. Without Jethro noticing I checked to see if he had a heart beat. There was none. That was the only time my hand touched his shirt.

K: His shirt.

S: So it went in to the point where you could touch your hand and then you pulled back?

K: That's when I wanted out of there. I had no business doing that, it wasn't effective. **Smith had been telling me I must say I assisted and wasn't effective so I wouldn't be charged with murder! It took Smith hours, off and on, to get me to submit to these statements.**

S: Was there a little bit of a time when you put it back up to him again? *It never happened.*

K: I jerked, when I pulled back I jerked and I opened my eyes to see what I had done. I didn't see I'd done anything. *Because I didn't. Smith twisted me enough to get me to say what he needed and to remember it! I just wish I could explain it.* I just stopped what I was doing and backed up and I got out of there. Just as I was doing it there was another round pulled off.

S: Was his tee-shirt visible when you did that?

K: Uh huh. I believe so. *See, I couldn't answer that Smith had left that open. I didn't know what I was supposed to say.*

S: Let's see, can you remember the knife going in to the point where your hand could touch his tee-shirt, did you have your eyes open then? *No, because it didn't happen that way at all...*

K: I remember just going in, making the motion to put effort into putting the blade into him. I wanted him out. I didn't obviously didn't know what I'm doing. *Smith's words.*

S: Why did you want, why did you want that knife to go in?

K: I didn't. I just wanted him out of his misery. I've never wanted to hurt James. I'd already hurt him *when I punched him* and felt bad about that. And then Jethro was on him and I felt completely out of control of the situation There wasn't anything I could do...

S: Did, what, did he say anything when you put that knife in him? *This never happened.*

K: No, he was already...

S: Did he moan, did he flinch a little bit?

K: No, There wasn't anything. He was gone. And, I do believe the last "pop" that Jethro had put into him that was his last breath or his last motion for breath there was nothing.

S: After you pulled the knife back away?

K: Right. *When I read through these statements Smith has programed, this is the only time I say, "Right."*

S: And then,

K: And I still don't even know for sure. you know, because I did make the motion. I did put it all the way into him to stop him from hurting. *I don't know why I am saying this because it never happened. I don't ever remember saying this.* I wanted him just to stop feeling anything. I didn't, I don't, I didn't do any harm. I didn't do any good, it's ridiculous that it even went to that point because it wasn't anything. It wasn't effective. I didn't have, to me the knife didn't seem to me to need to be cleaned off or anything but I did take it to the sink. I did turn the water on *Smith's words* and I put it back in the sink. And I put it back up on the counter so, I know if the knife was there it went with the other things that Jethro had taken... *It stayed with the dishes....*

    S: So can you think of anything else that was different today when we talked than from other times when we talked about the chain of events that happened?

    K: Well, just the simple fact that I didn't want to visualize myself being in that position understanding that everybody understood my situation, my position, and helping me to relive it, reliving somebody's death over and over again. It's not easy and I wouldn't wish it on my worst enemy. But uh, to say that I did not try to penetrate him or to penetrate him **has obviously showed up on the polygraph** as not the truth and I did not want any part of this to be fabricated or lied about. *This is the clue to the power of their badgering.* ***They convinced me that what I said must match with the polygraph or it would not be a valid testimony against Jethro.*** I need to see justice done in very many directions in any, even with myself. I would like to (serve??) other people with my knowledge and uh, in this field that other women that have been helped by a person like this. I would like my knowledge to be useful. And I don't want anything to be deceptive here. I mean, all the things brought out. I knew it would take some time, I told you all the truth will come out, it just took a lot of work.

    I see what you've done here, Smith, and I remember your ways. When I learn how to explain it, your job is gone. If I was so careless as to stab somebody, why would I come forward? Why was I so depressed and afraid to speak? Somebody, please listen and step into my shoes. Smith has done a lot of rearranging to get this picture, and I'm left with a conviction I don't deserve.

    After the taping I reminded Steve that the Captain says I have to apologize to you for believing in me, that by his years of experience, his logic, I stabbed James. But that's not the way it happened. Steve said, "Okay. It'll be all right," and we prepared to return me to my children.

The Fourth Interrogation

    Reader, please be warned! Captain Jerry Smith was teaching a course at Lane Community College on criminal procedures and was delving into the techniques of hypnosis when this prosecution was in process. A young woman who furnished documents to me on this case was there and knew of his reputation among female students.

    What Karlyn will tell you here is maddening. That he would use not only psychological, but sexual traumatization to get her to say what he wanted is just part of the dishonor perpetrated against her.

    The worst part, however, was the dishonesty, the manipulation, and the lies. In looking ahead to the brief by John Manning, filed April 29, 2003, outlining the final appeal of her post conviction, a great part of it is devoted to the known judicial record of Jerry Smith and his reputation for dishonesty, lying under oath, and manufacturing false confessions, including especially parts of the Deposition of James Hargreaves for Proctor and Boots which cost Springfield $2M. The brief also challenged the double life sentence imposed upon her.

However, without the illegality of her coerced testimony, the suborned witnesses, and the many *Brady* violations brought to the fore—in other words, those "improper submissions" the writer finally brought to Manning's attention—her last appeal would also be denied. Her attorneys did not know of the violations, and there was otherwise no proof attached that Jerry Smith lied in her prosecution. His reputation would therefore be one of the many things her defense did not object to. Her only hope would be in the *federal habeas corpus*, if her case could be brought before them.

The fourth video was made after a ride in the country followed by a session alone with Captain Jerry Smith. He was determined that she knew also details about the disposal of James' body and used techniques of hypnotism in order to try to get Karlyn to visualize where he was buried. This was when he had her lie back and held her hand while she answered his questions. She woke up to find him stroking himself. He then stood up and quickly left the room.

She said to herself, "Jeez! Is this why I've come all this way to tell the truth?"

Soon, in order to assuage his chagrin, he called in the other officers, humiliated Karlyn in front of them, and again demanded that she apologize for misleading all of them. However, additional details of the murder and the disposal of the body had been rehearsed that afternoon to his satisfaction, and she was counseled again to answer questions on the video according to the logic which he, in his experience, knew to be the case, to quit wasting their time, and to just get it over with.

Those details of body disposal are therefore repeated here according to what he had required her to say that afternoon. After James' body was found in the late fall, it could be seen that none of those details which he made her describe had been true. Also, there was no evidence ever that there had been any stabbing.

She was so demoralized after that long day of questioning and the sexual humiliation that her answers are shorter, less introspective. She readily describes happenings that had no meaning to her, things that in no way occurred. She had no alternative. Her resistance had to come to an end. Her pleas for help had been exhausted.

Excerpts of the last tape are as follows:

Okay, my name is Steve Walker. I'm a detective with Springfield police and today's date is May 5, 1994, and the time on my wristwatch is 6:14 P. M. Also present is ah Karlyn Eklof and Jerry Smith (garbled) Police Department.

SW: Karlyn, are you aware that the video recorder is on?

KE: Mhm (garbled).

SW: Images and voices are being recorded?

KE: Yes.

SW: Okay, we've ah talked for quite a while now and we talked about the events that took place involving James Salmu on the night of ah March 21, 1993 and determined that there was a ah pizza party at the house there, James' house, and what I'd like for you to do if you would in your own words, describe the chain of events that took place that evening and ah and maybe the day or two following the party and what happened following it. Do you understand?

KE: I understand. It's quite a schedule...

SW: Okay who were the last people there?

KE: Well there was James, myself, and Jethro and my son TJ and his little friend Steve, and ah which Spider had taken home with him for the night. Jethro and I *(Jethro)* wanted to be alone.

SW: Spider was still (garbled)?

KE: Right, Deb was there for a little while. She was kind of scared because I um kicked everybody out at ten o'clock and she wanted to stay later and her and Spider I guess weren't getting along but they they're okay though...

KE: ...I was very embarrassed cuz Jethro for one was getting hot; two it was in front of this Jethro, a guest, who I thought was a neat guy at the time, um three, I was really ashamed of my roommate for even presenting himself to a little girl like that. It made me very angry. *I was not angry. I had too good of a time at the party. When he head-butted me later on I reacted and punched him. I hadn't got angry with James. It seemed to me at this time that he could handle his mistake.* Well, he had gone back to his room and was going to get his jacket, keys or cigarettes, or something. I'm not really too sure. First he was leaving, then he wasn't leaving... *As Spider even noted we didn't think that it was going anywhere. It stopped, then it started back up, then it stopped. So I missed parts of why it started. Spider and I did actually move around the kitchen putting things away....*

SW: What happened when your fist hit him?

KE: It split wide open. This eye right here amazed me. It just split and of course there was blood (garbled) his mouth and then he'd get all over him instead of cleaning himself up.

SW: Did it drip down on his shirt?

KE: Yes it was.

SW: There was quite a bit of blood dripping down.

KE: Well grotesque, and he was letting it get in his mustache and stuff and he was running his mouth and... *Steve has allowed me to overexpress the issue. The cut to James' eye was no larger than this _____. My diamond ring started the opening, the impact from the punch continued it, so it had to have only been this wide. But it surprised me. I've never seen anybody open up like that. I did get scared and felt bad. He said, "Oh, I deserved it. I deserved it." Because he hit me first. We both stopped our argument. He was going to the bar like that. I tried to get his eye cleaned up before he left...*

SW: Did he wanna go in the bathroom?

KE: No. Truthfully. He really didn't care at first and then he just got anxious.

SW: How did you know he didn't wanna go in there?

KE: Because I forced him in there. I literally just pulled his ass in there. *These are Captain Smith's words again coming out of my mouth. I'm going back over these statements, and I can remember expressly the emotions of that night and the defeated feelings of telling the officers what they wanted to hear. I know now what they've done to me during the interrogation. Thanks guys. I was struggling so hard to cooperate, and you took me apart, what was left of me!*

The Fourth Interrogation

The following excerpts from the Fourth Interrogation videotaped reenactment were used extensively as exhibits in Karlyn's trial. Therefore those portions which were <u>underlined as exhibits are here underlined also</u>, and followed by Karlyn's comments:

SW What did Jethro do with that towel? You started talking about a towel folded up

KE <u>Right (garbled) He ah opened it up and pulled it, put that over (garbled) it was just a little little (garbled). He put it um up against the towel into his chest pulled off a round and um I don't... I'm not sure... I think he might have even checked the towel and opened up and seen what what the mark was. It looked like a little dark dark smear here where the bullet had gone through.</u> *This is when I bolted from the bathroom, went to the kitchen sink and held on.*

SW (garbled) through.

KE <u>Um I I couldn't take it. I went out of the bathroom. I stood against the refrigerator and the sink. I looked around for something to do and ah I picked up a steak knife, a little table steak knife with a wooden handle (garbled). I don't even remember why I did it. I didn't know if I was going after Jethro or what but when I got out of the bathroom I said to Jethro take him out of his misery or I will and um James was just like barely breathing. He was .. He couldn't say anything... He couldn't... He was too weak and I made the motion to to to get James right here or take the air.</u> *I never said those words, and I never penetrated him, never.* <u>I wanted him to stop hurting. I wanted the pain to stop that Jethro was getting off on. And ah and I saw Jethro over here fidgeting with this thing like it was cool what I was doing. It's not cool. Excuse me and um and he... I bolted right back out of there and Jeff said get something, and that's when the fourth and final bullet went into James...</u>

SW Can you show me where you put that knife?...

KE Right here... Right below his breast right right there. I closed my eyes and I wasn't really too sure if I made a puncture but logically um going over and over it again it's very very possible. I I would say, yes I did because I don't wanna be not care or deceitful here at all. I jerked back... *They had been telling me all day I was lying, telling me what really happened, and that I'd never see my children again if I didn't say it. This is all lies. Captain Smith drilled me so I keep agreeing. Although when I motioned or waved the steak knife I was just below his left breast. I realized that I was about to make a very big mistake and stopped. I returned back to the sink. I put the knife in the sink, then on the drainer with the rest of the clean dishes. I remember distinctly feeling foolish and overreacting. But I never penetrated him. I just realized what a horrible mistake I almost made. And thanked God I didn't.*

SW Did you feel... Did you feel his shirt...

KE (garbled) Yes I did. I remember feeling his shirt...
I wanted him to stop hurting...

SW So did that knife help?

KE No, it was really a ridiculous thought on my part. Um Jethro had... (garbled) this went on for about twenty minutes I'd say, the whole thing... bathroom, the whole thing. I'm not sure really. I (garbled) Jethro... just just when I realized I couldn't do it. **I just couldn't do it. I don't know what I was thinking.** I wasn't gonna make the same mess cuz it was already blood on the bath, blood on James. **I just didn't wanna... I didn't wanna be part of it** and look him and be in that position. I left the bathroom. Before I did though, I saw Jethro reach over around the corner as I was turning and he pulled off another round. I'm not sure where it hit him...

Editor's note: The whole basis for Karlyn's guilt is embodied in the above testimony, wrung from her through brainwashing and humiliation at the end of eight days of lies and denying her the right to counsel. **Do they really think this was a confession?**

Later in the interrogation Karlyn is asked to go over the description of where the body was that Jerry Smith had also forced her to put into words that afternoon while he had her lie back, shut her eyes, while he squeezed her hand and touched himself. Then he humiliated her by calling in the other officers to have her apologize.

SW: Did you ever go to the place where Jethro took James' body?

KE: I had often thought about it and I really... I would have swore that I hadn't been there, but I had remembered at one point a tree and a vehicle and two men, and I wasn't sure because of all the damage that Jethro had done to me down in San Diego. And his friends (garbled). I wasn't sure if that was the same thing and then (garbled) over and over and over this thing has been done. It finally slid into place that there was a truck, there was a shovel in the back of the truck. There was a tarp and there was a bag (garbled) like those fertilizer bags or cement bags and (garbled) bags like that, that kind of shape was tossed in the back of the truck and ah the guys said well, Let's take her with us. She can help and I was excited to go, because I didn't know what I was doing. I was like God, these guys are taking me somewhere, cool.

SW: What guys were that?

KE: Well, like you know this is so hard, and so awkward because I'm I'm really sure it was Spider but I can't be positive because um,

SW: Who else was there?

KE: It was Jethro. It was Jethro because, oh, what I do remember is that... excuse me. We walked over on the truck to back into the truck and there was a tree, a large tree right there (garbled) tree the leaves and ah we went over to this edge, it was like a little sand dirt dirt area and ah there was an embankment. It kind of went down into almost like a little beach, not quite enough where three or four people could have a little bit of a kickback (garbled) sun and there was these two huge like dirt clods, boulders looking things and ah if somebody just wanted to sunbathe and there was a little bit of water down below, not much and ah God It's just it's so so so vivid um the sleeping bag was pulled out between these two boulders these two um they're big dirt clods what what I call em and ah.

SW: It had been stuck down in there?

KE: Yeah. Stuck right between these two ah boulders, these two rocks, and ah whoever was with us and I I kind of I want (garbled) Spider but it's very very very much the only direction I could take it in because there's only two people, three all together that I knew with that kind of a truck and ah one of em's truck wasn't running and the other one wasn't around wouldn't be (garbled) but that that's that's (garbled). I'm still trying to work out who was out there with us that night because they were having me hold the sleeping b... I mean the the flashlight...

[It is pointless to continue this part of the deposition that Jerry Smith is conducting, since it goes on and on with garbled and truly unreal details that are like a stream of consciousness. It is surprising that he would continue with it, since he is obviously pushing her to improvise. It ends abruptly.]

JS: When you came back from there, did you go to your house or did you go to somebody else's house?

KE: Again it seems to me as I remember (garbled) my Cutlass and it was in front of Spider's. *Actually, I don't know. I told the police a thousand times I think it was a dream.*

JS: Steve.

The video was concluded at 7:27 P.M. after a few more routine questions.

Police Report of Steve Walker, Re: Karlyn Eklof

May 5, 1994: At approximately 10:00 hrs. Sgt. Mike Wisdom and I picked Karlyn and her children up at their motel. The children were left with child care and at Karlyn's request, we drove the rural areas looking for possible sites where Salmu's body might be.

We first drove up Hwy 126 again towards the county line of Linn County. We drove several side roads off the highway, but centered in the area of Leaburg Dam. Nothing was found that looked familiar to her. We then drove to the Marcola area and checked side roads up to and just past the county line. Nothing in this area looked familiar to her either.

While driving, we continued to talk about the case. Karlyn tried to be more specific in her account of events, including statements made, the phone calls, and how Salmu was killed.

Upon returning to the Springfield police station, Karlyn agreed to a videotaped interview with myself and Captain Jerry Smith. The following is a transcript of that tape.

After the tape was made, Karlyn was reunited with her children and dropped off at their motel.

*They fail to mention the pressure if I had not agreed. They brought the camera in and insisted they weren't taking very good notes and would like to film a session **after time alone with Smith**. Smith used techniques of very unprofessional behavior, things like holding my hand, sitting right next to me, telling me to lay back, close my eyes, take it easy, saying, "You'll feel better when you're through. Just say you stabbed him and all this would be over with. Come on, just say it. You can do it!" He'd say, "In all my years of experience you did it. Let's get this over with. Now! So you'll sleep better tonight. Come on." He went on like this for a while.*

When I would try to explain it didn't happen that way, he would tell me, "No, Karlyn, that's not at all what happened. Now you're going to tell me that you had to stab him. Jethro just isn't that type of guy to just let you witness something so incriminating and not be a part of it." He said, "It just doesn't work that way. Now, let's get this over with!" I tried to tell him it didn't happen that way, but he wouldn't listen.

He had me so frightened and worried if I didn't continue with interrogation his way I might not see my children. I wanted to talk to Steve about it. But I never had a chance to speak to him about it. I couldn't get away from Smith, and he kept on relentlessly.

Then he told me, "Just keep your eyes closed and concentrate. Just say it, Karlyn." He said things like girls in prison would really like me. And he was just so sure I wasn't that way. And who's going to raise your children? I'd been through so much. I was so scared. But he wouldn't listen to me anymore. When I opened my eyes he was pinching his personal self. When he saw that I saw him, he excused himself out of the room.

The Arrest

On May 6, 1994, Eklof was taken into custody and lodged at the Lane County Jail on a charge of aggravated murder.

After his initial declaration of arrest and her grave protests in Fred Hugi's office, she asked him, "Why?"

He said, "You are the small fish to fry, and Jeff, he's the big one to fry, and you stabbed James."

She said, "No, I didn't."

He said, "You're still under arrest," and he turned his head and looked out his window with his nose in the air.

She told the officers during interrogation a thousand times she didn't stab anyone. But that's not what's on the video. She couldn't believe it. She told everything. She had nothing to hide. She felt no guilt because she had done no damage. But not to hear her tell it after those guys were finished with her.

During interrogation Smith told her she had to apologize to Steve. He said Steve has believed in her and stood by her. Smith said he wouldn't have any part of that, and she'd better apologize to Steve now.

He called Steve in. Steve sat next to her on the interrogation couch. Smith was sitting across from her in a regular chair. She said, "Steve, the captain says I have to apologize to you."

He said, "For what?"

She said, "Smith tells me by his years of experience and his logic I stabbed James. It did not happen that way."

Steve said, "It's okay. It'll be all right."

Captain then said to her, "You won't embarrass my department or use officers by your cock-n'-bull story. It's ridiculous."

Steve takes her and sets her in a chair in Fred Hugi's office along with Rick Lewis, Tom Yates, Fred Hugi, Steve Walker, and of course the ringleader, Smith. Each one thanked her for helping solve the case, then said their feelings for her would always be caring, even though they thought Karlyn's feelings might change. She said, "Why would I change?"

Then Hugi says, "I'm very thankful you have cooperated as well as you have. Thank you. But I'm placing you under arrest. You are being charged with aggravated murder."

What! Why!

They brought her children in. She said to them she would have to go to jail. She told them that somehow she would see them again and she loved them very much. She told them to brush their teeth and to stick together, don't let anybody separate you. Steve took them out and a bouquet of flowers arrived from her son TJ. She burst into tears. She said, "Where's my attorney?"

Fred said she would get one later at the jail, and she said get my mom on the phone. He said, "Well then, this is over for you here. I'll call her in a while." Karlyn wanted her children taken to her. Then he said that foster care would be provided. Her words in her journal should be given:

Smith was a very smooth operator in all this, and he deserves to go to prison. I feel very abused. I also feel that they could have been honest. I came forward faithfully and was lied to and powerfully manipulated. The harder I tried to be honest about everything they asked of me, the more Smith turned it around, and also me, inside out.

My precious children were separated from me and then from each other. The heartache of looking back on the deceitfulness reminds me of the devastating pain I and my children went through when Jethro passed as around. There was no exit except for the one he left open, and when I took it somebody else would be there. We didn't go any further than where they wanted us. I will never forget the pain. The pain of it all.

The day of my arrest my rights were not read to me. It was too late for that. Steve, as we pulled into the Lane County carport, asked Rick if he could talk to me alone. He said, "Give us a minute." He said, "You know we all care about you." He said, "I didn't screw you. I didn't know about all this. I didn't know about this plan. I'm very sorry."

I told him, "I know. I'll be okay. Watch the Lord's work in all this. I did my best."

He said, "Yes, you did." He said, "I won't stop working on this and make sure your attorney does all he is supposed to do. Tell him to call me." I told him thanks and a few more things were said out of friendship.

And we went in. Just before the door Rick said, "I hate to do this, but I have to put these on—the cuffs—or they won't let you in." I was kind of confused why I was arrested and charged. I thought I did real well to describe what happened.

Until six months later and I saw the videos. I could have died. All that I could do was to be ill. As Mr. Evans the attorney finally appointed said, "I told you they have you saying much too much."

"But these things aren't true." I said.

He said, "I know how the police work."

I have hit every rock and hard place. I have been through enough. I am fed up with lazy, manipulating liars. I came here with an accusation towards Jeff, and it was turned around and parts added to it.

I also didn't get my rights read to me until Rick and Steve came into Lane County one week after my arrival in jail. Rick said he needed to say that, so that now, at least, I would be fully aware I hadn't been obliged to talk to them.

I said, "Now's a good time to tell me."

But see I honestly believed them when they said they believed me and would help me. I had no idea Smith's version or perspective of what happened was coming out of my mouth. I guess mentally I just gave up.

I'm so tired of being used.

I wish only to be heard and, if possible, believed. I stuck my neck out against my better judgment. I wanted James' mother to be comforted with the truth, and I wanted to help others because I'm carrying around a lot of knowledge of what Jethro and his people are very capable of.

Smith has signed, sealed and delivered me to a prison sentence on false statements. I honestly thought I was opening doors and getting help to other people, and nothing has happened except that I've been suppressed, and anybody needing my information has been left out. My family has had to go to great extremes to fill my place as mother to my children.

When I asked, during the interrogation, whether it was today I would see my attorney, I was told, "You don't want to talk to us any more? We can hold you in jail—instead of your cushy hotel room with your children—until you do." *I was so scared of being separated from them. We fought to get away from people, when nobody around could or would help. The police made no attempt to help us at that time.*

I did not write during the days of that gruelling interrogation, although I did begin to write the very first day of incarceration in Lane County, which happened immediately after the police took me and the children to a make believe Grand Jury, turned and separated us from one another, and walked me into Hugi's office wearing smirks on their faces. The rest you already know.

The journals that I wrote for the next seven months—to record what they told me in closed sessions concerning various motions to suppress, proportionality, and the plea bargains they offered which were not recorded—were taken over by my defense attorneys, who did not really defend me, and have never been returned.

And during that time, my attorney worked against me like digging for water in a dry well. Eight months, two weeks in waiting for a rescue from this, and nothing.

Captain Smith's Belated Report

July 20, 1994: Captain Jerry Smith states that on April 30, 1994 a polygraph examination was conducted with Karlyn Eklof at the Lane County Sheriff's Office by Detective Bill Kennedy. No mention is made of Steve Walker being present.

The very disturbing thing about this report is that it was written by Captain Jerry Smith, without the assistance of a court stenographer, three months after the polygraph took place.

It states that Karlyn stated verbatim during the polygraph and in the interrogation at the police station that she told Jeff, "Put him out of his misery or I will."

He then reports that on May 3, 1994 she told them she also "obtained a steak knife, returned to the bathroom... shoved the knife into Salmu... withdrew the knife and shoved it into his chest a second time."

Compare this report with the actual polygraph report itself, Karlyn's comments about their arguments with her at that time and all through the remaining afternoon and evening interrogations that she did not, in fact, do the things they were saying she did.

Compare this report, which is given at the beginning of this chapter, with that of Steve Walker who was present at her polygraph and made his report at that time.

Why is Jerry Smith reporting that she volunteered these statements, the statements he finally forced her to say in the remaining videos, but always, **always, reserving that she did not actually penetrate him? She caused him no harm.**

It is very curious that the erroneous use of polygraph evidence by the prosecution, alleged by Tiner's lawyers, that she "was not being truthful" in interviews (without mentioning the word "polygraph") referred to the actual polygraph report where her denial of touching the gun produced a negative.

Smith's report here is entirely fabricated. This report alone is evidence of his lies, evidence that Judge Hargreave could not "put his finger on" in barring him from his courtroom, to be reported later.

This is Karlyn's response to the report from her jail cell:

I didn't say a word that night. I was speechless. Smith has worked me over real well. This report was made three months after the interrogations. Mr. Smith has a real fine system when it comes to plugging in the statement and his perspective for a conviction on this report and on film. I've stated, "Take him out of his misery or I will." Those words never left my mouth the night of James' death. I've told the truth about this, and Smith has me plugged right into a conviction. I was speechless. I remember. But now that Smith has it all his way, Jethro will only confirm it, that is if he is required to make a statement at all.

These statements are not what I originally tried to explain to Smith. He twisted my statements, and pretty soon I believed he knew more about what happened than I did. So I agreed. I just wanted to get away from him. He's a pervert.

In her comments she goes on to recall an example of the ways they threw her off guard and taunted her with sexual innuendos during those nine days of interrogation: *He, Steve Walker and I were sitting in interrogation. He pops off some joke about his gender being short changed. God had shorted him. I thought he was talking about utensils of gardening or some sort, a subject we had previously referred to. I said it depends on how you use it. Steve says, "Karlyn, I'm sure you don't understand," and Smith is laughing so hard. He's not all there. He's demented.*

She told Smith she had a dream or was in a dreamy state and could see in her mind a place she could have been taken to in a truck with two people. He said, "You cock-'n-bull liar!" But it was no different from all the other things he made her say.

Many, many times she told of an event the way it happened. Smith then regroomed the story to his professional liking and forced her to say it.

During the interrogation she asked for and they knew she needed at attorney, but they continually sent into the room another officer every 45 minutes to an hour. This went on for eight days, approximately, 6 to 8 to 10 hours per day. She was belittled with slight threats, insulting remarks, humiliation, and, of course, in between all this was some comforting Pepsi served and some humor. All she wanted was help and somebody to stand by her.

If at any time she stopped cooperating, as Smith clearly indicated, the interrogation would be over and she would be under arrest. Her children would be taken and placed into foster care, which was done the very next day anyway. She struggled hard to stay calm and cooperative, though she knew she was very near to a nervous breakdown.

He broke me down using the precious people I love. So I closed my eyes and listened to the way he said he wanted to hear it from me. He told me the girls in prison would really like me, and that I shouldn't gain too much weight on him.

Chap XV: Jail Diaries 2/12/95

B ehind the citadel of justice, as we have called the Lane County Courthouse with grave doubts, and against the northern sky is the backdrop of the Hilton Hotel and in the distance a high-rise apartment building against Skinner's Butte and the river. Some blocks away is the citadel's companion, the Lane County Jail, which makes it all work.

Sixth Street runs behind the Hilton from an overpass to the east where there is an interchange of highways leading from the I-5 into the city, the suburbs, and the university area. The I-5 was built during the Eisenhower administration as part of a system of highways to expedite a smooth flow of traffic throughout the nation. There are points along the I-5, particularly through the Salem area, where it converges with the old 99E highway east of the Willamette river.

Fifth Street is behind Sixth, and both of these converge several miles to the west with the old highway 99W, running west of the river. Fifth is a kind of no man's land compared to those streets below it. The sidewalks are not repaired, and the grass grows up through the cracks. Here and there a specialty mercantile, a trendy restaurant, a gas station, or a set of public service offices emerge and endeavor to transform what, for the most part, are older buildings. Among those finding their way between these buildings are sometimes strange and derelict people.

What is strange and derelict about the area around the county jail is also true of the atmosphere within. Unlike in other public buildings, everyone is treated with suspicion. There are no welcome signs, nothing to orient one about which entrance to approach, and if you phone ahead nothing prepares you for the curtness, the turnoff, and the book of rules maintaining its isolation, unless you have someone vouching for your right to visit there.

The building itself, built to be adequate to its purpose, with strange glassed-in entries and an inner clear story, is deserted and seemingly controlled by intercom. The trees and shrubs on its grounds, though basically tended, are overshaded and overgrown. Needless to say, it is not, and was probably not intended to be, inviting.

It is interesting to note, however, the personal growth exhibited by Karlyn during her stay there, though the first seven months of her journals were taken by her second attorney, John Kolego and his investigator, Debra Martin, and never returned. Therefore the writer must try to fill in what had happened during the first nine months of her incarceration whenever questions arise.

She began writing the journals soon after her arrest, which followed the making of the four videotapes. The grinning faces of her prosecutors and the loss of her children put her in a state of shock for many days, but she felt it was important to document what they were telling her. Unfortunately, her accounts are missing. Those journals which follow, however, indicate much personal growth. One can see a new Karlyn emerging.

She is still very vulnerable, gullible almost, in taking immediate dislike to and resentment of her legal representatives or untoward admiration of them. Of those who prosecuted her, she focuses on the lies and treachery of Jerry Smith and has not yet learned who is really manipulating the evidence and the State's witnesses behind the scenes. She will get to know Fred Hugi. She will learn that as DA he will also have the authority to deny any motion to suppress or dismiss that her attorneys can devise. In other words, he not only created and distorted the evidence against her, but he also was able to dismiss any motion denying its validity.

How could this be? Well, I'm not sure. But for example, her Motion to Dismiss the coerced interrogations was denied because the interrogations were already being fed to the Grand Jury. That was critical, of course. He wanted to have a woman on death row. Somehow the jury was chosen on that basis. He must have had unlimited power to deny *due process* in suborning numerous witnesses and official reports. She will learn. But she hadn't yet. Even with a coerced confession, she still expected *due process*.

The dilemma posed by this situation is one of the great unfairnesses of the system. By the time there is a trial, as far as the jury and the defense are concerned, the admissability of her coerced testimony has already been ruled upon. It is not under question. Supposedly, the prosecution must tell the defense any exculpatory factors that are known which might exonerate the plaintiff before the trial. They must expose all factors in their discovery. If, however, they are able to deny any motion challenging the validity of their evidence, it cannot be brought up in the trial. The defense is allowed to consider only the circumstantial evidence and the testimony of witnesses which would tend to confirm what has already been agreed upon.

Karlyn would never be allowed to speak for herself at her trial. She always assumed she would be. Her jurors would never know, until after their guilty verdict, that she even objected to the coerced testimony. because she was not allowed to object to it.

However, the Karlyn that is emerging throughout this so-called *due process*, this speedy trial, is one who can handle herself, one who can finally deliver to the jury that convicted her, to no avail of course, her story, complete and unwavering, one that would bring some of them to tears. There exists somewhere a manila envelope containing jury statements indicating that half of them would have reneged if they had known this.

This Karlyn that emerges leaves her victim mentality behind, except when she is tormented by her terrifying memories. Having endured such abuse, she spots it wherever she sees it, especially among her cell-mates there at the jail. She has been through it. She knows what happens to innocent people when the police need a culprit. She champions them, and they her. The real Karlyn is compassionate, sometimes witty, very sharp, and kind.

In addition, the depth of her faith has grown. It was a faith that began after a diving accident as a young woman that left her nearly paralyzed. It had been there all along, contrary to the snide remarks of her prosecutors ("She wrote her two journals and then got baptized.").

During her incarceration, however, without the desperate struggle for her own and her children's survival to occupy all her resources, she was able to exist daily in relation to scripture, to what she feels were her blessings, and to people who shared her gratitude and devotion.

Without the journals, documents instead are included here and abridged, mostly without her comments, in order to fill in the gap.

Response to Public Record

Letter from H. Thomas Evans to Frederick A. Hugi Re: Plea Bargain
August 18, 1994
Frederick A Hugi
Lane County District Attorney
125 East 8th Avenue
Eugene, OR 97401
Re: The State of Oregon vs. Karlyn "NMN" Eklof
Lane County Circuit Court Case No. 10-94-04750
Dear Fred:

I discussed your plea bargain with the defendant. She is adamant that she is not willing to plead guilty to a murder charge and has asked that I contact you and arrange to have the case set for trial as promptly as possible.

I have told her that without question the things that she has told me that she has done makes her responsible for committing the crimes of assault and obstruction of justice. Those call for jail penalties almost as severe as the ones that you proposed with her murder plea, depending upon what the judge believes occurred.

If there is a possibility of us agreeing to her pleading to other charges which she admits that she has done with some agreed sentence or possibly even an open sentence situation, would you please let me know and I will discuss it with her further. I think that this might be workable because I believe you are very interested in having her cooperate in testifying against her code-fendant and that is something she is very much interested in doing, but if you end up prosecuting her on the murder charge also, that probably won't work as smoothly for either of us.

Please let me know if there is something more we can talk about in terms of a deal and if there isn't, then let's get together and schedule a trial as soon as possible.

Sincerely,
H. Thomas Evans

Writer's comment: If her own attorney believes she is guilty of assault and obstruction of justice, who can be for her?

Discovery of Body of Deceased Victim
Report of Chief Bill DeForrest

November 15, 1994

Body was discovered in the McKenzie Bridge area of the Willamette National Forest by a mushroom picker.

Death certificate cites homicidal violence, including gunshot wounds of the head.

[This certificate has been shown to be, in the evidence the writer has uncovered, based entirely on police hearsay. DeForrest is accused of perjury.]

By this report, James was found where Jethro said he put him, between two big boulders. So I conclude that my dream about being where a truck, trees, and digging were was just a dream, as I told everybody, because other-wise the body would have been buried up on top of a cliff. I only had a bad dream, which Smith made me videotape along with his other distortions of the way it really happened. You're a crook, Smith, and I'm going to prove it.

But Smith told me different. He told me it was no dream, and I was there and part of it all. The more I told him it was a dream the harder he held my hand. My hand was purple when he finally let go. That's when he told me to lay my head back, close my eyes, and say it! Just say it! Say I stabbed him and the sooner I said it the better I'd feel and the quicker we'd be through, etc. I thought he was going to slap me. He also leaned in close to me, raised his hand, and put his elbow on his knee.

Autopsy Report

Pathological findings:

1) homicidal violence, including:

a. Gunshot wounds of the head
2) Postmortem injuries of fingers,
remains discovered November 15,
1994 by a mushroom picker

in Willamette National Forest

[These findings do not support the type of crime for which Karlyn has been indicted.]

Discovery in State v. Karlyn Eklof
December 15, 1994

(Abridged) Hugi writes to H. Thomas Evans concerning the discovery items that were requested. Of significance are those tape recordings of phone calls between Detective Lewis and Karlyn Eklof on March 27, 1994 and between Captain Smith and Karlyn Eklof on April 16, 1993. Those calls would have indicated the false assurances and promises they were making to Karlyn, assurances that she did not need an attorney, that her Grand Jury testimony was essential to convict Jethro, and other indications of immunity. He is unable to produce the documents.

Re: Psychiatric Examination
December 19, 1994

The letter to H. Thomas Evans from the examining officer, Norman M. Janzer, M. D. indicates that

"in absence of any salient evidence (of the Homicide which she allegedly witnessed and for which she is charged), her credibility and mental state were questioned.

"There was no indication of delusions or hallucinations except for asserting she had seen 'Revelations' while on a plane... Throughout her examination she calmly repeated her account of the death of James Salmu. The lack of empathy was striking. I eventually decided she was competent to aid and assist you in her legal defense.

"Some of (her) stories suggested impaired judgment... According to the Caldwell Report the common diagnoses with her profile is of passive-aggressive disturbances and paranoid personality... the clinical diagnosis is Borderline Personality Disorder. This 'explains' her life-style, but would not provide a mental illness defense for her against a charge of Homicide. However it would offer mitigating factors should they become significant."

Writer's note: The above assessment, that the " lack of empathy was striking," makes one wonder how many times she can be required to repeat this gruesome story and if she is supposed to break down and cry every time.

Psychological Evaluation
Friday, February 18 1995

Karlyn mentions this second psychological evaluation in her journal of that date, but the document is not available.

Letter: Evans to Scott Summers, investigator
Editor's note: The missing journals make it impossible to know what occurred previously between Karlyn and her attorneys H. Thomas Evans, Terri Wood, and the investigator, Scott Summers, who was in Action, California.

Excerpts from their two letters of correspondence, however, are here given:

January 20, 1995 Re: Karlyn Eklof

Dear Mr. Summers:

...I want to retain you to take statements from the above-named defendant's mother and grandmother concerning mental or physical trauma that she may have endured as a child...

Sincerely,

H. Thomas Evans

Karlyn's mother and sister were interviewed. Excerpts of their statements are given here.

Declaration of Peggy Minch

Karlyn's mother described her husband Karl Eklof, father to her children Karlyn, Val, and
Karl (Sparky) Eklof, who she was married to for 14 or 15 years. She also had a daughter named
Diane Eklof who she adopted prior to marrying Karl. She said he was not an alcoholic, but he was
psychotic after he came back from the war in Vietnam. She briefly described the horrors he went
through before he returned to her and the three children.

Most significant was his captivity and torture by the North Vietnamese who rolled him in
barbed wire, twisted it until it was tight, and then rolled him down the mountain many times. He
had got rid of all his identification except a picture of her and the four children. So they tormented
him and brainwashed him into believing that the children were not his, and that his wife was the
biggest tramp on the earth.

When she went to meet the ship it was found that Karl had jumped ship and was POW for
about four months. When he was finally located, the Navy released him to her but did not offer
any therapy. Karl completely denied the children after that. He would consistently say, "I don't
know who your mother slept with, but you aren't mine." He had always been very harsh on
discipline, but when he came back from Vietnam he was vicious. She tells about her own abuse
and the severe discipline he exacted upon the children.

She cites an incident wherein she comes home to find that Val had been severely beaten by
him and states that Diane, Karlyn and Sparky had witnessed the beating. It was the incident that
led to their separation.

After that time she was having problems with Karlyn. She was belligerent, hard to handle
and wouldn't study. She wanted Karl to come down and talk to her (his favorite daughter and first
born). He offered to pick her up for a few weeks.

Karlyn told her that she mouthed off to her father and he backhanded her, breaking her
jaw. That is the story her mother told. Her sister, however, said it was because of attempted sexual
abuse, and that she was 12 to 14 years old at the time.

Peggy describes Karlyn as being always high spirited, cocky, and impatient. But she was
never vicious.

Her mother said the only time she knew of Karlyn riding with the bikers was on charity
runs. She also did not know Karlyn to ever take drugs other than to smoke marijuana.

She did not know that Karlyn had been raped and beaten by unknown
men in Imperial Beach in June 1993 until detectives Steve Walker and Rick
Lewis called her.

Apparently Karlyn didn't tell her any more than that for a long time,
because she feared Jethro would show up again and it would be dangerous for
them to know.

Declaration of Diane Eklof

Diane essentially repeats her mother's stories of the kind of abuse the three other children endured from their father, and she, from her stepfather. She does, however, give some interesting insights into Karlyn's personality and early escapades.

"Karlyn was very popular in school and had a lot of friends. She was very pretty, almost like Mary Poppins. She was highly intelligent and very imaginative. During junior high school, Karlyn was in lots of fights. We went to a tough school and Karlyn didn't take gaff from anyone. She was not one to start a fight, but she wouldn't back down…"

One thing Diane stressed was how terrified the children were for their father when the police were called. Even though they were badly beaten, they begged the police not to take him away.

Medical Records from Grossmont Hospital Requested by H. Thomas Evans

Hospital report indicates Karlyn had her right leg cast on June 14, 1993 and again on June 25, 1993 after the splint got wet.

The admitting diagnosis was that she was assaulted, had two black eyes, and pain on weight bearing. It is stated, verbatim, "She does not know that she was unconscious at the time," and that her attack was by two unknown men. It was determined that she had injury to her face, left foot and ankle, a mildly displaced fracture.

Demurrer/Motion to Declare Oregon's Death Penalty System Unconstitutional; or Alternatively to Require a Proportionality Review; or Motion in Limine

COMES NOW the Defendant, by and through the undersigned attorneys, and moves this court for the following orders:

1. To declare Oregon's death penalty system unconstitutional for failing to ensure a proportionate review of the punishment upon Ms. Eklof compared with other state and county capital cases;
2. In the alternative, to require a proportionality review of the death penalty upon Ms. Eklof;
3. To declare the death penalty system unconstitutional for allowing the jury to impose a standardless and unreviewable decision; and
4. In the alternative, to grant a motion in limine to prohibit the State from arguing for an unconstitutional death penalty.

These motions are… well founded in law, and are not made nor filed for the purposes of hinderance or delay.

     Dated, this __day of February, 1995.
     Respectfully submitted,
     William G. Young, OSB # 90138 Attorney for Defendant
     H. Thomas Evans, OSB # 68045 Attorney for Defendant

Defendant's Affidavit in Support of Motion to Suppress

I, Karlyn Eklof, after being first duly sworn on oath, do hereby depose and state:

1. I am the Defendant in the above entitled case.
2. As part of the Springfield Police Department's investigation into the death of James Salmu, I was repeatedly questioned by the police, who used threats, psychological abuse and offers of immunity to induce me into making statements.
3. The Springfield Police Department also used the same kind of tactics with my children, friends and family members to induce me to make statements.
4. I requested an attorney be present for any questioning with the police on numerous occasions,

and my request was either denied or ignored.
5. I never waived my *Miranda* rights throughout my contact with the police.

    Karlyn Eklof
    Subscribed and sworn to before me
    this 23rd day of February, 1995
    H. Thomas Evans
    Notary Public for Oregon

The narrative continues here, based on her journals, keeping in mind the large gap of missing ones. In the interests of brevity, her many struggles of compassion and contemplation are kept to a minimum, except where examples exist of her growth and special awareness. Only a small portion of what occupies her daily life is given, except that which pertains to her ongoing case.

Monday, February 12, 1995

Mr. Evans and Bill [Young] came today. Before either one could say anything I asked Bill where did I ever give him the impression that I didn't want an investigation as he told Terri Woods last week. He said, "You didn't, Karlyn. Mr. Evans did." That's what I thought.

Just as Ms. Woods confirmed. Now Bill apologizes for the mix-up. But Mr. Evans tries to avoid any guilt by rewording his original statements. Lawyers truly are the best and worst liars.

So now that we're back on track again, the investigator should be in to see me. Oh, with Mr. Evans escorting her of course. He sure has gone way out of his way to keep me from speaking to anyone about what happened to me. It's your problem, dear. I feel rage inside so I turn it over to the Lord. I can't afford to show any anger. So from there he says he'll have her back again some evening of this week. And of course then he's busy with another case as usual.

He sets in front of me a few pages and says, "These are going consistent with your original statements." I've heard him say that before. The papers consist of: James' death certificate and coroner's report which were examined by two doctors and a dentist.

They confirmed that James was shot in the head twice and that there were no other injuries, especially none to the body or ribs. I am forever thankful that not all officials are like Smith. And this report also brings out exactly what damages or lengths Smith went to frame me. In brief.

It has snowed off and on since yesterday. So beautiful. The dorm is packed and everybody is in good spirits. We're not allowed to look out the little window.

February 15, 1995

Mr. Evans came alone. He knows I don't want to be alone with him. He doesn't take any proper notes, and he says cruel things... Mr. Evans said something about the prosecutor is going to really prosecute me. And he doesn't appreciate my critical remarks. I told him I see you defend yourself real well. How about defending me?. I told him their own police reports and coroner's report clear me.

He said, "Yes, those things do work for you, but the prosecutor is still going to prosecute you." Then he told me about a case—this is the third one that he and Fred have worked on together—and his words are exactly like this: "It's financial. Fred has dropped charges again. So I have more time to work on this."

As soon as he said that, however, he had to leave to work on another case for another client. So far, after nine months of his do-da-do-da, it becomes clear to me, as it has from the beginning, he would do as the DA requires instead of working with me. A very gut-wrenching feeling. I just want to fall apart. He says my investigator can't come see me if he isn't present. But the psychologist, a male, certainly can. Wonder why this is Mr. Evans is stopping any support worthy of helping me. I need to get help....

Mr. Evans is trying to keep the investigator from speaking to me alone. He's trying to keep the story just the way Smith has set it up. And I won't have it, especially when I can prove the manipulation by pointing it all out.

Thursday, February 17, 1995

Today Mr. Evans and the investigator, Debbie Martin, came and did listen to me. I spoke about what happened to me and my children My hope here is that a woman finally heard from me and will put things in motion. I've run across enough men who either don't care, don't believe me, or don't want anybody to know.

These men who think it's great to sexually abuse women and use them without any knowledge of what has happened to them are sick. It hurts so much inside, knowing there's been damage, I still don't know whom to trust. While originally officers sent to investigate were carelessly exposing the facts I remembered in situations to my detriment, now those in position to help aren't even listening. I have found peace in leaving it all up to the Lord and I pray my children stay protected and safe. But I'm working as hard and as patiently as I can to get the information properly acknowledged.

If any of these people think I'm going to accept their unwillingness to look into what happened, they are under an awful misconception. My own ethics, my beliefs, hold strong. I believe in exposing the truth any way I can.

Friday, February 18, 1995

I worked breakfast with Kyman and something very special happened. Deputy Cooper asked me if I was afraid of him. I must have showed a little fear when he stepped up to me. He was sharing a joke to bring humor into the morning after our work was done. And I must have stepped back.

Well, I answered him like this: "Yes, I am afraid of men. I was attacked."

He said, "I know, and if I could go back in time I would correct the situation." He was "the first" person to actually comfort me. He told me he was very proud of me for speaking directly about what happened and for staying strong and going forward with it. I told him I would always be thankful for his comfort and encouragement. I will keep trying until people listen, I told him. It just isn't easy. I want people to listen while I'm still able to talk about it.

I told him my attorney is, like, an elite-type guy and doesn't understand. Then I realized what I said, corrected myself and apologized. Mr. Cooper is the real elite-type man for his reaching out and for his protective encouragement. My attorney is a snobbish ass. I've been kissing his ass for so long, hoping he would just once say, "Karlyn, I'm sorry about what happened to you, your roommate, and your children. Please help me to understand." But he wouldn't, ever.

Thanks, Cooper. What an angel. I think Deputy Kelly has been listening and watching over me the longest. And I'd have to say, she has opened up the truth for others to see, which I do appreciate.

Captain Smith is a heartless, cold, son-of-a-bitch who stirred this thing up to where I may never get out from under it. Unfortunately, I helped him without understanding or realizing I was capable of giving the whole truth on my own. My mental state was a lot worse off than I'd planned for or recognized. The torment I went through took me way beyond my own state of recovery so he was able to create distortions.

I am determined to survive this thing and to bring my children around to a freedom and laughter we once knew. And to encourage others to take heed to the warning signs of any unlawful mischief. The hardest part is understanding when you don't remember what happened. What to recognize is a sudden lapse of time, body sensations, exhaustion, confusion, and "new friends" you didn't remember meeting.

Karlyn does go on and on about the unusual happenings of her sojourn in La Mesa. But she has described them before, and I will exclude them this time. Later, however, in assessing her visit with the psychologist, she comes back to her pain and her memories, which I will again include.

The psychologist was here today to screen me. I have told him some of the events that happened to me. He seemed to be listening. It's only taken me nine months to get this understood. Now it comes all at once. Going over all of this again and the mind games going with it weakens me. I feel so very sad. Too much has happened. If Captain Smith had not manipulated this case to get his creditability this would have been resolved. My children would not have been bounced around in foster care, and I wouldn't be undergoing verbal lobotomies.

Now I get to take the same 500-Question test I already took. Boy, are they helping me! But all I see is myself open wide, waiting for the next insult or denial. Gut wrenching! And the lighter side to all of this is if I keep trying somebody might listen. I don't really have much thirst to go forward. I do get recharged, but it doesn't go far. At least that's the way it looks from here. All I can do is praise God and try to pull through...

Doctor Barnhart tested me all afternoon: Ink blocks, cartoon squares, blocks red and white, counting backwards, ABC's. It's very humiliating that I'm being challenged this way. I would understand if they were rebuilding my skills which were subject to damages. I'm being evaluated for a murder capability anybody pushed far enough would be capable of. But James did not sustain such damages. He did not die by my hands.

I wish there was a way to replay my memory to prove what did happen.

Sunday, February 19, 1995

There are 59 days until my trial. I've been going over my visit from the psychologist Friday. I didn't eat for a whole day afterward, and I slept off and on. I enjoyed the mind being exercised. But it was humiliating also. Because a man, Roe— something I can't even pronounce and never met—is the authority on these test results, tests for which there aren't any right or wrong answers, they say, but which will evaluate my level of thinking.

Which has nothing to do with what happened to me. Instead of listening to me and allowing me to explain all I can the best way I know how, more time is wasted and less is understood. If these people are so smart in playing mind games, why does the test have to go back to their offices to find the results? I'm scared of that. All I wanted to do was to tell what happened to my roommate, myself, my children and those other women who were victims.

They keep trying to build a case they call a defense. Right. Without having all the facts, like how many phone calls were made between me and the police to insure my arrival and preparations for testifying. The police have submitted only certain tapes. And so the attorney is only going with what the DA wants known. It's not fair...

The aching, helpless pain of knowing somebody has violated a human being, especially a child, is unmentionable. The fear and anger one goes through. I will always do my best to protect their innocent, precious lives. I don't seem to be getting the help I came here to get. It is time to reach out to those who understand my fear and pain and to work together for awareness and protection in hopes it will open people's eyes...

The hypnosis and moving around that was used on me and my children could very well explain some other ongoing events. If my mind wasn't strong enough to keep trying to snap out of it, and by the Grace of God, we would never have survived, as I am very sure others have not. I am so sorry I couldn't get this message and point of view out sooner. I tried! We might not be able to find the ones that are missing, but we can put a stop to any more disappearing. We must come together as a nation to stop these pagan rites, this occult white slavery!

Thursday, February 23, 1995

Mr. Evans and Bill (Murdock) came today. He showed me his Motion to Suppress, e. g., the videotapes, because of the manner in which they were coerced. Mr. Evans doesn't believe he'll get them dismissed. And like everything else, he's negative. He again told me to take the eight-year plea bargain. I told him to—well never mind—I left.

After I read the paper work I made a few changes, called him back, and said a few other things that I thought he should know. He and Fred Hugi, the DA, are speaking so freely about my case while getting two other cases dismissed. And so on. I also asked him why he felt he was here only to judge me and not to defend me. He said he meant only that he was giving me his judgement or opinion and, at best, he was giving me his best defense. Bill says it's an uphill, tough case. But he did suggest that Evans ask Hugi for a plea to hindering prosecution. Evans cringed at the idea.

He and Bill returned at 2:00 P. M. and we went over the paper work that I had worked so hard on. All the transcripts that they've allowed me to have I've gone over, every page, and have made notes and tried to correct errors where the police had bombarded me with questions. In the state I was in, police made soup out of me. Mr. Evans seems to lose much of his interest and forget real easily a lot of important stuff.

He also plays mind games, like he'll ask me a question which I'll answer; then he'll ask me the same question but apply pressure—body language, voice tone—like my first answer isn't appropriate or isn't acceptable. We finished for a while at 3:30 P. M., and he returned with Bill at 6:30 P. M. We went over a few more things I requested him to suppress. I wanted to talk more to others, like the investigator, whom I will see again on Monday or Tuesday.

Bill has really busted his butt to gather information on the case. I wish Mr. Evans worked as positively... as hard. Mr. Evans magnifies the incriminating, false statements and the necessity of plea bargaining. He says, well, you told them this and that. And I say, yes, but look just ahead of this and that and see what they said and what they did to get me to that point. He says, yeah, well, I also point out the missing tapes and missing parts of tapes. He says, Oh, I don't think a judge is going to acknowledge that. Yes, if he opens it all up.

He's suffocating my areas of defense and magnifying areas of manipulation to convict me. So I say okay, Lord, it's your business. They tell me I'll get life in prison, or thirty years, so take the eight years, even though Evans knows what the captain did to obtain credit. He feels it is too humiliating for his credit to go into my defense. He's willing to just make it look like he has covered everything, pushing hard at the last minute, and, oh oops (!) forgetting the important stuff.

He'll get depressed again, as usual, and nothing will get accomplished. Or he'll lag on information to be discovered. Perhaps it's not his fault he's trying to assist in convicting me. After all, one third of the angels were thrown from the heavens for disobeying. They were locked here on earth to deceive and commit heartache and to deny people proper assistance and to accuse them falsely. That is why the Lord sends his own to work and reopen doors Satan has shut permanently. God restores any and all things according to His plan. After all, Thy Kingdom come, Thy will be done on earth as it is in heaven...

When I focus on what these people tell me, how they're going to put me away with false accusations, because they can, it breaks me up. I've been through too much already. And it sure doesn't take much to bring me down. It's a gut wrenching, frustrating feeling. I turn to praise God. I know he knows just what to do. I focus on why he has me here, and I know he has me covered. I know work here isn't easy. And it's painful. When liars and selfish people have a hold on you, I just want to fall apart and quit. And just about then a door to an answer opens up.

It's the same feeling I went through for interrogation, which was supposed to be Grand Jury. Well, God bless this mess, and bless all those who are working hard.

My prayer buddy, Martha, is having a really rough time of it. The DEA pulled her in on one of their sting operations, and they didn't have anything on her. So now they are going after her husband. They tell her they are sending her to prison for fourteen years if she doesn't take the seven-year plea bargain. They tell her they know she's innocent, but they have to have somebody *if it has to be her. Well, guess what? I don't think so. These halfassed, simple-minded, threatening slob son-of-a-bitches in the DEA are gonna get up off their lying asses and do the proper work this country is paying them to do.*

Pulling innocent people in, kicking in doors of people to harass them, just to fill a quota, isn't going to work, boys and girls.

They charge conspiracy. Seems to me I complained once that people who conspire against innocent victims merely redistribute malevolence. So how about when the police do it? What's it called then? Entrapment? Perhaps we should go over the structure of our laws just for the benefit of the future so there's no misuse or misunderstanding. It also seems to me that an awful lot of people are in jails and prisons, all because of the entrapments in the law...

I did laundry roll-ups with Martha after Bible study. The girls made certain requests in the sizes I need, 38 bra instead of 36. One needs S pants, one needed L tee-shirts, one needed an XL tee-shirt, and one needed... And I remembered. I could remember them all! I have been restored. I can remember. I can concentrate. I can focus. Praise the Lord, thank you. I feel great. Ever since Dr. Barnhart did those tests I have felt a balance I haven't had for over a year. I just want to share this new feeling or emotion.

Memorandum to Suppress due to Sexual Harassment

February 23, 1995 The Memorandum is missing; however the date and incident were important because of the retaliatory charges brought against her thereafter.

Chap XVI: Jail Diaries 2/24/95

A s it becomes less necessary to define the changes and adjust ments that Karlyn is going through, her personal relationships there at the jail will be kept to a minimum. All that pertains to her case will be retained:

Saturday, February 25, 1995
Today I received a response to my grievance against Captain Smith. Chief DeForrest told me that Officer Smith, as well as others, I guess, are in denial about what occurred with me. Well, would I expect anything else?...

Monday, February 27, 1995
Sam and I worked lunch. She got confused about how to manage the count cup and was frustrated. She ended up going to the dorm and saying she wouldn't work with me talking about her. So that gave everybody something to talk about.

Well, then she did work with me and apologized. She, like others who have done drugs for a while and have had to do without, overeat and jerk themselves around. Frustration comes real easy. She apologized. But I told her, "Sam, because of my charges, they monitor me. Plus I put in a grievance against Captain Smith, so I expect his coworkers to weigh every opportunity to write me up. I try really hard to be on my own and on my bunk. I don't socialize for the simple fact that I don't need to be caught up in the swing of gossip or mischief. So when you stir things up like that in front of a deputy and the girls, I'm the one they automatically blame. It's unfair, but true."

So she said, "I have PMS overload. Sorry..."

Tomi, whose laugh is like that of a seal, told the girls about a dream she had. She dreamed I married Jesus, and she patented a game about the chapters in the Bible.

Mr. Evans came to see me on Tuesday night. He told me that Fred Hugi, the assistant DA, wants to know if I would consider speaking to him and the judge, something about evaluating the case. I said, of course I would; I asked for that in the beginning. Mr. Evans said he didn't expect it, "This isn't normal or even usual." But he's very glad. Especially since I do agree.

I asked him why is this happening? Do they see it from my side or are they going to hurt me by idle threats. He said the judge will assess the case and tell us both the answer! I guess I would hope for a breakthrough for the best. But I expect another Captain Smith move. And Mr. Evans better not be behind it all...

The investigator, Debra Martin, and Mr. Evans came and asked me a lot of questions. I asked her to give my information to the police down in San Diego. I just want to get help. I want somebody to know what happened to me.

March 3, 1995

When the deputy came in to tell me what time to be ready the girls clapped. I've been here so long Kris tells me, "Don't escape from the Court House!"

I told her, "It's not over 'til I say it's over."

At 2:30 I was called. We were watching a videotape on the fourth step of AA. Deputy Lankin walked me to the blue iron door or gate. I went to the court house in a white van with six other men.

A deputy walked me to a single cell. It was dark, and the iron bars shut loud. The hallway was available for me to see into, but so could anyone see into my cell. A toilet and bunk platform without a mattress is where I began to pray on my knees.

Forty minutes went by and a deputy said, "You've been cancelled." Then he cuffed me, walked me out to the van, and drove me back to Lane County jail...

Mr. Evans came to speak with me and said he and Fred Hugi, the DA, did get together along with two other judges. They agreed I requested a female to be involved in my case, so they interrupted a female judge during her busy schedule. Fred gave her the videotapes to view over the weekend, and they will speak to her about her opinion of the case on Monday or Tuesday.

I have a problem with Fred passing around the manipulated tapes. He tries to get in his cheap shot so people will be on his side. I asked Mr. Evans, "What is the important factor here? Does Fred only care about crediting Smith, or does he care about the truth? Why is it he is passing these interrogation tapes around so proudly instead of halting the whole idea and realizing what Smith has done? Why won't anybody listen to me?"

Nobody is telling the whole story. And they keep encouraging a false image of what really happened. I'm so frustrated and so hurt and angry that nobody cares about what really happened. They just talk about these stupid tapes Smith created so proudly. And, yes, they are based on 89% of the facts of the case. But they are all magnified to show the ugliness of it. Indeed it was ugly, but I was being pressed beyond my endurance to satisfy their demands to say what they wanted me to say so we could be finished. I appear overwrought and hypnotized. At one point you can see a hand being waved in front of my face...

I have tried to get police to understand, and they have denied me and manipulated my statements. I have informed them of several accountable witnesses to the damages that we suffered, but to no avail. Now would somebody please help me?

Sunday, March 5, 1995

Speaking to my mother on the phone tonight was frustrating. Sparky tried to get in, and then he burned rubber out of the park mother lives in. The manager called her and complained. And the roof leaks in several places, not to mention the floor has a warp in it.

My children sounded very depressed. But their beautiful souls are holding strong. God please release me. If you love me at all, send me back to my children. Please!

Monday, March 6, 1995

Mr. Evans came at 8:30 this morning. We completed going through the transcripts of the videotapes. I feel I've worked my best to speak on my own behalf, without ever seeing them or the notes used in the interrogations. I made a real struggle to cover the conversations. What was easier about correcting the interrogation transcripts by memory is the fact that I had to work at believing in myself, knowing that all the damages and suffering had to be put aside in order to find the courage and strength I needed to complete this stage of the work. I had to do it if I ever expected to survive this thing I'd been through, in hopes I could get help for other people.

Tuesday, February 7, 1995

Today I read in the paper an article that was of particular interest to me. It concerned the case against Procter and Boots of aggravated murder, the two young men who did eight years in prison for a murder they did not commit. Today on the news and in the paper the two men were dismissed from the charges against them. Praise the Lord!

The evidence used was nil, but because they had stolen beer from a store not knowing that a clerk lay dead in the refrigerator, Captain Jerry Smith headed an investigation which lead to the conviction of innocent men.

I have complained about Jerry Smith's manipulating my case long before I knew anything about Proctor and Boots. It seems to me it's about time to get rid of Jerry Smith from the captain's chair at the Springfield Police Department....

By the way, the two men recently were released and are pursuing options for compensation. The paper said that on the Proctor and Boots case Mr. Jerry Smith had no comment. He did say it would be of no use and would do nobody any good to converse across the media about the case.

What a wonderful time to shut up. He certainly doesn't mind cornering people and taunting them, using police department power to humiliate people. And when it comes time for his turn to be accused he squats off to another direction.

Thursday, March 9, 1995

Well, I'm depressed. I was finally called to the court house. I met with Judge Aiken. I saw Steve and Fred Hugi. Judge Aiken formally presented the case and all of the above were present, including a stenographer court reporter who was dismissed. Judge took her robe off and sat before me with all conviction in her eye. (This meeting was definitely off the record, but I didn't understand that until later.)

I couldn't find strength or a starting point, because she said right from the start, "Don't start from the beginning. I've already spent a full Saturday going over the information." Things got worse from there on. As I made efforts to express my feelings, she was determined to feed me that same line, like this was repeated about five or six times in two hours of conversing. She stated first that the DA is willing to drop my charge to felony murder, and her offer was to take the ten years with 20% off for good behavior to do eight years in prison. Oh, and testify against Jethro.

Or, I could take a chance on a trial, where she would guarantee I'd do thirty years or life and never see the light of day or my children. And that I would live in maximum security in a single cell with no view and be fed under the door through a hole. She continually told me the jury would find me guilty and that the maximum sentence would be thrown at me.

I continued to explain to her the manipulations of Captain Smith. She said it didn't matter. We went back and forth like that for a few times. She glared at me and sipped her coffee. She leaned back in her chair and held her chin up with her fist.

*She by no means wanted to hear what I had to say. She said, "Go ahead
and explain it to us." As I tried to, she said, "It doesn't matter. Nothing you
have to say matters, but go ahead."*

*So I figured they staged this thing to get a reaction from me in order to
know where to attack me from. Now Mr. Evans never defended me. He barked
when the judge said to bark. Also, before he, she, and I were left alone to
speak, Fred and Steve were there for a few minutes. They both did a double
take and said, "You look great" and "Good to see you." Yeah!*

*Well, in the first few minutes of the presentation, as the judge addressed
the two counselors and before the two men were dismissed, Fred was right up
on his feet. Mr. Evans didn't budge. I asked him why is Fred so jumpy. He said,
"You're supposed to address the judge on your feet."*

I asked him, "Why didn't you?" (Remember, this is my first time in court.)

*He said, "Oh, I was just... um... informal, and that isn't considered a
violation." I was asked to get prepared.*

*He told me he gets paid $55 an hour and would probably get paid $6000,
so he was planning a trip to the Virgin Islands. Isn't that sweet? And then he
asked me, like this, "What do you think is going to happen?" (Now that you've
stepped on a rusty nail and contracted gangrene? So when do we cut the leg
off?)*

*Well, after this awful and very unexpected day, being escorted to and
from the court by the deputy, I got on the elevator and he said, "I haven't seen
the tapes either, but from what I heard, you'd do very well to take the eight-
year plea bargain." No one seems to understand that the whole story is being
based on an officer's perspective, coercion, and manipulation. And I'm fighting for the truth.*

The following comments are taken from a letter written March 6, 1999
by Karlyn which suggests further insights about her first court appearance she
didn't realize at the time.

*The court session with Judge Ann Aiken was very disappointing as I had
repeatedly requested a female attorney, but I only received what Judge Merten
thought would break me...*

*She gave me twenty-four hours to think about it, but as I told her then
and will say again, "It isn't fair to James Salmu to take his death and rear-
range the facts just to justify a police version." Ann Aiken said, "That's not my
problem."*

*Due to the fact that she dismissed the court reporter so no further wit-
nesses would be there except the officer who escorted me from county jail and
Attorney T. Evans, the only way I can prove that the event ever happened is*

that during the Pretrial Kosyder slithered up to stand beside Hugi, stating he was enforcing a No Policy Unwritten Statement to impose Death Penalty.

He prohibited the fact that Ann Aiken privately spoke to me, and moved to strike it from the record, saying it was Privilege, if I remember correctly.

The writer believes that this warning meant they would not be able to impose the death penalty if they tried to make her plea bargain. That they did present the jury with the option of the death penalty will become apparent, however; indeed, it was made a basis for their selection.

Friday, March 10, 1995

I was called again today. Like yesterday, I was able to wear a regular outfit of clothing. I came in with a white blouse and skirt, shoes, etc. Again I was driven to the court house in a van. I was placed in a jail cell with bars. Aretha and Anita were in other cells.

I was called to the conference room. I sat in there with Bill, Mr. Evans and the deputy, and we spoke for a few minutes. He showed me the letter sent down to a detective to investigate my attackers, filmings, etc. So that's in motion.

We went before Judge Aiken, Fred Hugi, and Steve Walker. She asked if I understood the plea which consisted of ten years sentence, 20% off for good behavior, and testify against Jethro. I understood but declined their offer. I gave a short speech on tyranny and, in particular, that of Captain Smith. And I requested that I stand trial **as well as to testify against Jethro!**

Fred showed a gesture of praise, and the judge looked a little proud of me. Everybody adjourned.

I doubt they were very happy. They would not be able to have her agree to a murder based on their handiwork in exchange for leniency. They would have to carry their treachery the whole bloody way.

Saturday, March 11, 1995

This weekend is a tough one. Martha, my prayer buddy, is having to make one of the biggest decisions of her life. She passed her polygraph with flying colors, but the DA insisted on giving her time because she accepted the trip here from what she thought were her friends, but who turned out to be a malicious DEA cover. An innocent person is being threatened with thirty months in the Federal Penitentiary. If she tries to take it to trial, they will falsely prosecute her for five times that amount of time. She has bruises on her ankle where cuffs were placed...

I wrote nine pages of my experiences of damage done to me and my children and turned it over to Deputy Tammy to give to this detective who wants to help me after my trial is over.

Tuesday, March 14, 1995

I haven't had much to say or write since visiting with the judge last Thursday and Friday. Surprisingly enough, I was quite prepared at that time and have been finding simple waves of awareness ever since. What I don't like is how Captain Smith molded me and my experience to glorify himself. And so the story goes, snowballing in that direction with the help and support of his coworkers.

Since it is a crime what he has done, is it not a crime for the others to follow his lead? After all, I do believe it is. And I also understand that the big issue in my case is that I allowed Jethro to move me. I didn't know what he was doing.

The next thing that is bothering me is the way the judge spoke to me. She had spent all of Saturday going over my case and was convinced of my guilt. These professionals are covering up a guilty man's work and threatening me with prison even if I testify, and if not, I wouldn't see the light of day or my children. Pooff!

And they use the one-liner, "Oh, everybody is lying except Karlyn!" Yes, as a matter of fact, yes!...

I gave a short speech on tyranny in my excitement at finally seeing the interior of a court room. My dear and precious friend, Deb [Debra Martin], came to visit me. She's moved back here from Modesto. She is flying my TJ here to see me before the trial. I think that is so neat. I just don't know what to say about it yet...

After court and all its excitement, Friday evening came around and a most beautiful surprise came about. Debbie came to visit. She was so beautiful to me. She was so full of sorrow from losing her mother, and she still thought enough of me to visit. Then she tells me how bad she felt for not being here sooner. It's a wonder. Doesn't she ever do anything for herself? Well, I'm sure she does, but not much. Always for her children or somebody else.

I spoke to Mother, TJ, Caroline, and Duders on Sunday as usual. That is my only highlight around here, and it is difficult sometimes. I miss them so much...

Wednesday, March 15, 1995

Deputy Tammy confirmed tonight that she did pass my notes to Chris Jacobs, the detective who is concerned about the things my children and I went through. I am so very grateful that by the grace of God I am being heard. It's slow, it's scary, and it's hard to bring into focus the direction where this all is headed. But it is headed toward a rude awakening and awareness for all.

I am surprised that a few deputies are extending their concern about what happened to me. An overwhelming gratitude wells up from deep within my heart. Though limited by their jobs in their ability to help me, they have given me hope through their listening ears. Because of the security that is maintained here, I have been able to recover from some of the damages done to me. A rough way to go about it, but accomplished just the same.

Thursday, March 16, 1995

One month, two days before my trial. Deputy Tammy came to work today with great news for me. She sent off my short report to a detective friend of hers who immediately responded by calling San Diego and getting involved. Praise the Lord. Thank You!

Monday, March 20, 1995

Mr. Evans came to see me. He's back from a week's vacation down in Monterey. He was in the middle of the storm of the century but saw very little of it. He also said he traveled to the Hurst Castle but the roads to it were closed.

Oh, well, I had a great week not having to deal with him. He asked me to make a list of questions that would give me problems if asked by other witnesses. I guess I am doing my trial on my own.

It is very strange that Evans led Karlyn to think she would be on the witness stand. How much more he might have helped her if she had known she'd have no part in her defense whatsoever. That false hope led her to turn down any other options.

By the grace of God, he wants my mother here, my son here, and, oh, my grandmother, who is too old and frail to fly. He says we just need somebody, anybody, to vouch for me. I was requested to make a list of people who could be witnesses, and then told we can't fly anyone in unless the DA says so.

This is so incredible! Her mother and son were there, but not asked any questions that would verify her fear and abuse by Jethro. Even the prosecution's potential witnesses who had been at Grand Jury were not asked to come, the prostitute from Las Vegas who could have been cross-examined to verify her terror of him and the tales he told about the homicide they chose not to believe.

Well, I cried myself to sleep. I give too much to Evans. And he drops it in a dry well. I will call him today and tell him I don't need anybody to testify for my credibility. We will just have to work with whoever they subpoena.

He says then what do you want to do? Always asking me the same ques-

tion, and he knows I have given my all. Well, so now there's talk about me going before Grand Jury. I said I will testify against Jethro after my trial. They were trying to slide me into a worse position and didn't offer me anything in return.

I called Terri and asked her what I should do. Mr. Evans doesn't give me a straight answer, and he teeter-totters. She wholeheartedly agreed about his deceitfulness and useless work. She is very concerned and said she would vouch for me and go to the judge to get me a new attorney. I wrote her a two-page letter requesting a new attorney...

It's a real scary thought I can't find someone worthy of the authority they carry to help me, one who will support my truth with the legal words I lack. My fight is an obvious one.

I just want to get through this. Then I can separate myself from all this. Two years ago this very day I witnessed an unlawful act against another human being. Since then I have seen and been through more misery and torment than I ever imagined. My apologies to James and his family, friends, and neighbors. I have done everything I can to resolve this matter properly. But I also need much restoring and so do my children.

Thursday, March 23, 1995

This has been an interesting couple of days. Grand Jury for Jethro has been going on, and Fred, the DA, wanted me to come. I told them I would testify at Jethro's trial. Mr. Evans told me if I went it would be used against me. But if I was convicted at my trial, testifying against him could help my appeal. So, since he gives me no hope and fills me with doubt and fear, I decided to call Terri Woods.

She has been a breath of fresh air to me. I sent her a letter requesting a female attorney, stating also the fact that I had fired Evans three or four times. But that he would not or had not allowed me to fire him. With a little bit of hope or a tidbit he would string me along. Gut wrenching. I have waited a day-and-a-half to go to court to receive a new attorney. Now Terri has said she will go before the judge herself. Thank you, Lord. These notes are in brief. Since Evans is allowing me to be crucified, I can't begin to express my depression when it comes to him...

I can "poop" regularly! I feel the damages that were done to me are slowly fading. It's a strange feeling to feel and see my body slowly recovering. I've got so much bottled up inside me. All I can do is write about it and hope that somebody reads my notes. I don't feel that I've hesitated at all in my descriptions, although sometimes I feel humiliated when questioned and have a loss for words. I think it's a mental block, a fear of some sort, that continu-

ally waves through my mind and body. My head hurts sometimes, like getting slapped, but not feeling the hit. It's so hard to concentrate when I hurt.

Lord, believe me, how I praise your name. Please send me just one person to believe me and see me through. I need to stay strong, but fear is setting in. My neck vertebras are sliding on each other, and it is so painful. The top three are bothering me!

Friday, March 24, 1995

Today is Friday, and I am still waiting to be called to court to receive another attorney. I spoke to Lee for some time today. We had a wonderful conversation, and he is the only one who remembered the date of James' death. One person! He's very familiar with this case. He also told me for the past three years he has investigated Captain Smith because of all the complaints from women. I am not surprised. He said he waited to tell me, because he wanted to hear all I had to say. He believes me, everything I say. Thank the Lord. A comfort and a blessing! Praise God!...

Well, I was called to visiting. I asked who, my attorney? No way, I have nothing to say to him. The girls were clever. They asked, "Is it Evans or a new one?" Well, instead of all this confusion, I went to see who it was. It was Evans!

As deputy Pat stood by, I refused to go in to the visiting room. But he had papers for me. Indictments! Nine counts, which all belong to Jethro. I went in. Well, he also showed me pictures of the area where James was found. I did not recognize it. The place is not the same as in my dream. Not even close. I know Steve can verify that by my description. I was kind of numb, but then the Lord revealed to me his plan, and I got excited.

Then I stood up, there at visiting, speaking to Evans, and I said, "You are fired. You have never given me any hope. You have given me only fear and doubt. I'm scared of you. I don't trust you. You have not prepared a defense. If you had this would not be happening."

I came into the dorm. I cried. Martha, Jennifer, and Tomi comforted me. As we went through the papers, Jen and I discussed my past. All the girls are concerned.

It's pretty obvious what's going on. I didn't testify at Jethro's Grand Jury, so I get all of his charges. My goodness! The filth in the DA's office is childish and grotesque. I wish Fred Hugi could go through what I am going through.

My thoughts are going round and round, for a friend, for someone. So I pray. I don't want to upset Mother. Debbie wasn't home. Ms. Woods is out.

I praise God for the nine new charges for my case. I am so happy all is out in the open. What if I had gone into that little room and Mr Evans had handed me those charges and, without God, WHAM, he would definitely have gotten a little bit surprised himself. Praise God! I was prepared.

Response to Public Record
Sommer Investigations
March 11, 1995

A letter to Debbie Martin, Chase Investigations, Inc. indicates that Karlyn's lawyer at that time, Mr. H. Thomas Evans, requested that they ascertain if Mr. Jethro Timer had any involvement with a drug, prostitution or pornography ring in the San Diego/Imperial Beach communities. They stated they had begun their inquiries into that matter.

Memorandum of Law in Support of Motion to Suppress
March 10, 1995

H. Thomas Evans, Att. at Law, Memorandum to Suppress No. 10-94-04750: p. 8

THE LAW OF CONFESSIONS

Under the Due Process Clause of the 14th Amendment of the U. S. Constitution, criminal defendants have a right to a hearing outside the presence of the jury on the voluntariness of their confession. *Jackson v. Denno*, 378 US 368. 377. 84 S Ct 1774, 12 L Ed 2d 908 (1964). To determine voluntariness, a Court must examine:

...all of the surrounding circumstances—the duration and conditions of detention (if the confessor has been detained), the manifest attitude of the police toward him, his physical and mental state, the diverse pressures which sap or sustain his powers of resistance and self-control—is relevant. The ultimate test remains that which has been the only clearly established test in Anglo-American courts for two hundred years: the test of voluntariness. Is the confession the product of an essentially free and unconstrained choice by its maker? If it is, if he has willed to confess, it may be used against him. If it is not, if his will has been overborne and his capacity for self-determination critically impaired, the use of his confession offends due process...

The Oregon Constitution, Article 1, Section 12, provides for the privilege against self-incrimination which prohibits the use of an involuntary confession. In Oregon, the defendant may contest the voluntariness of the confession pretrial. *State v. Brewton*, 238 Or 590. 603, 395 P2d 874 (1964). ORS 135.425 (1) provides:

A confession or admission of a defendant, whether in the course of a judicial proceeding or otherwise, cannot be given in evidence against the defendant when it was made under the influence of fear produced by threats...

The test is "whether, under the totality of the circumstances, the waiver of rights and confession were the product of an essentially free, unconstrained and informed choice or whether the accused's capacity for self-determination was critical(ly) impaired." *State v. Burks*, 107 Or App 588, 592, 813 P2d 1071, rev. denied, 312 Or 151 (1991).

A court must also examine the following:

...relevant surrounding circumstances including both the character of the accused and the details of the interrogation. Some of the factors taken into account include the age, education and intelligence of the accused, the length and location of the interrogation, and whether the accused was advised of his constitutional rights or subjected to physical or psychological coercion.

State v. Davis, 98 Or App 752 P2d (1989), rev. denied, 309 Or 333 (1990).

However, a confession will be held to be involuntary under the totality of the circumstances if the defendant's will was overborne by deceitful police conduct. *State v. Burdick*, 57 Or App 601, 646 P2d 91 (1982); In the *Burdick* case, the police used lies and other trickery in order to get the defendant to make a confession. Although the defendant voluntarily appeared at the police station, he was subjected to coercive interrogations for several hours. The defendant's physical condition was impaired from lack of sleep and the consumption of alcohol. In addition, the police implied the defendant might be charged with a lesser crime and used vulgar insults to obtain a confession. The Court held the defendant's confession was involuntarily made because of these deceptive and coercive police tactics.

In this case, the totality of the circumstances will show that Ms. Eklof's confessions were not voluntarily given and must be suppressed under the Federal and Oregon Constitutions. The surrounding circumstances of this case reveal that the police considered Ms. Eklof to be a prime suspect in Mr. Salmu's disappearance. The police harassed Ms. Eklof's friends, family members and children to pressure her into making a confession. As in the *Burdick* case, the court must examine Ms. Eklof's physical and mental condition when she confessed to the police. Ms. Eklof was under severe mental stress and disability due to the physical and mental abuse inflicted upon her by Jeffrey Tiner. In fact, the police contributed to this situation by telling Mr. Tiner that Ms. Eklof had talked with them. The police knew Ms. Eklof would be beaten, and when she escaped from Mr. Tiner she was psychologically unstable.

Ms. Eklof never testified at Grand Jury, and instead was subjected to multiple interrogations. This is a similar situation as the *Cochran* case, where the police deceived the defendant as to whether or not an interrogation was actually taking place. The police lied to Ms. Eklof by promising that everything would be taken care of if she testified at Grand Jury. Additionally, the police told her the interrogations were necessary to prepare her for Grand Jury. When Ms. Eklof asked for an attorney, the police told her that it was unnecessary as long as she was telling the truth. All of these lies by the police created a false impression that Ms. Eklof was not being interrogated.

Ms. Eklof was subjected to multiple interrogation that lasted eight to ten hours each day for eight days in a row.

As in the *Burdick* case, the length and duration of the interrogation resulted in the defendant's free will being overborne. Although Ms. Eklof was staying at a private motel, the police were controlling her. The police paid for her room, food, transportation, provided child care, and telephone calls were being monitored. She was under close police supervision. Ms. Eklof was not free to leave.

Unlike the *Davis* case, Ms. Eklof was not only subject to psychological encouragement to confess, but also Captain Smith suggested what should be included in her confessions. Ms. Eklof, like the defendant in the *Burdick* case, was subjected to vulgar insults and psychological abuse by the police. For example, Captain Smith told her not to get too fat, otherwise the girls in prison would not like her. The police also coerced Ms. Eklof by threatening to take her children away from her and having them raised by someone else. All of this police misconduct was specifically prohibited in the *Burdick* case, and this Ms. Eklof's coerced confessions must be suppressed.

Since Ms. Eklof's initial confessions are coerced and thus involuntary, then subsequent confessions are considered to be fruit of the poisonous tree unless there has been a removal of the unlawful police conduct, *i.e.*, break in the chain of events. *State v. Mendacino*, 288 Or 231, 603 P2d 1376 (1979). In *Mendacino*, the defendant made two prior confessions that were illegally coerced. *Id.* at 238. The defendant's third confession was found to be the fruit of the poisonous tree because of the prior illegal confessions. The third confession did not involve a sufficient change in time and location to break the stream of unlawful police conduct.

A confession must also be found to be involuntary where it was induced through a direct or implied promise of immunity. *State v. Ely*, 237 Or 329, 390 P 2d 348 (1964); *State v. Capwell*, 64 Or App 710, 669 P 2d 808 (1983). In the *Capwell* case, the court held a confession was involuntarily obtained where an officer implied promised treatment as opposed to criminal prosecution if the defendant, who was not in custody, admitted to the allegations. *Id*, at 716. The court noted that it was reasonable for the defendant to have relied upon the officer's implied promise of immunity in making his confession.

Here the Springfield Police Department promised to send Ms. Eklof anywhere, and to protect her from Mr. Tiner. The police offered to get Ms. Eklof into a witness protection program if she testified at Grand Jury against Mr. Tiner. As in the *Capwell* case, the police offered immunity from prosecution which the defendant relied upon in making statements. In light of all the circumstances, it was reasonable for Ms. Eklof to rely upon the police's offer of immunity in exchange for information against Mr. Tiner. Of course, the information provided by Ms. Eklof included statements that she would not have made, but for the police's promise of immunity.

LAW OF MIRANDA

...In Oregon, *Miranda* warnings are... required under the Oregon Constitution, Article 1, Section 12, when an individual is placed in custody or in a "setting which judges would and officers should recognize to be compelling." *State v. Smith*, 310 Or 1, 7, 791 P2c 335 (1990). In Smith, the defendant made statements to the police at a voluntary treatment center which the Court found to be noncustodial setting and thus *Miranda* warnings were not required...

Unlike the situation in the Smith case, the defendant in this case, Ms. Eklof, was a prime suspect in Mr. Salmu's disappearance from the beginning of the investigation. Moreover, since Ms. Eklof arrived in Oregon from Utah in April of 1994, she was put in a custodial and compelling situation by the police. For example, Ms. Eklof was not in familiar surroundings and was under close supervision by the police. She was escorted everywhere by the police. The police persistently badgered, coerced, compelled and pressured Ms. Eklof to answer their questions by alternating promises and threats and bullying tactics. The police questioned Ms. Eklof at the police station for eight to ten hours a day for eight days.

The police tricked Ms. Eklof into believing that she was in Eugene only to testify at Grand Jury and then would be flown anywhere she desired to be protected from Mr. Tiner. Second, the police not only paid for Ms. Eklof's food and lodging, but also monitored her calls at the motel. Third, Ms. Eklof was taken to the police station daily by officers who subjected her to eight to ten days of interrogation almost always in the presence of several officers. Fourth and finally, she was under the close supervision of the police and was not free to leave the area. This is borne out by her arrest after the police had all the statements they desired...

In this case, the police advised Ms. Eklof of her *Miranda* rights in Utah. When Ms. Eklof asserted her right to an attorney, the police temporarily stopped questioning her. Rather than waiving her *Miranda* rights, Ms. Eklof demanded her right to an attorney throughout her contact with the police. It was only because the police misled Ms. Eklof into believing an attorney would be provided that she continued the interrogations. She was denied her 6th Amendment right to counsel.

CONCLUSION

In conclusion, Ms. Eklof's statements to the police must be suppressed because they were illegally coerced and thus involuntary. Moreover, Ms. Eklof's 6th Amendment rights were violated when the police either refused or ignored her request for an attorney and failed to give *Miranda* warnings when she was in a compelling setting. For all of the above reasons, Ms. Eklof's statements must be suppressed by the court.

Dated, this 3rd day of March, 1995.
Respectfully submitted,
William G. Young, OSB # 90138 Attorney for Defendant
H. Thomas Evans, OSB # 68045 Attorney for Defendant

Evans' Motion was not signed and may be preliminary. However, the

Motion produced by Karlyn's subsequent lawyer, Jeffrey Murdock, is not in her files.

State's Response to Defendant's Motion to Suppress

Filed July 14, 1995

The State of Oregon, by Frederick A. Hugi, Assistant District Attorney for Lane County, Oregon, moves the Court to deny the defendant's Motion to Suppress in its entirety.

This motion is based upon the attached affidavit and the following:

Memorandum in Opposition to the Defendant's Motion to Suppress

In response to the grounds raised by the defendant's affidavit:

1) The defendant was not in custody prior to May 6, 1994.
2) The defendant knowingly, voluntarily and intelligently agreed to speak with police officers at all times without counsel.
3) The defendant never asserted or invoked her right to counsel.

All statements made and all items seized were done with the consent of the defendant or the person whose consent was required to seize the item.

State's Response to Affidavit...

I was prepared at all times and am now prepared to give the defendant an opportunity to address the Lane County Grand Jury hearing this matter.

I was prepared to direct the defendant to the Lane County Public Defender's Office in the event she requested counsel on this matter.

No threats, psychological abuse or offers of immunity were authorized, made, or implied.

The defendant voluntarily provided all the information she gave to the police concerning this case.

Dated this 14th of July, 1995, at
Eugene, Lane County, Oregon
Frederick A. Hugi, OSB #73145

Demurrer to Aggravated Murder

Filed in February, signed copy not available, by H. Thomas Evans, stating that

1) the facts do not constitute an offense as required by ORS 135.630 (4)
2) The accusatory instrument is not definite and certain as required by ORS 135.630 (6)
3) The indictment does not contain a statement of the acts constituting the offense in such a manner as to enable a person of common understanding to know what is intended as required by ORS 132.550 (7)
4) The language contained in the counts charging aggravated murder fails to adequately put defendant on notice as to the nature and cause of the accusation against her as required by Article I, section 11 of the Oregon Constitution.
5) The statute, ORS 163.095, 163.105, 163.150, is unconstitutional under the 8th and 14th Amendments of the U. S. Constitution; Article I, Sections 16 and 20 of the Oregon Constitution.

Dated this ___ day of February, 1995
Respectfully submitted,
H. Thomas Evans, OSB #68045
Attorney for Defendant

State's Response to Discovery Request to Ensure Proportionality of Death

Penalty and Demurrer

The discover request marked States Exhibit 1, attached, was received on March 10, 1995. The State declines to provide any information for the following reasons.

I. Discovery Request

1) No case or statue requires that the State produce this information;

2) The defendant has not made and can not make the required showing that the sought after material is exculpatory and material; and,

3) The State has no better access to the requested information than does the defendant.

II. Demurrer/Motion

Defendant has provided no facts, statutes, or case law that support its position which therefore should be denied.

Dated this 13th day of March, 1995

F. Douglass Harcleroad, District Attorney

By Frederick A. Hugi, OSB #73145

Assistant District Attorney

Indictment

Filed March 24, 1995

The State of Oregon, Plaintiff

vs.

Karlyn "NMN" Eklof, Defendant

AGGRAVATED MURDER

AGGRAVATED MURDER

AGGRAVATED MURDER

AGGRAVATED FELONY MURDER

ASSAULT IN THE FIRST DEGREE

KIDNAPPING IN THE FIRST DEGREE

UNAUTHORIZED USE OF MOTOR VEHICLE

FELON IN POSSESSION OF A FIREARM

ABUSE OF CORPSE

The defendant on or about the 21st day of March, 1993, in Lane County, Oregon, acting in pursuance of a common intent with Jeffrey Dale Tiner, _____, did unlawfully and intentionally cause the death of James Michael Salmu, a human being; contrary to statute and against the peace and dignity of the State of Oregon;

Count 1) in an effort to conceal the commission of the crime of assault,

Count 2) in an effort to conceal the identity of the perpetrators of the crime of assault,

Count 3) in the course of torturing the victim

Count 4) in the course of attempting to commit kidnapping,

Count 5) did unlawfully and intentionally cause serious physical injury to James Michael Salmu, by means of a dangerous weapon, a knife;

Count 6) did... take James Michael Salmu from one place to another to cause physical injury,

Count 7) did... take, operate, exercise control over and ride in a 1965 Chevrolet motor vehicle, without the consent of the owner, James Michael Salmu;

Count 8) did... possess and have under his custody and control a .25 caliber firearm (there follows a list of Jeffrey Dale Tiner's felonies),

Count 9) did... abuse and carry away the corpse of James Michael Salmu;

Chap XVII: Jail Diaries 3/27/95

M onday, March 27, 1995

Reverend Lee came to see me. Martha told him about Mr. Evans' visit and the new charges.

When I told him I thought it was great, that I'd like to have them all, whatever it is they are going to do they should do it, he was surprised and said he was proud of me. He also explained what I already know to be true. That is, that they have no case against me and can't afford to lose this case. And because I wouldn't accept the so-called bargain, they threw in the most amount of charges they could. Well, we both agree. The DA has blown it. He should have stopped when he had the chance, etc.

I called Mr. Evans and told him to give Deb my journals. She had already been there, and he would not release them. For reasons, he says, that are important. And I'm okay with that. He said if he is replaced by another attorney, that attorney should have a look at them. And in the event he remains my attorney, he wants a head doctor, Barnhart, to look at them.

He also says that if he isn't my attorney, he will be called to testify. I said, "So what! Who cares. I told the same story to all these people. It only happened one way."

He then said, "Oh, but a little more mud for you! Remember when you put a grievance against Captain Smith with Chief DeForrest? Well, he is using a statement against you. Although he said he wouldn't do that, he is."

I said, "Well, of course he is! Anything else?"

Evans said, "Yeah, I told you to take the ten-year plea bargain."

I said, "Yeah, you did, you stupid _____!" and I hung up.

The statement being used is this: DeForrest asked, "Did you tell Cap-

tain Smith the truth?" I said, "Yes, I did, but the statements on the films are not correct. They are based on the facts but expressed the way Smith wanted them. Smith had repeatedly told me the way he thought things happened, and the more he worked with me, the more the story changed dramatically against me. He has brought out my original statements, but forced me, through his behavior that day and his threats, to add things which did not happen." Turns out they heard only the first three words I said.

Wednesday, March 29, 1995

I went to court today. I received "nine" charges, all of the charges that should be Jethro's charges. Mr. Evans spoke to me before the judge was seated. He told me Mr. Hugi was probably going to try another bargain. Oh, I thought. All bargains are off since I didn't take his plea.

So I told Mr. Evans, "You make deals with the devil, and since I'm not the devil, go straight to ___" He went and sat off with Steve Walker and Mr. Hugi. Just what I thought. They're all in this together.

The judge was real tough on the two cases that were before me. I got nervous. But to my surprise, he smiled and looked really serious at the DA. He asked about the changes in my charges and then listened to Mr. Evans. Evans stated that I had made a request for another attorney. He even went so far as to say that on several occasions I fired him, but then requested that he stay with the case.

He continued with the fact that I refused to step into visiting privately with him because I stated I am afraid of him. And then he stated that because of my attitude lately it would be difficult to work with me. And of course the judge and I were listening and watching each other.

The judge then spoke. He stated that he had known Mr. Evans for twenty-plus years, and that in requesting a new attorney I could get someone worse. He said Mr. Evans won a murder case against the judge once, and it didn't make him very happy.

The judge then asked me if I had anything to say. "Yes, Your Honor, I do. If it pleases the court, I would request a female attorney. Because of the damages that were done to me I don't feel comfortable with men, and Mr. Evans stopped the investigation which I believe was needed, an extreme investigation which I wanted in this case ripped wide open from all levels."

The judge said he would grant the female attorney. Then he asked Hugi, did he have a problem with that? Fred had to step up to the table because he had pushed his chair back against the wall. To his surprise I was about to receive all I needed.

Fred leaned on the table, tried to look at the judge, and said with his head towards the table, *"I didn't know we had to work with gender, but a... but a... well, I don't have an argument for this request."*

The judge said, *"I have warned you that it is possible to get somebody worse. But I will give to you the next available female attorney. Do you mind if we converse about a schedule outside your presence? We won't discuss your case, I assure you. Just a schedule?"* I most certainly did agree....

Today Mr. Evans was polite and respectful to me. As a matter of fact, the whole team throughout the day was incredibly respectful. It was a great day. The last thing Mr. Evans said to me was, *"Is it all right if I speak to your attorney about your case?"*

I said, *"No, it is not, but it would be excellent if you were available if she has any questions."* Good-bye, Mr. Evans!

When I got back to the dorm Lori and Martha said that I had had a visitor. I thought it was Lee, but an hour after being back I was called again to visiting. I got nervous. I thought it was the new attorney already. But it was Deb, the investigator, and she'd already been waiting for an hour. It was so good to see her.

Then that beautiful woman gave me the second best news of the day, but the most important news to me: She can confirm my damages! Praise the Lord. She and Scott have been cross-referencing my complaints and have verified them. The monies the courts gave to have them work on this case ran out two-and-a-half weeks ago, but they were so interested in the case that they have continued.

Because so much information has come in they want this case. I said, *"Mr. Evans and Smith refused to believe me. Smith said I was a liar, and Evans, well, we know what they are about!"*

She said, *"Karlyn, you are no liar, and I can prove it."* I had tears come to my eyes. *"But we have a lot of work accomplished which brings us to a barrier."* It seems the court, through my new attorney, has to request her. Well, you know that's exactly what I will request. And she said, *"We know about those people. It's all true, and if the new female attorney has another investigator in mind, I will gladly turn all my information over to her."*

Today I feel so at ease. No more those gut-wrenching disappointments and hellish fear, which I had from Evans.

Friday, March 31, 1995

A man called, an attorney named John Kolego, and said we needed to talk. He said, *"The judge didn't have a female attorney, but I have an assistant who is a mother, fifty-four years old, who will work well with you."* Oh no! Then he went on to say that he'll speak to Terri Woods and so on and so on. He brought up difficult parts of my story and pinpointed others.

Here the judge had told me nobody would be discussing my case outside my presence, and then this guy tells me all about my case, point by point, plus he tells me that Hugi, Evans, Smith, and Woods say I think they are working against me. What else.

All I said was that Evans is giving the DA everything he wants and has not prepared me a defense, but Mrs. Woods has been like a breath of fresh air and quite supportive.

Kolego said, "I noticed your hesitation."

Then I said, "I'm not trying to be difficult. I'm just scared and uncomfortable with men. And I do know I have to get over my fear if I ever expect to get any help." But this man is not it. He also told me I had no choice but to work with him.

Well I just don't think so. I told him I would wait until a woman was available. He said, "No, it doesn't work that way." We will see.

I called Deb and asked her to call the judge and Terri to find out why I can't have a female attorney. Terri was out and so was the judge. This new attorney had said he would go by Evans' office and pick up my paperwork. Oh no!

I called there and told the secretary not to give him anything. I have been so upset. I talked to my mother, who was very supportive. Tuesday there will be a hearing.

I don't like being told no woman is available when I was told by the judge he would grant me the very next woman available. Those were the conditions.

Monday, April 3, 1995

I'm still steaming about Mr. Kolego visiting me Friday. I've tried to call Terri to get the scoop, but she's not in. I'm sitting steady, waiting for tomorrow's court.

Tuesday, April 4, 1995

I went to court today. Mr. Kolego is officially my attorney. The judge spoke very highly of him and stated that he did his best to obtain a female attorney, and by no fault of his or the courts, there is no one available at this time. And to his surprise, there were only two females available for these particular charges. He also stated he preferred not to give me one who was inexperienced, so he placed my case in the most capable hands available. So we have it: Mr. Kolego is my trial attorney.

Before the judge or Mr. Kolego appeared, Fred Hugi questioned me *about Captain Smith, and I did express myself about the manner in which he manipulated my testimony that last day of videotaping. Fred sat next to Steve Walker with his foot up on the desk. Pretty cocky, I'd say: That's the same way Mr. Smith presented himself too. He was so different when he pretended to be my friend.*

Mr. Kolego said he did speak to Terri about taking the case. She was just too booked and the other woman wouldn't or couldn't take it either. So! Politics, I'm sure. But he reassured me of his compassion for my case and concern for my personal well being. He also shook my hand and looked long and straight into my eyes, with no smile. And, I felt warm, and I decided, that's okay with me. He said he would get my reports from Evans and see me this afternoon.

Well, I left the court house, and he was speaking to the DA, Walker, Lewis, and—Yates? Whose team is he on?...

I fell asleep waiting for my visit, so I called Mr. Kolego. He had been very busy with the investigator and quite encouraged to have her to work side by side with him. Praise the Lord. He'll see me tomorrow. He's viewing the films tonight. What a joy that ought to be.

I just don't know how to act. I actually have people concerned and working for me. Thank you, Lord.

Wednesday, April 5, 1995

I spoke to my lawyer today. He is rather enthused about working hard. As a matter of fact. He told me, "If it's still a matter of gender, I can get you a sweet old lady to hold your hand. Or I can give you a great defense by a dirty street fighter who will help me back you up in this. We are going up against the police department and the DA's. Right?"

I said to strong arm it. Needless to say, I am supremely impressed. Praise the Lord. Mr. Kolego also reassured me that nobody is running over the top of me anymore.

Friday, April 7, 1995

Mr. Kolego came to visit. He is pursuing this case with a strong back up. I encouraged him to succeed. I really like his power and authority, and he really pays attention. I gave him some notes to go over. He did say something about my not needing Deb, the investigator. We'll speak again on Monday. He wishes to introduce me to the partner he wants on the case...

Saturday, April 15, 1995

TJ is here. I will see him next week on Friday. I hope nobody, like the police, will be trying to talk to him. I understand that now Steve Walker is back on the case. He has been going after the boys to talk.

I talked to the shift supervisor about my visit with TJ. The supervisor said, "A contact visit, no. But perhaps an extended visit." Supervisor wanted to know why I requested the extended request when I'm allowed two visits this week just like anybody else. Well, because TJ will be on the coast with the family he is staying with on Tuesday, so I'd have only one opportunity for a visit.

My emotions are tipping a little. The last time I saw my precious son was on his birthday in 1993.

Monday, April 17, 1995
   Mr. Kolego didn't show with his partner I was supposed to meet with.

Monday, April 24, 1995
   There is an article in today's paper that describes a rape victim and her traumatic syndrome. She sees a therapist who is using a hypnotic technique, waving hand motions and eye motion to the beat of her heart.

I personally describe Mr. Smith using these same movements. But I did not know this is what it was called. When he put his elbow on his knee and waved it I thought he was going to slap me. But he didn't. He told me to lay my head back, close my eyes, and relax. He also told me just to say it, say that I stabbed him and we would be through and I could go see my children. He also told me the sooner I said it the better I would feel, and we would be through.

My cock-'n-bull story wasn't going to fly and embarrass his department and use them. The sooner I said it the sooner he'd be gone, and I could sleep easier. I told him it didn't happen that way, and he said, "Now Karlyn, you know you are not cooperating. Now let's go over it again. Just say it. Just say you stabbed him. Come on, for James' mama. Come on for James' mama!"

He said his years of experience, his logic, his perspective was the only way it happened. I told him, "But I didn't stab anybody."

He said, "Let's go over it again. You had to have. Jethro wasn't going to let you not be a part of it. Now I know the truth, don't I, Karlyn?"

I said, "No you don't. That's not the way it happened."

"We could be out of here if you'd just say it..."

I spoke to my attorney, Mr. Kolego about what a blessing he is to me. His partner is very much interested in working on this case. Jeff Murdock is his name. Mr. Kolego asked me a couple of questions, and I responded well. Like the way he has worked so hard on the case in just six days. Wow! I am really impressed.

The reason I mention that I responded well is because there's security when he speaks to me. Not like Evans and Smith. How they belittled me, humiliated me, and called me a liar. I almost lost my direction and strength because of these two stupid people, and I'm very sure Hugi has played a big part in the humiliation.

Wednesday, April 12, 1995

I've had plenty of rest all week. My attorney, Mr. John Kolego, is excellent. We spoke yesterday for a few minutes. He comforts me. He's strong in his defense for me. As I see it he will be excellent in the court room.

I spoke to TJ tonight. He is also sounding much older and missing me very much. He says he can't remember what it is like to have me around. That hurts.

Friday, April 14, 1995

Visiting took forever to get here. TJ was at the last window. I didn't recognize him. He was thinner than I expected, and he was taller. He is so beautiful and grown-up. I miss him so very much.

His eyes wandered around. He's so lost. I felt so bad, but I couldn't let him see that. I spoke cheerfully. We stood during the first few minutes. He finally slowly sat and relaxed into a great conversation. He said, "I miss your beautiful smile, Mom. I need you." I love him so much. He visited my attorney and liked him. He was nervous a little; he dropped his hat.

Sunday, April 16, 1995

I spoke to Mother, and she tells me Betty called and said Jethro is doing beautiful work in the penitentiary, painting and getting his degree. Isn't he just so clever? Then Smoky said Jethro won't let Karlyn take the charges. He just isn't that kind of guy. CRAP!

It is so sad to the writer that Jethro is able to con her own family, all because she could never tell them what he really did to her. Their anger would have put them in great danger if Jethro ever came around.

Tuesday, April 18, 1995

Today is my mother's birthday. I think about her a lot. The things she has done for me. The terrible things to watch out for. The long wait for my arrival. Life will surely be different outside of here.

I will certainly always carry the fear that somebody might take my children. I will never trust for them to simply go to school or out with friends.

Even the one officer who I trusted can't rebuild my faith and trust. Every day I see the faces of people who position themselves around me and my children to do harm, and how friendly they were in doing it. Makes me ill.

Wednesday, April 19, 1995

I spoke to Mother last night. She was depressed. Bob took off to Chula Vista. Sparky called and made threats. It was her birthday. Caroline's tutor, Julie, and all the children made Mother birthday cards. Praise the Lord.

She came home from work and it was all wet inside. Their roof leaks. She calls it a pig-in-a-poke. Nana wasn't well, so I guess everything is disgusting.

Monday, April 24, 1995

I called my attorney. He said he'd be in to see me, but nobody came. I worked dinner with Jen and Nicole and then went to the yard. Then I folded laundry, then cleaned rooms, then did sugar roll ups.

Sunday, April 30, 1995

I am giving much thought to restoring the damages which were inflicted upon me through hypnosis and subliminal programing. I am still trying to recover from a lot of areas and levels. Two of the damages which have lingered are the hardening of my ears and the aches and pains of my eyes and neck muscles. I finally connected last night what the words or thoughts were that were causing me pain and suffering. Thank God!

Once I recognized the timing of words and their connection to my pain, I could conquer their hypnotic hold on me. It is very painful to know that hurting is coming from the effects of mind control which linger on. But to say anything about it to anyone here would only sound crazy and get me in deeper than I already am for expressing the crazy things done to me and my children. And when I recognize the moment of change, and what the thoughts are which caused it, the connection quits. This thing with my ears hardening and my eyes blurring has recurred many times and has been very frustrating.

All I want to do is show some people what I went through, where it happened, and who did it to me and my children. Plus the things that were said and done. And Debbie Martin seems to be the only one who has even paid half way attention to me.

For the longest time questions were asked of me as though I were the biggest liar and my answers weren't even worth listening to. Because they'd already got it figured out by their years of experience and logic. Mr Evans is the twin to Smith as far as idiots go. If anyone ever says they are there to help you and then changes or denies your story, run!

I called home. Immanuel was sick, vomiting. He's sick too often. I asked

Mother to have him tested for AIDS. I'm concerned, even to the point of demanding that they test him. I pray, dear Lord, that you heal our baby. He's sick; that's very obvious.

Mother's fine; Bob's okay; TJ went to the Padres and Astros game; and Caroline is being lippy. Well, sounds normal.

Tuesday, May 2, 1995

Another month has slipped past me. It's May 2nd, and I had no idea it was even May. I knew it was coming. I'm having a bad day emotionally. My attorney says the psychologist wants to work with me through the summer. September? I probably won't make it. I'm driven way too far in one direction. There's nothing left. I need help. I need to be with Immanuel.

I want to be there when he is tested. The other night TJ handed him the phone, and he said, "I'm sick, Momma!"

"I know, Duder. Man, you be strong. You'll get better. Okay?" I want to be with my children. Lil' Duders hasn't lived long enough to have forgotten what all was done to him. The reality is I'm suffering so much pain that I know Duders is too. And reality sets in and says all this did happen to us. Why am I still in Lane County trying to convince people...

...I returned to the pictures of my grandparents. I thanked God for their sixty-fifth anniversary party. Although I wasn't able to attend, I understand the love and the caring and sharing of family and friends who were there. In spite of my calamities, I have a set of grandparents who have always stuck by me and provided for my children and me and a mother who has amazingly worked her life's schedule in order to support and protect my children. And there are two sets of aunts and uncles who have at different times guided me through life's rough spots.

One aunt and uncle once wrote me out a blank check to do with as I pleased. Well, I don't really regret not using it. And I will always be grateful for what they tried to do. I understand it clearly now. And, as for my other aunt and uncle, they have always made me feel welcome in their home, year after year. I know that I am from good people, the best. And that is a great comfort to me. For I know that is who I really am. No one can take that from me.

May 5, 1995

I have been here one year today...

Martha, my prayer buddy, watches over me closely. As I started to cry last night after lights out, she jumped to be next to me. I sent her away. I just needed to cry. I have a lot of disappointment and anger locked up inside of me.

I can't even believe all that has happened. And I'm real sick and tired of trying to tell my story to professional people who aren't even listening. I will never trust or take a problem to law enforcement again.

Saturday, May 6, 1995

After being in jail for a whole year with nothing accomplished, I feel I should never have come forward to get help, or to try to help solve the terrible things that happened. I remember Steve talking to me after my arrest. It was a couple of weeks later when he told me to ask the DA: "What do you want out of me?" Steve knows what Smith did, but Rick tried to act in denial, as though the captain would never do such things. But it's all too obvious.

At least I've been given a new strength I haven't had before. Well, it's no easy matter to be called upon to speak in front of a congregation of people, as happened to me recently in church. But I do have something to share. And if you don't think so, just you wait a minute and listen.

The Lord revealed himself to me and by his Grace has given me answers to ultimate problems, like: Why we are here and what his word means. So if you'll just wait a minute while I catch up with my diary, I'll tell you more about it.

Sunday, May 7, 1995

Well, all weekend long I've thought about what the attorney said about the psychologist needing all summer to evaluate me. No way...

I have been driven way too far in one direction. First it was the dreadful awareness of what Jethro was about, the control he had, my unspeakable fear, the deception he used, the careless, untrustworthy actions, the beating, the molestation of Immanuel, the entire way he structured the abuse of me and my family for his own income and profit. That final reality of other people touching my children and constantly pulling us apart sickens me.

But then there was the crap that Smith pulled, that horror and disappointment. The strength I've held onto waiting for the proper help has run out. I just want my damn release...

I went to church today. I almost didn't go. Three quarters of the way through the service the preacher said, "The Lord tells me there is a woman here, and a man, with whom he is working in order to prove his love and righteousness in their lives. Would those two people please share with others at this time the ways that God is blessing them?"

A man stood up and was vibrant in his love for the Lord and told us how the Lord revealed himself and the work he has done. Then I waited. Nobody else moved. Before I realized it, I spoke up and said, "I can testify to that!"

and went on to announce a few more things that were miracles in my life. All three of the preachers spoke in full agreement of what I said. It was brief but direct. It was the second time I had spoken out recently...

Monday, May 8, 1995
    I went to class today, and as usual was called out to visiting. Deb was there to go over the information she had found. I'm very much encouraged by her research or investigation... But in the middle of telling her about the two men I am completely afraid of she got up and pushed the call button. I don't really know what to think about that. She is busy and very thorough, so I won't worry. Perhaps we're all just trying to avoid emotions.

    I called my mom, and she's having trouble with TJ. It seems Sparky has been going to TJ's school everyday, and now TJ can't or won't get along with Mother. He said he wants to go live with his dad. What line of crap is Sparky feeding my son? Won't people please leave my family alone. Please, God! What more? I can't take any more. No more! No more! No more! I've had enough. I'm raw and bleeding...

    Something else about today: When Deb cut me off, I remember when Jeff, the assistant attorney, said that police are allowed to do overtime, but that attorneys are only allowed a certain amount of time and that's it...

    I spoke to TJ. I blew it. I called him a stupid _____and laid into him about Sparky. But I told him it was okay to get rides home. But I'm scared that while he is walking home somebody might try to grab him. We talked through the better part of three sets of calls, one-half hour each.

    We discussed everything. Then he realized that the same man who had called him and Steve liars before the Grand Jury was Smith, who had caused great harm to my case. He also said, "And why did they tell us we would be protected and flown anywhere we wanted to go if we would just help them solve the case?" I'm glad he still remembers.

Wednesday, May 10, 1995
    Last night as I was ready to fall asleep I got that recurring pain that hardens my ears, blurs my vision, and gets me confused and depressed. Ever since Jethro and those people got ahold of me and the children, I've had a lot of pain. Sometimes I've noticed that when certain words are said I have a reaction. So I've tried to monitor myself and find the subliminals that are causing my problem.

    When I first left San Diego I could hardly read. My focus and concentration were gone. My drive to find help was desperate. So I trusted the few people I was in the most trouble with, the police. But in my state of mind I felt that with them I'd be safe and not out bouncing around to the whim and fancy of every subliminal predator. But it turned out to be my greatest mistake. I was attacked from all sides.

*Two years have gone by and I still can't recover. Some days it's about to drive me crazy. It's a real disadvantage when I am the object of inquiry with people who are actually trying to confuse me. **Sometimes I am experiencing fear and being out-of-focus when simply visiting with people.** Simple questions leave me dumbfounded. I know that whoever is sitting before me probably thinks I'm lying, and in this case that's not good. I try so hard not to get humiliated and to force myself out of the confusion.*

But the visits are short. I wish these people knew what I was going through. If I had help I could be so strong. I almost feel retarded at times. I feel I am withdrawing from frustration and depression. It's like a wall has been built around me, and I have to find the key words to get rid of it. Unfortunately it's a long process, on my own, brick by brick, trying to remove the subliminals. If this stuff were used the right way, it could be a powerful tool to build a better world. But it is dangerous!

Tuesday, May 16, 1995

Today, again, my head is just screaming. Sometimes I see everything before my eyes, and I know how hard I have tried to get help. I can't believe Captain Smith's ego is so large that he won't apologize for his wrongdoing, correct his mistakes, and get on with a solution. Likewise, I hope Jethro will tell what really happened and also admit to touching Immanuel. But that hasn't happened either.

I had a dream. I saw Jethro. We were in a classroom-like building and he was being very gentle and nice to me. I acted as though I didn't remember anything, so the closer he tried to get to me I would move away to try to find an outside door. Another couple was in my dream. They were watching and waiting to see whether he would talk about anything. I wasn't strong enough to hide my fear and confusion, so about then he wasn't nice and young looking anymore. His nostrils flared. And the couple got me out of there.

When I think how I trusted him, I remember how perfectly nice and gentle and normal acting he can be, especially after he's done something horrible—cool and innocent as a cucumber. First it's a real eerie feeling to be that unaware of a person's activities, but then it is worse to be afraid to react ...

Debi came to see me tonight. We talked about her birthday. And about TJ and his friend, Steve. It seems Steve's mom isn't taking care of him. Sounds a bit familiar, since I took care of him for seven months.

I also spoke to Mother and TJ. I don't feel right. Mother is going to talk to TJ's principal. It should be me. And I spoke to Nana. She sounds great. Bumpa isn't doing so well...

Friday, May 19, 1995

Well, it's been an average day: court calls, meals served, count, girls frustrated by their incarceration, driving me to the point of wanting to care less, instead of speaking to them encouragingly and focusing them.

Deputy T. tells me a detective spoke to her and said, "Gee, Karlyn has spoken to a lot of people." I thought at first I did something wrong, cuz before trial somebody is always telling you don't talk to anybody. But in my case if I hadn't talked, I'd never have got the concern of others working for me. And that means help.

Nicole and I did laundry. She said, "You have impressed a lot of people. You are doing a great job." Wow!...

Monday, May 22, 1995

I think I've asked every way I can for counseling. Rosi has gone to the phone to call Women Space. I need help. More than a counselor can give, but it would be a start.

I called the children. Everybody sounds so far away. Caroline and I sang songs. Duders and I counted numbers.

I am trying so hard to settle in and prepare for the questions that will come with this trial. I've tried so hard to give all I could and to bring an awareness to everything that happened. However, I can't escape a cornered feeling, and I feel left out now that things are rolling. I feel that the people who did all the damage, and especially the ones who touched me and my children, will never be investigated and brought to trial...

The two attorneys I have now will either make or break me as far as my faith in men and people in general are from now on. I fervently wish that they will fight for me, bring forward the truth, and that everybody, the DA included, will address the reality of this situation...

Well, Debi, the investigator, was here at 8:20 this morning. Seems she's been in trial and was very tired. She focused on her hair a lot of the fifteen minutes we somewhat talked. I gave her direction. She said, "Oh, we'll cover that later in the mechanics of the case." I tried to tell her I was mentally blocked and struggling to understand. She said, "Oh, just try to remember or come up with anything that might help...."

I do trust that everything will go well, but the days are passing, and the steps taken are long and empty ones.

Chap XVIII: Jail Diaries 5/26/95

Friday, May 26, 1995

Martha woke up today and just fell apart. She hates this place. I know, but what drives her nuts are all those things that happened to her that she could not control. The heroin addict in here who doesn't even get time, and yet Martha is charged with a crime she didn't do. People who are users just come and go, and we just watch them. Here they are the support structure for the drug problem, but they are given only small fines, short sentences—if any— and alternative programs.

Sunday, May 28, 1995

I didn't go to church this Sunday. I'm just not interested in all that's going on around here. I spoke to Mother, Caroline, and Immanuel. They sound great, and Mother finally did get the roof fixed. A dear old friend of mine, Jim, from the Lakeside Hotel, helped her. Thank you, Lord. You know, I asked for the leaky roof to be fixed, and it was. Thank you! Duders talked real clear. TJ was at Uncle Al's.

Tuesday, June 6, 1995

Debra, the investigator, came today. She is preparing the case nicely. She always looks great, although last time she seemed to be distracted from resolving her other cases. Just tired, perhaps. I can't complain because she always lifts me up, and she is doing all that I could possibly ask for.

Today's visit was quite comforting. She'll look into the matter of a girl *who was running her mouth to Pam in booking about my case and about Al Hope. She sent Johnny Bowman's attorneys my information. She also told me it was good to see me smile... I love my present defense team. I know they'll do great...*

Oh, also Debi is going to talk with Elaine from Woman Space. And she wants my journals. What a blessing. My experiences must be made known to others. She also guarantees to me that they aren't forgetting me. Yes, I know that. It is obvious, and I can feel the difference.

Sunday, June 12, 1995

There has been a lot of news in the paper this week about the Colombian Cartel and the Miami sting operation. That is what reeled Martha in and over our way...

TJ spoke about how Jethro acted, charming, but then bragged about how many girls he did. TJ lost respect, which was never really there with TJ. But he emphasized tonight on the phone how Jethro would be gentle-speaking, and then speak trash! I never knew he ever spoke to TJ any way but respectfully. But then TJ mentioned this to me briefly once before. He knows me. I would never be able to tolerate anybody foul-mouthing around my children. My precious children and I have been through too much.

Monday, June 12, 1995

I stayed in my bunk until 1:30 P. M. Just as I got out of the shower, my investigator, Debi, was here. She looks great, sounds eager, and I signed a release slip for the information from the shelters. I turned over to her a brief of the events I wrote about in Journals 1 through 10.... [The ones that will never be returned]

Tuesday, June 13, 1995

A tour came through here again today. And I spoke to Kolego. I certainly didn't expect to go into a full conversation. But he has his work cut out for him, and I do appreciate that. He is very concerned. I've lived with this mess every day, with constant reminders. He even offered to put $20 on my books. Now that's neat, really neat!

Thursday, June 15, 1995

At 10 A. M. this morning Dr. Barnhart was here to evaluate me. He also took a moment out to encourage me to be watchful of the company I keep. What was encouraging was—because I have tried so hard and given so much effort to monitoring and restoring myself—he said, "You have achieved about seventeen levels of progress." Wow, I took that as a verifiable level. We did various tests: a counting, a color, a shape, a word and a story test.

Friday, June 16, 1995
I didn't receive the $20 Mr. Kolego said he'd put on my books. Today was commissary. Perhaps next week?

Saturday, June 17, 1995
I spoke to the children. All is well. Mother is taking them to Disneyland. Willy is going with them, Debi's son.

Sunday, Father's Day, June 18, 1995
I spoke to my grandfather and Nana. They're doing fine. Mother had the children there.

Wednesday, June 22, 1995
Sister Marguerite paid postage for me on a card from Bobbi, a lady who cares. I saw Debi, the investigator. She is working through my case quite well. She was ill for a couple of days and is back on track. She'll visit with my attorney and co-counsel, Jeff, on Friday. I believe all is well.

One thing I've noticed. My feelings and depth of pain have hardened. Tears come, but I don't cry. I don't know if that is good or bad. My overall stay here has been quite smooth and some of it even kind of fun.

Thursday, June 23, 1995
This morning promises to be a beautiful day. I received my kite back from medical. I requested advice about my neck. It's tired of holding itself up. My neck muscles hurt...

Yesterday, when Debi, the investigator, was here, she said fall would be a great time for a trial, not summer. Well, I hate hearing that. I want my trial to be over. I also want Smith's resignation. Martha reminded me that he's going for governor. Oh! No!

Fred has been hard on me, so several people have said. He has been hard on me because of the Diane Downe's case. He doesn't trust women. And so perhaps he might as well understand I don't trust men...

I spoke to my attorney, John. He's ready to kick butt. He spoke to Fred, who insists on a conviction. But, what is interesting is that he says I instigated the argument. Did I? So, what is really on his mind?

Saturday, June 24, 1995

I have stayed on my bunk all day. I called to my Nana's and Caroline is recovering from chicken pox. My blessed Aunt Omie and Fran brought an ointment over for Caroline, a clear ointment. I'm so very thankful because if she flashes on the white ointment as I have I'm not sure what her reaction might be. I'm still feeling very low and show much disappointment. The girls are very caring.

Monday, June 26, 1995

This week started out with Deputy Jean waking me up to go to court. Very unexpected, so I hurried into my clothes, a white skirt and blouse that had been in property for two-and-a-half months.

I waited in a dark lonely cell that slammed shut, hard iron, for an hour. Then I was called into court for motions to suppress. Officers Walker and Lewis, Smith and DA Hugi took the stand. My attorneys Kolego and Murdock were excellent. Issues were brought out on their tactics of interrogation. Hugi took the stand, mentioning the open invitation for Grand Jury to testify against Jethro. All said, his actions are proof this case was abused and misused, plus other things not here to mention. He was also drawing large letters on a pad: YOUR FRIEND!

This trial has started out with motive manipulation. But very interesting, Smith took the stand before Hugi. He greeted me with a "Hi" and a nod. Then he took a few minutes to cover his credentials which were impressive, but also showed his education in manipulation.

I was impressed by the thoroughness of my attorney. And also temporarily amazed that each of the detectives lied, out-and-out lied. Lewis was clever. He just left out parts of his original statements. Also Kolego called Hugi slippery. Everybody laughed.

Wednesday June 28, 1995.

On Tuesday Martha received forty-eight months.

Today Lee came to see us. Martha was too exhausted to get up. He explained what happened to me. The courts closed Martha's sentencing unannounced. They set her up. The DA came out of the hearing like the cat that ate the canary.

Her attorney spoke with Lee and said she received seventy months, not forty-eight. What the hay? More deception. I've asked Martha to get her paperwork, and get proof of what they gave her. Julie came to see Martha. I hope she can encourage her.

Thursday, June 29, 1995

Debi, the investigator, came. I had to sign releases for information. She received from me my writings, books 11, 12, 13, 14, 15, 16, 17 and 18...

Deputy Toni was left a note not to work Martha because she is a federal inmate...

Tuesday, July 4, 1995

I was told, don't talk to anybody about my case. Well, if I hadn't, I'd be sitting in a penitentiary for ten years. I want everybody to know what's going on. Perhaps not every case should be exposed the way I went about this one, but I was literally left without any other direction. My problems were being covered up and not solved.

Still, after fourteen months of incarceration, we have not received proper counseling or inquiry into the events which occurred. I am painfully aware the wrong people were involved from the beginning of this case. I have fought hard to get help. I have had nothing to hide. I gave up all that I could, and that has helped me endure the hoops I have had to jump through. I hope my case will bring a change to the justice system.

Thursday, July 6, 1995

I had a very interesting visit with Lee. It seems Martha's case was a completely unauthorized misuse of the system. Somebody out of D.C. has actually stepped in to reprimand the corrupt misuse of official authority and funds—vehicles, entertainment, phones, restaurants, airfare, and time—all unauthorized. There were people there who disregarded a direct order to lead her out of the country with a warning and instead spent $1,000,000 building a false case while they were enjoying themselves. Too much monkey business...

I received a visit from Mike, an investigator who was sent by my attorneys. He has simply amazed me. He openly expresses Francis's apology and concern. He says her daughter, Brenda, said before Francis died she told people she knew I didn't hurt James. She was the one who in the beginning turned against me, accusing me of being a black belt murdering biker bitch.

Well, those words have rung in my ears with the witch hunt she put officers and James' family on. I thought I would never survive it. Until now, the sweet words of "She didn't hurt James" coming from the only other female friend from that night bring solace words can't express...

Sunday, July 9, 1995

I spoke to my children. Duders has the chicken pox all over his body, from the tip of his nose to his precious little toes. Mother says Betty called and said Willy got killed on his motorcycle. I am truly sorry to hear that. Willy helped me. He gave me the station wagon that helped me to get away from Jethro, and Will is also the one who found me when I turned up so brutally beaten and got people together to find out who did it. Well, William Beard, I am one who will always remember you. Thank you.

Caroline is very excited. Her seventh birthday is in ten days. She says I'll be home after her birthday. I hope so.

Saturday July 22, 1995

I spoke to the children at Nana's. Caroline's birthday was celebrated at the beach with them. TJ stayed home with Sparky and a friends of TJ's.

I spoke to Nana and she has prepared a birthday party for Caroline on Saturday. Caroline writes letters to her daddy Carl. Our lives are so empty and lost, out of balance and abused. I almost wish I could die from all the anguish that my family has to endure. I know what happened to James isn't right, so I have done all I can do to get this resolved. But for crying out loud, why did I ever come forward? Oh yeah, it was the right thing to do. And I came in order to be a part of something very important...

Kim Wolfe spoke about a tattoo she received at a shop in 1986 called Spider's Tattoo Shop. She also claims that she blacked out for some time. She feels a drug was used on her. Also, Spider was running with a Gardener family that is well-known for child pornography, a reality and truth I can't deny...

I called home today to wish my daughter a happy birthday, and Sparky answered the phone. Said he was depressed and missed his son. He went on about some other stuff, making half-assed statements. When I finally said, "What are you getting at?"

He says. "You want me up there at your trial or not?"

"Well," I say, "Where do you come from, asking me? It's my attorney that needs to evaluate that." So I ask again what's wrong, and then he slanders Mother and Nana for a while.

I say, "Okay, get to the point."

He tells me, "Oh, I gave your attorney a big speech on all you've done." Oh really, etc., etc. Well, my attorney told him to change his bad attitude. He says, "Yeah, I'm bad, and you know it."

He does all he can to rule my Mom and manipulate the children. He hurts me year in and year out. My mind calculates all the damages he has caused in my life, and the anger starts to boil. But the facts are, all I want is the best for him at making a life for himself. I wish he and I could get along.

Monday, July 24, 1995

I spoke to Nana last night. She sounded wonderful. Mom and the chil-

dren had just left. When they got home I spoke to Mom, and she says Scott, the investigator, was told to back off his investigation on Jethro. Then he has asked for the copy of that awful tape Smith had so much fun making with me. I told her not to pass it to him. Who knows who will see it. I'm a little bit sensitive about it. I made a damn fool of myself. Anyway, perhaps this means help is working...

The Pretrial Proceedings of August 2, 1995 are given at the beginning of the next chapter along with Karlyn's comments. Karlyn was not present.

Tuesday, August 1, 1995

Well, transport was today. Tomorrow is court again, Motion to Suppress.

My investigator came. She's real impressed with my behavior and so are the attorneys. I think we all agree it's gonna be a wonderful trial, and a lot will be accomplished, no thanks to Smith or Evans. Goofs!

Wednesday, August 2, 1995

I went to the court booking office. They were going to take me in greens. Oh, no! I will dress. And that set us back a moment or two. This place and the courts are a racket. It takes a full two minutes to go from here to the courthouse, since we go from the van to the courtroom, wasting no time. Everybody was waiting.

Bill Kennedy and Chief DeForrest were the two officers left to testify. Hugi spoke from some notes. He was clever. The way these guys warp their statements to give false impressions is amazing. Innocent people actually go to prison by these tactics.

August 3, 1995 Thursday

Yesterday the judge denied my Motion to Suppress, based on the premise that my statements were voluntary. He prefers to deny the fact I had no choice in my struggle to go forward while Smith was threatening me about not seeing my children. As much as I wanted to help resolve this case, I have a major complaint against the tactics of Jerry Smith. I have said that his interrogation was unduly coercive, while the DA says, "Yes, that's probably true. He's not as patient as Walker and Lewis." So?

The judge also says I act like a lady and am strong-willed. He can't believe anyone would bully me or pressure me. Little does he know. Yes, I have been bullied and abused. I was before and after, but I'm not now. And I'm not making it easy for them.

*The judge said yesterday he believes the only reason I spoke up to offic-
ers was because a person was missing and I needed to lessen my involvement.
Won't he be a slight bit surprised when he gets the full details?*

Response to Public Record

Order Denying Defendant's Motion to Suppress

August 8, 1995 Re: videotapes and transcripts and reports of the defendant's statements.

"This matter came before the court on the defendant's Motion to Suppress the defendant's
statements. The State filed a written response. Hearing was held on Tuesday, July 25, 1995 and
concluded on Wednesday August 2, 1995. The defendant appeared personally and by John Kolego
and Jeff Murdock..."

The defendant's motion is DENIED.

Wednesday, August 9, 1995

*I finally spoke to Nana and Bumpa and wished him a Happy Birthday.
He sounded great. Sparky is supposed to be going to Diane's. Thank you,
Lord.*

Monday, August 14, 1995

*Sparky left Mom's to go to Diane's in San Francisco. Mickey Mantel
died, a baseball hero. I've been trying my hand at shorthand writing. I miss
my children.*

*I want my Carl back. I usually keep that to myself. I'm just not sure who
I am to him or if I will ever see him again. But I do hope so, because I think
about him a lot. For a long time I have hidden my feelings, but they show too
well to those who know how empty and shattered my life has been without his
physical presence. I needed him so much just to be close, and I loved him more
than I could ever show. My head aches with the pain of hidden emotions,
longing for his presence. He is so truly missed. Memories of him are so dear.
I did love him so much.*

Tuesday, August 15, 1995

*My attorney, Jeff, came and says a letter was sent by them to Jethro but
was returned as "refused" mail. He is also up for parole, October of next
year.*

*Fred Hugi admits during the Motions to Suppress he was wrong and so
was the judge on a call. A lot of good that does me. Fred also says that he can
indict Jethro any time so not to worry. Jethro won't be released. **Fred also
admits he wishes Smith hadn't had anything to do with this case.** The attorneys are already preparing for the Court of Appeals. I'm sure my attorneys*

are the best, but I do not like any of this.

I am thinking that a "prison experience" should be a time of personal development. It is a time for learning to use time wisely and for seeking out one's self esteem and efficiency through love. Life is an echo. You get back what you put into it. Therefore, don't let things happen. Make them happen. Turn away from criticism or resentment. Bring forward lovely things, like kindness, sympathy, forbearance, a winsome attitude, love, and a noble heart, righteous and pure.

Friday, August 18, 1995

I called my attorney. John is real alert, and he is generally aware of my status, which nobody else seems to want to give me a clue to. Anyway, Fred, the DA, is on vacation in Maine.

*He also **reestablished an investigation on Spider**. I am totally pleased. John says he's going to put $20 on my books again, and that's neat.*

I got a visit. Debbie came to see me. She looks great, tired, but great. She bought a house next to the Canadian border. Praise the Lord.

One wonders why Kolego wasn't able to discover that there was a leniency deal going on between Spider's attorney and Hugi. This came to light in this writer's discoveries.

Sunday, August 20, 1995

I spoke to Mother tonight. She sounded great. They just returned from camping. She said the children were angels. But she was tired and wants a break. She's pissed at Fred [Hugi] for lying to her. He said to her he was my friend and hers too. Now I'm finding out the DA's office is telling people I'm in protective custody. Nope, I don't think so. I may have been for a year, until they charged me.

You know, these pinheads, these goofs, couldn't protect a jug of fleas sealed in a cooler.

Fred says he was sorry Smith ever had anything to do with this case. Yeah, when? I'm not sorry. He's the greatest example of what a professional with too much time to play can do when left unsupervised. I've gone through being a victim of a very professional crime ring, to a police hit team, and now to a dorm full of mischievous women. And as much as I long to go home, I'm scared to allow the child or mother in me to get too close. I'm too emotionally suppressed. Real true love and affection could bring me to an emotional breakddown.

Tuesday, August 22, 1995

Deb, the investigator, came in to see me. She looked wonderful as usual, wore a beautiful amethyst, rich purple, as well as her wardrobe, purple. She looked great.

I spoke to her about a problem I had. The last few times Deputy Tammy M. came in the dorm she was extremely rude. She ignored me, glared, and kept walking. I responded with, "Hey! Not even a hello?"

Then she said, "Oh I didn't see you." She used to make a point of coming straight in to see me. But as of three weeks ago she's not even nice. One morning she stabbed me with her keys and asked me if I wanted to work. I was terrified and gasped for air. I almost wet myself. I did get up to work. Last week she did it again, and I gasped for air. I don't deserve that...

Well, what's going on? For the longest time Tammy spoke very highly of me, but three weeks ago, poof!

But then Tammy said, "Keep my husband out of all this." Out of what? ...He works for Captain Smith. I truly believe he has put Tammy in a very awkward position. Probably by showing his wonderful art work of videos.

Wednesday, August 23, 1995

Every once in a while there's a smell that shoots out of the vents. I get a headache...

This week Mary and I went to booking to collect garbage. Yes, bags of garbage. Deputy Anna Marie walked us through. The holding cells were overpacked, men in some, and women in others, lying on the floor and benches. It looked like they had been there for a day or so—no shower, no blankets, no food, overcrowding. The system needs to adjust for future growth.

Wednesday, August 30, 1995

I went to medical. My headache just won't go away. My temperature is 101.5. Karen, the nurse, says in all her years of working here I'm the only one she has ever seen not asking for medical help. I just lie up on my bunk and try to fight it on my own. She gave me a white pill yesterday. I took two today. They were pink.

Dr. Alcott saw me today. He went over the past symptoms I was having. I was feeling better, but sore-eyed and exhausted with a slight headache. I feel it is an inner ear infection trying to surface. Before I left Utah I had an awful night with one. The doctor said to take Ibuprophen and ice if I had any further pain. The ice works. Now I'm fine. I worked dinner and folded laundry. I felt a little clammy and light-headed.

Tuesday, September 5, 1995

I felt much better yesterday. I just laid around. I tried calling Jeff Murdock, my attorney, today. He was out to lunch. His secretary gave me words of confidence and fellowship. She said our papers are together and that I had a lot of people working in my corner. What a comfort and blessing.

An hour later I called and spoke to Jeff. He ran down the structure of court witnesses and agenda. One point I'd like to make is that no one can describe the fear I've been through. I'm still not stable... He... is preparing for court tomorrow. I feel weak. Martha braided a ring on top of my head.

Wednesday, September 6, 1995

At ten-ish, I went to the court where there were just the judge and the DA attorney's clerk. They discussed my attire and made arrangements for the jail to receive the dresses I had when I was at the motel with the children when I came here to testify. So the attorneys received my clothes and sent them to the cleaners.

There was a Pretrial Hearing on September 6, 1995 which, apparently, Karlyn was not requested to attend. Her comments on the transcript appear at the beginning of the next chapter.

Thursday, September 7, 1995

Eighty people came into the courtroom for jury picking. Very interesting. Each person was called into the jury setting. Twelve of them were given an extensive questionnaire to provide information on their background and their opinion on the death penalty. Wow, some responses were quite strong pro and con.

Most people are concerned with the leniency of the law after incarceration, primarily why people sentenced to do twenty years get out in five. Judges reply that it is due to overcrowding. He said that every time he has to sentence somebody he has to think real hard who will they let out to receive this one in. He stated that people, "citizens," just aren't willing to foot the bill for a new prison.

So next is the challenge, that's what the DA and the attorneys call a jury pick. The strategy is to get people with an open mind. Interesting how people react when questioned about their responses in the questionnaire. Some don't even know what they wrote.

Friday, September 8, 1995

So, after a day and a half, my jury consists of a church elder, a security guard, a cattleman, a housewife, a Radio Shack employee, among others. Just various persons who truly don't want to make decisions but have an open mind. The judge completed, with such grace, the jury picking in express time. He's pleased. I'm okay with it. I did not receive my dress yet.

Monday, September 11, 1995

My attorney brought a skirt and blouse from those I brought from Salt Lake. It's too small. Is anything going to be in its place. I expect a great outcome and won't expect anything less. Well, tomorrow is the trial...

This is Monday, the day Jethro has been brought here from Nevada to be asked one question: Will he testify? I called my attorney, Murdock, to find out what happened.

Jethro said, "No." Took the Fifth. I'm a little pissed he didn't just confess and get this over with. So now he's been flown back to Nevada.

The girls and I feel that the honcho's wouldn't let Jethro or advised him not to talk because they don't want to admit what they've done to me. So I'm sure it was just fine for them that he didn't. I'm limited in my knowledge of what is truly happening, but I'm not slow to the obvious either. Politics, stupid, politics! If I had been out while preparing for my trial, my attorneys and I could have communicated. But as it is, I lack a court strategy.

I called Debs and spoke to Willie. He and Steve Chase were there. Steve got on the phone and said, "We gotta talk." He was scared of Jethro, and the police told him not to talk to me. I told him I was scared too, but I was strong and I could take Jethro down even though the police are charging me.

He and Willie are also supportive of me, and since he has to testify, I told him not to worry. Just tell the truth. It's the only way to get through this. He said he lied at first, but tried to express afterwards what he could remember. I told him that was fine, but also remember the police are trying to project their opinion of what happened onto him and not to let them twist his words. I also told him he can't be wrong or right in his statements because he wasn't there when it happened, and everything would be all right.

Then he said he'd wanted to talk to me for some time, but they told him not to. Well, I reminded him they cannot do that, and that I cared very much about him, not to worry, just tell the truth. Then we talked for a minute about the weekend when he was ill and his mother's friend gathered up the boys, thirteen of them, and planned an overnighter. Well, then plans fell through and everybody ended up at my little apartment for three days. I had wall-to-wall boys.

After our talk, I felt he sounded relieved and could face this trial more easily. I told him no matter what happens not to worry. I was strong and I could do this.

When Deb came to see me Friday she said Steve Walker came by wanting some pictures of me and wanted to know if TJ had talked to Willie. Deb felt insulted that the police were so driven and lacked compassion for the children.

Today is Caroline's first day at school in the second grade. I spoke to Mother and the children through three calls. The phone hangs up after each half hour. Caroline jabber-jaw wastes no time talking. She tells it all. She is so beautiful, so precious, and so brilliant. Immanuel David, mumbled gibberish, and TJ is a nervous wreck. He mentioned a couple of strange things, stuff like what happened to me and the two little ones at my apartment. And just by him mentioning it, my heart, mind, body and soul went into a frenzy.

I told him to focus on Jesus and let him handle the spirituality, but also to be aware of those people who had less than their own life to live and were bothersome to others. But now I know my family is still being effected by that circle of people.

Chap XIX: Trial Diary
8/12/95

K arlyn was not privy to the following Pretrial Proceeding. There
fore, there is no mention of it in her diaries. Her comments are
from a much later date.

Pretrial Proceeding, July 25, 1995

In the opening statement Smith claimed Karlyn became a suspect. This was Kolego's
argument: Well, if so, why after several collect calls was she lead to believe she had friends and a
support group?...

Smith stated that she first called in April of 1993 "as a result of us trying to locate her." *I
paid dearly for violating Jethro's security. I asked detectives to please come down and help me.
They also told Jethro, at his parole officer's, that I was cooperating with them. Walker and Lewis
did finally show up six weeks later. I was broken and bruised. Lewis' first statement was that this
was the soonest we could get cleared to come...*

Smith stated that until April 29th Karlyn's only contact was with Walker and other officers. *When I arrived on the plane and saw just the two of them I said, "What, no attorney?" Walker
said everything had been arranged...*

Smith claimed she did sound bizarre and irrational at times but regained her stability.
*Smith was running me on a roller coaster of pushing buttons: Who's gonna raise your children?
Just tell us the truth. Send another officer in to sit with her. She's full of hot air. Let's go over it
again....*

Kolego picked up on the misconduct, maliciousness, playing with the *Miranda* rules, and
that the attorney requirement was, quote, "Just a rule we have to play by," end quote. Then,
immediately after that, "Why? Did you misinterpret that?" end quote. *This is what they did to me!
They wouldn't allow me to protest...*

Kolego laid it out to Smith that she was led to believe that she was a witness, even after
explaining about the knife and the carpet, and that she had nothing to worry about. *Plane tickets
were bought, an attorney would be provided, and a hotel and meals, everything on a first name
basis...*

Smith claimed she couldn't prove her injuries. No police report. *Well, Walker and Lewis
saw me. Try fear, Smith, fear will freeze anybody from doing what's best...*

Walker stated that I was comfortable being on their team. He was asked if that implied immunity. He denied this. Not being treated like a suspect, was she part of the prosecution team at that point? Steve said there was no implied immunity there.

Rick Lewis stated that his visit with Karlyn, while Walker was talking to Tommy, was extremely limited... less than a half-hour. *Rick lies, we spoke nothing like a half-hour, and he doesn't mention that I was brutally beaten. But they did come back the next day...*

Rick said he read Karlyn her rights. *Well, if you could call it that, playing word games. They had no authority to arrest me... so how could they do that?...*

Rick said he believed she understood that his job was to obtain information for the homicide, not necessarily what was in her best legal interest. *Not exactly, Rick, you guys played a game.*

****

Karlyn was present on August 2, 1995, for the following Pretrial Proceeding. She mentions it in her diary, but her comments here are of a much later date.

Pretrial Proceeding, August 2, 1995

Bill Kennedy... claimed Karlyn agreed to the poly without threat... *well, I didn't have any options nor did Steve tell me where he was taking me until we were in the underground parking lot, as if, now if you refuse you'll be under arrest...*

He is questioned whether Karlyn ever waived her rights to an attorney before the polygraph examination. He said, "No, I cannot say that she was wanting to talk to me under any circumstances. I can't say that." *Right. I wasn't asked...*

Bill DeForrest's testimony on her misconduct report against Smith for sexual remarks and manipulation of himself. *The day afterward, I met with Bill and Evans the attorney and was given all nine charges for Jethro's crimes....*

Kolego and Smith recited pages of conversations where Karlyn asked continually for an attorney. Smith agreed to one, to flying her out, and that a waiver of her rights was never signed, *which would be necessary for poisonous tree, free will of choice...*

Hugi said Karlyn should have just shut up. *How's that when officers are alternating and pushing me up a roller coaster and back down. So now it's my fault. The detectives are caught playing with the case, cat and mouse. I continued to cooperate as I was told to do...*

Hugi claimed she knew how to refuse to answer about Laughlin, NV. *Hugi is vindictive.* He said they didn't even have a body or evidence. Soon as they found out about the carpet and linoleum they put things together the best they could. Karlyn supposedly hung herself when she hung around these people... *prejudgment, bullying...*

Hugi claimed police were nothing but nice, and that Karlyn just made the calls as a pest. *They were bearing down like vultures. That's why plenty of people were aware that Spfd. P. D. wanted Karlyn for murder. Gosh, Hugi, lie some more.* The police gave designated days to call. *My concern was what would happen if I didn't call...* Hugi said she agreed to do the video. Nobody was overbearing. *Yeah, Smith's threats aren't on film, how clever...*

Kolego referred to her March 21, 1994 request to Smith that she have an attorney present. The Court responded that it was a "musing" on her part. *What about the arguments they gave me every time I asked?*

September 12, 1995, Tuesday

Trial, first day. I rose early, ate breakfast, and did my day room chores with the assistance of Rosie and Tracy. I curled my hair the night before. As I tried to lie here and meditate, the girls were giggly and rude. Rosie blared the TV. Please, girl, not until 9:00 A. M. I couldn't sit, so I started fussing with my hair. I cried out of frustration, as I watched those curls straighten right out. Sheri, Mary, and then Martha came. What happened? Sheri combed it up. That wasn't it. I took it out. Martha braided some of it. Mary was comforting and trying to focus me.

The deputy made the first call for court, then the final. Well, I gotta go. We walked in to booking. As we passed the fish tank, several men were there dressed in white overalls. Sherri's husband was one of them, going to the penitentiary for forty-eight months. Sherri burst into tears. I had to tell her to control herself. The deputies would shackle her, and I didn't want to be seen shackled.

The deputy on duty to dress us was Vikki. She and the sergeant told me my dress was delivered, but not to this department. Then they handed me the one freshly cleaned but too small. So I dressed in the outfit I had had here for sixteen months. No good! I cried, "Deputy, I waited 16 months for this day!" They just said, "Seven minutes to departure."

Sherri and I both were crying. Then she grabbed me and hugged me, and I looked in the mirror. My hair flowed naturally. I wanted it up. My dress had locker-room odor and was wrinkled. I looked awful.

About that time Deputy Vikki and the Sergeant opened the door and handed me my beautiful turquoise button-up dress. I was so surprised. I thanked them over and over again. Time to go. Handcuffs were applied to us and into a van we went...

Sherri went to court. Then I was called. An officer recuffed me. Oh, also the belt to my dress was cleared to be worn, but I never did receive it. My counsel and Reverend Lee were there in the court room, and Debi, who had been subpoenaed. The jurors and judge came in, and the opening statements were given.

Fred greatly unnerved me. I wasn't expecting what was about to unfold. He painted the most ungodly grotesque details of James' murder and portrayed me to be a murdering black-belt biker bitch from hell. By the time two hours had gone by he had twisted and repeated and reconnected damaging statements into the utmost and ugliest form. I wanted to execute or convict the person he described. But it was me! Now, wait a minute! The jury was furious, legs crossed, arms folded, jaws tight.

He also presented seven bulletin boards that described Jethro; one column, James; and another column, me. Oh, it wasn't pretty. Then the judge called lunch.

Fred's opening statements referred to all my statements, and did he have a heyday! One thing touched me. He told jurors I didn't cut the fingers of James' hand off. But he told how I shared every bit ... of Jethro's charges.... He described me as coldly and ... a black-hearted person who could be capable of enjoying such activities. I can't say these words

That's not me at all. I couldn't believe it! Next is my attorney, Jeffrey Murdock. He did agree to the event as if it were proof—a murder with me at the scene. Troubled and in such horror, with Jethro as the sole perpetrator. His speech was a relief to the jurors, and they relaxed and unfolded. I felt relieved finally and uplifted. For the first time I was actually defended and recognized as a victim also.

Jury broke. Twenty pictures of Jethro were produced and, low and behold, pictures of me. When Robert took me camping I had just had Caroline and felt free. I took my blouse off and had on a long fringe vest and opened it. A 1988 picture. The only time I'd ever done anything like that, for crying out loud. We were friends since I was a little girl, and we were camping. The DA is hitting hard and below the belt in his call of duty.

Deputy Welch and I sat in a jury room until the break was over, along with Deputy Bill and some other deputy. They didn't cuff me. But they did check the bathroom thoroughly.

Witnesses, as you would expect from the prosecution, gave rehearsed statements and answers. But Jeffrey Murdock quizzed them also and loosened Fred's grip. The landlord, Keith, Steve Chase, the girl Joie, Al Hope, and the next door neighbor were first. The landlord and Keith used Smith's version of unhealthy remarks. The girl denied any involvement. Al couldn't remember his original statements, or who he sold a gun to.

Steve did okay, but he did do something I didn't expect. He told the jury I slapped him once. And grabbed him up out of the back seat of the car the day TJ took off. Then he said his mother gave me permission. I took that child in when he had or said he had no place to go. His mother needed help with him or couldn't be bothered. Debi has had him since.

So I guess you can kind of figure how this day went. Mother was called by Debi and Jeffrey. I spoke to Mom. She was encouraging but a nervous wreck like everybody else.

Wednesday, September 13, 1995,

Second day of the trial. I wore my turquoise dress with a white fluffy blouse underneath. The Court started out by calling witnesses: James Davis, Kathy Miller, carpet salesman, David Tiner, a couple of officers, Spider, and Dave Wilson.

I was on the news last night and in the paper today.

The prosecution, Fred Hugi, is coming on full force. Any little argument I've ever had with anybody is drawn out to be a vicious bloody mess. All these people have described my faults and tantrums.

Dave Tiner says I engaged in a conversation with Jethro and him. I never spoke to him about what happened. He, at the time, offered to help me get an apartment. He was very upset and did interrupt and argue with John Kolego, and the judge, in turn, also warned him, saying he asked for it. The judge has already gone 100% in favor of the DA. It doesn't look good for me at all.

Jethro was here over the weekend and spoke to John by phone. He was going to confess, but when it came down to it he didn't, and I can betcha I know why. The story Smith has perpetrated is an ugly matter. The situation of course isn't pretty. But because of all his twisting and turning and conditioning, he can't afford to lose. What was freakish tragedy has turned into a bloody premeditated murder.

Tomorrow the tapes get played of my "confessions."

I called Mother. She was out at a funeral. The children were with TJ. I read the news article. He was not happy, but he needed to know how words were being used. The paper stated I had just started reading the Bible. But I noticed at court the DA didn't ask anyone if I went to church or had a Bible. So I wonder where that came from.

Anyway I talked to TJ. He's ready to come up. He wants to pull eyebrows. He's very supportive, and I was encouraged that the children were under his wing.

My thoughts are slipping. I'm going in waves. I spoke to Caroline. She let out some tears. Grammie doesn't let them cry. While TJ and I were talking the two little ones escaped outside to play freebee. I had to tell them not to, and emotion flooded the phone. Little Immanuel let out a deep cry. He said, "You need to come home." Caroline said, "You've been gone too long, Momma." All of us will be back together I promised them.

Fred is only doing his job, but he has also abused his authority and helped mislead people, digging up as much dirt as possible on me. It truly looks real bad. The girls here are more upset than I am. They're very support-

ive. Deputy Burke says, "Hey, you need support. Just ask. We are here." Amazing!

The cuffs being put on me were tighter today. My attorneys are frustrated by the judge's favoritism. So what, we're gonna win!

Let me not forget to mention the wonderful Judge Ann Aiken was in the court. So pleasant to see her. She's the one who offered me ten years with 20% off. That's when I got all of Jethro's charges.

Oh, today in court Spider did give himself up big time. He bolted from his chair when asked where were you at 1:00 A. M. the night of the murder. He immediately stated Karlyn has been trying to say I helped bury the body, and with that he stated she told me in interrogation that she had to take him out of his misery. He lied. He told the attorney I know where you are going with this. His eyes were bugged.

Thursday, September 14, 1995

Third day of trial. I was in court today seven hours. No judge, and tapes of telephone conversations were played. My cries to get welfare and help are heard. That my memory had been tampered with is extremely obvious to me. I can remember and feel what I felt then. I answered questions before that didn't appear on the tape or transcripts. The police have altered the tape.

Anyway, nobody was in the court. Not a newspaper reporter not a witness, not a friend, not even his family or Jeff, my attorney. And not the judge either. These tapes showed my fear and memory loss, truly, in my voice.

Christopher Boots was in the court room. *There was one person who knew what I was going through. It had happened to him!*

We go back at two. Deputy Jean called for a thorough in-house cleaning and no phones.

I read today's paper. It was brutal and incorrect. Although its description of Dave's false testimony was accurate, they left out the word false. I could go on, but what's the use?

Friday, September 15, 1995

Fourth day of trial. Phone conversations were played. Again these were from Utah, about my coming, about trying to remember. I was struggling. There were crazy emotions from all that had happened, and I was trying to get to the truth. I mentioned several times that the Lord will reveal the truth even if I can't, and so I would write all that I could remember. I revealed the ritual that I found myself in and all that I could remember about other girls being hurt. I could hear the children's voices in the background.

During lunch break I was escorted handcuffed through the back corri-

dors of the court through the lobby and onto the elevator to a single cell with iron bars, where I was uncuffed and had the iron door slammed shut.

When I returned to the court room, a video was played, one where I walked through the house and tried to express or expose what happened that night. I got all screwed up. I left out a couple of things by getting way ahead of myself.

I sat right under the TV writing. And the jury, attorneys, and the judge were all on the other side of the room. I tried not to forget what I was writing on, but I cried. I tried not to. I had stressed the importance of my participation all along before the officers got a hold of me, and I'm sure the jury can see my cooperation in the interrogation. The pages turned in sequence in the jurors' hands. The judge stated in his twenty years in office he has never seen a more cooperative and complete jury.

The two tapes that I've been requesting of phone conversations finally did turn up, and guess what? Neither of my attorneys were given the transcripts. It was a member of the jury who had eleven pages of it missing and spoke up. We took a break to copy those words. The deputy brought me tissue. Steve brought me water. He's starting to show general concern as before. The DA stood behind me and questioned Steve. I snapped at my attorney, "Does he have to stand behind me?" Fred has been hanging onto James' family.

The papers also left out that the attorneys, even Fred the DA, got the witnesses to contradict their statements. Questioning them from different directions proved it.

Tuesday, September 19, 1995

When I arrived in booking, no new dress, so I put on my old sixteen-month stinky one. The van upon delivering me was greeted by a photographer. I was not pleased. I was locked in a cell next to Rosie, who is losing her children due to drugs. Court today was consumed in the playing of the rest of the videos, and they played throughout the day.

But there were witnesses, among them the pathologists, an anthropologist, a girl from Dave Tiner's apartment who stated I gave her black eyes, Brenda the bartender, the man who found the remains, and Detective Steve Walker. Slides were shown and the skull of James was brought in.

I won't go into my feelings or emotion. What is important to me right now is James' family. As the day went on, the findings totally revealed that a gunshot or gunshots were the cause of death.

However, video after video was shown in which I'm describing a stabbing that never happened—the brilliant works of Smith. As all this came flooding into the court room, I felt James' family in complete hatred for me. By the

*time these tapes are finished I'm confessing to a stabbing, and a burial, that
never happened.*

*And under direct questioning Steve Walker had to state that the body
was in fact not buried and their own forensics blew the confession out of the
water by denying that there was any blood or stabbing wounds. None at all.
So the poor detective Walker was beet red from all this, and nobody to blame.
Tomorrow Smith is on the stand.*

Wednesday, September 20, 1995

*I wore a tan-gold dress to court. The DA presented his last speech and
final witnesses, Dennis, Corina, Mike, Andreas, Shawn, Paula, her husband,
Steve Walker, and Smith.*

They also played the phone conversation with Jethro.

Without warning, the prosecution had put Karlyn on the phone to talk to
Jethro. This was while they were still in the process of manipulating her. In it
he is mainly warning her about all the treachery around her. Karlyn didn't
come off very well because she is still terrified of him, and she ingratiates
herself as though they were on the same side because she had not had time to
assess the reasons for the call.

In this phone conversation Jethro clearly states, "You did nothing wrong!"
He also is the first one to tell her that these people interrogating her are not her
friends; they are there to trap her.

*The DA rests his attorneys and, after a short conference with Kolego, I
agree to rest. We believe that their case has fallen apart right before them.*

It is a very perplexing point in the trial when Kolego rests his case rather
than to defend her. He even had Karlyn believing that the jury would see right
through these things. Hugi and his prosecutors and suborned witnesses had
told so many lies, however, even suggesting that Karlyn's coerced testimony
was all lies, that the jury expected much in terms of refuting their testimonies.

Juries can consist of rather uninformed, easily lead people. The evidence was not there, and playing two sets of wholly inconsistent inculpatory/
exculpatory tapes should have alerted them that police coercion effectively
forced Eklof to testify against herself.

Kolego evidently thought the jury could see the way the prosecution's
case had fallen apart and how they had tried to convince them of her guilt
based on "bad character" acts alone. But they were never aware of the coercion.

Nor were they aware that one of the two key witnesses, had already
been arrested, and Hugi had suborned his perjury by delaying and promising
leniency in his prosecution. Therefore, Al Hope said she procured the gun

before she went to San Diego. The other key witness had a deal through his lawyer that he would not be questioned about his involvement at the crime scene. Distabile, therefore, stated that she told him she "had to put him out of his misery". Jerry Smith also stated Karlyn "said" she stabbed James 30 or 40 times, which was a lie. But the jury did not know these were lies!

I am sure with God's blessings that his Grace is sufficient for me. So we won't be bringing any witnesses for me to confuse matters. We feel strongly about our argument and final statement.

Fred was not prepared for this and whined to the judge that he'd been deceived. Steve looked slightly bewildered. And the judge just leaned back in his chair. The jurors looked as if: Oh, this moment came way too quickly. The judge had just finished telling them we had a ways to go in the trial. Well, the moment I was waiting for has finally arrived!

Reverend Lee has been in the court room every day. When I arrived back at the jail, the girls and I with Martha circled in prayer. It was beautiful.

I was told Fred had no choice. The department had to prove where so much time and money went, and so on the story goes. So truth and justice are buried at Lane County in favor of pride and manipulation.

Jurors deliberate tomorrow. The judge wanted me to sit all day in their cells. I said, "Oh, no." So he left it up to the officers.

I asked Fred in the court room, "My, I compliment you on your grand-standing. What, the facts weren't awful enough. You distorted the truth. You grotesquely exaggerated and made horrible statements about me."

He said, "Get into the spirit of things, Karlyn. What's wrong?"

Friday, September 22, 1995

Richard Sherman shook my hand and wished me luck. I was called to court, sat in a cell until 4:00 P. M. The jurors verdict came: Guilty!

October 2, 1995

They reconvene to vote for death-by-injection sentencing.

I truly had no idea. So now that I am on the receiving end of media broadcasting and court manipulation, they state the horror that I won't be walking the streets anymore.

The girls here in the dorm are so supportive. A couple of them have also been victimized by Fred and his misuse of authority, and they feel so bad for me, knowing what they have been through.

The news media and newspapers have jumped on this ungodly band-wagon. One news commentator who was speaking slightly for my side was demoted and relieved of my story...

As I came back from court the news was out. Deputy Simons questioned me if I was suicidal. The facility expected me to come back in pieces. But this is what I have to say. They won this round, by fudging with me and my statements and adding grotesque horror. So I am giving thanks to the Lord that I have the strength and am ready to go round two.

I wish Jethro were allowed to give his statement.

See it didn't matter to Fred I didn't cause James' death. He in time would work the pieces around to that, as long as I admit to being there. That's all it took. He really believes he solved this case.

By this Saturday afternoon the dorm is emotional. I'm fine. They say they've never seen such strength. Well, do I fall apart before battle? No!

The paper said they cleared me, and then Fred's speech slammaunked me. Richard called to see if I'm OK. He wants to see me Monday. Bev Shopman checked on me last night. I wish people knew the truth.

Sometimes I feel like giving up. The force of these men covering their mistakes and feeding statements to people, rehearsing them so as to build an illusion into the case, whose misfortunes were already more than I could handle.

I feel so humiliated. I spilt my drink down the front of me and Mary Guerin wiped me off. I cried, so Kelly walked me out to the yard to cry alone. I don't feel too well. All I can pray for is to win my appeal. Please, God, please. I can't stand feeling the manipulation, and I scream at Smith and Hugi.

I know I am not the first one to be overpowered and thrown out like garbage just so a DA 's captain doesn't lose his job. But what I don't understand is how they can live with themselves and the extent they will go to cover their greed. They mislead the public with their grotesque horror. I feel raped again, very much destroyed and taken advantage of.

I have reason to believe that Elaine from Woman Space, who could have counseled me, denied me because of Judge Ann Aiken. When I called for help the woman on the phone said they wouldn't let go. They would be there to help. No show! I found out this weekend Judge Ann Aiken rode in a parade with the grand marshal who represented Woman Space.

Well, as I've watched how these professionals misuse their authority and push their knowledge around, I feel that many people have suffered under these conditions. Over the years a person might hear rumors and say, "Whoa! What is going on down there?" But when personally affected by the tremendous twisting manipulations, there is no help. A person can only suffer their effects alone. And I thought the occult was violently wicked!

There was no reason nor evidence for Fred to [degrade] me so slanderously. I realized from the beginning that Smith would always cover up his professional surgery to my statements. I felt that what happened to James was *vile and awful and that Jethro needed to pay for this grotesque error.*

I came forward after many horrible struggles, and I trusted valuable information to officers who said they needed my help. But before too long, Smith took apart my statements, ran others together, and without evidence or proof, designed a horror story that I couldn't even believe!

I tried to explain that to Judge Ann Aiken, but she wouldn't hear of my accusations against Smith and gave to me all nine of Jethro's charges. I can't believe it. This just gets worse. Then the trial comes, and in Fred's outrageous speech against me, he completes Smith's work. What school do these two go to?

I recognize the pattern they used by past cases. They picked horrible facts from other cases and speculated and accused, sliding them in between my words, which were altered by Smith's techniques of interrogation.

It's brilliant surgery and bullshit! This is not suppose to happen in America. I truly can't say I've learned. Because I would come forward again if ever in this situation. Which I pray never happens...

I did try my best to answer their questions and to the questions I could not answer they filled in with their own speculation. I was mentally unable to answer all their questions, because of the damages I went through. Their twisted words have convicted me.

Monday, September 25, 1995,

I received a visit from John. He is very upset. He says he is going to appeal and that Judge Merten was prejudiced and committed a reversal error. John is emotional and didn't sleep all weekend.

Lord, I expect miracles like 4th of July fireworks in this case! Come on! Deputy Lankin said I looked like a Pentecostal Princess.

Chap XX: The Trial in Retrospect

I n the previous chapter we have seen how little of the trial Karlyn could actually remember, analyze, and write about in her journals. Her comments on the Pretrial Proceeding of July 25, 1995 and her Pretrial Hearing on August 2, 1995 are a little better, in that she is responding to the written word.

Her journal writings and her responses, however, tell the real story. No amount of trial transcripts could ever tell so well the real devastation, the heartbreak, and the torture she went through. Even when she doesn't react as those around her would expect, it is obvious she is in a state of shock. Her ways of handling herself, of reacting on whatever level she can, tell so much about her inner strength.

Because of the limited nature of her reactions, however, it is essential that the events of the trial be set forth here, sometimes paraphrased or summarized, but nevertheless made part of the record for her. The most egregious happenings, as has been hinted, were taking place behind the scenes and will be dealt with eventually. This, however, is not the place for them.

In the Pretrial Hearing which follows, Karlyn was apparently not in attendance. She wrote in her diary on that day that she spoke to the judge and the DA at the court only in regard to her attire for the upcoming trial. Her comments to the transcript are based on what she learned as time went on.

Pretrial Hearing September 6, 1995

In the Colloquy Murdock requested individual *voir dire*, something which denied a public hearing of a jury request due to the length of time it would add to the case. The Court stated if there's a problem with a juror they would face it out front in the open like in the real world. *Yet when a juror requested to see the judge about her concerns, the judge asked the clerk to direct the juror to come in at a separate time, and he cautioned the clerk not to let the other jurors know...*

Kolego states that the defense opposed a pretrial ruling on the admissibility of the statements of Jeffrey Tiner. He objects that Mr. Hugi offered as evidence a transcript of conversations with David Tiner and Captain Jerry Smith. Those statements weren't under oath... some are inconsistent with others... (and) they were not subject to cross-examination...

Hugi stated that some of these statements were made in Karlyn's presence by Jethro to Dave. So those were adopted by her. She acquiesced to them. She agreed to them. *I left Dave's kitchen and went outside. That's not exactly going along with it...*

Hugi stated that other statements were made by Jethro to Dave in her absence. And those are coconspirator statements and they're admissions against penal interest and therefore admissible. In his memorandum he set forth why they are admissible. The requirement for statements against penal interest is for the declarant to be unavailable. *And he'd see to that. Even if they brought Jethro here, he'd take the Fifth...*

So during pretrial they discussed that the issues for conviction were to be that Karlyn was a coconspirator and aided concealment. *So they brought Tiner in and the DA took the Fifth for him...*

Hugi was trying to land evidence that Karlyn was a coconspirator, that they were running away from the scene together. *That's so far beyond the truth. First, when the landlord kicked me out I begged Steve Walker not to allow it. Then he assured me we would be okay. But the landlord spoke with Smith and the children and I were out.*

Kolego asked about a pretrial settlement conference in front of Judge Aiken. Hugi stated "there was never an offer" of a plea bargain. *But Judge Ann Aiken gave me 24 hours to decide on a plea bargain of eight years and Thomas Evans tried to urge me to take it as well. Terri Woods also viewed the record and said eight years isn't a bad deal, but if what I was stating is true, stick to your guns.* Mr. Kosydar slithered in from the back of the room and stood next to Hugi arguing with Kolego for about ten pages or so of transcript about case studies. He stated that plea bargains are confidential as well as other analyses of evidence. *The State does not acknowledge they offered a plea bargain...*

Kolego stated that he thinks the State would concede that Karlyn was not the person who inflicted the fatal injury. Yet she is facing the death penalty...

Kolego requested of the court to know why this case merited the death penalty *when they know I wasn't the cause of death or the fatal injury?* **The Court replied they would allow a limited hearing and that Kolego should be ready to make objections.** Kolego replied that it's a Catch 22 situation.

The Court adjourned.

Trial Record
Monday, September 11, 1995

Court convened for the purpose of establishing that Jeffrey Dale Tiner, who was brought here from the Nevada Penitentiary and represented by Mr. Ross Shepard, would not testify for either party.

Tuesday, September 12, 1995

Jury selection was complete.

Opening Statement for the State

DA Fred Hugi's Opening Statement for the State consumed fifty pages of transcript. His description of Karlyn was prejudicial:... has never been self-sufficient... three different fathers... biker type individual... common attire, etc.

Hugi said Karlyn asked Al about getting a gun, said she paid for the gun.... *Where do these lies come from?*

[Hope's indictment on child molestation was delayed two years, by Hugi, until after he had testified against Eklof. Hugi concealed the pending Hope charges from Eklof's attorney, thus concealing/withholding crucial impeachment evidence. When he was indicted, it was as a " participant in a homicide in Lane County." The complete story will be revealed.]

Opening Statement for the Defense

Murdock stated in his sixteen page Opening Statement for the Defense that cause of death was a gunshot to the head and the only shooter was Jeffrey Tiner. He stated that Karlyn was present at the scene of the murder but at no time acted like someone planning a murder. That she acted just the opposite.

He would bring forward witnesses to testify that Karlyn and James had a very good relationship and that there was no reason for her to want James Salmu dead. Though present at the murder, she did not intervene or stop the murder. She covered up out of self-preservation and to preserve her family. Mentioning Spider, he stated that the jury was going to see that she was not the only human being covering up for Jeffrey Tiner. She was not the only human being scared to death of him, and that his own brother was scared to death of him. John Distabile was terrified of him, and even covered up for the same reason. In fact, if anyone could have saved James' life, it would have been John Distabile.

When Deborah Distabile left there was no observable tension or conflict between Karlyn and James. What happened was not something that had been premeditated or planned in any way by herself. And maybe not by Jeffrey Tiner. He might have been so soulless and heartless that it didn't take long for him to decide to kill someone.

Murdock expected there to be testimony in this case of Karlyn's fear of Jeffrey Tiner. Of his intimidation of her, of his control of her, of her obedience to him. He indicated that her son TJ would testify... even more important would be TJ's testimony about the trip south after this murder occurred. And TJ would testify about that trip, about her efforts and desire to get away, how Jeffrey Tiner, at all times, either had the keys, the car, the kids, or all three. Her brother would testify.

[Karlyn has made one comment in regard to the trial transcript at this point:] *TJ was called a liar in his Grand Jury testimony. At the trial he simply wasn't asked any questions which would have confirmed the above. My brother's testimony was of no value. His (Murdock's) boasts were as bad as Jethro's.*

Mr. Murdock said that at first Karlyn, Dave Tiner and John Distabile all covered up for Jethro. But the farther away she got the more open she became, more open about her fear and more open about the events. He pointed out that Dave Tiner would admit, as he had under oath previously, that it was just Tiner telling him—Dave Tiner—what she had done, that it was not herself telling Dave Tiner what she had done... And there was nothing Jethro liked more than referring to his biker bitch girlfriend. Mr. and Mrs. Tough. That was what he wanted the world to think. And by spreading responsibility to her, he satisfied that need of his and that desire.

Mr. Murdock then said that his client came from a very hard culture. *This very description would be used later in the trial as a reason for the "bad act" witnesses, in order to refute any good image he had tried to create here.*

Mr. Murdock cited the many ways that Karlyn expressed fear of Jethro: covering for him, lying, because she didn't want him angry with her; that she feared he would dump her with his ex-convict friends; and by the very fact that he ordered her to tear up the carpet, wash the car, and kept the keys and children from her on the trip.

Mr. Murdock then abruptly concluded that Karlyn was painfully close and present at the killing, but he was confident that the jury would find her mere presence insufficient proof to find her guilty in this case. He thanked them.

After the presentation of these grossly unbalanced opening statements, a great deal of time was consumed in hearing taped phone interviews and in the showing of the four videotapes to the jury over the next few days...

The first of the "bad act" *witnesses,* Kevin Leroy Ray, James' neighbor, said James told him Karlyn's car belonged to a boyfriend of hers and that there were a lot of parties at their house. *Both are lies...*

Kathryn Shults, the landlord, claimed James was reliable in doing repairs. *He was four months behind and I did the repairs...* She then accused Karlyn of stealing. *She yelled this at me while I was removing my stuff...*

Al Hope said Karlyn asked to purchase a gun. *Not true. Al was afraid he'd be charged with selling firearms to an ex-felon and have to do six months in jail.* [When Karlyn wrote these comments, she had no idea the extent of Hope's crimes.]

Steven Michael Chase, TJ's friend, said he heard Jethro tell James to go and said he had a gun. *I didn't see or hear the first part of this trouble....* Did Steve see Karlyn hit James? Ans. No. Could he see her inside the house? Ans. No...

Asked if Jethro told James he was going to shoot James if he didn't leave? Ans. Correct... Was the house... a happy place to hang out? Ans. Yeah.

"Did Karlyn ever slap you?" Ans. Yeah. For what? Ans. "... we didn't do the dishes right one time. She would wrestle and teach us stuff. TJ took off the day of the party, and James and Jethro thought I knew where he was..."

Keith Smith, James' friend, testified, said James wanted Karlyn out, otherwise he'd move to California. He said there were fifteen to twenty people at the party, which was mine and Spider's. *This refuted Kevin Leroy Ray's claim that there were thirty to forty.*

Asked by Hugi if he'd ever seen Karlyn knock James down. Ans. ..."We went to Swinger's bar... and James was kind of pushing himself on her, and she just pushed him out of his chair..."

Wednesday, September 13, 1995

Linda Smith testified that she never noticed any conflict between me and James...

John Distabile claimed he first met Jethro at the airport in Eugene. *Willy states that they knew each other for ten or more years in Imperial Beach.* Spider claimed Karlyn wanted a party so they had one, just to get people together. Spider claimed both Jethro and

Karlyn encouraged James to go to a motel. *Well, that's not true. Spider put his foot on a chair next to the heater and offered him Jethro's money and told him just do what you are told.* Spider claimed total innocence. *Which isn't true. He and Jethro went to the back patio and marched back in together. Due to the experience I sustained, I believe now that Spider wanted to use the house to drug women and film them in sexual assaults. So that's why Spider was the first one to approach James about leaving, which backfired in Spider's face. Then Jethro uses force which I didn't see. Spider says he saw Jethro sock James.* Spider claimed that he saw Jethro flash a chrome piece and ask who had a loose zipper. Then he claimed Jethro straddled James and spoke to him in a low voice. *Jethro must have heard me coming in from the back yard. He let James up. All I saw was Jethro sitting next to James who was sitting on the couch. Spider was watching. He was standing just about where I saw him last.* Spider left the house taking the boys with him for the night. *But Steve went home instead. TJ should have been brought back, but wasn't.* Spider claimed Karlyn shut the door, implying that she was keeping James from leaving... *When the door opened James had every opportunity to leave and the same throughout the evening because he had also available the back door which was always open and very close. James was not being held in the house...* Spider claimed a conversation between himself and Karlyn that *never happened. Obviously he can't decide where they were standing. He can't remember.* Spider claimed he did not observe her do anything that may have caused James death...

Q. And Jethro Tiner was from the San Diego area; correct? Ans. I never met him there. Q. ... you met each other in a pizza party up here in Springfield; correct? Ans. Yeah. Q. Small world, isn't it? *That's not what Willy said, in Imperial Beach!* Murdock asked Spider if Jethro told him about Karlyn's part in killing James. He replied, "He didn't tell me, Karlyn told me herself. She put him out of his misery, she said." Murdock asked, "Did you say that in front of the Grand Jury on May 2nd, when you supposedly told them the full truth? Ans. "I don't remember them asking me that question." Murdock then asked, "Whether or not Karlyn had any involvement, wouldn't that have been an important fact when you were under oath?" Ans. "They never asked me the question..."

Q. "You're telling us that for the first time?" Spider answered that Steve and Captain Smith brought him down to the station house in Springfield, put him in the same room with Karlyn **and she had said that she had to put him out... of his misery.** Q. Do you remember saying that in front of the Grand Jury? Ans. I don't remember the question being asked. *The reason Spider didn't state this at Grand Jury is because the Police Department gave it to him at the interrogation.* **He had three polygraphs and three interrogations. He learned what the prosecution wanted him to say.** *Would I say that to him when they put him in the same room with me? Huh uh! Elsewhere I've told what he really said, to me!*

[Here again no one knew what was going on that caused John Distabile to keep changing his testimony. Hugi had a transactional immunity deal with

Distabile. This would constitute absolute *Brady* material as key impeachment evidence which should have been produced to Eklof's counsel prior to trial. A letter from Robert Cole Tozer to Fred Hugi, 6/14/94 to that effect was hidden from Eklof and her counsel. Hugi never revealed the deal to the jury. Spider's above statement to the jury, however, was critical in convincing them of her guilt.]

"Spider, did you lie at Grand Jury?" "Yes." "Why?" "Afraid of Karlyn?" "No." "You didn't report the death of James. Scared of Jethro?" "He's a doer. He does what he says he's going to do."

Spider claimed Karlyn accused him of disposing of the body. *Where did he learn that? The same place he learned that they wanted him to say I put James out of his misery. Yeah, Smith turns everybody into a twisted mess, thanks...*

Dave Wilson attested that the party was family oriented and that there was no tension between Karlyn and James.

Glen O'Del Dent claimed Karlyn needed the vinyl and carpet fast, and if he couldn't take care of it, she'd go elsewhere, also that Jethro was short and stocky. *I had no idea at first what Jethro wanted in the store. Mr. Dent never spoke to me and he lied about what I said. Jethro is not shorter than me.*

Glen said the male seemed calm, totally calm. He paid. He came to counter for further instructions.

Kathleen Miller, a long time friend, talked about albums of Karlyn's father's which she showed her and a nickname Jethro gave her, Sluggo. *He didn't tell her in my presence. I was across the yard.* She said they exchanged words [in anger] a couple of times. She said Karlyn got physical and she asked her to leave, which she did finally. She also stored some of Karlyn's things when Jethro took them south. She also said Jethro had just gotten out of prison, that Jethro told her it was for killing a child molester, and that she didn't have any reaction. *I never heard Jethro say anything to Kathy about child molesting. Lies.*

Kathy stated she didn't see James again after the party. She stated the last time she saw Jethro and Karlyn was the day they left. Jethro came with the kids, then she came after that *because I was with the detectives.* Kathy stated she left her belongings at her place, Jethro took off to Dairy Queen, then came back. Then they packed the car and left... She observed no conflict at the party.

James Davis saw Jethro the next day after the party. Jethro was wanting to paint the car. They purchased paint. Spider, James Davis, and Jethro painted and repaired the car. *What I get from this is that Jethro never intended to fly back...*

In the cross examination of State's witness, Dave Tiner, Kolego declared that the conditions for establishing a foundation for conspiracy had not been laid and that statements made by Jethro to Dave were not in Karlyn's presence.

Dave said Jethro said he killed James because James molested a child. Dave said they beat on James, she stabbed him, so Jethro shot him. *Which is not true, and Dave wasn't there to see what did happen. And if that were true then why did Dave, when he returned from the three or four-hour drive with Jethro, tell me I was in danger? He also told me he would help me get a place here., and drove all of us to a duplex with a fenced-in yard for rent.*

Dave claimed, variously, that they were laughing, they shot, they cut. *(that is not the truth), then* he claimed Jethro told him never use a .25. Dave said that's the way he related the story to him. *That's right because Karlyn did not talk about it. Jethro's story was the only story being heard.*

Hugi asked, "She was upset because the knife was full of blood and she ended up losing the knife?" Dave said they threw it away, *which isn't true, nor was it used as a weapon. I found it in the leather bag when we were lodged in an Imperial Beach motel. As a matter of fact I had it when I carved a candle that had the gold ornaments in it, which was after Dave's. Wow! Listen to Hugi!*

Dave claimed Keith wasn't allowed to come in. *Well, since Dave wasn't there and this is the police's story, it's a very good example of what police did to get this witness pumped up. Keith was allowed in when I showed him in and asked him to get the shotgun out of the house. If the carpet had been soiled either he or TJ certainly would have noticed.*

Dave started to say **he**, then stops and says **they** *(police rehearsal)*, and stated that Karlyn bragged about her father being in the Hell's Angels. *Guess what, when Jethro told me to go get my albums, I did. While sitting in the kitchen looking at them, Jethro popped off with her dad is a Hell's Angel, and I immediately corrected that statement, giving it the history that was given to me. He was in the club for about a year in the early 60s, then gave back his patch in a shoebox by delivery. End of story.*

Hugi asked, "I guess she beat on him for a while and then started stabbing him with this buck knife?" Dave doesn't answer that question. He said instead, "And Jeff shot him... in the chest... in the head... in the mouth so they wouldn't have a dental record... and "cut off his fingers so they couldn't get any fingerprints. Could I get a drink of water, your Honor?" *I should think so. But look how Hugi baits him.*

Dave claimed **they** called James a child molester. *That's not true, although I heard James tell Jethro the reason he couldn't go to Keith's for the night was that he kissed Joey with his tongue...*

Dave told Hugi the fingers and gun went off the bridge. *My question is why were the fingers found at the scene? Dave will say anything. He also said the dog was thrown off, and of course he turned up.*

Dave said Jethro was a violent guy and he would come looking. Jethro called Dave at his new house and made idle threats about coming up and taking him for a ride, *his last ride.* Dave was scared that Jethro would show up. *Yeah, I know that feeling!* Dave said I clocked his neighbor *and he makes up a lot stuff. He claims the incident was over speed. I don't believe so.*

In a brief cross examination Kolego was interrupted by Dave twice while asking him a question. The Court replied, "You're getting it answered. I've warned you. You've got enough of it. Now, I've warned you, if you keep this up, he's going to keep it up, and I can't stop it, because you're inviting it." *Dave is very defensive about Kolego saying that during all this bragging that was going on he wasn't acting disapproving, he wasn't contra-*

dicting, he wasn't saying anything. But the Court is also defensive.

Michael McCarty of Springfield Police Department reported that he came by on March 24, 1993 after Keith made the missing person report and removed James loaded shotgun. *The original carpet was still installed, meaning if foul play had occurred the carpet would have been out that night.*

The Court scheduled the playing of the videotapes, and Hugi stated that Kolego was concerned about his record. Kolego stated, "I am concerned about the record, and out of an abundance of caution, I know that. I am aware of the Court pretrial ruling but **I want to note the continuing objection of any and all recorded statements. Ms. Eklof wants that clear on the record.**"

The Court replied, "It is abundantly clear on the record. As far as I'm concerned, Mr. Kolego, you don't have to keep popping up. Don't keep popping up." Kolego's reply was, "Good enough for me," Hugi's, "We've got no problem with the continuing objection either."

The Court continued that we could have a reporter in here… to make a statement that this is a recording of something or other.

Thursday, September 13, 1995

Steve Walker gave the background of Karlyn's call on June 3, 1993 and his and Lewis' contacts with her on June 14th and 15th while she was suffering from severe injuries. He recounted their visit also to San Diego to talk with TJ in Lakeside, after which they visited her in Salt Lake the week of January 26th. *I was glad to see them but my memory was lacking. TJ told them his mom saw James get hit. I will not call TJ a liar, however, I never saw James get hit at all.*

Rick Lewis recapped their visit to me in Salt Lake City, when she admitted that Jethro shot James. She cried.

Jerry Smith agreed Karlyn didn't understand what the Grand Jury was. He was surprised that Lewis told her to get an attorney. He thought she didn't need one. He offered her one but didn't follow through once she arrived. He said he told her to tell the truth and it would have an impact on what they would do, referring to the DA.

Smith agreed it was apparent Karlyn had had no recent contact with Jeff Tiner. He told me that he had been in a car accident, with his new girlfriend left paralyzed, and was in jail. He said she was surprised and pleased he was in jail. *But Tiner still wasn't arrested as yet for this homicide. I had gone as far away as I could but now I could quit worrying. I could try to get it together to come forward.*

Rick Lewis agreed he misled Karlyn into believing she was a witness against Jethro. A tape recording was played of a conversation she had with him on March 22, 1994. Kolego asks Lewis, "You told her about coming up to a Grand Jury against Mr. Tiner?" Ans. Yes, I did.

Hugi redirected to Lewis, "That offer is open to and is still open to Karlyn Eklof, isn't it?" Ans. Yes, it is. *Yes, but not if they don't allow the truth to come forward about what they did!*

Hugi admonished the jury not to watch the local news… nothing had happened outside your presence… In absence of a jury the court discussed written instructions for the jury on all the charges…

Friday, September 15, 1995

Officer Pete Ackom attested that in Spider's February 10th interview he said Jethro had struck James in the face and was very adamant about there being only one blow. He also said Karlyn told him James was up the river.

Kolego asked Ackom if he was aware of discrepancies in Spider's testimony and that Spider might have had some role in disposing of the body. *The police told Spider I blamed him for disposing of the body, which wasn't true. However, it got Spider to tell their lies.*

Bill Kennedy was asked by Hugi if he had me sign an advisement of rights before the polygraph. He said he did. *The only thing I signed was the poly test sheets. The question about the gun was misleading. I jumped, because I had touched the bullets Jethro dropped in my hand.* Kennedy said he told her she was holding back about cutting Mr. Salmu, but he clearly stated that she said she did not cut him with a knife at all... that she did say she had a knife in her hand when James was shot the last time, but that she did not have anything to do with cutting him.

[It was revealed in the Tiner trial that police-delivered hearsay was extrapolated from the findings of the polygraph without acknowledging its source and used in the statements about Eklof and Distabile not being truthful and lying to the police in an interview.]

After the playing an audio tape (Ex. 17 - 4-8-94) Kolego asked Walker if in this conversation I was rambling, more disassociated, and... decompensating psychologically. He replied that I was centralizing on events that took place... in the San Diego area... less "sensical" than before. Ans. "Not to her, I'm sure." Q. Well, to you? Ans. Yes...

Kolego asked Walker about the first video: "And she indicated what her involvement was in that videotaped statement and you keep questioning her, right?" Walker agreed.

Q. "And was that because you had gotten some information from David Tiner? Her version didn't match Dave Tiner's?"

A. "We had gotten information from David Tiner several months before this."

Q. "So you kept after her about her testimony, about their version of the events, so that... it would be more consistent with what Mr. Tiner said?"

A. "Not necessarily. There are pieces left out and I was just looking for the truth and everything that took place."

Q. "But she'd given you a complete taped statement at this point and you did three other videotaped statements after that, didn't you?

A. Yes." *You should have stopped here, Mr. Kolego. You were doing fine!*

Q. "Okay. And you just kept doing it until you heard what you wanted to hear?"

A. "That's not true. Every time that we talked she was able to remember more things, and each day that we talked she did remember more things, and it changed. And that's why the videotapes were made to capture that information she had."

So that's the answer the prosecution wanted the jury to hear.

Exhibits were admitted into evidence. Again Kolego reminded the Court that here is a continuing objection *concerning the coerced testimony.* The Court replies: Yeah. There's a continuing objection. *I hope the jury understood this, however. I wish they had known* **why** *there was.*

Kolego stipulated to the admission of a conversation with Jethro. *A juror requested information on her safety. Two times another juror was dozing off due to his medical condition. The judge asked the clerk to instruct juror to come in at a*

separate time to discuss her concerns.
Court adjourned for a three-day weekend.

Tuesday, September 19, 1995

Terry Bekkedahl of forensics took the stand to discuss certain exhibits. He had FBI training and had been in the lab for eighteen years, *Smith's buddy.* He discussed Exhibit No. 37 which was a photo blood spatter on the dryer.

Bekkedahl stated: 37 is a photograph. He also located some blood staining and run on a dryer located in what he described as the utility room towards the back end of the house. And that depicts that red staining on that dryer... this particular material right here was determined to human blood also. *I believe this to be a phony picture, a big spot of water, because this area was nowhere near the crime. Could we have those tests, filing fees, and date of payment?*

The witness again referred to blood spatter on door jam, never referring again to blood on the dryer. *Because it is phony, but it inflames the jury.*

Expert discussed cast-off splatter on the wall... "So if we're having a dripping situation or a transferring going on, I would expect more than what I saw... You can get cast-off though I wouldn't describe this... as... the same scenario you've described." Looking at the carpet and pulling it to look at the pad, he found no blood stains.

[Bekkedahl went on to give a positive identification of the blood stains, saying that the DNA from Mr. Salmu's bones matched the blood stains. Hugi solicited it. This forensic guy lied under oath, at Hugi's prompting, because the actual report, Aug. 17, 1995, three weeks before the trial, stated that "no conclusions can be drawn." This constituted State-suborned perjury of OSP Criminal Investigator Terry J. Bekkedahl. It is also gross prosecutorial misconduct for Hugi to solicit Bekkedahl's perjury while concealing the exculpatory DNA results.]

State's witness Brenda Lee Culp, manager at Driftwood, testified Karlyn once came in wearing a knife and that she asked her to give it to her or take it home, which she did. She also said James wanted her out of the house, but later said he could handle it. She confirmed he never told her Karlyn hit him because he jumped into bed with her, or that she was part of a group that organized a birthday party for him after that. *This was Francis' daughter. Francis was first to make calls when James was missing, but on her dying bed she told her daughter I didn't do it. This was told to the investigator, but is not told here...*

Hugi was back to the movies, second videotape, made on May 2, 1994. *He thinks he's a producer.* Kolego cross-examined Walker about the events in between, the polygraph, the questioning, their concern that my statements didn't match what they had been told by Dave Tiner. Walker agreed that was one of the concerns.

Before the third videotape was played, in absence of the jury, Kolego objected, "I know the Court's already ruled on the admissibility of statements, but in the 5-3- statement... there's a reference to the polygraph. There's just one sentence that we have a problem with."

[His objection was to the following statement of Karlyn on the video:]

"But, uh, to say that I did not try to penetrate him or to penetrate him **has obviously showed up on the polygraph as not the truth.** And I did not want any part of the trial... didn't want any part of this to be fabricated or lied about."

Therefore, Kolego states, " I think that reference to the polygraph is inadmissible." It was then established that it had been whited out in the books and removed from the tape.

[Now this is very strange! Why would her own counsel want to remove her reference to the polygraph? That is exactly why she kept going with the interrogation. They had convinced her that she must get it right, and that it must match the polygraph. They are the ones who used the polygraph to force her to lie. This is a fact the jury should know.]

Melinda Daughtery, State's witness described the incident at Dave Tiner's, said Karlyn walked up her and started to hit her. When questioned why it happened *which would have helped me,* Hugi objects to hearsay statements of an observer.

Kolego established that Ms. Daughtery was in custody on a probation violation for welfare fraud and had been subpoenaed to testify.

Samuel Vickers, medical examiner, described tool markings which indicate fingers had been severed and had been found with the body. *Jethro lied to Dave about throwing them into the river.*

Vickers confirmed he had viewed the videotape where I was confessing to perpetrating, and that there was no evidence of trauma to the ribs, only bullet wounds... Confirmed that there were no wounds to destroy dental work. *Another lie bites the dust.*

John Lundy, forensic anthropologist for the Oregon State Medical Examiner, when questioned if there was any evidence of knife wounds, replied in the negative. Lundy establishes that there are plus or minus 206 bones in the human body and that if an individual were stabbed 30 to 50 times there would be a high probability of some evidence of knife wounds or that body.

[In the Tiner trial, Samuel Vickers, medical examiner, could not state a cause of Salmu's death, based on physical evidence, and he would not support the Salmu death certificate. He admitted the official Incident Report was police-supplied hearsay and admitted that the reports were not based on first-hand knowledge or upon his own investigation.

It has been established that writing, such as in a death certificate, may constitute hearsay. However, the prerequisite to use any given entry in an official record as evidence is that the official making the entry must have had either personal knowledge of the facts or the opportunity to ascertain the truth of those facts. Any judicial record may be impeached, or the presumption arriving therefrom be overcome, by evidence of collusion between the parties or fraud in the party offering the record.]

After the playing of the third videotape, of May 3, 1994, Kolego asked Walker how many hours he would estimate that he'd been talking to me, interrogating or interviewing, on that day. Establishing that it had been at least four hours, he was asked what was being said during those four hours.

Establishing that the DA's office was reviewing the tapes as they were made, Walker was asked if they had indicated there wasn't enough to charge her with prior to this. He answered that their responsibility was to indicate to him when or if an arrest would take place, which hadn't happened.

Kolego persisted and said that it is their contention that some of these details were supplied to her and that their goal was to supply her with enough details or have her say enough so that she could be charged. Walker denied that they told her about details they'd gotten from Dave Tiner. He denied telling her she wasn't recalling all that she should. *What rot!*

Questioned further about the hours of interrogations before each video, and whether they had been supplying her with details about things they'd heard from other sources, Walker stated he didn't recall, and that he was very careful not to do that. *Steve sure has a funny way of not being able to answer Kolego, but when Hugi cross examines him he goes right into a schedule...*

Walker told Hugi that before the last video on that day, on the 5th of May, at about 10:00 in the morning, he and Mike Wisdom from the police department went to the motel and picked Karlyn and her children up... They drove all the way up Highway 126, up the McKenzie, to the county line, etc. etc. *He has it all in hand, but not the additional harassing, humiliation, and coercion.* He stated that on May 5th they conducted another interview and another videotape was made of the results of that interview.

Kolego established that basically she had no money. She gave them statements and they provided her with meals and a baby-sitter, that they picked her up at 10:00 in the morning on that day and the video was finished at 7:27 that night. Walker agreed.

Kolego asked if Karlyn confessed on the videotape about burying the body four feet deep (Walker didn't think it was that deep) or agreed that Jethro was flicking a cigarette into the grave, carrying the body uphill, and wedging it between two boulders? Walker said yes to all of these questions. Kolego asked if he was at the scene when the body was found or if he ever found any evidence of a grave? The answer was yes. *He also spent considerable time viewing the remains in forensics and learned there was no evidence of a knifing..*

Kolego asked, "Wasn't the story that you got from Dave Tiner that there were two boulders? The body was by two boulders?" Ans. I believe he mentioned boulders. Kolego went into an examination of the area where the body was found.

Kolego asked, "Do you know why it is if Ms. Eklof would confess to burying a body if she didn't?" Ans. You'd have to ask her. He reviewed a former question, " 'Were you supplying details about a knife?' And you said you tried not to; correct?" Ans. Correct.

They reviewed an April 8, 1994 transcript where Walker referred to Dave's testimony and said, "He made some inference that James had been cut up a little bit." Walker finally located it in the record.

Kolego established that Walker had supplied that particular detail, and that he also said, "I think we talked about that a long time ago?" Walker answers, "Uh-huh. And she said, 'Not in front of me.'" *Exactly, Mr. Walker. You supplied it to me.*

Following the proceedings there was a discussion about letting alternate jurors go, which was not normally done until they entered the guilt phase. Kolego pointed out they didn't yet know if there was going to be a penalty phase and asked if they were "cut loose" or not. The Court responded, "I know it..." In other words, there would be a guilt phase, and they would be cut loose with an admonition not to talk about the case in case they were recalled, even though they hadn't been in attendance.

Wednesday, September 20, 1995

Smith took the stand and described how they came to believe there was foul play, that Salmu had friends, left no word and had a check coming from work.

He described how Karlyn added information day to day during the interrogation and eventually revealed she had been there when the body was deposited. Their interest at that time was in trying to recover Salmu's remains.

Smith went point by point through what she had added to the testimony: He said she told Jeff to put him out of his misery or she would, her belief that by stabbing Salmu she would take the air out of him to stop him from hurting, that she rinsed the knife, that Tiner disposed of the knife, about the grave—*all of these were his own versions, his twisting of a stabbing that never happened.* They arranged a phone call between Jeff Tiner and Karlyn on May 7, 1995 to talk to him and elicit statements from him to get him implicated and convicted. *I was too scared to ask.*

Kolego cross-examined Smith about the forensic evidence, about Karlyn's willingness to talk, the length of time during the final interrogation, and her actual words which, supposedly, described the stabbing. Kolego went over them and said, "She didn't actually confess to stabbing him; she made these kinds of statements." Smith answered that the recording indicated she backed off from the accuracy of her descriptions that she had provided earlier and that she indicated earlier that she had thrust the knife into James on two occasions. Kolego established that this last taping was after eight hours of questioning.

Hugi asked Smith if, when Karlyn was interviewed in person, she said things that she either omitted or minimized her involvement in during the videotaping? Ans. Yes.

Corina Birch, State's witness, Karlyn's former neighbor, was questioned about an altercation just before Jethro arrived. Kolego objected, unless it has to do with Jethro. Hugi explained that the counsel's opening statements had opened up a propensity toward violence and they wanted to show she assaulted other people and why she would go to such lengths to make her relationship with Jethro work. The objection was overruled. The altercation was described in which Karlyn physically challenged her to return her ten dollars in food stamps. When police were called no report was filed, because Karlyn had left.

The initial questioning of Dennis Heide led to a Colloquy, in absence of the jury, in which the Court discussed the reasons for overruling the counsel's objections. The Court stated that "in the opening statement, the defense portrayed for the jury a mild-mannered, fragile female who was protecting her children and had come under the influence of an evil man who made her do everything that she did against her will. And a lot of this evidence he saw that the State was bringing in was in contravention of that opening statement. And that's why he'd been overruling a lot of objections.

The Court continued, "I thought that door was kicked open so wide you could drive a bulldozer through it. I'm a little bit fearful now of what we're going into. Is it going to be relevant to say, 'Yeah, she moved in with me and punched me, too?'"

Kolego countered with, "The opening statements aren't evidence… and this is more properly rebuttal evidence… I don't think there was ever a reference to nonviolence. There was a reference to fear… I don't think… there is … say a bald assertion, that this is a lily. She's a survivor, she's tough, she's from hard culture… I don't think that kicks the door wide open for any time she ever got in a beef with anyone."

The arguments in this Colloquy were the same that were used in the Open Argument of my appeal, these and the question of allowing victims' impact statements before my sentencing. Neither of these issues, however, carried any weight with the Court of Appeals, and my appeals would be denied without comment.

The Court continued to discuss the relevancy of my relationship with Dennis, and stated that when he heard the opening statement, he was saying to himself as a trial judge: 'Good God! I wonder who the State's got out there that they're going to bring in that they weren't otherwise going to bring in?" Kolego stated a continuing objection. The Court said, "You got it. Let's not take the long road to San Diego."

Dennis was questioned about various assaults involving Karlyn, the last being when he said if he had known what plane she was coming in on he'd have beat the shit out of her.

Michael Andrus, who hired her to deal cards at the White Horse Tavern, described a few fights that broke out in the bar, and she'd kind of break it up. She hadn't been hired to do that, and he had to let her go.

Hugi asked if she indicated to him that she preferred being a bouncer to being a card dealer. He answered Yeah, I believe so. Yeah, she liked it. Kolego asked him if he was worried about his liability... Ans. Yeah. And partly for her safety; correct: Ans. Right.

Court was in recess during the noon hour.

Bill DeForrest was asked about an interview with Karlyn on January 26, 1995. Nothing is mentioned about her complaint against Smith. With Tom Evans, her attorney, present, she told him that she had told the truth during the course of her interviews with Smith, or if anything had caused her to tell anything but the truth during the course of the interviews. She said, "No. Everything I said was the truth." *But I hadn't seen the videos, and my attorney, who had, should have been answering for me...*

Various States witnesses were called, Shawna Brunson, Paula Haskins, Tommy Haskins, and Barry McNichols, who all attested to some form of altercation on Karlyn's part...

In a Colloquy Kolego moved for an acquittal. He stated that under ORS 136.425, sub. (1) there had to be corroboration, that a confession could not be given in evidence when it was made under the influence of fear or threats, nor was it sufficient without some other proof.

He stated that it was the position of the defense that the statements of Jethro Tiner to his brother should not have been admitted by the Court, contrary to the Court's ruling, and 2) that the statements of an alleged coconspirator aren't sufficient to corroborate.

Mr. Hugi replied that his understanding was that they were received as statements against penalty interest, not as conspirators testimony. There was also a dual ground. They were received as admissions from the party's opponent for those particular statements that were made and ratified by herself... And that was the reason they brought Mr. Tiner back and went through the invocation of the 5th amendment was to make him unavailable, which was a requirement to get the statements against penalty interest admitted.

Kolego replies that it was our position that those violated my client's confrontational right...

The Court: I know that. I'm not asking you to concede your objection. Mr. Hugi, can you point to any other corroboration?

Hugi cites Dave Tiner's statements, redoing the carpets, blood found on the door, remains that were found and cause of death by homicide.

The Court: I think what he's implying is when the statute said there must be corroboration of a confession that the crime was committed... There must be corroboration of a confession that the crime was committed and that the confessor did it. *This is the gigantic error. All of the arguments of the prosecution overlook this requirement. There is no evidence that I, the confessor, who was coerced in my confession, did it.*

Hugi goes on and on with his "corroborating" evidence, that she participated in re-carpeting, that innumerable elements of her testimony were found to be true, etc. *notwithstanding the fact that innumerable elements of my testimony were found **not** to be true.*

The Court: In a nutshell, you oppose the motion. The motion is denied. *This is a corrupt court. This can't be happening in our legal system. Where are the rights of an individual to due process and a fair trial?*

When the judge responded with the above, after a short private discussion with co-coun-

sel and the myself, Kolego stated: Your honor, and I didn't mean to be coy with the Court—
having considered everything and having discussed it at lunchtime with co-counsel, and having
discussed it with co-counsel now, **the defense is going to rest.**

The Court: **And not call...**

Mr. Kolego: **Any witnesses.**

*As I wrote in my Trial Diary: Fred was not prepared for this and whined
to the judge that he'd been deceived. Steve looked slightly bewildered. And the
judge just leaned back in his chair.*

The court then discussed the possible length of closing statements and asked Kolego for
any closing remarks. He stated a preference for arguing the case to the jury while it was still fresh
in their minds, and they decided to have arguments on Thursday and planned the time of conven-
ing after a discussion with the jury, which must be unanimous for murder, and of drafting instructions for the "lesser includeds."

After the jury reconvened, the court announced that the State had rested its case... , and
Kolego announced:

Your Honor, we've elected not to put on a case and the defense rests. *So, with the
above rulings, what good would it have been? The jurors looked as if: Oh, this
moment came way too quickly. The judge had just finished telling them we had
a ways to go in the trial. Well, the moment I was waiting for had finally arrived.*

Thursday, September 21, 1995
Hugi presented the Opening Argument for the State.

Hugi indicated that what lawyers say is not evidence. They should trust what they remember if there's a conflict between that and what the lawyer represented. He said Mr. Kolego wouldn't
intentionally mislead you... *Hugi, you're right, but what about the State? Hugi
tried to use witnesses to prove his version, which is manipulation and misrepresentation. Again Hugi is trying to convince the jurors that all conversations
proved the case fit together.*

Hugi proceeded to discredit Karlyn by using her public assistance, Hell's Angels, her
children's fathers and her dress. Then he compared Jethro's prior history with hers—*there's no
comparison, Hugi*—and said the High Tide was where Jeff hung out and that's where she
met him. *Not true, I met Jeff at Willy's house.* Hugi claimed Jeff's brother calls Jeff a
Norse God back to kill child molesters.

Hugi then used Al Hope's testimony to prove she purchased the gun. *I did not.* [Major
error, Hugi, suborning Hope's perjury. **Chinese proverb: The laws sometimes sleep, but never die.** The attorneys for Tiner's trial reveal the extent of
Hugi's leniency offer in lieu of child pornography charges, requiring six pages,
which will be revealed in succeeding chapters.]

He stated that she was a "biker bitch" to which Kolego objected. The objection was overruled by the Court who stated, "It's in the evidence." He continued to try to convince the jurors
that she played a role as a biker bitch and continued to do so until she went to Salt Lake City
where a transformation occurred. *Yes, when I learned from Walker and Lewis that
Jethro was in jail and I could finally try to tell what happened without fear*

that he'd come after me.

Hugi went over the scene of the murder, mixing up characters and rooms, leaving Spider out like a frightened mouse when he's the one who teamed up with Jeff when they marched in from out back and told James to take Jeff's money. John Distabile was the only person who could testify to what happened in the living room after the phone call to Linda.

Hugi tried to persuade the jury that Karlyn had aided and abetted in planning the crime, suggesting she aided in the procurement of items so that the crime could be accomplished. He continued to anguish the jurors by stating she lost her buck knife due to the blood bath, *which never happened. In fact, forensics said there was no evidence of a blood bath. However, Jeff took it upon himself to alter a different part of the house to keep detectives going in circles.*

Then Hugi shifted gears, realizing they found no such evidence, and stated that Salmu got tortured in the tub. *Forensics proved there was no evidence in the tub, not even in the drain.* Hugi then accused her of being ordered by Jeff to get the pruning shears. *He forces the jurors to believe that Jeff cut James fingers in the house. I'm not sure where he wants that part to have happened, in the living room or the bathroom. Fred, which is it?*

Then Hugi really tore into her about a stabbing that never happened, but admitted there's no proof. *Yet he first states that my position in the stabbing was ineffective because he was already dead. But he accuses me of one, then two stabbings, and, in the Closing Argument of the Penalty Phase, he says 30 times! Hugi's many versions of James death proved that I was being coerced and was suffering from the spin that the State had added to my story.*

Hugi's many versions proved that nobody had a chance at the truth. He covered up for Smith's interrogation misconduct and the fact that due process was violated. He continued making up solutions for problems that had never been solved. Hugi talked about a possible interim place, a sandbox, where James might have been buried, using skirmish, overhaul, and overkill. *Well, Hugi, which one of your stories is it, or shall we go with what I saw?*

Hugi stated she got her butt kicked and Jeff got a new woman. He left out that the detectives and she stayed in contact.

Hugi went over the moving of James' car and three interpretations of how the dog might have been killed, *which he had done to this whole story all the way through.*

He stated she tried to talk Keith into taking James' shotgun out of the house. *I feared for my life. And how did this fit with my not allowing him in the house? Jeff painted the car, and I wasn't even there or told 'til later. It was done.*

I called Rick and Steve the second week, as soon as I could get far enough away from Jethro to do so. Six weeks passed by and I was found horribly beaten with broken bones. Hugi stated Rick and Steve were in Chula Vista two days later. *After I was beaten, yes, and that was too late to help me.*

Hugi said she returned to Springfield, stayed two days with Spider and then hit the road. *How many times did police talk with Spider, and why did he tell me not to bring attention to this case?* Hugi told jurors she placed a spin on the case. She even put it in writing. *Then the coercion interrogation altered the case,* and he said she made all those tapes and her actions were inconsistent with her words.

He went round and round about the bullets and the cause of death, and what could have been fatal, but said they can't know. But the intent was certainly there. Why did Jeff kill James? No reason; he just did it. Because he could, and that's the reason she did it. *Hugi's going around in circles, just blah blah blah.*

Mr. Kolego finally objected, when Hugi stated that nobody had ever told her what to do since she was thirteen years old, and reminded the jury that the defense said "J would testify about how Jethro controlled me. Kolego objected and said we made a tactical decision not to bring forth witnesses and it shouldn't be commented on. But the Court said, "It's overruled... what... was going to come out of that person's mouth would not be evidence, because that person didn't testify." *That's a pity, John Kolego. I wish you had allowed me to have one witness of the abuse we suffered!*

Hugi didn't apologize for the interrogation and tried to convince jurors that by the looks of it everybody was treating a killer real well. Then he misinterpreted the phone call to Jeff in prison. *They threw it at me. However would I get him to admit to his crime? That call brought back all my trauma and fear. Emotionally I was trying to blend in with the woodwork.*

Hugi accused her of getting the gun from Al. He accused her of labeling James a child molester. *These things were so untrue.*

First he said she tried to get James out of the house; then he said she kept him there. *Well, Fred, which is it?*

Hugi stated James wanted to leave and she prevented him from doing that. Then he likened this to a rapist who would knock someone off a bike path into a blackberry bush where you could do it and not be seen from the bike path... which would be a kidnapping.

Kolego objected that Hugi was instructing the jury as to what the law is, and he thought that was erroneous. The Court: Overruled.

Hugi also stated he was not saying Karlyn cut James' fingers off... they were saying abuse of corpse included treatment of corpse by any person in a manner not recognized by generally accepted standards of the community. He didn't say she was the felon. He was saying she aided and abetted this felon to have the firearm.

[I don't know how the jury could accept that rationale. Here he is saying she wasn't the felon, but aided and abetted him. Why then is she being convicted of all his charges?]

Hugi ended by saying that "because we don't know everything doesn't mean the defendant is not guilty and we haven't proved her guilty of the charges in the indictment beyond a reasonable doubt." *Of unlawfully and intentionally causing the death of James Michael Salmu, a human being—you have not proven that beyond a reasonable doubt! You have not! Your web of lies has not proven that! I did not knowingly and intentionally aid and abet a felon to commit a murder. There is no proof that I knew what he intended to do.*

Kolego presented Closing Argument for the Defense.

John Kolego reminded the jury that Karlyn was innocent and remained innocent unless and until the State should prove the guilt of each and every crime that she was charged with, and each element of those crimes, beyond a reasonable doubt. He also reminded them that we all agreed that if the State didn't meet that burden, that their obligation was to return a not guilty verdict.

Kolego was very clear in saying that what Mr. Hugi said wasn't evidence, and that what he told them the evidence was wasn't the evidence. He also told them that what Hugi told them about her, that she was a biker bitch, had children from three different husbands, and was receiving public assistance—those issues were not relevant on any of the crimes that she was charged with. He had told them that to inflame them.

He said Spider talked about how this thing began. *Indicating Spider was a witness; yet he's the one who set James up.*

Jethro was like a piranha in a goldfish tank. These people were not equipped to deal with him. He questioned her choice in men.

There was no evidence she wasn't paying half the rent, and James was a thoroughly decent guy, lonely, and there was some tension sometimes. He told people he didn't like her friends.

But there was no reason to think that she deliberately planned and had James killed so she could have this rental. The State was asking the jury to find that she did, beyond a reasonable doubt, based on those statements.

The State was also asking them to believe that but for her, James would not have been killed, if he hadn't met her, it wouldn't have happened. But they were talking about intentionally causing.

One, did she intentionally cause the death of Salmu; two, conceal the crime of assault during the course of a kidnapping; or three in the course of the crime of assault: or four, did she do that intentionally? Did she have a conscious desire to kill or did she set in motion a chain of events which resulted in the death of James? You can't use guesswork and speculation. You're stuck with the evidence the State has given you. And there are a couple of different (conflicting) pieces of evidence that they've given you.

One of the things was Al Hopes's testimony. Al said, "I can't remember. I can't remember who gave me the money and who I gave the gun to. And I think it might have been Karlyn." Then Al's own criminal activity was questioned, giving a gun to known felon. Kolego submitted that the above was plenty reason for Al to lie [and walk free for two years on child pornography].

Another of the big, big pieces of evidence was David Tiner's statements. His brother told him about committing a brutal murder and he didn't say, "You ought to turn yourself in." He just nodded and yucked it up. So when they got back there was this bragging going on: A) they killed the dog; B) they threw the dog in the river; C) Jeff shot James in the mouth to destroy dental records. And that she stabbed him 30 to 50 times and Mr Hugi said it was a bloodbath there. Then Dave said they rolled the carpet up because there was blood all over the carpets. And they had to get rid of it."

As Mr. Kolego pointed out, we don't have the burden of proof... *He decided not to put on evidence because none of the above had been proved. And if it ain't broke don't fix it.*

Kolego stated that if there were so many things wrong with Dave Tiner's statements to convict her of aggravated murder beyond a reasonable doubt, if you were going to pick and choose, you were going to pick the parts you like and throw out the parts you don't like, and say that that's proof beyond a reasonable doubt.

Then there were Karlyn's statements. Kolego took the jury through her interrogation, the requests for a lawyer, the neglect of *Miranda* warnings, and then the repeated threat that they would take her back to the motel, to her children, **and to Grand Jury** after she told them what they wanted to hear.

Kolego had a problem with Hugi dehumanizing her to the jurors about the way she dressed. He suggested she was a biker bitch, and they ought to find her guilty. He asked them to look at Al Hope's testimony. Look at Dave Tiner's testimony. Look at the totality of circumstances and the quality of the evidence. Then if they're not convinced beyond a reasonable doubt—"I don't care if you think she probably had something to do with it"—if they couldn't prove to you beyond a reasonable doubt each and every single element of this, then you've got no alternative. You had to return a not guilty verdict.

Kolego said that Jethro's brother was afraid of him. Why shouldn't she be also. She was holding the bag. And about that phone call to Jethro, *which upset me a lot because I was unprepared for trying to make him confess,* Kolego put that in the right perspective: "She was told to call him up, at the very end, and he correctly, correctly, for the very first time, pointed out to her, 'Karlyn, these people are not your friends. Karlyn, these people might be trying to kill you. Karlyn, you shouldn't talk to these people because they're not out to help you.'

"And she sat. And he said, 'I'm not just going to take the rap light off you. Sit tight. I'll be up, I'll take care of things.'

"And yeah, she melted because she doesn't have very good judgment of men. She can't judge men very well. She liked Rick and Steve... She felt they were real great... They were doing a job and they were playing a number on her... You can see what kind of judgment she's got."

So she's holding the bag and the State was arguing they'd got proof beyond a reasonable doubt, and she shouldn't have been afraid of Jethro. Kolego pointed out the perjury of Spider... He lied, because Jethro's not even here and he's afraid of him. His brother hasn't seen him for five months before he finally got the courage to call.

Kolego maintained that the proof doesn't rise to the level beyond a reasonable doubt on any of the charges. And she hadn't even been charged with hindering the prosecution. But the others? Kolego told the jury they would either have to acquit or convict her of those. But if they would look at the evidence, it didn't rise to the necessary level of proof. So then they had to acquit her.

Kolego discussed the lesser charges and what the choices of the jury might be.

He stated that they didn't raise a defense or put on any witnesses because they didn't have to. The use of the vehicle, the disposing of the corpse, those were things that she did while acting under duress. The man she thought was prince charming was really a killer and she guessed wrong again. First victimized by Tiner and then by the police. So the defense duress, Kolego thinks the evidence is raising it. Not a defense to murder, but a duress that had to do with participating in the unauthorized use of the motor vehicle and disposing of Salmu's remains.

The commission of acts under coercion had to be by use or threatened use of unlawful physical force of such nature as to overcome earnest resistance.

The danger had to be present, imminent, and impending. The burden of proof was on the State to prove beyond a reasonable doubt that that defense did not apply. And Kolego submitted to the jury that they couldn't prove that... and that any reasonable person would under those circumstances have done exactly as they were told. He concluded that deciding solely on the evidence, the jury ought to return not guilty verdicts on all eight counts.

Hugi presented Closing Argument for the State

Hugi's final half hour could best be described by the adjectives, epithets, and cliches he used. He'd already said it all in the Opening Argument. He started out with: biker bitch, jerk, birds of a feather, tough guys, bad ass, baloney, liar.

Then some of his more bald statements included: "Al Hope; what was his lie? He said, 'Yeah, I'm an ex-con. I got the gun for her... she gave me the money, and I gave it to her and Jethro'"; "She confessed to burying him: That's one of the things we're never going to know"; "Dave Tiner was here and he told the truth... Karlyn Eklof has not told the truth"; "Why did she want the shotgun out of there? If they came in and looked around they were going to take her ex-con husband away in handcuffs. That's why".

And he thought there was no evidence at all in any of this that the police did anything untoward to her. They scrupulously protected her rights; "Witnesses have done their job... Dave Tiner... he can be in danger... but he came in here and he did his job... The police have done their job... Judge Merten is going to do his job," he said.

"It's up to you to do your job to return a verdict that shows your ability to find the truth out of all this evidence. The verdict that will let the Salmu family finally get some peace and know that justice has been done."

Kolego objected, rightly, to this as a naked plea for sympathy that he didn't think appropriate. The Court interpreted it a different way, but still instructed the jury that no verdict should be reached for the defendant, for the member of the public, or for the public at large. *This objection, similar and in addition to the Court's allowing victims' impact statements before my sentencing, were issues that were challenged in my appeals.*

Thursday, September 21, 1995 Jury Instructions

The Court urged the jury that they must make an individual decision regarding each element of the charges and determine whether the evidence indicated guilt beyond a reasonable doubt. He gave instructions to the jury on each of the nine counts. He stated that, in addition to the written instructions, he would give them additional instructions verbally and in hand writing.

The Court discussed Count 1: aggravated murder, when a person intentionally causes the death of another human being in an effort to conceal the commission of the crime of assault. Lesser included offenses, if on Count 1 that person was deemed not guilty, are intentional murder, manslaughter in the first degree, manslaughter in the second degree, and criminally negligent homicide.

Count 2: consisted of aggravated murder with intent to conceal identity of the perpetrators, and lesser includeds.

Count 3: consisted of aggravated murder in the course of assault, intentional assault, maiming, or torture, and lesser includeds.

Count 4: aggravated murder, including kidnapping.

Count 5: assault in the first degree. The judge said that she" or another participant caused the death of James Michael Salmu," finally indicating in his instructions to the jury that someone else was involved.

In discussing assault in its four degrees Eklof was named as allegedly causing the death to James by means of a dangerous weapon, a knife.

Count 6: charged kidnapping in the first degree, charging that she took James from one place to another with the intent to interfere with his personal liberty.

Count 7: was unauthorized use of a vehicle

Count 8: charged possession of a firearm by a felon. *Well, I'm not a felon, and I didn't possess one. But it is alleged that I aided and abetted Jethro to have one.*

Count 9: charged abuse of corpse in the second degree.

At the end there were separate instructions for the alternate jurors and the 12 member jury panel.

During the Colloquy which followed the above, the concern of a member of the jury was heard by the court, which was a fear of her so-called connection with the Hell's Angels. Would they come for her if she were convicted.

In questioning the juror, the judge was concerned whether she would find her guilty just because of that connection. Determining that she would not, he assured her that he himself would have absolutely no fear for her or her family no matter what verdict she would reach. Absolutely none.

In the absence of the jury the court discussed further instructions to the _jury in the deliberation. The Court concluded with the reminder that the motion to prohibit the State from arguing the death penalty was denied, and that there was no evidence to indicate this case was treated disproportionately to other aggravated murder cases charged in Lane County, which might or might not be a moot issue. *Is it possible I could have received the death penalty? You bet!*

Friday, September 22, 1995 The Verdict

The court convened at 3:15 P. M. with the jury still deliberating to answer the jury's question: "Does the term 'personally' equate to 'solely' in the phrase, 'The defendant personally and intentionally caused the death.'?"

In the discussion of this question Mr. Hugi stated they had covered that argument: the correct answer was no. Mr. Kolego opposed, saying it was tantamount to commenting on the evidence to give any advice at all. The Court, however, chose to answer, instead of not answering, the question. It would be a simple no. This deliberation took only 5 minutes.

At 4:26 P. M. the jury had reached a verdict. With the presiding juror answering, the Court asked for their verdicts, which, one by one, were:

Count 1: aggravated intentional murder, not guilty, Lesser included: Intentional murder, guilty, 12-0

Count 2: aggravated intentional murder, not guilty, Lesser included: Intentional murder, guilty, 12-0

Count 3: aggravated intentional murder, guilty, 12-0

Count 4: aggravated felony murder, guilty, 12 to 0

Count 5: assault in the first degree, guilty, 11 to 1

Count 6: kidnapping in the first degree, not guilty, 2 to 10, Lesser included: Second degree, 12-0

Count 7: unauthorized use of vehicle, guilty, 12-0

Count 8: felon in possession of firearm, guilty, 12-0

Count 9: abuse of corpse in the second degree, guilty, 12 to 0

The Court instructed the jurors: Because of two guilty verdicts on the two aggravated murder charges, a penalty phase hearing was required, which would start October 2, 1995... and he ordered that they be in attendance. Okay? The judge asked that there be no discussion of the case among themselves or anyone else. The alternate jurors were informed of the verdict and also advised.

Chap XXI: Penalty Phase and Sentencing

I n this chapter Karlyn will finally have a chance to speak to the jury. Alas, it is after they have convicted her of all the crimes Tiner com mitted. It is too late for them ever to retract their verdict which will result in her being considered for the death penalty and then given two life sentences. Her words, her story, finally given but too late for her defense, are so important that they will be presented in **bold type**. The analysis of documents continues:

In a Colloquy, the rules on allocation were discussed, that is, the defendant's right to make a statement prior to execution or sentencing. Mr. Kolego also anticipated arguing to the jury concerning circumstances of the crime, of which they found Karlyn guilty beyond a reasonable doubt, although that was not beyond all doubt, and that they should consider that before sentencing someone to death.

In addition, although in a previous review within Lane County the counsel was prohibited from rearguing proportionality, it was determined that the Court should instruct the jury to answer the question 'no', if one or more of the jurors found any aspect of the circumstances or of the defendant's character to justify a sentence less than death...

An interesting exchange took place:

Kolego: ... The fact that you convicted somebody doesn't mean that there is no doubt. And there have been cases of innocent people being convicted of crimes, even here with the Springfield Police Department.

The Court: Okay.

Hugi: I'll take exception to that. I don't know of any cases of innocent people being convicted.

The Defendant: I do.

Kolego: So, essentially, we think that that's a legitimate topic for argument...

The Court: *After a further page of discussion* ... Therefore this residual doubt is a contrary instruction to my instruction of beyond a reasonable doubt. You're precluded from doing that... it would potentially conjure up how cases were prosecuted under different district attorneys with different ideas... of the death penalty... [*Karlyn writes in a smiley face.*]

Kolego brought up the aspect of asking for a mistrial because of the court's admitting "bad act" testimonies against Karlyn, overruling his objection at the time. In reviewing a transcript of Murdock's opening statements—supposedly opening the door to that evidence by asserting her peaceful character—he saw nothing that would open the door.

This was opposed by Hugi. The judge immediately stated he read the opening statement also, and found a number of occasions that supported his ruling. The motion was denied...

With the jury then called in, the Court instructed them in the penalty phase, which is not often necessary, since all murders don't qualify for this phase. He stated that the jurors should consider all the evidence they had heard, plus additional statements from the prosecution and the defense and the statements of additional witnesses.

He stated that here they would be dealing with just four questions, and that it would take only one vote by one of the twelve jurors to spare the life of the defendant.

The definition of the four questions was outlined by the prosecution in his Opening Remarks for the State, and Hugi used the occasion to go over all the evidence that had been outlined for them which ought to be used in determining their answer to each question, and telling them in detail why their answer should be 'yes' to each question.

The four questions would be: 1) Was the conduct of the defendant committed deliberately and with reasonable expectation that the death of James would result? 2) Is there a probability that the defendant would commit criminal acts of violence that would be a continuing threat to society? 3) Was the conduct of the defendant in killing James in response to provocation by him? 4) Should the defendant receive the death sentence?

In the examples, Hugi selected from the most odious of the testimonies, no matter how they conflicted with other testimonies, or the evidence. *He gave his version as the "evidence," yet in the beginning of the trial he stated that nothing attorneys say is evidence.* At least twice Kolego objected to the evidence that was alleged, and finally to a consideration of Eklof's character based on the "bad act" witnesses brought forward and Hugi's suggestion that the manner in which James was killed—'this knifing'—would be enough. Kolego's objections were overruled.

Opening Remarks for the Defense were brief. Kolego reviewed the three possible outcomes of the sentencing: 1) death, 2) life without parole, and 3) life with the possibility of parole after thirty years. He also reminded the jury that there were no trials or convictions in any of the "bad act" episodes brought forth during the trial, and that she had only two charges on record, before this case, those of giving false information to a police officer and a misdemeanor battery conviction, both in 1990, and that the victim in the latter case would be brought in to be heard during this penalty phase. He also listed the deputies who would be brought in to attest that she had not created one problem while in custody.

The questions were barely mentioned, but the jury was assured of her value to other people, for example, fellow inmates and, in particular, her emotional value to her son.

****

Although we are at present describing the penalty phase and what went on in the courtroom at that time, twice there were references to the "bad act" testimonies allowed in during Karlyn's trial. They were dealt with in that long chapter, but there were certain aspects of those charges against Karlyn that were not given. In addition, they became issues again during the penalty phase.

Kolego just reminded the jury that there were no trials or convictions relating to the "bad acts" Hugi brought forward, and only two charges on record. One of those is as follows:

Tiana Jordan was brought forward for the prosecution to describe the incident for which Karlyn was given a misdemeanor battery conviction. Officer Jeff Ziegler testified concerning the above incident, during which she was arrested, got loose, and was again reapprehended.

There was also the testimony of Mike Mansfield, which was used initially to blacken the name of Eklof and to create a media blitz that she might be the one responsible for Salmu's disappearance. The police, during the first week after the disappearance, allegedly paid a large sum of money to Francis, bartender at the White Horse Tavern, who was a friend of Salmu's and jealous of Karlyn, to name and enlist her employer's cooperation in this story, the first major story to hit the newspapers. She called her a "black belt, murdering biker bitch." [To the writer this tells more about the Springfield police department than about Karlyn.]

Laura and Mike, the couple who had known Karlyn in San Diego and invited her to come up, introduced her to Mike Mansfield, and he turned out to be a very generous person. He purchased secondhand beds at a bargain price, which helped her set herself up in an apartment quite nicely. She thought he was her friend, until he appeared at her trial.

As a witness against her, Mike gave the State just about anything they wanted. The State offered him relief from some drug charges. He would do a year on his sixty-month sentence and he'd walk. Well, he jumped at the opportunity, and so did a few other folks.

Mike stated for the record that he had known Karlyn from the first day she arrived up from San Diego and that he had even employed her at one of his card tables at the White Horse Tavern in Springfield. But he went on to say that he had to let her go due to the fact, as he stated, "She was hired to do cards," and that she had tried to be a bouncer (which Karlyn states was not exactly true).

What actually occurred was that a very angry and aggressive customer one night threw a chair at the pool table lamp. Karlyn raised her arms and in a very assertive voice told him he had won and the fight was over. The customer responded calmly to her voice and exited the bar. The police caught up to him outside and took him into custody so he wouldn't drive home drunk.

Mike also testified that he saw Dennis, the man she was dating at that time and later almost married, with a fat lip one time. Dennis claimed it happened when he was asleep and that Karlyn had done it. Karlyn wasn't sure how.

Francis' daughter Brenda visited Karlyn in prison to tell her that her mother was dying of cancer and wanted her to know she was very sorry what she had done. She said she knew that Karlyn was not responsible for the murder. When the prosecution has big bucks to spend and cases against many people, they can get them to say whatever they want.

Karlyn was pictured as "combative" with no provocation and mean-spirited. The jury could look at her with grave concern. Yet she was not allowed to react or say anything to the one-sided bully stories being built up against her.

Then came Dennis with his testimony. He reflected very angrily about the time they traveled together from Springfield to San Diego. Karlyn is convinced that Dennis didn't have a clue about what had encroached upon her during their sojourn there.

He was, therefore, not much interested in defending her or making her look good when he was called to be a trial witness. The jury was left with the impression she had somehow punched him, and I believe she did at one point when he rudely put his hands under her buttocks while dancing at a tavern.

Then there was the "Raccoon Eyes" episode, which happened at Dave Tiner's apartment in Fresno after Jethro took them down the I-5 after the murder. The incident was described in the chapter, Under Surveillance, but is again summarized here:

Tiner sent Karlyn across the walk to pay for a phone bill that Tiner had ran up and then followed her over to the apartment. That sudden surprise caused Karlyn to raise her arms to cover her head which caused her to elbow the woman standing next to her. Immediately apologies were made. But Tiner had already seen that Karlyn was a nervous wreck and gave her that look to get it together.

Another witness, Corina Birch, was brought forward who had been one of Karlyn's first friends when she came to Eugene. She was also one of those who helped care for her children when she, Dennis, and Patrick took that trip to San Diego.

Somehow, in the anxious days while Jethro was in Springfield and tensions were building up there was an altercation between Karlyn and Corina. Although it never progressed to being physical, her testimony was allowed to influence the jury that it might have been. It was alleged that Karlyn became volatile toward Birch when she refused to replace food stamps.

Karlyn's trial lawyer, John Kolego, initially objected to the above "bad act" testimonies. However they were allowed in, in violation of a rule calling for their review. John even rested during them, while the jurors were at the very edge of their seats, gut-wrenched and determined to do the prosecutor proud. Hugi wanted the death penalty.

****

Six deputies were brought in who attested to her good behavior, cooperation and value to other inmates during her incarceration.

In spite of the testimonies in the penalty phase which were positive, Mr. Hugi at one point inserted into one of them the following comment: "Were you aware that she's threatened to kill an inmate and said she already killed a man and had nothing to lose?" *This is the typical type of vindictive bullying that we can expect from State officials. They're vigilantes, tyrants! He said that without any proof, and wasn't required to give any. There was no objection.*

Officers who have observed me in one-and-a-half years of incarceration stated I have a calming effect on people and am generally helpful, work thoroughly, and no close supervision was required. Hugi caused further damage in a PSI report sent to prison officials in which it was said I threatened and abused people in the Lane County jail system. This really hurt, even after all the damages from the interrogation. Again, he was not required to produce witnesses to those allegations, which nonetheless prejudiced the prison officials.

Monday, October 2, 1995

Karlyn's mother, Peggy Minch, was called as defense witness. The first questions she was asked were about Karlyn's godfather, Bob Dahle, and she denied that he was her father. She also said her 'real' father was not only strict, but abused his three children after he came back from being a POW in Vietnam. She described her phone calls to her children and the emotional value that has for them.

TJ was asked about letters and phone calls from his mother and their effect on him and Immanuel and Caroline. He said she taught him to be grateful, to make friends, and to cook. He described her taking in a homeless person. *Although Murdock conducted this direct examination, nothing to support the abuse and fear I suffered from Jethro is ever asked, which he had promised in his Opening Statement by the Defense.*

Another witnesses by the Defense was called, Deputy Matthew Keetle, who attested to her good character...

In a Colloquy the court discussed the placement of the allocution, before or after a possible rebuttal. It was decided the rebuttal would be afterward. There was an interesting exchange which took place:

The Court: Is your client prepared to make her statement today?
Mr. Kolego: I believe she is, your Honor, yes.

The Court: I've read the cases on allocution, Mr. Hugi, and I can't quite figure out where you get the idea there's a case that says the proper scope of the statement. Nobody suggests what that proper scope is.

Mr. Hugi: I think it's wrong. It's not evidentiary. And dealing with the facts of the case that it's fair game, I think she can say, "Don't kill me." I think she can say, "I'm sorry." But I think if she says, "Hey I didn't do it. Jethro did it, and here's the story," that's out of bounds.

The Defendant: What are you afraid of?

Mr. Kolego answered that if you've been convicted you still have the right to say whether you are denying guilt or not and to plead mitigation of sentence.

Another witness by the defense is heard via telephone, Deputy Rick Maya, who testified that she had never threatened or been aggressive toward other inmates or jail staff.

In a colloquy with the jury present Hugi questioned whether the victim's family would be given the right to address the jury as well. Kolego stated that there is no common law right of allocution for victims in capital cases. The Court pointed out that there are no cases when it was denied. Kolego then requested a recess in order to research it. *Due to the fact that I requested to make a statement to sentencing jurors, Mr. Hugi, on a whim, pushed for the family to come on as witnesses which the court and defense attorney are questioning as improper procedure.*

The judge proposed that they proceed with Karlyn's statement, and then he would tell them what he was going to do about this. It turned out that he went immediately to the victim's impact statements without any further study.

****

Statement by the Defendant

[Karlyn appeared before the jury and delivered her prepared allocation, which was, of course, after she was convicted on all counts. A few statements and paragraphs have been removed in the interests of brevity, and an occasional word or phrase correction has been entered. These corrections were very few, and Karlyn's handwritten copy of her intended statements were used as a guide.]

The Court: Well, let's proceed with your client's statement and I'll tell you what I'm going to do when I get done with that.

Members of the jury, in much the same way that a convicted defendant may address the sentencing judge, because, as I will instruct you, you are the sentencing body in this case, the defendant may address you. This statement is not made under oath nor is the defendant able to be questioned about it. In other words, she's not subject to cross-examination. The statement is not evidence in the case. You may consider the statement for whatever you deem it to be worth.

The Defendant: May I sit where the witnesses sit?

The Court: Yes.

The Defendant: Thank you. This hasn't been very easy for any of us, nor certainly for yourself more than myself. I must give the greatest apology and the most deepest and sincerest apology to the Salmu family, his friends, and coworkers for an error of judgment. Not only on my behalf, but also on Jethro Tiner.

I did not intentionally kill James, nor did I stab him, nor did I say I would take him out of his misery. It was never my intention to see any harm to him. He was my friend and he was very good to me.

I have come forward on my own through many struggles after some very traumatic things that happened including that I was taken deeply advantage of but I understand the reasons why for that. I have prepared this statement hoping I can bring awareness to the

things that I have fallen into and the things that are capable of prosecution.

Your Honor, at this time, if I may please the Court, may I continue with this?

The Court: Go ahead.

The Defendant: Thank you. It is important to me at this time you try to understand a few things. First, I pray to our lord Jesus to give me strength and the wisdom to speak the truth to your hearts to give you peace and comfort at this time.

I am from a very loving family. My grandparents have been married 65 years and they are going strong. They're inseparable and they have a very strong religious background through the Lord. This is not an omission of guilt; this just as a reference of background. My mother's a very devoted woman. She's very strong. She supports me very much. They believe in justice but they do not support the State employees and what they have done to deceive you in this case.

I do not expect any of you to believe me at this time. But if you would, could you keep in mind the things I am about to say. You have an image in your mind of what happened, it is gross and it is also an error. Due to the dramatic, theatrical, speculation statements of State employee, Fred Hugi, which is due to the manipulation of Jerry Smith. During my first two hours of interrogation, Jerry Smith told another officer, quote, unquote, "We just can't allow her to walk in here and solve this case. It would be politically embarrassing."

I came in with written statements. Things that happened that were very strange, unusual, and very painful happened to me and my children afterwards. James was just the beginning of some horror for me. My original statements have been altered by employee tactics of harsh, lengthy interrogation.

There's a whole lot more to this case that could and would prove my innocence but the State employee, Fred Hugi, doesn't want you to know that. They don't want you to know the whole truth. I presented detectives with written statements. I trusted them with valuable information. I tried answering their questions, and when I didn't have answers, they filled them in themselves with speculations and accusations. And I fear that's what's been used in this case to convict me.

I was told I was being prepared for Grand Jury. Jerry Smith thanked me for solving their case which did not have a body yet. He told me he didn't want me to get impeached. He insisted we go over again and boy, I was exhausted and emotionally struggling. As we spoke, Jerry would take parts of my statements and twist them and say, "That's what you mean." I didn't have anybody to defend me. There was nobody to help; I was scared.

Jerry Smith kept looking at his watch. He started rotating officers in to question me. Jerry's perspectives were being added to my statements. I've been scared for a very, very long time. I might come from a rough background, slightly outspoken, slightly wild. It was never my intention was to see James hurt. I don't believe in guns and I don't believe in what happened. I don't condone it. I don't believe in what happened at all.

Words enough cannot apologize for what happened here. I am doing the best I can do in bringing the full truth forward. I did not kill James; I did not stab him. I did not sick Jethro on him. I did not take him out of his misery, and it was never my intention to see any harm come to him. I have come forward to give you facts. In my life, I have made errors and poor judgment calls, but I also know right from wrong. And I have made different efforts to bring you that information.

This was an unexpected situation that tossed me into a helplessness and emotional devastation which has put me at a mental loss. I was very withdrawn. It has taken a lot of courage to overcome my fear and I don't want you suffering anymore. I have to suffer with this for a long time. This isn't over yet, not by any means.

You have been given... their version of what they only want you to believe. Cleverly they have used this case. In interrogation, Jerry Smith's tactics were pushing the truth out of my statements. He told me his years of experience, his perspectives, were the only logical way things happened. Then he rotated officers in to question. I felt misled and abused but I stayed confident. I was trying to do the right thing.

Officers would just say, "A few more questions." Detective Walker questioned me, Rick Lewis questioned me and Tom Yates, too. I understood them, but I didn't understand what was happening. I was called a cock-a-bull liar and he would tell me we're going to be there a long while. The other officers told me I was being very cooperative and I appreciated it.

When Jerry came in, he would explain facts about other cases and apply them to this case. This was horrifying to me. He placed a chair in front of me, and leaned forward, and placed a hand against his knee, and started swinging an arm back and forth. It was very intimidating. Jerry said I better cooperate with him. He needed the truth, and I better tell it. I told him I had given it to him. I was trying very much to be helpful. Again, detectives rotated in, questioned me, and checked on me.

Jerry Smith closed the door and sat next to me on the couch, and for a while, he carried a casual conversation. He told me to relax, lay back my head, close my eyes. He was holding my hand. He'd say, "Karlyn, now we need to know where's James."

He'd say, "I know this is pretty hard on you. Jethro put you through a lot and we want to help you with that. First, let's get this over with. This isn't getting any better. You can remember, Karlyn, you just need some help. Come on, do it."

He'd say, "You just want to be helpful and I know you don't want to remember. And when you do, just say it. Let's go over it again. Relax and just say you did it and this will all be over tonight. Come on, you're almost there. We will be there. And I've got an officer to take you to your children, and I'll get out of here too." He was referring to me to cooperating to a stabbing.

I tried to tell him it didn't happen that way. I didn't do it. He said I was a cock-a-bill liar and he said I wasn't concentrating. That I needed to cooperate with him and I told him I was trying and I wanted to be helpful. I need to talk to James' family and this wasn't going anywhere.

Jerry Smith told me to describe the place where James' body was. I told him I did not know. He said, "Come on, you're just not concentrating for James' mama." That was ripping me apart...

For a while, I didn't know, and he repeated some things to me. "You were riding in the car, riding in the truck." Well, maybe I was. "Whose truck?" I didn't know. I hadn't seen it... "Who was driving? Describe the dashboard. Anything." I don't know. I could see the truck and being in the front seat of a truck. My head was in Jethro's lap. He asked me to describe... the inside of the truck... The two men don't want me sitting up. He didn't want me to see where they're headed...

The Court: Ma'am, you're going to have to slow down.

The Defendant: Yes, your Honor, thank you... I told him I think it's just a bad dream. I asked him if we could make this into an easier process. He reassured me I was doing fine.

Jerry said, "You stabbed James. You did it." I said, "No. I did not." He said, "Well, you did. You had to of." I told him, "No. I did not. I came here to let you know. I came here to let James' family know what happened."

I was trying to do the right thing. Jerry told me to relax. He offered me something to drink. He always brought me a Pepsi. He told me to lay my head back and close my eyes. He sat next to me holding my hand to comfort me. It wasn't long before he had a real tight grip on my hand and he was touching himself, and he realized that I saw. He stood up and told me that I would not disrespect his department. He said I won't be using his officers now and I would be apologizing to them now. He said they believe in you.

He left out the door and he came back in. He went out the door again. My years of experience, my logic, I told you, she did it. Jerry Smith returned with Detective Steve Walker and he told me to apologize to Steve. The captain says I was to apologize to you. It's possible that I might have stabbed James, and I have taken advantage of you, and I apologize. And I told him I was sure at that time that it didn't happen that way. Steve was satisfied. It would be all right. It would be okay.

Then they brought a video camera in and that was taken over and over again asking questions. And I was taken back to my children. The next couple of days were like that, five to seven hours of rotating officers, then the video camera. Spider was brought in once during interrogation and he said just tell them I didn't know or do anything. I didn't have anything. Just tell them. He was so nervous. I told him to leave, get away from me. Dave Tiner was brought in. He said, "You know, my brother's going to kill us." I said, "I know what your brother's capable of. I'm scared too."

Then on Friday, the tenth day of being here, my children and I were escorted to Grand Jury. Two ladies were asked to watch my children. One stated, "There's no Grand Jury today. It won't take long." I was escorted into Fred Hugi's office and then was handed a beautiful bouquet of flowers sent by my son. I was told thanks for solving the case and placed under arrest for murder. Fred said their feelings wouldn't change. They still cared very much about me and they told me that their feelings wouldn't change for me.

I asked Fred, "Why?" And he said, "You're a small fish to fry." He said, "You stabbed James." And I said, "No, I did not." He said, "No matter. We're not after you, we're after the big fish, Jethro." And I burst into tears and I requested an attorney. He said I would get one at Lane county. My children were brought in to me. I was told to say good-bye. I love them more than words can express. I hugged them and I kissed them. I said stay together with granny and TJ would get them. Rick said they were just doing their job. I was confident everything would work. I knew I was doing the right thing by coming here.

I was lodged in Lane County Jail on aggravated murder. A call was made to Jethro. He had made promises to turn himself in. Well, he didn't. So when I regained my stability, I came here to inform the Salmu family what happened... I'm scared of Jethro. I didn't want him to know how long I'd been here with the police.

At the end of that week, Rick and Steve, the detectives, came and advised me. Rick read me my rights. He said it was something that had been overlooked somehow and they had a few questions. I didn't mind. I wanted to cooperate. I wanted to get through it. This is still important to me then as it is now. I still want to be helpful. I still need to prove some things.

Mr. Evans was the counselor presented to me. He advised me no more further contact with the police and I wanted to stay on top of the case. The officers; they said they were my friends and they wanted to help, and I believed them. I still do. The reverend saw me once a week. He was more comfort than counsel, more than Mr. Evans. I couldn't understand why.

I requested a grievance against Captain Smith for misconduct and I told them why. Six months went by and I requested to view those tapes. Mr. Evans advised me to take the eight-year plea bargain... I didn't understand why until I saw those tapes. I was ill. He said it was typical and that's what police do. Did they know the rotating pressure and roller coaster of emotions led to these incriminating statements? Mr. Evans reassured me that they knew exactly what they were doing and that's why I wasn't allowed to review the tapes when they were finished.

I can prove I didn't stab James. I can prove I didn't bring any harm to him. I was in error of negligence as far as defending him. Mr. Evans didn't feel any reason at that point to go any further unless some of his remains were found. I had already been put through so much. Where do I start?

He gave me no hope and with his assistant, Bill Young, they went right to work on something called motions to suppress. These are motions to suppress and these are grievances against the department. I asked for transcripts and a grievance for an investigation. He ignored my request. I had high hopes of reestablishing the truth by the grave where the remains were found...

By the grace of God the remains were found! I had high hopes of reestablishing the truth. Even though their investigation cleared me, nothing changed. Mr. Evans and I went back and forth. He didn't want to prove my innocence, he was there to judge me. I then requested a woman attorney, someone who could prove my side and comfort the family.

Mr. Evans at this time agreed to investigate. I met with the chief and just made informal written complaints against Jerry Smith for his misconduct. He wanted to know why it wasn't done sooner. Mr. Evans said he didn't think the timing was right and that I had requested it several times before. I wanted to get my information to the family along with an apology. I was told that's what trials are for.

There isn't a day that doesn't go by that I don't wish I would have done things differently. I should have paid closer attention. I should have stood up for James. I didn't realize where things were headed. I didn't know what Jethro was capable of. I am really sorry and truly sorry that James is gone at this time. James was good to me. He was my friend. He's been better to me than most people. I probably took advantage of that. But I never meant any harm to come to him. He was the first person I ever allowed my son to take off with. He taught my son how to fish. He was my friend.

I apologize. I'm sorry isn't enough. It doesn't touch what I'm feeling. It doesn't touch what you've gone through. It doesn't bring him back. I waited a long time to get this chance to speak with you. I'm very ashamed of the situation and I'm doing the best I can to bring the information to you. This is truly my hope that God's grace will cover your hearts and in time bring good memories instead of this; what you're going through now. I ask you for forgiveness. I am truly sorry this has happened. This is not an admission of guilt. This is a mercy call for forgiveness, just simply that.

I have a couple more things I'd like to say for the record. Again, it is my deepest and most sincerest apology to the Salmu family, friends, and coworkers. And I don't know what else to give you at this time. I wish for further investigation to be done on this. Mr. Evans agreed to investigate further my complaint against Jethro. I carried a lot of fear and I needed help. I was emotionally struggling.

The officers saw the damage that was done to me by Jethro and his friends to keep me from remembering or keep me from going forward. Very unusual painful things that were done to me and my children. Well, he started to say he would investigate on his trip to Disneyland. I had remembered some very strange things but I asked him not to reveal them.

When he returned, he stated he couldn't find any information to verify my complaint, and he said that he was rather direct with a few people in their questioning. He told them I remembered some things. I said, "So you told them I remembered?"

I requested a woman attorney. I called Terry Woods. She agreed to meet me. She was given twenty hours to review this case. She also agreed after viewing the tapes that eight years wasn't a bad offer. When I stressed my concerns and grievances and told her in brief that things I believed to cause this weren't being brought out, it's an awful tragedy, and I need the truth to be presented, she tried to understand and she agreed a full investigation should be conducted. Then she requested it in writing.

But Mr. Evans still wouldn't work with me on the grievances, the possibility that Spider, Potato, and/or Jethro had a control system that they don't want revealed. That's the only thing I can explain about my fear and what happened that night.

Next, Judge Ann Aiken was presented the concerns of this case. She wasn't the woman attorney I requested though she viewed the tapes. She was rather direct and she warned me of the consequences of not taking the plea offer. I was given 24 hours to think on it. I returned to the jail in denial. I did not want to do anything until the truth was stated in this case.

I fired Mr. Evans and with that I received all of Jethro's charges the next day... eight new counts. I then went to Judge Merten who granted my request for a woman attorney but it was to his amazement that no woman was available. Then came John Kolego and wonderful Jeff Murdock who have worked together and supported me in this case.

I would also like to add there was Deb Martin, who investigated, who had plenty of knowledge and concerns in this case about things not revealed to you by the employees alternating in this case. I needed much help consulting the Salmu family, and take it from me, they twisted and used it against me. I have tried to do the right thing. It is the best thing to do, to reveal what has happened.

Do the jurors know Jethro was brought here the first day of my trial? He was here to confess. Fred Hugi, in front of the judge and in front of counsel, if I may quote him, they made Jethro take the fifth. These are the same tactics that were used in the Proctor and Boots case that hindered them and imprisoned them unjustly for over eight years. I don't know much about law but I do know right from wrong.

The prosecution has taken advantage of me for media purposes and incredible glorification. It takes a lot and a peaceful heart to endure things that this trial has gone through. I need to prove the facts of this case. Thank you for listening.

Your Honor, may I step down, please?

The Court: Yes.

****

Immediately after the allocution the Court asked: Mr. Hugi, do you have a representative of the victim present? With that established, Kolego stated:

Your Honor, I understand the Court is going to allow this. I would like to make an exception for the record. An objection on the record... Ms. Eklof's right of allocution is within the four questions... These are aggravated circumstances that... don't even apply (to the victim's family)... we want to note an objection.

With James' brother on the stand, the parameters of what he might say are discussed.

The statement by the victim is interspersed with a continuing dialogue with the judge about what he is allowed to say, which, it appears, are answers to questions the judge asks. *I believe this conversation was used to keep alive in the jurors' minds the vividness of horror Hugi used to sway the jurors. Later Judge Merten would give jury instructions using graphic wording, which would leave an impression on their minds of determination.* The rebuttal or Opening Argument for the State immediately followed.

Dealing first with Karlyn's statement, Hugi said, "It's... I don't know how to respond to that. She's got this opportunity to just lie to you unchecked. And we don't get to present evidence, nothing. We just sit here and take it and listen to it. And I guess it speaks for itself."

Mr. Hugi complained about my statement, calling me a liar, wanting to check it with the evidence. *What did this guy want? They blasted me out of the water by hours of coerced statements which were false and misrepresented the case. They spent close to three years preparing them. This is vindictive bullying.*

Hugi claimed that Karlyn was trying to find a third party, a bushy-haired stranger, who really did this crime. *He must still be thinking of Diane Downes.* Then he went on to use Dave Tiner's statements. *I never spray painted the car; I never laughed about this; I never thought it was just a game.* He said Karlyn was sick, but not as a mental defense, then listed what the exhibits were about, and concluded it was not about jail officers or her phony-baloney story, it was about the butchering of a person.

Kolego objected that these were not relevant inquiries on the four questions... He had made a comment about the allocution, that was fair. But this was not addressing the four questions. His objection was overruled.

Hugi said Karlyn had a sociopathic personality, to which Kolego objected. This was overruled, assuming the term was used in everyday common meaning. *Hugi accuses me of killing James. No proof of that. He states that I bragged about it afterwards. Yet the interrogation clearly indicates I have no memory of that, so how could I brag. Dave Tiner's cousin in Tennessee and the prostitute in Nevada clearly stated that it was Jethro who bragged.* Hugi said some guards in jail came in here and said she was no problem on their shift. That was like a rattlesnake that had lost its rattles. Well, let them deal with her. *Hugi is getting pumped up, yelling at the jurors. Then he apologizes for raising his voice.*

Hugi convinced the jurors of cuts and slices *that truly never occurred,* stating it was up close, stating there was no sense of contrition or penitence. He started to suggest that there were going to be deputies available... *(who might testify against me?)*

Kolego objected and said there was no evidence of that... He could have called somebody from the institution. The Court sustained the objection, and Kolego asked that the jury be instructed to disregard Hugi's statement.

Hugi called Jeff's and Karlyn's relationship a perfect match made in heaven. Whatever he would do, she would do. Hugi recalled her phone conversation with Jeff from jail stating she didn't accuse him of shooting James *because he might have accused me of stabbing him 30 times. Hugi accused me of melting: Oh Jeff, you got married! These were questions the officers promoted, and I was too scared of Jeff to accuse him. If anything, my children aren't safe, Hugi!*

Hugi stated there was no motive here—*the first truthful statement from this bully—then he realized what he said and tried to clean it up by stating they were not required to show a motive, which makes it worse.* Hugi pushed jurors to believe a woman can be manipulative, can be dangerous... even when they're incarcerated... so what we have left is... a fighting machine. And what could we do about it? We could answer the four questions yes...

Kolego pleaded her case with the jurors through the first and third questions—if they believed she deliberately killed James with no provocation from him—that his primary concern was with the second and fourth questions, the probability that she would be a continuing threat to society and that she should receive the death sentence. He argued that there was no criminal violence on her part before 1990, and we were not going to litigate each of the assaults. Also that we didn't have evidence of prior uses of weapons.

He was not going to say she's innocent—they had obviously found me guilty—but they should look at the evidence and remember that the State had a burden of proof beyond a reasonable doubt on the question of future dangerousness, and he didn't believe they had met that burden.

Mr. Hugi stated they didn't have expert witnesses; they hadn't wanted to insult the jury's intelligence. There were four simple questions to be answered, which were to be answered yes.

The community depended on them as representatives to do the job. Kolego objected that the community was depending on them to kill her, but it was overruled.

Hugi said she had a motive to behave in jail, so she'd have witnesses to come in for her, but had had no others. *They were waived from the beginning. I was given no defense.* Hugi went on to say she acknowledged no wrongdoing, but that Mr. Kolego had said she had some conscience because she came forward and talked to the police, that any lawyer would have told her not to talk.

Then Hugi said, "Well, so, **she didn't hide behind the shyster,** you know." Kolego objected to this as improper argument and the Court asked for a different word, Mr. Hugi. *Here in a nutshell is what Hugi is saying: Don't thwart us and don't expose us, so we can frame people and solve cases.*

After Hugi's Closing Statement, the Colloquy was at first devoted to questions the jury might have about the timing of their deliberations…

In absence of the jury, the court then heard Mr. Kolego call for a mistrial for allowing the victim's relative to testify and for Mr. Hugi's saying that Karlyn could have hid behind a shyster—and to imply they were shysters— which he thought was prejudicial and should entitle them to a mistrial.

Hugi explained that Kolego himself had said any attorney would tell her to not talk to the police, which he didn't view as responsible behavior on the part of attorneys. *Exactly. That's part of their tactics down there in Lane County. They deny people their rights and justify it this way.* Both of Kolego's motions were denied, *of course.*

[That was the point wherein Judge Merten should have called Hugi on his remark. People do have the right to remain silent, I believe, though Judge Merten evidently doesn't think so. Hugi and his deputies have proven exactly why they should.]

Jury instructions were given. These included an additional one: If they were to answer one or more of the questions 'no', they must decide a fifth question, whether the defendant should be sentenced to life imprisonment with or without the possibility of parole or release. The verdict was to be done on a master copy, not separate votes.

The verdict revealed the following answers to the four questions:

1) Was the conduct of the defendant committed deliberately and with reasonable expectation that the death of James would result? Foreperson: The jury voted no, your Honor. The Court asked whether or not they had answered the other three questions, and they had. Therefore,

2) Is there a probability that the defendant would commit criminal acts of violence that would be a continuing threat to society? The jury voted no, your Honor.

3) Was the conduct of the defendant in killing James in response to provocation by him? The jury voted yes, your Honor.

4) Should the defendant receive the death sentence? The jury voted no, your Honor.

Therefore, with three 'no' answers, the fifth question had to be answered.

5) Are there sufficient mitigating circumstances to warrant a sentence of life imprisonment with the possibility of parole or release? On the last question, the jury was equally divided. Six yes, six no.

Kolego questioned the court if they would again poll the jury, which resulted in their passing a verdict form which they again filled in, but with their names recorded. The result was the same. These forms, however, were to be put in a sealed envelope, not to be opened except if recalled by the appellate court with jurisdiction.

Tuesday, December 12, 1995 Sentencing

The judge called for any family members to address him. *James' mother came forward and stood next to me. She immediately confronted me. I had no warning of this. Merten just played it off. As she began venting, she claimed she never saw me cry or show remorse. My attorney's both clearly instructed me not to show any emotions. Do not cry!*

Then she claimed that James had requested that if anything ever happened to him just bring him home. *Thomas Evans showed me a written will and testament from James which was written over a year before he met me. The will claimed somebody might shoot him from the bar.*

James' mother gave me a message from his younger son, which was, "Fuck off, die, and go to hell, Karlyn." *If James had a son why didn't he ever say anything? Why weren't there any pictures or phone calls?*

David Salmu was again called forward as a family member who wanted to address me. He pretty much goes into detail what people had told him that James had said about the last few months of his life. He mentioned Francis who originally called his family and stirred people up, *who on her deathbed said she knew I didn't kill James.*

James sister also told of her grief and, in person, made her accusations. She stated that little by little they found out what happened the night her brother was murdered. *These bits and pieces were spoon fed to this family to keep them pumped up to believe in the police version. I was always the suspect, and I was never given the chance to defend myself. The DA here is proven to have never needed me as a witness, but always as a suspect.*

Karlyn was given the opportunity to read another prepared apology, but she still requested help in revealing the truth of what happened. *Because I did not commit this terrible crime, I am accused again and again of a lack of remorse. I have expressed my sorrow all that I can for what James' family has been through. But Judge Merten can only respond, immediately:*

The Court: "I find the following aggravating factors: Deliberate cruelty to the victim, repetitive assaults, use of a weapon in the commission of the offense, lack of remorse by the defendant and lack of provocation by the victim."

The Sentencing was as follows: Counts 1, 2, and 3, and to Count 3, aggravated murder, for which she was sentenced to life without the possibility of parole.

Count 4 merged with Count 6, aggravated murder, kidnapping, for which she was sentenced to life without parole, consecutive to all other sentences.

Count 5, assault in the first degree, she was sentenced to 130 months consecutive to all sentences; Count 7, unauthorized use of a vehicle, 12 months; Count 8, felon in possession, 36 months; and Count 9, abuse of corpse, 24 months.

She was told she had rights to appeal, and to write for a notice of appeal in the next 30 days.

Chap XXII: Post Trial Diary

K arlyn's story thus far has been based primarily on her journals
and the legal documents she wrote comments on Since her
sentencing she has written long summaries of her story and of
those traumatic days of her interrogation, and trial. She has also written appeals for herself, as anyone in her position might do. Since the writer has had
access to these additions, minor points and refinements have been worked
into the telling of her story .

In regard to her journal writing, however, that activity soon came to an
end. First there is a gap in her writing. Then a journal appears two months
after the trial. New people emerge without explanation indicating there may
be another missing journal. The reader should be warned that this is her last
journal and that the rest of her story will be told by the writer, what I learned
when I first came into contact with Karlyn, in the spring of 1997. and about
what had happened since then, including excerpts from letters from her.

The reader should also keep in mind that this journal began after the
penalty phase and before her sentencing, which took place in December. Although the court transcript of her sentencing and her comments have been
given previously, her journal will give some indication of what was going on
in her mind before, during and after the sentencing .

Since this is her last journal, the writer will leave it in first person and
make but few cuts, in order to bring her closer and allow the reader to enter
into her confusion and heartbreak.

Thursday, November 16, 1995

*I received two birthday cards. Nana sent $10. She was at emergency all
night. Bumpa has pneumonia. I spoke to him. Although he sounded wonderful, he said he didn't feel too good. In all my life he has never complained.
This hurts so much. I miss them.*

Martha sent me a card. It is beautiful!

Mother received a follow-up call at work from the Governor's secretary. The secretary wasn't very nice. She told Mother I wasn't even here, at the Lane County Jail, and she didn't know who I was.

Paya spoke to Larry and is sending the box of papers down. He wants the transcript. Marcia is working too. Murdock is also.

[It would appear that Paya and Karlyn have met, that Marcia is another independent person interested in her case, and that Jeffrey Murdock is still working as her public defender.]

Paya made a comment, looking at Thomas Evans' work for Motion to Suppress, "I can't tell who he's writing for, you or the prosecution."

People attach themselves to a notorious case, like Karlyn's, and enter into the atrocities of her police betrayal and her vivid experiences as victim of ritual abuse. Paya and Marcia entered in that order, Paya, because she was taking a course from Jerry Smith at LCC on criminal justice and realized he was breaking all the rules after she chose Karlyn's case for her case study; and Marcia, professor at OSU, who was doing research on ritual abuse and white slavery. I believe they were both at her trial.

Friday, November 17, 1995

It was a late visit, but bless her heart, Marcia came. I appreciate her so much. Our visit was very encouraging and uplifting. She seems to have all the right questions.

I received birthday cards from my children, a beautiful angel and a letter from TJ, school pictures, handprints, and a card from Paya and also Marcia. Very thoughtful.

Sunday I spoke to Mother for an hour. A lot of complications, TJ's not in school. He was suspended. Caroline is throwing fits and Immanuel is just as sweet and onery as he can be. Bumpa has pneumonia. Nana moved a chair and fractured her vertebrae. She and Bumpa both were in the hospital this week. As the ambulance was called, Bumpa checked the car. There were two flat tires, stuck with huge safety pins. The neighbor went to buy tires and installed them. And I sit in Lane County Jail awaiting a life sentence to a murder I was a witness to. If these are God's blessings, I certainly don't want a curse.

Tuesday November 21, 1995

Marcia came to visit. That precious woman follows all my complaints. And encourages me to follow through with my hopes. Although I am an inmate here I do require a reasonable amount of notice for preparation in arriving for appointments. Due to the lack of consideration, all paperwork is one-sided.

She urged me to require a certain amount of notice.

Fred Hugi requested a PSI (Pre-Sentencing Investigation) to be done before sentencing. So I called John today. No answer. I called Jeff (Murdock). He's in and says tomorrow at 12:30 P. M. is the appointment. Well, that's news to me. But he also says that he's in trial and requested John to be available. Now tomorrow should be interesting. Will an attorney show or not is the question. Although Jeff gave me clear instructions, do not talk to them unless an attorney was with me, he also inquired if I would make a statement. A complaint, more like it. I guess the PSI people want a statement.

Wednesday, November 22, 1995

The notary came at 9:30 A. M. today and put her stamp on the Sexual Assault Support Services (SASS) paperwork so Debi Martin could release my journals. Then the PSI guy came, and, guess what, no attorney, so no appointment!

Well, I am back into the dorm. Tomorrow is Mary's birthday. I feel a lot better, and I can breathe again. Spending a few days getting reacquainted with the Lord has made a wonderful difference...

Thursday, November 23, 1995 Happy Thanksgiving.

Nana is in the convalescent hospital. How I wish I were there to help her. She watched over me when I broke my neck.

Friday, November 24, 1995

At 2 o'clock the deputy calls to me. Attorney visit, will I go? It's John Kolego, and he starts with the PSI guy, Jean Spears, who was coming in to do an investigation on me. He says Fred was in his office saying he was sure I would get my conviction overturned and go home. But he insisted on sticking me with something; well, of course, why not? Fred is going for any of the other charges which are already time served. But he wants something, anything. Kolego asked if I wanted to make a statement but advised me not to because it would only add fuel to the fire. No kidding!

So we talked about the other charges that are on Fred's list, and as I said clearly over and over again, it all happened the way it happened, and I came forward to do the right thing. I have given all I can give and they rudely took advantage of me. I did the best I could.

I asked how I could put in a grievance against Fred. Kolego said Fred is allowed to use any distractions; he has no law. Well, we'll see about that. I've been wrongly and falsely convicted. Anyway, Jean Spears showed up. John Kolego went out of the visiting room and said we had no statement and were going for an appeal. As they walked off together to leave, I could see John apologizing to Jean all the way out the door...

This is all very confusing. Hugi requested the PSI guy so he'd be covered if her charges were dismissed. As a matter of fact, she was found not guilty of the first two counts. But she was given the lesser charges of those two counts and all the other charges. Many times she has mentioned to me that they should have been dismissed those other charges.

Tonight Marcia came. She's always so supportive. I called Debi Martin at 6:00 P. M. She was working on a murder case late. I explained that SASS wanted the journals, so we decided to copy and release the remaining papers. [This, I believe, is the group Marcia works through, wanting Karlyn's story of abuse through the white slavery ring.]

I spoke to Paya. She is ready to send written copies of a press release to the Governor, Hugi, and several of news media. [That's Paya, all right! When I met her I was flabbergasted. She was not afraid of anybody. She marched right into Hugi's office, Jerry Smith's, and got the governor and the news media on the phone.]

Tuesday November 28, 1995

Final Justice aired a show at 10:00 P. M. about women who are hypnotized and kept captive for sexual and violent reasons, chained and blindfolded, but also kept up on outside daily activities and ran around town to do errands.

Hard Copy aired a story about a pornography videotape out of Japan of women being forced into rooms and raped by three or more men. [**Hard Copy** was going to interview Karlyn about her story recently, but they never did...]

Friday, December 1, 1995

Emma and Marcia came. They met yesterday with the director of SASS, whose name is Phyllis. She is very concerned and willing to represent me. I complained of the "prince charming and the spirit you've been waiting for" Jethro used which was probably the same spirit I saw that night of the ritual.

I spoke to Jeff (Murdock) by phone. He comforted me. I was starting to get very negative. He reassured me I would get my appeal and retrial. He said Paya and Marcia visited Kolego, and Paya flagged him down at the court house and pleasantly conversed. He said she is very loyal.

I spoke to Paya for about one-and-a-half hours by phone. She drilled me on not being negative. We covered a lot. I feel better although she did tell me that due to her interest in this case her grades have dropped. She picked up my bags from booking. I feel refreshed by her support and concern. She has spoken to several people on my behalf.

Sunday, December 3, 1995

Mother stated that a friend of hers, Shawn Diane, bought the children this year's Christmas tree and a train to go around it. I called while they were decorating it. Caroline was so excited to see the lights from outside she hung up.

Friday, December 8, 1995

Paya visited. She looks great and sounds great. I could tell she was pleased to see that I felt better after our previous phone call. Marcia showed up late. She was horse riding and had hay barn on her jacket. These two gals are wonderful to keep up on the steps involved in my story.

I called Paya. She is procrastinating on her Bio study, but sounds great.

Day before sentencing
Monday, December 11, 1995

Today was my visit with Emma, Marcia, and Paya and it was wonderful. We sat at the round table in the multipurpose room. Phyllis didn't show. I would have liked to meet her. As we spoke I felt a sense of lasting friendship. I wish I could have met these wonderful women in another way. But of course that's not possible now. I just hope they can achieve all that they're out for. I appreciate their love and support. How I wish I could do something special for them.

John Kolego saw me for a visit on behalf of Hugi. He says the DA wants to subpoena me to Grand Jury. He says that if I respond he'll go to the Governor on my behalf to commute my sentence down to eight years. So I said, "No."

I will be at his trial. No sooner. Also, James' brother will speak and his mother and sister sent a video. Oh, yeah, Fred is going to speak also. All I want is the truth, until this case is presented with facts only. Then, and only then, will I be at peace.

Steve Walker and Rick Lewis were waiting outside when Paya, Marcia, and Emma left today. John questioned Paya on her knowledge of the case or interpretation. She told him there were areas of question on police procedure. Steve, also, sent word to me that if I would like to have him visit he would. As long as we don't discuss Jethro, right?...

At a different time Karlyn wrote about the day before sentencing, which had more to do with legal aspects between herself and her attorneys. Those writings now follow:

December 11, 1995

The day before sentencing John Kolego, appointed defense attorney during the trial came to see me. He asked if I had any questions. I said, "Sure, why didn't you defend me in the trial?"

He said, "We've gone over that. You'll get your appeal." He stated that Fred Hugi approached him and their conversation was that Fred offered to commute my sentence to the governor. I didn't know what that meant, but he continued. He described a few things that he would say on my behalf.

I asked him what was Fred up to now? He wants you to testify against Jethro Tiner before Grand Jury. I told him, as he already knew, "I have always been available to testify against him to the Grand Jury. But not until the truth of this case was brought out. Down to the truth!"

I asked, "What is this commute thing?" He said that it was a deal that the governor would agree to a much lesser sentence, and probably it would be the original eight-year offer. I said, "No! I want the truth of this case revealed, not Fred Hugi's story! I would have taken the eight year bargain in the beginning if the facts were being represented correctly, not twisted and reprogrammed!"

I asked him why he didn't he go to the Governor himself to commute my sentence. Instead of answering, he said he would accept my calls collect and that he truly felt bad about the way things went. He felt Fred did him wrong. Kolego said Fred said that he wasn't sure the case would get overturned or that he wanted to get me for any lesser charge. He had to keep his hooks in me!

Somehow it came about that we discussed what Dennis Heide said to him in the court room. John asked Dennis what kind of a girlfriend I was. Dennis replied, "She's gullible!" That means, I believe, that I'll believe anything, at first, anyway. Dennis took me to the Hilton on Halloween 1992. Dennis took me to San Diego. Dennis is starting to prove he can be involved.

Abruptly Kolego said he would forward paperwork to appeal my case, and then he couldn't be my attorney anymore.

I asked him why is Fred doing this to me. Haven't I already been through enough? He said, "You'll get your appeal." He said, "Everybody knows Jethro did this." He explained the appeal and went out. I'm sure there's more to this conversation, but not much more.

So altogether I asked him three times what Fred was talking about and how is it he keeps offering me these convenient bargains just before court. When he knows I am adamant about revealing the truth. And that I will not give in to his political influences. It just gets worse every time he speaks. I understand the complication from being at a crime scene. But where does that give the right for altering the facts to create such distortion?

Day of Sentencing
Tuesday, December 12, 1995

Sentencing was horrifying. James' mother, brother and victims assault group spoke. They called me and my children names of deep disgust. James' beloved mother shook uncontrollably while she accused me of killing James. The name calling and questioning of my morals was all she could think of to do. I wanted to help her so much to see what truly happened but I could only sit there. My attorney, Murdock, could only apologize to me for having to listen to it. As his brother spoke I could only think of Fred and his wrongdoing in misleading this family and using their misery to glorify himself.

I spoke out with an apology and a direct description of the misconduct on the part of the authorities.

Then Judge Merten spoke, just barely. He sentenced me to 130 months plus 412 months back to back. Fourteen years, ten months, if I heard him correctly. *When he was finished, both attorneys fled from the court room, John stating he was going to apply for my appeal and Jeff to another case. I prayed the pain would end soon for all people involved.*

It is obvious Karlyn was stunned beyond understanding. She didn't hear the sentence correctly in the pain of what she had endured. Is it possible she went through the remaining events of the entire day, still without fully comprehending?

*I want to express my feelings about what I read in the newspaper tonight. I was sentenced to two life sentences plus 202 months. **I didn't hear any of this in the court room**, and the article says I rambled!*

With all the heart in the world I can't see that this will ever get resolved! I'm so pissed I can't even cry. I wish all the pain I've been put through would zap Hugi and Smith. Then perhaps a reality would surface in them.

[At a third time Karlyn wrote of her visit with Rick and Steve on the day of her sentencing. In her first journal writing of that day she did not yet understand. It may have become clear only when she read it in the evening paper. Her third analysis of that meeting, though repetitive, is included here because of her additional understanding of what happened to her:]

After sentencing I was returned to Lane County Jail. Detectives Steve Walker and Rick Lewis interrupted my lunch. In the dressing room Steve sat next to me. Rick stood directly across. He kept his head down, humbly shifting his feet. Interrogation started.

Steve started right off with, "I know this has been a traumatic day for you. I know you must not be feeling well."

I said, "I wanted James' family's pain to stop." I also spoke up to Rick stating, "You said I would not be arrested if I kept cooperating."

Steve then jumped in with, "Well, Karlyn, you know we need you to testify. It's Grand Jury today."

"Oh, no," I said, "Not until this story is back down to the truth."

Rick said Jethro is going to say I did it. I guessed so. He said, "We know he's the one who did James... I'm going to be blunt with you. You have to testify."

I said, "I'll be at his trial. I will give him no reason to call me a liar. But how come I'm to support the prosecution now when the story Fred gave is ridiculous?"

Rick asked me if I remembered the phone call to Jethro after I was arrested. Of course I do. He said, "You know he lied to you about marrying that girl."

"Yeah, so he lied about a lot of things." Rick then went into questioning me about the place where James was found and spelled the name of the road. He told me to get a map and go over the area. I told him, "I do not know the area, and what about Spider? Why was Spider getting off? He was the one who provoked Jethro, not me, as the paper stated. And another thing. Didn't he give himself up on the stand? Even Fred says he knew where the remains were."

Rick said he wasn't in the court room when that happened. Steve then made the effort to explain to Rick what did go on with Spider's statement at the trial and how he lied at two Grand Juries and three polygraphs. He also said that when the detectives have tried to question Debra, Spider's wife, she just cries. I said how convenient!

If it hadn't been for my son TJ being at their house that night to see that Spider had left after midnight and woke up again when he and Debra argued, then I wouldn't have known.

I asked them, "Do you remember I told you I thought Jethro came back sooner than I expected him to that night when he left with James in the trunk?" They both said yes.

Then I cried. I can't stand all the damage Jethro has done. Steve asked about blood, the only real evidence of blood was a small splotch on the door which could have been there for a long time before. I reminded them of a Polaroid picture they had seen in Utah of my three children with bruises and black eyes along with white ointment. I told them I learned it was called Silver Clone, obviously cream used to cover the laser burns that covered their injuries.

*They again turned to me to testify against Jethro. I told them Hugi of-
fered Kolego a deal. They seemed surprised, said they knew nothing about it,
and asked if I considered it. I again said, "The truth to this tragedy is yet to be
revealed. It will be at his trial." So Rick says you will testify no matter what! I
said, "Look! He raped my son, Immanuel."*

Steve said, "You didn't tell us that."

*I said, "It's in my writings. Immanuel complained the bad man hurt him
in his butt." I burst into tears.*

Wednesday December 13, 1995

*The day after sentencing I don't feel well at all. Salt and pepper were
too heavy to hold.*

*I spoke to Paya last night. We discussed the visit I received after sen-
tencing by Steve and Rick. She wasn't happy, also she gave me quite a direct,
disciplined speech from the heart I needed, and she certainly doesn't mind
repeating herself if I've missed something, which I do appreciate. She guarantees I need a complete restructuring of friends and life. Oh, yes I agree. I
hadn't planned on going backwards. But it sure is wonderful having a thorough push from the right direction for the right reasons and from the right
person.*

Chap XXIII: The Right to Appeal

After her sentencing, that is, after the full horror of her sentencing soaked in, Karlyn suffered great fear, shock and anger. Just as any person who is fully committed to the truth and refuses to confess to a crime they did not commit, she had maintained throughout that if she did the right thing, surely she would merit the right outcome. She had witnessed a horrendous crime and became herself victimized by the madman who committed it and his abuse ring, but she finally had the courage to overcome the siege they laid upon her—using her body and controlling her movement—and to come forward to bear witness.

As Plutarch wrote, "The measure of a man is the way he bears up under misfortune." Well, Karlyn has been a lesson in tenacity, in commitment to her goal, in breaking free and bringing forth the truth of the disappearance of James Salmu. Remember, when she came to testify against Tiner, James' body was not yet found. She did not understand that the Springfield police would break their necks to convict her, instead of accepting the truth she struggled to bring forward.

After her long ordeal of interrogations, arrest, and her trial and its preparation, look at what Hugi was doing before her sentencing. He knew, finally, that Jerry Smith went way beyond what was expected of him—merely carrying out Hugi's directions, however—and he had a "confession" which they knew was false, full of holes, upon which they were then obliged to convict her. Look how he courted her, that "I'm Your Friend" sign, his statements indicating her sentence would be overthrown, if she would just plead guilty to their fabricated story.

She wouldn't do it. And they were flabbergasted, up a tree. Looking ahead, Hugi knew that if Tiner's lawyers had to use their fabricated story in order to convict him, they would soon find out how deceitful and corrupt they had been to convince the jury of her guilt, based on the lies of Jerry Smith and the perjury of the witnesses. He sent Walker and Lewis to beg her for him. But she finally knew what they had done. All they needed now was her Grand Jury witness, once and for all, to attest that Tiner was the principal perpetrator of that crime, and then they would never have to go back and revisit the atrocities they had committed.

As long as she pleaded guilty as a coconspirator, that is, so they could show leniency to her and commute her sentence. That's what the Governor's office turnoff was all about, which the writer and Karlyn's mother experienced. Hugi must have loaded the gun, so to speak, in dumping more lies upon them in case anyone came forward to protest her trial. They were all so angry that she would not plead guilty and save the State a lot of trouble.

The writer sees a very upset district attorney who had seen his house of cards begin to crumble. The City of Springfield had not yet been sued for $2M, but it was known that their police department had withheld exculpatory evidence in convicting Proctor and Boots, who were now finally walking free. And he was still so traumatized by the shaky evidence and brainwashing of Diane Downe's children in convicting her that he got mixed up in Karlyn's trial and accused her of foisting her crime on some "bushy haired stranger" which didn't fit at all.

But that wasn't the beginning of it. He was completely aware of Jerry Smith's "witness" scam, knew of his judicial reputation for dishonesty, lying under oath, and manufacturing false confessions, which was cause enough for dismissal of a celebrated case *United States v. Bravo* (1992), and the fact that in a sworn deposition of Lane County Circuit Court Judge J. R. Hargreaves, Smith was "86'd" for life from his courtroom. There had been at least two prior reversals of court cases involving Smith, a homicide case where he snatched suspect away from counsel *State v. Haynes* (1979) and another coercion of "confessions" in *State v. Guayante* (1983).

He still allowed Smith to coerce this young woman for nine days running, when they could have had her Grand Jury testimony against Tiner for free. And in order to make it stick, they had to further corrupt themselves by creating State-suborned perjury in the testimonies of Al Hope, John Distabile, and OSP criminal investigator Terry J. Bekkedahl, at least, and the suborned false entry, tampering with public records, and false testimony under oath of Dr. L. Samuel Vickers.

These procedures constitute corruption of the vilest sort. Still, one cannot consider them "evil" in the same sense as the criminal act of Jeffrey Tiner.

Their corruption is more akin to "folly", certainly not harmless, but expedient in the manner expected by the courts in bringing about convictions to satisfy the public's need to have crimes solved. The courts want to look the other way. But the need for expediency leads them to conduct sting operations and to pressure for plea bargains in violation of the civil rights of defendants. One may argue for expediency.

However, the result of this "folly" is to completely mislead the juries who must ultimately decide upon the guilt of the defendant. In *Letters from Prison*, Protestant Lutheran Minister Dietrich Bonhoeffer, who was finally hung by the Nazis for an alleged plot against Hitler, said that "Folly is a more dangerous enemy to the good than evil. One can protest against evil, it can be unmasked and, if need be, prevented by force... Against folly we have no defence. Neither protests nor force can touch it, reasoning is no use; facts that contradict personal prejudices can simply be disbelieved... they can just be pushed aside as trivial exceptions."

The folly that was presented as evidence in the case of Karlyn Eklof remained moot. The evidence may be erroneous, but it is completely unassailable by a reasonable person on the outside. Once it has been presented in a court trial without objection it is under "procedural default," completely unavailable for review.

We have seen in the courtroom behavior of Hugi one who is completely self-satisfied. He is perpetrating a folly, a lack of moral principle, and, because of the power that he has, is inflicting it upon the jury. "It is a moral rather than an intellectual defect..." as Bonhoeffer would say, and "the power of some needs the folly of the others. It is not that certain human capacities, intellectual capacities for instance, become stunted or destroyed, but rather that the upsurge of power makes such an overwhelming impression that men are deprived of their independent judgement, and—more or less unconsciously—give up trying to assess the new state of affairs for themselves."

Ultimately, the writer blames the courts for encouraging these kinds of deceit and expediency.

The most unforgivable part of Hugi's performance was that he knew what he was doing. He knew that Karlyn knew what he was doing. He knew she wasn't guilty, and he was smiling about it. She was "the small fish to fry. Tiner was the big one."

However, when her sentencing was immanent, he realized the danger he was in. **He used every means**, therefore, if she would not agree to testify at Grand Jury against Tiner while awaiting her sentence, **to bring about a maximum penalty against her,** including one she wasn't aware of until she read her oral argument, to be discussed later.

He expected he might reap the whirlwind, which he did. During Tiner's trial, after the key delineation of the Al Hope/Fred Hugi sweetheart deal/indictment delay/ leniency, Hugi quit the practice of law, behind the Tiner allegations. It was learned that the CSD videotapes of Hope's molesting his daughter were absolutely in Hugi's possession. Yet he sacrificed the public's safety by allowing that madman to walk the streets two more years so he would state that Karlyn procured the gun which killed Salmu before she ever met the killer!

****

Not knowing much about the laws protecting ineffective counsel and procedural default, Karlyn wrote up her own appeal for the injustice she had received in her trial, a commendable document of several pages Karlyn studied the law and her charges and drew it up based on the actual illegalities of the evidence and the coercion used against her. She didn't realize that the only defense appeals brought forward would be about minor courtroom errors.

However, Karlyn knew very little about what was available to challenge in her appeals after her defense counsels failed her so miserably during her trial.

If her counsel had known, however, the corruption behind the suborning of key witnesses and official reports, however, they might have been able to cross examine those witnesses and reports and make objections which could have been preserved for appeal. In addition, if they had been able to do that, the corruption would have been exposed, and the jury would have been aware there was reasonable doubt that she was responsible for Salmu's death.

The Oral Argument took place on May 29, 1998. We are skipping ahead a bit on something which will be again reviewed, because Karlyn was reacting to something she read in it which she had missed at the time of trial. It was about Hugi. As stated previously,

"He used every means, therefore, if she would not agree to testify at Grand Jury against Tiner while awaiting her sentence, **to bring about a maximum penalty against her…"**

In a letter from Karlyn written February 22, 1999 this is what she wrote:

I read back over Gartlan's Oral Argument. Do you know what I realized which nobody caught. The fact that I was acquitted on the first two charges of murder. Meaning that had Fred Hugi stuck to the first and only charge they indicted me on I would have walked out free from the trial. And to compound further embarrassment, not only was the first charge dismissed but a second top charge was dismissed.

It really hurts to know that he knew I wasn't guilty, and to avoid losing

he went out of his way to twist up the case just to insure a conviction. With everything he threw at the jurors, I'm surprised that Kolego didn't call a mistrial. When I was cleared of the first and original charge and then a second one, the trial should have been stopped. I never knew I was acquitted in the beginning...

She had received all her formal charges two days after she filed a complaint against Captain Jerry Smith alleging sexual harassment and coercion to produce the four videotaped "confessions" which would be the basis for her conviction. Her Motion to Dismiss those confessions was denied, but Kolego's blanket objection to them preserved them for future appeals. That is virtually the only item he did object to, but that was entirely neglected throughout her appeals.

The Oral Argument

The Oral Argument, on May 29, 1998, was concerned principally with the introduction of "bad act" testimonies against her character and a "victim impact" statement from murdered man's brother before the jury voted. In Karlyn's letter she was reacting to what Gartlan had written about her case in his opening statements, and she found information that had not really registered with her before about being acquitted of the first two charges.

Nevertheless, it is important to review the points that were covered by the public defender, Peter Gartlan, and the response attorney, Ann F. Kelley, in their briefs and in their oral arguments. The appeal was denied, without response, as were the appeals to the State and to the Federal Supreme Courts.

Peter Gartlan, of the Public Defender's Office, filed the Appellant's Brief in November 1997. Ann F. Kelley, Assistant Attorney General, filed the Respondent's Brief on March 10, 1998. Gartlan's list of nine "bad act" witness errors, one prejudicial statement, and one victim's impact non-witness are as follows, **along with Ann Kelley's responses**...:

1. Dennis Heide—trial court properly allowed Dennis Heide to describe his relationship with defendant.

2. Corina Birch—trial court properly admitted evidence of defendant's actions toward her.

3. Allegation of defendant beating up two men at the White Horse Tavern—trial court properly admitted evidence.

4. Shawn Brunson, witness to altercations with Corina Birch and Dennis Heide—properly admitted testimony.

5. Paula Haskins—properly admitted testimony.

6. Tommy Haskins—properly admitted testimony.

7. Barry Nichols—properly admitted testimony.

8. Kathleen Miller—properly admitted evidence.

9. Prosecutor's comment that defendant had three children by "three different fathers." The trial court properly overruled defendant's objection to the prosecutor's opening statement.

10. Permitting the victim's brother to address the jury as a non-witness under ORS 137.013. The trial court did not err when it permitted the victim's brother to address the jury.

So, that was the Oral Argument. These were all judged to be "harmless errors." She had been facing the possibility of a death penalty. In the Oral Argument there was an interesting exchange:

Gartlan: ... I'm taking issue with your statement that there's no question that she stabbed him, because there is a question that she...

Kelley: There is never any evidence *contrary* to her confessions that she stabbed him. I should have said it that way...

This is justice! The suborned coroner's report was *contrary* to that. First, we have a coerced confession, without any corroborating evidence except the killer's bragging... and then we don't have any evidence to the *contrary*! Is that logical?

The part that is upsetting to the writer is to have Peter Gartlan, who was Karlyn's defender, say in his brief:

"Defendant later told Detective Smith and Distabile that she stabbed the victim to put him out of his misery... At other times **defendant told police she stabbed the victim 30-50 times (Tr 472)."**

Of the latter, Smith forced her to say she held the kitchen knife; it was only Tiner who bragged about the stabbing; and Distabile was suborned to the perjury that she said it was to put him out of his misery. Then, we have Captain Jerry Smith himself on the stand at the trial, quoting from his second phone call to Dave Tiner, the killer's brother, describing what his brother Jethro bragged to him on a drive in the country after they arrived in Fresno.

No way did Karlyn ever say this to the police, not even in eight or ten gruelling days of saying and backing away from ever "penetrating" him. She never said anything to Dave. She was terrified.

Here we have Captain Jerry Smith, giving in his own words what he tried for ten gruelling days, using intimidation and sexual harassment, to get Karlyn to say: "She got a steak knife. She returned back into the bathroom and she held the knife against Mr. Salmu's chest and shoved the knife into Salmu. She said she pulled the knife back out and shoved it in a second time." **But she never said that!**

Here's what she did say, under duress. These excerpts from the transcript, also included in chapter 14, are repeated here, without underlines:

SW What did Jethro do with that towel? You started talking about a towel folded up.

KE Right (garbled) He ah opened it up and pulled it, put that over (garbled) it was just a little little (garbled). He put it um up against the towel into his chest pulled off a round and um I don't... I'm not sure... I think he might have even checked the towel and opened up and seen what what the mark was. It looked like a little dark dark smear here where the bullet had gone through. *This is when I bolted from the bathroom, went to the kitchen sink and held on.*

SW (garbled) through.

KE I I couldn't take it. I went out of the bathroom. I stood against the refrigerator and the sink. I looked around for something to do and ah I picked up a steak knife, a little table steak knife with a wooden handle (garbled). I don't even remember why I did it. I didn't know if I was going after Jethro or what but when I got out of the bathroom I said to Jethro take him out of his misery or I will and um James was just like barely breathing. He was... He couldn't say anything... He couldn't... He was too weak and I made the motion to to to get James right here or take the air. *I never said those words, and I never penetrated him, never.* I wanted him to stop hurting. I wanted the pain to stop that Jethro was getting off on. And ah and I saw Jethro over here fidgeting with this thing like it was cool what I was doing. It's not cool. Excuse me and um and he... I bolted right back out of there and Jeff said get something, and that's when the fourth and final bullet went into James...

SW Can you show me where you put that knife?...

KE Right here... Right below his breast right right there. I closed my eyes and I wasn't really too sure if I made a puncture but logically um going over and over it again it's very very possible.

I I would say, yes I did because I don't wanna be not care or deceitful here at all. I jerked back... *They had been telling me all day I was lying, telling me what really happened, and that I'd never see my children again if I didn't say it. This is all lies. Captain Smith drilled me so I keep agreeing. Although when I motioned or waved the steak knife I was just below his left breast. I realized that I was about to make a very big mistake and stopped. I returned back to the sink. I put the knife in the sink, then on the drainer with the rest of the clean dishes. I remember distinctly feeling foolish and overreacting. But I never penetrated him. I just realized what a horrible mistake I almost made. And thanked God I didn't.*

SW Did you feel... Did you feel his shirt...

KE (garbled) Yes I did. I remember feeling his shirt... I wanted him to stop hurting...

SW So did that knife help?

KE No, it was really a ridiculous thought on my part. Um Jethro had... (garbled) this went on for about twenty minutes I'd say, the whole thing... bathroom, the whole thing. I'm not sure really. I (garbled) Jethro... just just when I realized I couldn't do it. **I just couldn't do it. I don't know what I was thinking.** I wasn't gonna make the same mess cuz it was already blood on the bath, blood on James. **I just didn't wanna... I didn't wanna be part of it** and look him and be in that position. I left the bathroom. Before I did though, I saw Jethro reach over around the corner as I was turning and he pulled off another round. I'm not sure where it hit him...

The whole basis for Karlyn's guilt is embodied in the above testimony, wrung from her through brainwashing and humiliation at the end of nine days of lies and denying her the right to counsel. They had also just told her the polygraph just "proved" she had done it, so she'd better say it the way Captain Smith wanted it or she'd never see her children again.

What kind of a defense is this? When her own public defender in her oral argument makes such a statement? That **"At other times defendant told police she stabbed the victim 30-50 times (Tr 472)!"** That is Jerry Smith's big lie.

All of this is folly. Peter Gartlan failed absolutely in his duty to challenge the inadmissability of her involuntary "confession," which had been the only thing that John Kolego effectively preserved for review.

And what use is an appeal if the one thing preserved for a public defender to bring forward, the inadmissability of her involuntary "confession," is not challenged? Instead, is quoted by him, along with what the Court allows as corroborating testimony, that is, what the killer bragged to his brother, as **evidence**? There was no evidence.

PART TWO

Chap: XXIV Enter the Writer

Enter the writer, and a more unlikely participant in the foregoing scenario could not be found. I met Karlyn Eklof at Oregon Women's Correctional Center (OWCC) at a class on journal writing in the spring of 1997. Nine or so inmates were having a party to celebrate a one year anniversary that Cleta Brooks Lee had been coming to teach the class. I had started a small press and had published Cleta's book, *Therapeutic Journaling*, which the class used as a text. I had also typed a first draft of Karlyn's struggle with memory loss she entitled, *Capture the Moment*, the previous fall as a favor to Cleta. Therefore I was invited to this celebration.

I still have a picture of that meeting, in the conference room, through those locked doors, past those uniformed, holster-bearing young women who commandeered the place. First in the photo is Cleta, portly, aging, with a booming voice, penetrating eyes and the ability to convince anyone that his or her story is the most important one in the world. Also that the telling of it would yield the serendipity of many solutions to life's problems which he or she had not thought of. Really, she is a quite celebrated person, having published several books on her own life, based on over sixty years of journal writing, and holding a record at Border's for the longest-running class ever held there.

Her manner, in conducting this class, would reveal her many years of experience, her ability to draw out her group, and also her foresight to set rules to ward off clashes and jealousies, which her audience here was prone to.

Then there was Karlyn, lovely beyond expectation in her prison blue shirt and denims with dark hair flowing to her waist. Her manner, in first meeting, had been easy and correct, indicating a comfort with people of all sorts. She seemed petite, but it was probably the way she moved, and her high cheek bones were somewhat striking, indicating perhaps some native origin. But her face was amazingly delicate, symmetrical and expressive. Her hazel eyes were at first penetrating and then seemed to dart back and forth occasionally to observe anyone taking issue with her behavior. After all, my typing her manuscript was a favor not passed around. She smiled, she chuckled a slight bit, seeming to avoid showing damage, I believe, to her teeth.

I felt privileged to be there, for all of them, and to hear each of them read a bit of what they had experienced and still suffered from.

"Oh, they're all innocent, to hear them tell their story," I have heard most people say when and if they learn of my involvement to help Karlyn. Even an official chaplain I know who is connected with the prisons in Salem said this. But that is not the way I heard them. I heard of their wrong associations, wrong drugs, and wrong backgrounds that did not provide them with legitimate roles, appropriate and dignified ways of adjusting to their stations in life, and personal skills to stand up to those controlling them.

And I heard also of possible betrayal by those in authority. Why is it the courts are so careful to discern the relative guilt of men involved together in crime, and yet will dump the entire penalty on young women whose male partners are the chief perpetrators? Shelters for women and children who are being abused are not open to those whose partners are involved in crime if there is any indication they were also at the scene of the crime. A crime that is not yet solved will hold all persons who were in the vicinity liable to intense interrogation, often withholding their civil rights.

Finally, in the portrait around the conference table, there's me, only twelve years or so younger than Cleta, silver blond hair, in a navy suit with a white blouse, trying to play the part of a writer/self-publisher, a role I had never intended to get into in the first place.

Really, I am a musician, pianist, organist, once for a brief four years a professor of music education, never hired back in the schools because of being overqualified for an ordinary tenured position. So I have ended up substitute teaching at retirement age, playing the organ for pittances, and trying to make a little money any way I can. My first book, a biography of my father with a lot of local and genealogical history, received a few reviews and a lot of criticism. From that I went on to publishing a few other peoples' books, including Cleta's.

Having introduced myself, Karlyn, and Cleta at our meeting, I want to say a bit more about my change in values and my mistrust of the criminal defense processes as seen in the happenings in Lane County. I have been conveying this right along, of course, in my opening chapter on the citadel, and the various discoveries I have made on my own in regard to Karlyn's case. But I never thought my inquiries and research would take me so far afield.

I may describe to you, as the story proceeds, the moments of great fear I have had, the fear I have induced in others who are close to me, and moments of fear in Karlyn's own family, as I have proceeded in my inquiries. Even those who suffer the most are afraid of the probes into Karlyn's life, because they are deathly afraid of retaliation if her tormenter were ever freed. Better to leave Karlyn with two life sentences to serve and be able to welcome him as a friend if he should come.

I should be asking myself why on earth should I ever proceed in my challenge to the rule of law which has allowed this travesty to occur. And I do. I do thoughtfully analyze what reactions I might have had on many different levels. The essay I quoted from in a previous chapter on Bonhoeffer's *Letters from Prison* made such an analysis and gave me insights from which I will now freely paraphrase. Possible responses to authority are in seven or eight sections, which I will discuss according to my personal experiences:

First, there is the possibility of stepping aside before the inevitable stronger party, with the law on their side, no matter how they interpret it. That would be my position, for most of my life, until my encounter with Karlyn's case.

However, I must say that for someone brought up on traditional ethical principles it is quite bewildering to find evil disguised as social justice. I understand that for a society to work it is necessary to entrust our elected officials (*e. g.*, governors, senators) and those they appoint (*e. g.*, law enforcement officers, judges, district attorneys) with a certain amount of authority.

I was always the first one wanting to call the police if I saw a potential knifing in the parking lot, for instance, when friends thought it imprudent. But I have seen too many mistakes. Police gunned down a young man in my small town, who was mentally disabled like my son, who was threatening people with a stick he had stapled with bottle caps. He was known to them. The state hospital released him days before knowing he might go off his medication and become paranoid. His whereabouts and condition were reported to the police. Their reaction was to shoot him dead as he tried to climb onto their vehicle in the Safeway parking lot.

My neighbor, who was like a father to my youngest daughter after her father died, had a stroke in prison they didn't even notice. He came home a vegetable and died soon afterward. His age was about fifty-four. And his step-granddaughter who had accused him of molesting her finally confessed she had just been angry because he was trying to control her cousin's behavior in regard to drugs. I observed the case workers, patrolling him while he was still under observation, unfairly reporting his behavior. I observed his evaluation trial in the courtroom, after his rehabilitation, and heard how his trusted advisor deliberately misinterpreted his denial of the kind of thoughts they said he had.

No, I want to say, I have been through that stage of *deferring* to the party in authority. I've also been through the second stage, that of *fanaticism*, where I would actually confront and do battle with those tainted powers, thereby getting entangled in nonessentials and being backed down by cleverer people who knew the laws covering their negligence. I have learned much in trying to help Karlyn, especially my own limits.

At the third stage, I have seen others tear themselves to pieces over the heavy odds, their conscience striving against the powers that be, till at last they content themselves with a *salved* conscience instead of a clear one. "Maybe she did it!" is their final intuitive summary.

Well, yes, there is always that possibility. But what do you do with that thought? Do you say there's nothing more I can do for her but I'll stand by her, or do you use it as a reason to reject her and her right to have had a fair trial? If you are sure there is nothing more you can do for her, that is accepting a *bad* conscience, a fourth possibility, but that is better than accepting a deluded one. It is imperative, however, that you not reject her.

Then there is the fifth stage, especially if you have some duty or some vote which reinforces the existing criminal justice system. That is, you accept the *duty*, like a good jury member, of convicting an innocent person, even if you suspect the witnesses are lying and there's not a shred of evidence of their guilt. You accept the duty of obedience to the law, even when the prosecutors and the judge are misleading you, and you do not protest changes in the law that make it easy for them to neglect the civil rights of the accused. You have then done your duty, as a citizen. You have accepted the duty of obedience to the law, but you will also, in the end, have to do duty by the devil too.

A sixth point of view might be to accept the success of her conviction, realizing that the success of the legal system has some historical significance. You still have the *freedom* to accept the *success* of our legal system. Though greatly flawed, sometimes justifying evil deeds and shady means, success makes history. Control of crime is a good in itself, no matter how dogmatic and authoritarian.

However, though we may have the freedom to accept the present means to enforce the law, we are also accepting the corrupt means of doing so, to which we are blinding ourselves. The means used are those of a despot, and no matter how revered and successful a despot may be, there is no way to control what follows. Our freedom to accept the success of our legal system is an intact freedom. But our freedom to protest it may be taken away, insidiously, often without our being aware of it. Our protest may one day place us on a watch list. And that is totalitarianism. Accepting the success of our legal system, because we think it makes us safe, is a very dangerous position to take.

You could, however, protest those changes in the law, vote against those who are being elected who support those changes, who make huge cuts in criminal defense and make a speedy trial a thing of the past. How else, but in a long delay, could they devise such false evidences and create such a public clamor for the conviction of those accused.

In a recent study called "Harmful Error" of 223 prosecutors who had been cited by judges for two or more cases of unfair conduct—already selected from thousands of cases that were not protested—reported that only two of those were disbarred for mishandling of criminal cases, though some one quarter of those cases studied reported some dismissal of charges, reversal of convictions or reduction of sentences.

In all the others, even though the unfair conduct had been cited, judges labeled the behavior inappropriate but "harmless error." In the list of eleven harmful behaviors diagnosed in the study, at least ten were used to prosecute Karlyn Eklof. They included 1) making inflammatory comments in front of the jury, 2) introducing inadmissible evidence, 3) mischaracterizing evidence or facts to the court or jury, 4) making improper closing arguments, 5) tampering with court records, 6) failing to disclose exculpatory evidence, 7) tampering with witnesses, 8) using false or misleading evidence, 9) harassing, displaying bias toward or having a vendetta against a defendant, and 10) improper behavior during Grand Jury proceedings. It is not known whether they excluded jurors on discriminatory grounds, the final harmful behavior cited. They did, however, preselect them on the basis of their willingness to inflict the death penalty, which was out of all proportion to her alleged crime.

You could protest this unfair and illegal conduct, or you could accept your duty of obedience to the law. Or you could accept a bad conscience, refuse to vote or to have anything to do with it, which would be better, however, than accepting it.

A seventh position one can take, when things get really bad, when corruption rules our law enforcement, or our nation's foreign policies, we can always retreat into private *virtuousness*. We can look after our own households. We can base our lives on the Bible which merely confirms the fundamental wickedness of those living outside it. We can shut our mouths and our eyes to the injustice around us. In spite of all we do, however, it will be what we leave undone that will haunt us. We will either go to pieces because of this, or we will become the most hypocritical of all hypocrites.

There is only one answer, an eighth one. There is the possibility of *civil courage*. We may already have shown bravery and self-sacrifice when called upon to defend or support our country, right or wrong. We may already be used to obedience. Even in America we have been ready to follow a command from "above" rather than our own private opinions, perhaps a sign of legitimate self-distrust. We have accepted our roles, our callings, as the other side of the coin of freedom. Obedience has been our responsibility which alone makes freedom work. But we have not realized that our submissiveness and self-sacrifice could be exploited for evil ends.

In this we have become lost. We have lost sight of our need for free and responsible action. *Civil courage* can grow only out of the free responsibility of free men. When we are confronted with folly, with foolish action supported by others who are deprived of or have lost their will to independent judgment, we have a special responsibility to go beyond the judgments of folly. There may be thousands of persons who are wrongfully accused and incarcerated. But that is no excuse for not responding when one learns of the violation of the rights of *one human being*.

****

If it seems this writer felt compelled to react on one or another of these seven or eight levels of response to the denial of *due process* to Karlyn Eklof, it was not without a lot of prompting. People are inclined to cry wolf and then decide that that's all they were doing, crying wolf, after all.

People have called urging me to try to help her, pointing out sources of information and oversights in the appeals processes, and then have quietly left the scene, doubting her, doubting that they should have been involved in the first place. Or they have denied calling me, which happened with Tiner's lawyers, alerting me to their discoveries and wanting me to get in touch with Karlyn's lawyers.

But when Tiner's case was finally decided, they knew nothing about the source of a forty-two page "Confidential Document: Notes for Counsel" outlining and documenting numerous prosecutorial violations, which ought to have been considered in her post conviction, which they sent to a lawyer I had engaged to look into the case. He denied knowing about it also, after I found it among documents he returned to me.

Her appeals lawyers have been particularly hostile to my input, allowing me one brief phone call to advise me in their legal doublespeak into their ways of holding the defendant herself accountable for oversights on the part of her counsel and advising her to tell me that I should not call them again. Kolego, her trial lawyer, refused to return her journals even when she subpoenaed them; Peter Gartlan, who gave her oral argument, considered only the illegality of the "bad acts" witnesses and of the victim's statements which were ruled "harmless error;" Beverly Penz, who initially requested I never call again, in the end received all the documentation she was ready to consider from me through Karlyn, including the four videotapes, just days before the post conviction hearing; and John Manning, her PC appeals lawyer, who received the forty-two page document from me, and, after a year-and-a-half, ignored it completely in his brief.

The lawyer I engaged to look into her case, before her post conviction hearing, showed excitement, especially when I furnished him initial documents I recovered from the Supreme Court records in Salem concerning Al Hope and his delayed conviction for child pornography. I had first found Tiner's Motion to Dismiss at the records library based on his lawyer's thorough investigation of the coerced testimony of Karlyn, and I called Tiner's attorneys who had sponsored it. Tiner, himself, had apparently written it.

Then I received a phone call from a member of their team suggesting there were other transgressions and that I should contact her post conviction counsel. That was when my call to Beverly Penz was considered out-of-order (definitely an "improper submission"), and not to be repeated.

So the lawyer I engaged continued to communicate with Penz, trying to lead her in the right direction. I believe this is when he must have received, unsolicited, the forty-two page document, leading the way to an adequate post conviction appeal, from Tiner's lawyers. Or perhaps he wrote it himself. I'll never know.

But Penz was alternately being suspended for misdemeanors or browbeating Karlyn for not furnishing her documents only she could have recovered, and was not interested in doing any real work on her case.

She probably was not authorized or paid to do any. Her expenses showed that she duplicated the videotapes I sent, but she did not return them. When Karlyn's post conviction was denied, however, there was a letter from me, the writer, to the judge in Umatilla County, which I thought was citing the evidence of Hugi's suborning witnesses, which Penz was ignoring. It was included in the record as an "improper submission."

Later I learned, however, that that letter had been ignored and another, written as a cover letter for Karlyn on some ritual abuse clippings and her story of such abuse, had been listed as an exhibit, without comment. The dates for her judgment were altered in order to include it.

Therefore, the lawyer I engaged, deciding that Penz was not going to look into the "discoveries," in any case, forgot about them, and they lay buried and forgotten in the boxes of Karlyn's documents I finally had him return to me. He said, "Oh, but you can leave them all here. They're safe." But he had already refused to handle her post conviction appeal when she was moved from Pendleton back into the valley, citing, of course, a too-busy schedule.

He then told me—you've guessed it. He said, "Maybe she did it" and "she's her own worst enemy." Lawyers are not obliged to uncover truths, except for large fees. My thousand dollars was only a tiny foot in the door.

John Manning, who was eventually appointed, received the discovery items from me and held them for over a year while making a meek attempt to track down their authorship. My lawyer denied any knowledge of them. He also made one aborted attempt to remand her case back to the Umatilla court that had denied her appeal, which was, at least, good for the record.

Then he wrote an oversized brief, citing the known treachery of Jerry Smith, one item in the discoveries, and the illegality of her serving two life sentences, but with no other reference to the discoveries. I have called him only at Karlyn's request. He said, however, that those discoveries would be very important in her *habeas corpus*, at the federal level, if she is granted one.

I am getting ahead of my story. It is difficult to describe the step-by-step events in her appeals without summarizing their final outcome.

****

This chapter is an attempt to explain myself. Why would anyone get involved in such an unsavory mess? I have learned that those defenders who might have helped her are turned off by the horror of her situation. They might have worked harder on this case because of the obvious violation of her civil rights, particularly after they learned of these late "discoveries."

That would have been too easy. She insists that they recognize she was a victim of a larger criminal activity, a widespread network of drugging and violating women, a whole gamut of illegal networking from white slavery and pornography to ritual abuse. It is much easier for them to say to each other, which has been recorded over and over, and to me, when I have protested, "Well, she's a little bit crazy, isn't she?" Yes! She is even at times fixated on what happened to her that caused her to be at the scene of the crime. But they want very badly to deny this.

No matter that hundreds of disappearances of undocumented, homeless, and otherwise expendable young women are reported and ignored, and that hundreds of their bodies are found in that border area where her abuse occurred, which are attributed to drug deals gone bad. No matter that the sale of pornography, both on the internet and in the Mafia-controlled underground, is a serious problem. No matter that narcotics investigations into the sale and consumption of drugs commands untold amounts here and abroad. The agencies thus engaged don't want to know about the abuse of women which in a large measure finances the drug trade. That would make their job too difficult.

Sending detectives down there, or the FBI, with a few names and locales to look into only confirms their opinions. Those names are attached to people who otherwise live very normal lives, who network and cover for each other, and whose crimes are hard to detect.

Occasionally, however, they do detect such crime. And, in Karlyn's case, that's exactly what they did. They learned of Al Hope's production of pornography and possession of the gun that killed Salmu, before we did, and Distabile's presence for some unknown purpose at the scene of the crime, which would have made her story plausible.

Then the prosecution used the knowledge of these crimes to blackmail the two persons who were directly involved in the activity that led to the murder of James Salmu. They suborned their perjury by having them state the two lies that convinced the jury of Karlyn's guilt: first, that she arranged to purchase the gun from Al Hope that killed Salmu even before she met Tiner, and secondly, that she told Distabile in regard to the murder of Salmu, that she had to put him out of his misery.

I am telling you, in an overall outline, how this case was thrust upon me, in ways I couldn't in good conscience avoid. There was no way I could ignore, first what persons of prior involvement were asking me to do, and, finally, what Karlyn was asking me to do, as her only remaining source of hope.

I am not claiming any great wisdom in having succumbed to that last response category of Bonhoeffer, that of *civil courage*. I have been terrified at times, as I will recount in the pages which follow. I am still terrified. This book, finally, is the only resource left to me.

Having recounted the story Karlyn told which was reinforced by all her documents, then the story of our meeting and of the moral choices I have had to make, I will now proceed with the story in detail of my contacts with her and others who have tried to help her, of the various appeal processes she has been through, and, finally, the story of my inadvertent "discoveries," knowing that the reader has a framework in which to place the pieces.

Chap XXV: Paya

K arlyn wrote me a time or two after I typed her manuscript and met her at the journal writing class at OWCC, but I probably would have forgotten about her in time. Except that Paya called. And now I will never be able to forget Karlyn, or Paya.

Out of the blue I encountered a dynamic wonderful girl who would rouse an army, if necessary, to answer to her questions and outrage. She had chosen Karlyn as her case study when she was taking a class at Lane Community College in criminal law taught by Jerry Smith. He couldn't have been more unhappy, I am sure, to have her in and out of his offices, at LCC and the Springfield P. D., telling him what was wrong with the way they were handling Karlyn's case.

What a boon it must have been to Karlyn throughout her torment, her trial, to have a friend like Paya championing her case, totally positive about the eventual triumph of justice. There was no one exempt from the onslaught of Paya, not Hugi, Walker, nor Lewis, nor editors of the *Register Guard*, who were tuning into Hugi's big story and burying a story of one reporter who was pointing out that there was no real evidence against Karlyn. She also confronted the governor, the State District Attorney, the Boots and Proctor attorneys, and a slew of people I never got around to knowing.

In her first telephone call to me, soon after meeting Karlyn in the early summer of 1997, she named so many important people she had contacted, or planned to contact, it set my head spinning.

The only thing Paya was not good at was actually doing some of the things she envisioned. I was. She and Karlyn, especially, wrote up lists of ways that her defense lawyer, John Kolego, had failed to defend her properly. The plan was to have me send a complaint about him to the Oregon Bar Association.

We were misled about one thing, however, not by the bar association, but by every defense lawyer we contacted on Karlyn's behalf. The "voluntariness" of her coerced testimony could always have been revisited, even without the later discoveries of Tiner's lawyers. The evidence was there in the record, and her appeals lawyers should have sought it out and followed through with what had been the one and only real objection Kolego made.

****

I met Paya during my first visit to see Karlyn at OWCC. She wore earth sandals, a dirndl skirt, braids and southwest jewelry. She was brown and earthy like an Indian princess. So wild, so pretty and Bohemian, truly the most confident activist I have ever known.

I will digress here, and what I will muse upon tells much more about me, certainly, than about Paya. She would never dream what memories she evoked in my long and eventful life. But perhaps the reader should know what motivates me.

I was not close to the Bohemian world of the 60s, though my now deceased husband was very close, if not a part of it, as he went through architectural school at the University of Oregon. I understand he once organized a potlatch at the beach and presented an "environment" as his senior project that totally baffled the faculty. When they finally approved it, he refused his degree. That was at the beginning of the 60s and just before I met him.

I always felt somewhat remiss in his eyes for obsessing about my appearance and for being too busy earning a living to bake bread and cook vegetarian foods all the time. No matter, he would grind the flour, make the sauce and cook the spaghetti; and he never complained about my incessant practicing for concerts or my going back to the university for an advanced degree. There was nothing laid back about me, and he always supported what was different about me.

Paya brought it all back to me somehow, especially when I visited her at her little camp at the back of her parents' home in Philomath, that feeling of being obsessed with a cause, utterly devoted to a principle. I loved watching her make the spaghetti and sauce for her teenage son and getting him settled at the computer. Then she showed me all the boxes and boxes of documents she had amassed on the Eklof case and went on and on about its intricacies.

She brought back the memories of our cottage in the woods on Markham Hill in Portland, which burned while we were in Eugene working on my degree. Oh, the happiness of budgeting $15 a week at Ernie's market on the banks of the Willamette for groceries, spending much more than that for violin and cello lessons for my children, sewing our own clothes, and adjusting to an adorable baby girl he never planned for in the first place. Actually, she was born while I was a teaching assistant at U of O while he was designing and rebuilding our house in Portland.

I remembered our friends' wedding on a houseboat on Lake Union in Seattle; sending the wedding couple off in a boat to their own island in the San Juans; eating oatmeal, fruit and nuts for breakfast; and spending whole days of lying in the sun at the Wilson River and weekends camping at Todd Lake.

But we were devoted to causes: Ceasar Chavez and the grape boycott; a neighborhood discussion group to protest the Vietnam War; subscriptions to the New York Review and Commonweal, which I still subscribe to; and weekly trips to the Multnomah County Library to stock up on books. Even his designs for the duplexes on Camelot Court, for the townhouses on Sylvan Hill, and for the guesthouse at the monastery in Lafayette were made as statements against the conspicuous use of space.

It has been many years since my husband, prone to intense highs and severe depressions, first overdosed, and then died fourteen months later, in Canada, where I was an assistant professor at the University of Calgary. I'm sure the loss of his preferred environment was a big factor, but he could never bring himself to curb my insatiable ambition. Since then I have been devoid of causes, simply trying to survive in any way I could—since I became over-qualified for the schools I had taught in before—and to build a home in the country near Dallas, Oregon, near the cabin he built before I knew him, and to continue raising our nine-year-old near my older daughter who had married and was living in Salem.

I have lived a long and busy life and have made many adjustments. At one point when my youngest daughter was approaching college age, I went to New York City in order to be hired back in the schools to make a decent wage. In my seven years there I met my present husband. In 1990, however, we both returned to my beloved Oregon.

Little could Paya imagine the memories her presence evoked. Her pri-orities, her careful doling out of spaghetti, brought back to me that my de-ceased husband would definitely have wanted me to help her. He would have wanted me to be much more like her.

****

Really, criminal defense has never been my area. I never even read crime novels or fiction. So, knowing I would miss a lot while Paya talked on and on about the Eklof case, I asked if I could run my tape recorder while she talked. Well, she's not bothered, but there's small chance I'll ever get it all straight. I'm at an age where things sink in slowly. Every time I've talked to her she is miles ahead of me, always full of surprises.

When I went home I took the videotapes Karlyn had made. That's a shock! Here Karlyn is behaving like a puppet, saying over and over, "Absolutely! Absolutely! Yes, I am making these tapes of my own free will," etc.

Paya became obsessed over the return of Karlyn's missing journals which Debra, the investigator, had turned over to Kolego. After learning Debra's address, we decided to go confront her. One hot summer day I picked Paya up at her home in Philomath. She showed me a gorgeous patch of wild flowers and a lot of short cuts into Eugene. We parked near the citadel and had sushi at a street cafe nearby. Then we went to the records department and picked up all the latest from the Tiner files. I don't remember what it was we copied. I asked also for any files on Al Hope and Distabile. You see, we were very suspicious even then. At that time there were none.

Later we parked on Hilliard on a shady strip near the college and happened to run into Debra, just leaving her offices by a side door. Wow, was she annoyed! She had ignored our letters. But she stated that it was John Kolego who had Karlyn's journals, and we could just ask him. These people know and recognize Paya, and as far as they're concerned, they've had enough of her pressure. Karlyn had found Debra so adorable, and such a great friend. It's not hard to observe how it changes people to be off the payroll. I found this all very amusing.

****

When I phoned Kolego for return of the journals, as I have recalled previously, he stated, "But that was a long time ago!" It had been about three years.

Does he remember whether Hugi informed the defense counsel of the pending prosecution of Al Hope which he was personally delaying at the time of Eklof's trial?

"He got a deal or something?" Kolego asked Hugi facetiously during the trial, as though it weren't so.

Answer: "No." How could Kolego know of such perjury? There was a 10-Count indictment against Hope which Hugi parlayed until January 18, 1996, in order to avoid Hope's impeachment. He even had him secreted into the Douglas County jail, rather than Lane County, where Hope was arrested, argued for him to remain free pending the sentencing hearing, and made a motion to dismiss specifically Counts 4 and 5, vaginal and anal penetration with a foreign object.

As his defendant's representative, he was entitled to cross-examine the witness and, based on knowledge of the above and to establish that the Court had granted Hope transactional immunity from charges of sexual misconduct, even though the State had not yet filed criminal charges against the him. And the jury was entitled to know witness' possible bias or interest in order to evaluate his credibility. The fact that impeachment evidence was in Hope's own file rather than Eklof's was no excuse for nondisclosure.

Did Kolego know the writing of a death certificate may constitute police-supplied hearsay, and that Dr. L. Samuel Vickers should not have been able to state a cause of Salmu's death, based on physical evidence, which became an issue in Tiner's trial?

Did he know that a hidden parole office document of April 1, 1993 clearly showed that Eklof was a primary homicide suspect, negating all police claims that she wasn't, as they enticed her to come forward to testify at Tiner's (her own) Grand Jury?

Kolego was also there when Terry Bekkedahl perjured the evidence in the final OSP report of "inconclusive" DNA test stamped "Received" on August 24, 1995, three weeks prior to Opening Arguments in Eklof's trial, and stated that the DNA matched that from Salmu's bones. Bet money that the DNA "inconclusive" report was not provided to her trial counsel, or Kolego would have "called" Bekkedahl for his perjury.

****

The above areas of inquiry pertain primarily to John Kolego's role in Karlyn Eklof's trial in order to show how he might have acted if he had possessed the exculpatory evidence that should have been provided to him. I hope he kept good notes about what was shown to him since his memory is so short.

Karlyn, and possibly Paya, were fixated on the possible errors of Kolego in her early appeals processes, because of her great disappointment in the outcome of her trial. They were also challenging his ineffectiveness in not bringing forward witnesses who might have convinced the jury of Tiner's treachery. They wrote these things in a complaint about him to the Oregon Bar Association.

But he had no defense against what he didn't know. There was corruption there, and he knew it. But he could not put forth objections to any extent without the impeachment information. Because her trial was rigged in the first place, his effectiveness could not be challenged to any extent in her appeals.

His co-defense counsel, Jeffrey Murdock, however, was cited for possible error. His opening argument, remarking on her character, opened the door to the introduction of the eight or so "bad act" witnesses the prosecution brought forward. This was an issue, along with the State's allowing victim impact statements before her sentencing, in her oral argument. Yet these were deemed "harmless errors," as was expected.

Murdock's errors, however, were again challenged in Karlyn's post conviction hearing, this being the only obvious problem Beverly Perz could come up with. Murdock was shortly after Karlyn's trial suspended for his alcoholic and drug addiction, but his performance at her trial was deemed unaffected by this and well within the range of error allowable for any number of other possible attorneys.

****

For a year or more after I met Paya we kept in touch via e-mail. From February 1998 through January 1999 I was in the role of carrying out tasks that Paya assigned me, and she was in the role of making decisions to assist Karlyn in her defense.

By the time that year and Karlyn's oral arguments were over, we were both deciding that nothing was working out. I made the decision to begin ghost-writing a book for Karlyn, based on her journals and documents, and Paya, well, for a while I believe she was misinterpreting things Karlyn said, causing me panic attacks, and indicating to both of us that she had misgivings about continuing on her behalf. It must be noted, however, that Paya lost a very important job opportunity because of her activism on Karlyn's behalf, which should have been sufficient reason to discontinue. More will be said of this a bit later and in the next chapter.

I mentioned earlier an FBI inquiry into Karlyn's claims of ritual abuse and Paya's role in setting up an interview with her at OWCC. In February 1998, instead of meeting with Paya and Karlyn at the prison, the FBI person set up a conference call with her and another person. Karlyn just didn't want to discuss it on the phone with the recordings, etc. because there had been so much mishandling of the information she had given to Kolego and Martin leading to fear for her family and possible retaliation by friends of Tiner's still in Imperial Beach. Unfortunately, Karlyn's failure to come forward with names in this impersonal situation caused criticism on Paya's part and a letting go of involvement on the part of Marcia, the OSU professor.

Suddenly, in April 1998 Paya took a job in Bali and our e-mail exchange slowed down for a while. She did, however, have an e-mail address there and I was able to update her on May 8th about the progress on Karlyn's case.

I told her I had twice visited Karlyn and had once talked to her new attorney, Peter Gartlan, about her upcoming appeals. How I wish I had known then that he was absolutely wrong that her "voluntary" confessions could not be revisited. I was lulled by him into a sense that nothing could be done that was not being done, while Karlyn and Paya were giving me a strong sense that there were things he could do, even at that time, which he would not do. Unfortunately, however, they were no better than I at that time in sorting out the really critical elements.

But this attorney, Gartlan, indicated to me that only the trial itself could be subject to review. All he would agree on was that a complete story of her ordeal and the trial itself would probably help her gain clemency at some point in the future. But not now. He really did not want anyone putting pressure on it at this point.

I gave Paya the great news that Boots and Proctor had received $2 million for having spent eight years in prison. The City of Springfield admitted no wrongdoing in its settlement and stated that the city stood behind its police department and the two officers named in the lawsuit. Others said it was clear evidence against the death penalty. They also stated that there were safeguards in the laws, which had been violated, leading to their wrongful imprisonment.

By June 1998 Paya was back from Bali, waiting to be admitted to grad school at Oregon State University on a provisional entry. She was also acquiring the forms necessary to send the Oregon Bar Association for Karlyn to challenge the performance of John Kolego.

Their reply, however, was that they handled misdemeanors and gross incompetencies of attorneys which would lead to their disbarment only, and if Karlyn wasn't happy with the way Kolego handled her trial, another lawyer would be the way to investigate the "quality" of his performance.

At this time Paya was still in correspondence with the OSU Professor of Political Science, Marcia, who was interested in Jerry Smith's sexual harassment of Karlyn as well as her experience with the ritual abuse of Jethro and his cohorts.

The ritual abuse issue was the main reason Marcia got involved. She was a survivor of this type of abuse and lectured on it for Sexual Assault Support Services (SASS). Otherwise, she had no other interest to be involved, but thought she could offer sympathy for the wrongs done Karlyn and her children. She even explored with a lawyer from SASS the possibility of Karlyn's filing for criminal charges for the rape of her children by Tiner, but found it not possible.

Her correspondence with Karlyn soon ended. Karlyn's complaint against Smith was denied long before, and the failed FBI inquiry probably led Marcia to exit from the case. She did write a letter informing her that her job assignment would take her to Europe for a while, and she wished Karlyn the best in her appeals. She was not mentioned again.

Karlyn's complaint against Smith, however, had some significance down the line. Her written complaint of coercion of false confessions and denial of access to requested counsel was key impeachment evidence against Jerry Smith in the Tiner trial.

The prosecutor outright refused to produce the documents of their coercion for Tiner. The trial judge, Darryl Larson, appeared to be covering up the issue. At one time there was a 16 Count judicial ethics complaint pending against Larson, who refused to recuse himself. We know also that her confession was at one point in Tiner's pretrials almost thrown out as "involuntary."

How that error was somehow glossed over, we do not know. But the State was much in danger of doing so. The State will not admit its folly. And they were finally obliged to seek out Karlyn's live testimony against Tiner in his trial.

After years of taking the Fifth amendment when asked to testify against him, it was only her terrible fear of his being set free to terrorize her family that caused her finally to do so. This would happen in the year 2000.

Karlyn's "oral argument" took place on May 29, 1998. The content of it has been reviewed, but not the logistics. It had to be on the calendar 30 days ahead of time, but she didn't know it. Gartlan never told her, and he didn't tell me when I called him. Eventually we realized it had taken place already, and after much delay I finally acquired a tape recording of it, which I transcribed and made available to Paya and Karlyn.

This has been the pattern all through my efforts to assist her. If I'm ever lucky enough to have her counsel return my calls, no information is given to me which might be helpful in following the case, and I must go to the court records department to request documents after the fact. Twice I have been called upon to furnish my transcript of her oral argument to the attorneys assigned to her appeals which followed, because it was not otherwise transcribed.

The incredible thing is that, even so, I have been the first to inform Karlyn, long after the event occurred. I have since learned that Tiner has always been thoroughly involved in each step of his defense and that Karlyn's attorneys have given her as little information about what they have decided to do as they seem to give me, a thoroughly rejected bystander.

Please understand that this is largely because she will not, either intellectually or emotionally, separate herself and her case from the trauma of her abuse by the police interrogators or the drugging and hypnotism by the criminal and his cohorts, which were the cause of her being at the scene of the crime.

Quite naturally, her defense counsel would like to ignore this. And they do, despite her. That is why they are left with the police-constructed version of the crime based on the criminal's bragging and their suborned witnesses and decide, as in the oral argument, that the "bad act" witnesses and the illegal victim's statements were but "harmless error," and that, as state's respondent Ann Kelley stated, "There was no evidence that she *didn't* do it." Well, the forensics and the autopsy report actually proved that. But they were suborned also, and the jury was told they proved she did it when they actually proved just the opposite.

****

It was during the summer of 1998 that I alerted Paya to Diane Downe's book, *Best Kept Secrets* and Ann Rule's rebuttal, so to speak, *Small Sacrifices*, which was made into a book on tape and a movie, trumpeting Hugi's side of the story.

Hugi's way of building up a case against Diane with the media is very similar to what he did with Karlyn's. He had a big investment there, since, as Rule says, he immediately "fell in love" with Diane's daughter, whom he later adopted. One can see how he and his team ran Diane into the ground, perfecting their techniques back then, and have kept doing the same kind of framing and overkill on suspects after that.

But Diane was not as malleable a person as Karlyn, and they did not have enough to convict her for at least a year. All they could do was keep her away from her children and build up a media case against her. Reports of others sighting the "shaggy haired stranger" in the vicinity were completely ignored.

But she was also not so nice as Karlyn. Her behavior turned the public against her. She even got herself pregnant, deliberately, as a comfort to replace her lost children. The concrete evidence they constructed against her, however, makes no sense to me. Diane loved guns and kept them in her apartment. The police went there and found shell casements on her bed which they mixed up with the ones found at the scene of the crime and, completely disregarding the rule of law in the gathering of evidence, swore that this proved her guilt.

This "evidence" was not submitted in the time frame and in the legal manner it should have been, but they made it stick. They also felt obliged to back their forensics man who said "blood spatter" proved the child who was killed was pulled back into the car after being thrown out.

Everyone, and I mean everyone, tells me, well, anyway she was guilty. So I know what I am up against with Karlyn. But how can they believe that she conspired with a man she had met two weeks before the crime to kill her friend and housemate, and that she knew what he and his cohorts were planning to do, with her body, with her life, after that? No way can I believe that.

In an e-mail Paya sent me in July 1998 she indicated that she had been in the Lane County records archives and read a motion filed by Hugi for the State which stated that "the ultimate outcome of Salmu's death was by the stabbing of Eklof, attempting to put him out of his misery". Well, the more times and the more ways that he can say it, the more difficult it would ever be to erase that impression. It brings to mind my recent encounter with a Lane County records clerk who said, "She was there, you know, she knifed him!"

Paya remarked that she had tried for two years to get anything at all from Debra Martin, who had come back from San Diego full of encouragement for Karlyn about what she discovered. But now, all we have from her is unprofessional conduct.

In the e-mail Paya told me to tell Karlyn that Deb Martin stated to her "she is surprised by some people's (meaning Paya's) lack of concern for confidentiality in discussing Karlyn's case." Of this Paya wrote, "What a total _____! Blame the customer for her rude behavior and lack of professional conduct as if she cares for Karlyn..."

Continuing her e-mail, Paya wrote, "Please Erma, don't let her off the hook, keep calling her to mysteriously 'find' those 'missing' journals which would reveal Deb Martin's work of going to El Cahon and Imperial Beach during which she exposed Karlyn's problems to the abuse ring... Concern for confidentiality, my ___!"

The next day she wrote, "Yes, I told you before we met Deb Martin what a butthead she was going to be, So, now you know what I had to deal with for at least one-and-a-half years. What makes me mad is her total DE-NIAL of who I was, and denying all previous letters and phone calls... amazing. I got dead-end responses many times. Our best medicine is to just keep forging on—we have many of Karlyn's journals, and if we never get the other ones, so be it."

Another remark Paya made some time in July after reading the Downe's book was that, to her, the similarity in the cases was that they both motormouthed incessantly to the detectives. They did not shut up and demand an attorney present... that Karlyn's own testimony and cooperation over a long period of sessions—outside and beyond those days where the tapes were made—are beginning to lead her (Paya) to a different conclusion about whether or not we can help her... she gave away the store.

I do not agree, of course. Her testimonies, in addition to being cooperative except for her frequent requests for an attorney, were all exculpatory, as were the two journals she brought with her from Salt Lake City, which were hidden, ignored, and lost until after the trial and which should have been sufficient exculpatory evidence. With so much exculpatory evidence, the probability of her being coerced beyond her ability to withstand is even more evident. She was forced into lying about her involvement.

During the fall of 1998 we also sent a six-page letter of appeal to Centurion Ministries, started by Jim McClosky, who had succeeded in freeing 14 people from life sentences and establishing their innocence. His reply was that they could help no one who was at the scene of a crime.

Paya also assigned me the task of researching attorneys who had won post conviction releases to see if one might be retained as a public defender for Karlyn. This was about a year before I began, on my own, to actually interview some.

I was concluding that no efforts on our part were making any difference in her appeals, and that her own story of what happened to her must be told and made available to someone who would take it into consideration. After my ghost-written book for Karlyn was completed, I would be able to seek that person more effectively.

Meanwhile, in the fall, events were leading up to a complete break, or what seemed like a complete break, with Paya. I will summarize, however, some of those events.

In August of 1998 Paya had an opportunity for a really splendid job, as mediation and volunteer coordinator for the Corvallis/Benton County Juvenile Justice Center. She would be helping offenders and victim's families get together and decide on restitution of community service contracts. She asked me to do a personal, local reference for her, which I am sure I must have done.

The upshot of this was that Paya lost this opportunity after being highest on their list of applicants when they learned she was trying to help Karlyn. Evidently in her graduate program at OSU it was forbidden that she be involved in assisting any convicted criminal. The result of this lost opportunity was not immediate. She went on working to assist me in helping Karlyn until she finally realized the full effects of this denial. She had a young son to support and an older daughter who was a student in Italy. She took a job at the Ramada Inn.

When I requested of her that I wanted to have the first two journals which Karlyn wrote in Salt Lake which told her story in the way she wanted to present it at that time, she invited me to come down to her place in Philomath and pick up all of the journals and transcripts, boxes of them, and said that she might have to let go of all her attempts to help Karlyn.

On September 22, 1998 she wrote, apologizing for not visiting Karlyn. She had awakened, thinking about her and wishing she were closer for a visit, but she said she couldn't afford the gas to go anywhere. She had injured her back after starting the new job and was in bed for eleven days. Now she was looking for another job and would also be starting night school in Eugene soon.

I believe that stress was building up for both Paya and Karlyn at this time. Paya was so concerned about Karlyn's reactions to her appeal that she had her put on a suicide watch when it was denied.

Looking through my notes to Paya I find that on October 23, 1998, my husband went with me to Philomath to pick up all of Karlyn s documents. Later I apologized for my husband's reactions, which were to express a lot of fear about what we were involved in. She replied the next day, "Not to worry... It is a dangerous situation until Tiner is convicted... Another thing, please tell Karlyn my suggestion is to consider writing or calling Judge Larson's office that she would be willing to cooperate for testifying as a witness in Tiner's trial. This would give her another chance to defend herself and the limitations of her involvement. She has lost her appeal so it won't affect any legal action coming."

I knew Karlyn did not agree with this. To Karlyn, such an idea cancelled out all the integrity she had exhibited thus far. I did not respond to Paya on this issue.

Gradually in our correspondence I sensed a very exhausted Paya, who had depleted all her resources and emotional energy in defending Karlyn and had drawn me into an involvement she was beginning to question. Not ever being the kind of trusting person Karlyn was, she began to question how it was ever possible for Karlyn to be led so far into her own destruction.

She said, "Whether or not the one coerced reenactment by Jerry Smith to get her to 'confess' to stabbing Salmu in any capacity did or did not oc- cur— she still volunteered all the other details of the killing freely having very strong emotional involvement with Detectives Walker and Lewis who 'took care of her and children' to help her feel comfortable while she sang like a bird. She was led to believe by them that she was a witness to a brutal mur- der and could cooperate with the prosecution to solve the crime.

"I hate to say it, but these tactics ARE NOT UNUSUAL and occur daily within the parameters of police work. The real terrible treatment was by Smith who constantly badgered her and wore her out in order to get a coerced state- ment about a supposed stabbing—which so far, I haven't been convinced, didn't happen."

Time was taking its toll on Paya. How could she be saying this? Didn't she know what it must have been like for that exhausted girl on the afternoon of her final debasement by Jerry Smith, who was told to lie back, tell the story they wanted to hear, and that it had to match the polygraph which says she was lying or her testimony would be impeached when she went before the Grand Jury. "Look, we all want to go home!"

Then she opened her eyes and saw him rubbing his male member between his thumb and forefinger and stood up. "You are not going to embarrass this department!" he yelled at her. He called in Walker and made her apologize to *him*, for leading them all on. Walker was really sorry for her and told her not to worry. Then he put her before the cameras one last time and prompted her to repeat their police version, also to repeat the erroneous burial of the body, three feet deep, and other scenarios they had rehearsed her to say.

I have seen the video; I have the transcription of it; I have included it in this book so that you can see what she was actually made to say and again in response to further lies on the prosecutions' part. When the murder occurred, she was terrified of what Jethro was doing, and **there were no words exchanged between them.** What is recorded is what the police forced her to say which might have been her feelings at that time. She had picked up a steak knife, yes, but her motive was to stop Jethro or, at the very least, a fleeting concern for the suffering of her friend. However, nothing occurred in regard to that steak knife. All the rest was forced upon her by her interrogators. Since they would not accept her true feelings, it had to be their interpretation of them.

I am leading up to panic attacks by all who are concerned at this time: Karlyn who reacts badly in her journal writing class when she finally understands the hopelessness of her situation; Cleta who cancels the class because of all the bad behavior, Karlyn's included; Paya whose loss of faith is so overwhelming she bows out; and finally myself, who has a panic attack in the middle of the highway after visiting with Cleta one rainy night.

Chap XXVI: Panic Attacks

After Karlyn's first appeal, the Oral Argument, was denied, three of us most involved in trying to help her, as well as Karlyn herself, experienced rather weird panic attacks. For my part, there was a feeling of despair that I would ever understand the ways of the courts. I had tried from the first to pose questions and get answers to what we thought important. Only minor issues were addressed.

When I finally did get through to Gartlan after the Oral Argument, he took five minutes to explain ongoing procedures to me. My questions were not over, but this much I took notes on:

He said that Karlyn was nowhere near her post-conviction relief, that she was still on direct appeal. There were three steps in that direct appeal: 1) the Trial Court, 2) the Court of Appeals Open Argument, and finally 3) a Petition for Review by the Court of Appeals to the Supreme Court which he was in the process of filing.

In regard to what was at issue in this Petition for Review, he said it was to determine if the judge made errors. What was in the Trial Court and the Open Argument was at this time fixed, so there would be no going back to consider if Kolego represented her correctly.

After this third step, which could take months and months, she could then file for Post Conviction Relief. He would still represent her, and it sounded like various Supreme Court attorneys would continue to go through the Open Argument and its briefs to see if the judge acted correctly. He said something about it taking forty-five days for the judge's decision about the Open Argument. But that would have been long ago.

He did talk more freely to me than in the previous spring, but I wasn't asking him any specific questions then. You can see, however, that these processes I still cannot cope with. It is like having the courts do their thing behind a wall, but are not willing to have anyone know what issues are being looked into. Then suddenly they are formulated, there is an open argument, and they are denied. It is as though they plan them in reverse order: Now let's see, what is it we can be sure the courts will deny? But if they reviewed these things so well, how could Tiner's lawyers have uncovered so much hanky panky in their review of the same occurrences.

I am still puzzled that in those three processes, none of their specific considerations were made known to Karlyn, or to me. Karlyn talked to Gartlan, but she was no closer to understanding than I was.

****

Just when Paya was having so many second thoughts about Karlyn, and Gartlan had seemingly failed in his appeal for her, we went to visit her at OWCC together.

I regret that evening so much, because I can look back and feel the strain Karlyn was under, not only absorbing the defeat of her appeals, but also trying to keep up her own morale by entertaining us with yet more unexplained clues concerning the criminal scene. It is understandable that she was always consumed by the shock of that murder scene and obsessed with trying to understand what might have been going on.

But Paya was asking me to look at this as an indication that she might have known more about what Jethro and John were planning than she was letting on. I don't believe this. Her first stories did not implicate John so much, but more and more as time went on they did. The shock of her holding the bag for the whole scenario left her no choice, especially when it became clear that John had lied in a way to implicate her completely. He shouldn't have had to do that. Why had he lied, and what was he hiding?

John was wise enough to get a lawyer for himself after the three Grand Jury interviews showed radical discrepancies and the three polygraphs confirmed his deceit. No matter, Hugi didn't want to prosecute him anyway. He wanted rather to bargain with him, through his attorney, into giving them the story they wanted. Since they had been able to keep Karlyn away from an attorney, they had all the story they needed to solve their crime.

They had no need to know why it had happened. They didn't mind that Karlyn had no reason to conspire against Salmu as long as they could manipulate Dave Tiner's, Al Hope's, and John's testimonies against her and cause her to recreate their fantasies.

I began to feel guilty myself in talking to Karlyn about it, not wanting her to fantasize about the story or add to it. In my early attempts to write her story, in her own words, using the many times she had told it, I was fearful this might happen. What was a marvel to me was the essential consistency of it. But she had to wonder why it was that she was charged with helping to cover up the crime and no one else was.

On this particular evening we must have encouraged Karlyn when she again wanted to recreate that tragic scene. Karlyn speculated that perhaps James "may have heard something he shouldn't have" in Jethro's and John's conferring on the patio, "and therefore needed to be 'offed,' and that they might have intended to take over the house to bring women (victims) in for sale."

Now this did not upset me, because I know that it came from a long time of wondering and didn't add much at all to what we had suspected. But it upset Paya. She said it indicated that perhaps Karlyn was in on the conspiracy, even if against her will, and therefore we had a lot to worry about from the "outside." Suppose she and Tiner were on the inside, there were serious connections on the outside to retaliate against us.

Paya, in her free associations, was getting to me. There was no way that Karlyn was "in on" what they were doing. But her assumptions about outside connections coming after us were beginning to scare me to death.

I had only wanted to sift through Karlyn's story, checking and double-checking with her for the details of it. If I were to write this story for her, my name would not be on it. And nobody could sue me. And no one could sue her or prosecute her further, because she'd already lost everything. So she might as well speculate and name names. Why shouldn't she be allowed to wonder why they had broadsided her with the worst story they could concoct?

I wrote to Paya just before that meeting saying that I didn't want to destroy Karlyn's confidence in me by raising questions about her speculations. I said it was not up to Paya or me to determine her guilt or innocence. I said, "Let her tell her story and continue to tell it. As she refines it, the TRUTH WILL OUT! The more times she tells it, the better able she will be to face any truths she has not already faced. If she can be listened to, no matter what her defenses were at that time, she will free herself from whatever inaccuracies there are.

I told Paya to "please continue to believe in her, or if you can't, withdraw for a while. Certainly you must convey confidence in her when you talk to Kolego, Gartlan, or this new DA, etc. You are so competent and so much needed."

My words were not heeded. Instead she advised me to withdraw also from the situation, as she was resolving to do, to "write Karlyn and tell her you have more teaching than expected and with the holidays coming you will be setting the writing of her story aside until after Christmas. That way if you do actually put it aside, believe me you will have new insights by letting all of this information 'settle' inside. When I spent lonely days and evenings in Bali this last spring, I had plenty of time to rethink my own life and my involvement with various things like Karlyn. I came back determined to see something differently."

After the meeting, Paya again indicated her resolve to withdraw. I could have accepted that. But a day or so later she said she felt compelled to write to Karlyn. I tried to persuade her not to, saying that it was so unnecessary. But she wrote to Karlyn:

"Your story has not changed since I met you three years ago and neither has your... strength to fight for your freedom. My personal story is changing and the environment needed to keep up with the changes is something I need to face. I am feeling like I can not continue with helping you. I don't feel efficient, and neither do I have a legal degree to truly be of use, which seems to be what is completely needed..."

"Since being received into the graduate program for counseling— I had signed a notice that upon beginning it, I would not support, advise or counsel anyone anywhere for free or monetary value. Apart from that opportunity still coming, I have lost very important volunteer opportunities by mentioning my involvement in your case as a support person. Erma can fill in on her next visit.... I need to take care of my more than five years of school and career-hunt by insuring that I am not ruining things for myself by my involvement."

Nothing Paya could say after that would ever make any difference to Karlyn. It was the ultimate denial of the lifeline she had counted on all the way through her trial and afterward. I believe Karlyn sensed far more than is expressed in the letter. She would brood on it and occasionally write about it for a long time.

What I want to emphasize here is important. TIME WILL TELL and it has. Hugi did suborn Spider for his perjury at her trial. We know that now. And Al Hope also. Al was even said to be "involved in a crime in Springfield, Oregon," as we shall see when I reveal all that was learned from the Tiner lawyers. There is every reason to believe all that Karlyn suspected, now that time has verified it.

Paya alone was responsible for the continuing support Karlyn had throughout her trial and the ordeals she has encountered since then. Without Paya as her mentor, I don't know what Karlyn would have done. And Paya literally commanded me to get involved, at least in helping her in her tasks and research, and finally in convincing me to take over when I was able to complete tasks she was unable to do. Paya is very dear to me, because she made me aware of an injustice and showed me strengths I never thought I had.

I am pleased that I have been able to contain some of Paya's anguish and to protect Karlyn from what would have been the full weight of her lack of faith. In doing so I have restored Paya's confidence and amazed her with what I have been able to accomplish in the past few years.

My confidence has also sustained Karlyn, never allowing the anger and betrayal she has sometimes felt toward Paya to go unchallenged. Since Paya was giving too much, and it was affecting her success in life, there was still someone left who truly believed in her. I would accept that role and would never let her down. Therefore her faith in God, an integral help in her terrible plight, would continue to be something she could share with a real person on the outside. Together we would take optimism and hope to a higher level.

I am certain that Paya has moved many steps up from the deluded conscience she once settled for to regret her bad conscience in rejecting Karlyn. In her very busy and hectic life she calls once or twice a year and rejoices in the progress we have made toward Karlyn's defense.

****

That was Paya's panic. Now I must tell you the effects on Karlyn of her grave disappointment, because her appeal was denied and because of Paya's letter. Although her behavior didn't change in regard to me, she did contribute to a bad scene there at Cleta's class and therefore lost weekly contact with one of her most valued mentors. She was not the only one who misbehaved, but it was the last straw for Cleta.

Cleta had been absent for six weeks because of a back operation, and it was during her first class after arriving back that some incidents occurred. The class members were all reading their five-minute stories for the week, with a person I will call Debbie doing the timing. There was a new member present for the first time, and Karlyn went and got her a folder and gave it to her. This was against the rule, since new members had to attend class three times before receiving a folder.

Debbie passed a note to the secretary reminding her of the rule that was being broken. Karlyn got up and went around to whisper something in Debbie's ear and again took her seat. Since Karlyn looked angry and Debbie looked hurt, Cleta told the class that if anyone wanted to talk about anything they could remain after class.

At the end various members gave Cleta a hug as they left. Karlyn always gave her a hug, both in coming and going. Then a guard came in and told Cleta she was not to touch any inmate for any reason. This had never come up before.

Since Cleta had asked anyone wanting to talk to remain, Debbie stayed. But the guard came in again and informed Cleta that no one could remain alone after class to see her, so Debbie left without telling her what had happened. Both Debbie and Karlyn wrote Cleta notes, however, explaining the incidents from their individual points of view.

Debbie wrote that Karlyn had whispered to her that she'd never heard of this rule and Debbie was just trying to get her into trouble. She also wrote that Karlyn was waiting for her at the end of the hall and hissed, "Well, you didn't get to see Cleta after all, did you?" obviously being the one who reported to the guard that Debbie had stayed to be "alone" with Cleta. Then Karlyn wrote an eight-page tirade against Debbie which Cleta didn't even finish it was so vicious.

Unfortunately Karlyn had told the whole class about my spending "hundreds of hours" helping her with her "story", which was not wise. I certainly wasn't, at least not at that time, though I was helping her with her appeals. I feel badly because Debbie had knitted me a shawl for Christmas the year before, though I had written thanking her. I could not, of course, get involved with helping other people. Now she was retaliating by telling Cleta that I should watch out for Karlyn, that Karlyn had stolen some of her handywork, etc.

At the next meeting Cleta told the class that she couldn't teach the class any more and had resigned. There were always arguments trying to break out. Her rules and wonderful presence weren't enough. The timing of each one's reading and reminders that there was to be "no cross talk" had been disobeyed once too often. Therefore, the notes these two had written her, the incidents in class, plus the indignity of being chastised twice by the guard, finally got to her. She was through, and this would be a big disappointment in the otherwise bleak lives of the class members.

In addition, her spinal operation on a problem dating back many years had been serious, and she felt she had to guard her energies. The journal writing seminar she conducted at Border's Book Store was the most popular event they had going, and she didn't want to jeopardize that.

Cleta, whom I adore, had her own reasons for not continuing the class, and that minor incident was not the only one, just the last straw. The class was always very difficult to teach. There was so much strife and tension.

Cleta also had had her doubts about my giving Karlyn so much help for a long time. You must understand, she wanted me working on reprints of her first two books instead. But I didn't want to get involved while she still had another friend thinking that it was "her" project. Unfortunately, this friend was not doing a great job on the editing, and Cleta didn't want to offend her.

However, I did get involved in publishing the two books for Cleta the following year. After I had finished Karlyn's book, the ghost-written account upon which I based this book, I spent the next whole grueling summer publishing her *Sing Above the Pain, Books One and Two*. Her friend, however, talked her into leaving my publishing company out of the brochures and denying me the opportunity of marketing them.

No one can be really unhappy with Cleta, however. I have learned so much from her, and she introduced me to a lot of people and helped me secure reviews for my own first book and the three I published for her in Salem's *Statesman Journal*.

After what I will call the panic attacks of Paya and Cleta, described above, I wrote Karlyn what I hoped was a soothing letter. I told her I felt very bad about what Peter Gartlan had said and that her case appeared to be etched in stone as far as any appeals were concerned. I also told her that I knew she was feeling very low at this time and that I would be there for her as best I could for as long as I could. I knew how hard it must be for her that, on top of her defeat in the Oral Argument, it seemed that other very important people were now abandoning her.

I reminded her that "nothing has changed. Nobody is perfect. Everybody has their own reasons for the decisions they make and it's not you, or even partly you. You can make mistakes too and still be loved... What you have told me hasn't changed. I would never be able to bear what you have had to bear, and still have to bear."

My goal in writing to Karlyn in this way was to help her integrate, to absorb what seemed a rejection by two trusted friends and to accept her own mistakes and bad behavior. I did not want her to go inward and reject herself or doubt her right to go on telling her own regrettable story. Telling her story, with all the dangers of overstating it and making errors in judgment of what happened, would be vital in remaining intact. Without integrity she would die.

You can see, also, that I was trying to understand more and more about her story, to fill in the blanks, so to speak, so that I could write the book that would free her.

When I observe what I said in my letter to her I shudder at the corruption that had gone on behind the scenes I didn't know about then. I would not now blame her defense team so much. Judge Merten may have appointed an innocuous counsel to punish her for rejecting Evans and refusing to plea bargain. But he appeared to use prejudice against her during her trial and was probably more responsible that she did not receive a fair trial than Kolego was by not objecting to it.

****

After my friends each had their panic attacks, I had mine. When Cleta told me Debbie said I should watch out for Karlyn, I did not tell my husband or he would have jumped all over me. This would have been proof that I should never have become involved. I didn't believe I was in any danger, but Cleta's story frightened me.

On my way into Salem to pick Cleta up for our meeting where she told me about the bad things that happened in her class, my Mazda lost power a few times. I then asked her to drive herself to the restaurant so she wouldn't be stranded if I had trouble again.

As I wrote Paya, "Then I drove home. It was raining. Oh, my God! I got right in the middle of a difficult strip beyond the 50 mph zone out of Salem and the car lost power and stranded me in the median. I was terrified. I managed to get the lights flashing and wondered what on earth I would do. There was no residence or business in sight around that difficult turn in the road, and there were four lanes of continuous traffic all around me. The rain was pouring down, and there was no light on that bend in the highway. I thought I was going to die.

"I sat there idling and finally remembered that each time this had happened the car had finally started again after I had turned the key off. Why not again? It was just that I was terrified and couldn't remember that. I turned the key and it was all right. I kept to the slow lane all the way home in case it went out again and made it...

"I have come to the point where I can understand your fear. I have had to feel it a bit myself in order to come to that point. Just telling about it I begin to feel the panic all over again."

Unfortunately, this was not the end of my panic. Reacting to the fears of those around me was nothing compared to the fear I was to feel when I inadvertently made discoveries that would break this case wide open!

Chap: XXVII   Exercises in Futility

K arlyn was transferred to the Eastern Oregon Correctional Fa
cility at Pendleton soon after our last meeting with Paya. Her
mother was quite hysterical about it, knowing that our visits
kept her going.

I made a special effort to write often to her, sometimes every two weeks.
My letters to her and her replies help me to remember the sequence of events,
as Paya's e-mails did previously. I inquired early in the year about the out-
come of her Supreme Court reviews. I see in her Case Register that it was in
January 1999 that both State and Federal Supreme Court appeals were denied.
I'm sure it was all just paper work and that she was told nothing about it.

It would appear then that Karlyn, because of miscommunication with
Gartlan, filed for her own Petition for Post Conviction Relief on May 19,
1999. It was stamped received on July 20, 1999. Would she then be denied
relief because of the things she did not mention?

I see, however, that her appointed Post Conviction attorney did file a
"formal" one. Whatever was selected for appeal would then limit any future
appeals, and her attorney's errors would be used to explain it.

The year did, however, bring about many interesting events and insights.
I happened to be seeing my personal lawyer about a property probate matter
and for advice about publishing Karlyn's book. Since I had all her documents
and journals, save those Kolego would not return, much of my correspondence with her that year was in regard to questions about facts and sequences.

I believe this was extremely painful to her, to go back over what she had
written about her family, her life, and even the scenes she had so often described. I gave her as many pages of the work I had done as I could, at least

initially, but when I realized she was just not responding to them or sending them back with corrections, I decided I'd best organize her words, her many tellings on my own, making sense of it as best I could while being careful not to add anything she hadn't said. Naturally I tried to smooth out any really rough places.

It was not an easy task for me, since I was substitute teaching two to five days a week, playing the organ at a small church, taking care of my disabled son and managing, with my husband, our two-acre place in Dallas.

Then I broke my ankle, falling from a ladder while cutting a tree limb with an electric chain saw, and I had to take leave from both my jobs. It was a boon. Really, it was the pain that caused me to work way into the night at the computer when I couldn't sleep, and in that six weeks I managed to get Karlyn's book finished. Of course, it was an editing job, not a writing one, but I did have to organize it and intervene often to make her words intelligible. My sister in Portland read the book for errors, and I had five galley copies made for further reviews and editing.

I did everything right, because I was expecting a miracle, getting it copyrighted, getting the ISBN, and having it listed in *Books in Print*. I was expecting that Karlyn's story from her point of view would be sufficient to exonerate her. .

Well, I was wrong. What I thought was a clear defense of her was anathema to the five people who read it and one other who merely looked at it and thrust it back into my hands like a hot potato.

Well, I'm exaggerating. My sister did read it and was overwhelmed with the trauma of it. But did she believe her story? That will always be the question. Do you believe her? My sister did believe her, but was upset by all the trouble the girl had gotten herself into.

Belief is the question that is always asked as though it were the only question. I don't think so. The question is, was she adequately defended, did she receive *due process*, or was she duped, violated, and debased when she came forward to try to tell the truth? Truth itself must always be relative to *due process*.

The most important person, Karlyn, read it and said it was not what she had in mind for her book. She wrestled with it through the first five chapters. As she went forward into the sixth, seventh and eighth chapters she found herself twisting in her seat. She could not find in it her story the way she needed to have it told. She wrote, "I feel it enhances the police version and places them back at the wheel."

I believe she's right. Too much depends upon your believing her, because at that time there were no documents proving how they were duping her, how they were suborning witness after witness, how they were misrepresenting evidence that ought to have been exculpatory. So, it was absolutely necessary at that time that you believe her, that the police abused and betrayed her as she said they did.

When I compare this book, *Capture the Moment: A Police Betrayal* with the original small story I typed for her before we met, I could agree with her. Her story could never be, in all its details, the pretty story she would have it be. Unfortunately, she ended up with a psychotic tyrant of the most despicable sort who used her, abused her, terrorized her beyond any extension of will on her part.

I am saying that if she is turned away from her own story in the same way other people are, she must at least learn to come to terms with herself and the way it happened as she has written in her journals. She allowed herself an "improper submission" to someone her so-called friend, Potato. introduced her to, who she felt safe and amused by. If she didn't know what was happening at the time, on later reflection she should have. Her terrible misgivings about Tiner when he insisted on coming up to Oregon would indicate that. Unfortunately, she couldn't refuse him once she heard his voice, which awakened the hypnotic state he had had her in.

When she found herself again in Imperial Beach and spent three months or so there, while Tiner regularly checked her whereabouts, she ended up with persons whom she later called her friends. The fact is that she gave the detectives—and me when I was writing her story—a whole list of names of people who were friends of hers there, who rescued her, and who tried to watch out for her when they knew what Tiner was doing to her. It was Tiner who sold her, abused her, and started a vendetta against her when he thought he was losing control over her.

They were, however, all pretty dangerous people, often covering for each other and cooperating with each other, if necessary, to carry out illegal activities—including drugging, raping and filming women and children. They could be called upon, through fear, intimidation, or money, to assist Tiner or look the other way in most anything he might do.

I believe one of the most telling remarks of the frightening experiences she reported was the one made by her friend, Willy Beard, the one who met her, Dennis and Potato at the airport and who first took her to certain areas in Imperial Beach, where she had been warned never to go. When he helped rescue her from the abuse ritual on June 12, 1993 from behind the High Tide Tavern where she had been dumped after a severe beating, he said, "I used to drug and film women like that."

Well, he was her friend, a lot of them were her friends even when she later remembered they were in the ritual. Some of them may have been doing it all the time, in some out-of-the-way shack, with nameless abducted women, only this time Karlyn was included, at Tiner's request. Some of the dialogue indicates that they were aghast that the perpetrators of the ritual would do this to Karlyn.

Yes, Willy Beard was her friend, and she was in sorrow a few years ago when she heard he had been killed on a motorcycle. But Tiner took her back to Imperial Beach and there was no way she could have resisted his supervision of her whereabouts. She tried to adjust as best she could. Aside from the friends she made, there was an incessant sucking away of her own volition. Tiner was using her for his own purposes, and they all knew it.

When you read in the newspapers that hundreds of young women disappear over the border between California, Arizona and Mexico, do they ever suspect that there exists there an unrelenting, insidious, trafficking of women's bodies by persons there on the scene, with otherwise responsible lives and occupations? No!

Kolego and detectives Martin and Walker thought they could just go there and they'd all blab on each other. Most of these folks had prison records. Did Kolego, Martin and Walker ever think of that? How did they get prison records, and what else were they doing that they never got caught at? Is it possible Karlyn could exist there, under the watchful eye of Tiner, who had already been told by Walker, et al, that she'd been talking to them, without really knowing for sure what they were all involved in? Yes, of course. Her being there, under whatever duress, didn't make her a "part of it."

We don't know, of course, what the detectives did find out. Any verification of Karlyn's story would tend to create sympathy for her with the jury. The prosecution couldn't allow that. Debra Martin's story was never heard. So all that did sift down from their investigations were remarks that reflected badly upon Karlyn herself.

She was both "lying" and "mixed up in it" herself. She couldn't be both, and I believe she was neither. I believe she deluded herself into thinking that some of these were her friends, since she was not free to leave because of Tiner, and that she was safe with them. These "friends" of hers remembered the night of her ritual beating when the detectives inquired about it, but they backed away when it was suggested that she recognized and remembered the faces of those involved.

The illogic which one of the detectives presented to me, when I spoke to him in the hall during Tiner's pretrial, was that Karlyn was "mixed up in it" and had been for a long time. First of all, everyone has supported the premise that she met Tiner for the first time when she, Dennis and Potato went to San

Diego a few weeks before the crime.

Secondly, does he imagine that when she was taken, out of fear for her own and her children's lives, back to Imperial Beach that they sat her down at the table in some bar and said, "Look, here's how you can help us recruit women so we can drug, rape and abuse them"? She was there out of fear, but she is a survivor. She adapted herself to whichever friends she thought she could count on during her abuse.

What I am trying to say, because of Karlyn's rejecting her book, is that I do not reject it, any more than I reject her story. She doesn't lie. You can't make her lie, as they found out when she wouldn't plea bargain. But she discredits herself when she tries to dress up her story in order to portray herself as being always the victim. She placed an unholy trust in her friends, and some of them betrayed her.

Karlyn quite rightly reacts with horror to what she supposedly said in the last two videos. It must be presented. That is what this is all about. It must be repeated as often as necessary that the fact is she didn't say ANYTHING to Tiner as he confronted her with that puny knife. Neither did he. His eyes said it all: "What do you think you're doing with that?"

She put it away because there was no stopping him. The police grilled her for nine days and terrorized her in order to get her to repeat what in their minds she must have been thinking. Smith kept telling her about a gruesome case he knew of and she had to have said and done the things he was telling her to say, according to all his years of experience in crime detection. They had her saying things she didn't ever remember saying, perhaps under a threat induced by hypnosis.

She was even saying, yes, she told the truth in those videos. Until she saw them nine months or so later. They wouldn't let her see them all that time. Since she thought she had told the truth, isn't that proof enough that she was hypnotized? The Grand Jury was in session on the very days she made the inculpatory videos, and she was not asked to testify for herself, Tiner, or anybody else. That is illegal. They were forcing her to lie against herself in her testimony on the videos and denying her her own voice with the Grand Jury.

The third one to reject her story was her mother. Some things mothers and daughters never tell each other. Well, it all came out, and her mother wanted to sue me. After about three phone calls I believe she began to simmer down, and the book may have brought about some new understanding, especially about what she endured in abuse from Tiner. I must say, however, there was no end to the fear they both had of him, their having once accepted him into their family life, however briefly, when she first met him, and again during those first few weeks back in Imperial Beach.

The fourth and next to last person to have read her story was an old and trusted friend of mine from Portland. She was a close friend of my deceased husband, and I knew and admired her husband, who was a well-known jazz pianist. She was the daughter of an editor of the Oregonian and an avid reader. I considered her one of the most liberal people I knew, and I valued her opinion.

I wasn't prepared for her reaction, and I fear I still have not recovered. She was so shocked and disbelieving of it that I had to pick the copy up in person. She feared to take it to the post office in the event it should ever be traced back to her. She was terrified to be in any way associated with a defense that would, undoubtedly, be watched closely by the establishment.

What had seemed so wise and knowing about her—her grasp of politics, history, and writers of all sorts—did not extend to criticism of the ways of the courts. I was somewhat assuaged that two other old friends, one an architect and the other a builder, who were associated with my late husband, listened avidly to my description of it and encouraged me in every way they could. It was like a message to me from the grave.

I have, however, come to terms with my well-read friend's rejection of Karlyn. My friend's rejection has given me the patience to await the outcome of her appeals and to discover for myself the truths behind her wrongful conviction. I have learned much in knowing that my friend could not accept that Karlyn knowingly or unknowingly submitted herself to her own degradation by Tiner, and that she was as susceptible to drugs and hypnosis as she would have us believe.

I was in an experiment on hypnosis in a psychology class in college. I was called up, as was a girl from my dorm. I could only shake my head and wonder how they thought I could ever be so stupid, while my friend was performing antics all over the stage. Some people are really susceptible. But Karlyn was aware of certain lapses of time, and she should have figured it out and avoided those situations when they first began. But I don't reject her for it.

Karlyn did not commit this crime. The story of "why" it happened and "how" she got blamed for it is a story that needs to be heard. It is certainly more interesting and dramatic and tells more about human nature—especially of the ways of the police and the court system—than many another story of true crime. Knowing what we know about the percentages of innocent people who are convicted ought to wake us up to the fact that all criminal investigations don't proceed according to Anne Rule and John Grisham.

The person who pushed the book back into my hands was my own personal lawyer who had advised me not to write it. He was nice enough when he advised me on the legal aspects of writing it. But finding I had gone ahead, he wouldn't touch it or look at it. You'd have thought the state attorney general was there in his office and that he was facing disbarment.

He did, however, give me the names of two criminal lawyers he recommended to help me learn whether she had any chance at all in her Post Conviction Relief. I was able to follow through with one of them, quite soon thereafter, since I am not one to sit on my apprehensions.

The one I chose was a prominent individual. I am surprised that he gave me any time at all. I'll call him Mr. X. When he finally returned my call he said he would not even look at the case without a thousand dollar retainer. I came up with it, hiding the fact from my friends and family, and, I believe, surprising him a little. It was in July 1999 that he drew up a contract setting limits on what he would do.

He wanted all her documents, the trial transcript which I had organized in notebooks, and the book I had written, which, I believe, provided him with a chronological guide through the materials. I had a visit or two and perhaps an occasional phone call from him through the summer and early fall.

I must say, he was really not giving me any feedback into her situation until I began to provide him with some of my own. I discovered the missing links in her defense before he did and brought them to him. That he investigated them and buried them is unfortunate.

First of all, I was looking in Tiner's files in the Supreme Court archives and found his Motion to Dismiss Interlocutor Appeal with his signature at the end. It had been written in January, and it contained the most complete expose of the illegalities, lying and coercion that had gone into Karlyn's videotaped "confessions" I could ever have imagined.

I called the attorneys Thomsen and Gough in Eugene whose names were on the edge of the document. I don't remember what they said. My understanding at this time was that the State District Attorney authorized the dismissal of the Court's own interlocutory appeal as a result of it.

Soon I received an unsolicited phone call from someone in Eugene. They were asking me—yes, me, the writer— to help them get in touch with Karlyn Eklof's Post Conviction attorney. They had some very new discoveries which would be important to her case. They mentioned to me over the phone the evidence of leniency offers to Al Hope and Distabile.

The call was from the husband of an investigator who was trying to locate me following my call to Thomsen and Gough's office. He told me she had laryngitis but would call again in a week or so.

It was after that phone call that I stopped by and asked Mr. X if I might refer the matter to him when she called. He said by all means. He also said he had read Karlyn's book and was now reading the appeal briefs. When this investigator called, Patricia Jaqua, I told her about my current investigator and assured her I would endeavor, through him, to get the information to Karlyn's appointed PC lawyer. It was later designated that Beverly Penz in LaGrande was assigned her case, but I'm not sure when that was finalized.

I brought to Mr. X the information I had learned in the telephone call from Eugene, copies of Tiner's Motion to Dismiss, and the case history of Al Hope which I found in his file at the Supreme Court records office. He said he would be ready to talk to me in early September to tell me what he thought he could do for Karlyn.

In regard to the information Patricia Jaqua alluded to, he said that the information discovery was as available to him as to anyone. It would be a matter of knowing whether to go ahead with the case or not. He was in no way bound to any agreements with Tiner's lawyers.

I still do not know whether the "Confidential Documents: Notes for Counsel," which he inadvertently included in Karlyn's documents when they were returned to me a couple of years later, were of his research or of someone in his office, or were forwarded to him from Jaqua's office. Mr. X has denied any knowledge of the document.

In the fall of 1999 Karlyn received a hand-printed letter from Tiner himself. She sent me a copy. Honestly, the letter sent chills up and down my spine in response to what she must have felt upon receiving it—from the man who had murdered her friend; tortured, used and sold her body; beat her abominably three times; and raped her baby. I believe the letter came in September.

I was so traumatized by his even writing to her that I interpreted what he was saying, first of all as a threat to her, and secondly as boasting of the grandest sort, of his discoveries, what to watch out for, and what to draw into her PC relief. We, I mean Karlyn, myself and her family, were all so frightened of him at that time, before his conviction, that we saw him walking away with his own defense and going scot free. He nearly did, and it could have happened. And he'd have come after us, any of us who might have tried to help her make her story stick.

I also read it as arrogant bragging, designed to scare the wits out of her. When I organized the records I have of what transpired in 1999, it was right on, however. It was exactly, in outline, the information Mr. X's office received from Jaqua's, after I put him in touch with her. Tiner could even have written it, based on the documents and research his lawyers were furnishing to him at that time.

But Mr. X never forwarded it to Bev Penz. He told me at that time that he had not called her, but that he had talked to Jaqua. He said he was just getting it together what he wanted to suggest to Penz. Then, suddenly, he didn't seem to want to talk about it, and I didn't know why.

I, myself, was somewhat resting on her case that summer, full of disappointment because of the reactions I had received from those who had read the galley copy of her book. Therefore, I got involved helping Cleta republish two volumes of her autobiography.

Again I was editing day and night, since I wasn't teaching, to produce *Book One and Two* of *Sing Above the Pain* in time for the State Fair. There were scores of pictures to scan in, the cover design to compile, the usual copyright and ISBN legalities and researching the best company to print the books, which we located in Portland.

More than that, there was the great problem of editing. The original editions did not read well in some sections. Her concerns at one time did not carry well into the present time. I wanted it to be funny and delicious to read. I believe we succeeded. The books have been a great success.

In the end, however, she decided to do all the marketing herself, with the other "friend" as her financial manager. I really did it all for free. The marketing experience I desired did not come about, though I had devoted my whole summer to it.

In the fall then, after receiving a copy of Tiner's letter, I realized there had been no communication between Jaqua and Beverly Penz. The information about Distabile in his letter was new to me. It was part of what Jaqua said they had learned that was important to me and to Karlyn, but of no interest to Penz, who by this time was not receiving my calls.

I believe Mr. X's communication with Penz was soon sidetracked by some grave personal difficulties she was undergoing, which I will discuss in the next chapter. I believe she once talked to Mr. X when Karlyn was called to testify at Tiner's pretrial hearing and trial in 2000, and she eventually secured the four videos from me through him.

I regret I did not force her to contact me, after her rude dismissal of my first call and directive not to contact her again. I did write her a letter accompanying and requesting return of the videos and another to send her a transcript copy of Karlyn's testimony at Tiner's trial.

It was a rather bitter year altogether. Paya wrote or called me a few times, inquiring about Karlyn's progress. There were requests from Karlyn about trying to retrieve her journals from Kolego and Martin and learning the status of her PC relief.

With Mr. X, however, was my biggest discouragement, and perhaps greatest missed opportunity. As I look back, I realize from my notes to myself and letters to Karlyn that he knew all that I have since "discovered." But he could not go forward without money. I was hoping for the miracle that he would be appointed to defend her *pro bono*, especially after her PC was denied and she was moved back into the valley.

I believe he first ascertained that I was in no position to fund Karlyn in an expensive defense, and then gave me the impression that there were no guarantees anyone could overturn what had already occurred in her case. He knew he could placate me in ways I wouldn't even be fully aware of until some years later.

What is so discouraging to me is that some things were handed over to me on a silver platter, so to speak. I knew about them. I was told. But I could not get any attorney to acknowledge them, and I couldn't by myself determine how these discoveries could be used to overturn her conviction.

The process was so new and hard to understand; therefore I tried to put my trust in someone who would help me. I was told that in most cases of this sort nothing can be done. I went away convinced that "nothing can be done" instead of knowing for a certainty that if I had money to help her something could be done. I was supposed to just go away and forget about it.

I was given this impression so that my righteous anger would not arise. Anger, that is, that money could stand in the way of an adequate defense for someone who was indigent.

I really doubted myself. Especially after I had completed her book. I first thought that writing the book was the answer when I couldn't get anyone to help me defend her. Then I found that even a book thoroughly outlining the corruption that convicted her of this crime, far beyond what any fear and proximity might have led her into, would never be read. Her case would never be heard, because now it was thoroughly prejudiced.

While Tiner was in total control of his defense, directing his attorneys in some hundred motions and authoring his own Motion to Dismiss, Karlyn seldom heard from hers.

Who paid for all of this? The State, of course. Because here was a killer, whom they expected to be on death row. They would leave no stone unturned to make his a fair trial, since they did not want it to be overturned on appeal.

As to Karlyn's case, they knew it was messed up, early on. Maybe no one would ever discover this. There are hundreds of such cases. Each attorney assigned her did not want to be the one to blow the whistle, so each, in turn, misrepresented her. It had to come from the outside.

Chap XXVIII:
Karlyn Testifies

T he year 2000 presented a double track in the affairs of Karlyn Eklof, first her appearances and input into the trial of Tiner, and secondly an ongoing miscommunication between herself and her Post Conviction attorney, Beverly Penz.

Just for a starter in that matter, let me quote from a letter Penz sent to Karlyn November 29, 1999 in regard to myself: "Ms. Armstrong contacted our office the other day. She informed us that you had asked her to contact us because you felt that we were not working on your case. [I don't believe I said that.] In the future, we will not discuss your case with anyone calling on your behalf unless we have requested the person's assistance or if the person is a witness or has some direct connection with your case."

Well, how about if Karlyn had requested my assistance, which she did? I had a delightful chat with her legal assistant, informing her of the discoveries offered by the Tiner legal team and the document I had recovered concerning Al Hope. But when she told her employer about them Penz went into a paranoid fury about input from me of any kind.

In the letter, however, she went on to develop the possibilities of their investigation along the lines I had just provided, the leniency offer of Al Hope and the possibility of contacting Tiner's lawyers. She also requested Paya's address in order to retrieve Karlyn's documents and transcripts. Karlyn had to inform her that they were now in my lawyer's office and that I could go there at Karlyn's request from time to time to have items copied for her that she needed. My opinion is that she could just not quite get herself together, and she refused to ask for my help or to acknowledge my help when it was given. This was to be the pattern throughout the investigation.

Her first task in regard to Karlyn was to make her available to testify at Tiner's pretrial hearing in Eugene, which was scheduled for February 15 and 16, 2000. She also received a letter informing her that the present Lane County

DA intended to question her and that she no longer had a Fifth Amendment privilege. Ms. Penz also chose not to attend and was assured an attorney would represent Karlyn at the trial.

I wrote Karlyn twice in January telling her I would be there, also appraising her of what Mr. X was telling me about the difficulties of post conviction reversals. Since I was already traveling to Eugene one Friday-Saturday weekend a month to attend an organ/choir director workshop at the Episcopal Church of the Resurrection, I planned to visit her if possible. I asked for her size measurements and hoped I'd be able to bring her suitable clothes for her court appearances. She was so very sweet about it, but perhaps she already knew she'd never be allowed to wear them.

I was there February 15th when Steve Walker, Rick Lewis and Fred Hugi each took the stand and stated they did not know why their and other Grand Jury testimonies were not recorded.

When Hugi returned to Room 408 in the citadel at 1:00 P. M. February 15th, 2000, sweaty from playing basketball after defying the Court request to step briefly into the hall at the 11 o'clock hearing, he sat cross-legged with his head in one hand, flipping his glass case with the other. When asked why there was no court reporter present when Walker and Lewis testified before Grand Jury, he replied he saw no need for it.

"It was a pretty notorious case," he said as he screwed up his mouth when asked if the Grand Jury knew about Karlyn's conviction. He said also that he was sure the Eklof Grand Jury heard at least a portion of the Eklof's tapes. He was also sure that there was nothing about the Walker and Lewis testimonies he wanted to hide.

After a series of such questions to Hugi, in order to discover fraud in their Grand Jury proceedings, Defense Attorney Lance stated that the State has the ability to impeach witnesses, whereas the defense does not have this prerogative. He summed up that Walker and Lewis did, in fact, testify before the Grand Jury, and we were entitled to know what was said.

However, DA Lane then said there was no indication that the State tried to hide anything pertaining to the case, therefore, the Court should dismiss this objection. The motions are denied, stated the Court.

Various motions were brought before the Court which Tiner had initiated. They then moved on to examine Tiner's Motion to Suppress Audiotapes of the defendant, Tiner, of April 26, 1993 and June 3, 1993, when he was queried by phone as he visited his probation officer in San Diego, after which he was released from custody.

One facet of Tiner's Motion #8 was for the prosecutorial misconduct he had alleged in regard to Karlyn's videotaped confessions which had caused the State at one time to dismiss its own interlocutory appeal against Tiner and a vast delay in the proceedings.

The question for me became, how did they manage to get around it now? First they get a different judge. Then, for the record, that judge systematically ignores the issues.

Therefore each issue of Motion #8, charging prosecutorial misconduct, was summarily dismissed. DA Lane said he did not want the Court to assume he was shortening these issues… but any decision should be only on evidence presented, not by defendant's allegations.

[All evidences presented in Tiner's original Motion to Suppress were no longer considered. These parts of the prosecutorial misconduct they did not choose to deal with. In the following Jerry Smith is being questioned by DA Lane. I believe I forgot to inform the reader that as a reward for solving so many cases, Smith had been made Chief of Police.]

At 3:40 P. M. DA Lane called on "Chief Smith", still under oath, and he was asked about his contacts with Karlyn Eklof. "Did she agree to fly back to testify for Grand Jury?" Ans: "Yes."

"Did she testify?" Ans: "My understanding was that she did not.' Other questions that were asked included:

"Did you have any contact with witness Alven Hope?" Ans: "Yes"

"Did you take notes?" Ans: "My contact was very brief."

"Did you relate personally if there were any deals if he were to testify for the State?" Ans: "No. Any negotiation would be the responsibility of the DA's office."

"Do you know if any other officer took reports that were not provided to the State:… Did you tell officers not to take reports:… Or shape them to benefit the State:" Ans: "No."

There were also questions about taking photographs of Tiner's tattoos when he was brought up to testify at Karlyn's Grand Jury and about the DA's taking the Fifth Amendment for Tiner.

When Karlyn was brought in, Mr. Kent, her appointed lawyer, led with the question of whether she had the right to invoke the Fifth Amendment. They then asked her if she intended to invoke that right.

In response to their query she stated quietly and firmly, "What's been done in the courts is wrong, and I refuse to answer until right has been done."

To each question, Karlyn then answered, "I refuse to answer that question.'

To this DA Lane interpreted that she refused to answer in order to protect Mr. Tiner… Lance, the defendant's counsel, stated that the conjecture was not reasonable, not logical. He also stated that the State cannot call a witness knowing they will invoke the Fifth Amendment [and may not continue to question, as questions are prejudicial.]

The question was then subjected to the judge's ruling, which he promised by the first of March. Before the court's adjourning, Kent inquired about his appointment as Karlyn's counsel. Lansen, the presiding judge, indicated that he would be retained through the trial which was set for April 4th.

On Friday Tiner was on the stand stating that information was withheld about Alven Hope's being held on charges at the time he was called to be a Grand Jury witness. He also questioned statements alleging he himself was involved with "gang" activity at Folsom, which was the reason the detectives photographed his tattoos, in order to identify certain defining tattoos among gang members. He also drew attention to items not timely given to his defense, causing great delays: cash payments to Eklof, document stating steps of her coercion, promises given to her, etc. In regard to Alven Hope, Hugi wanted to dismiss the charges and act like there was no kind of deal made. What Tiner described was a cumulative denial of... *due process* in the conduct between the DA's office and the police department. [What we observe here is a systematic denial of misconduct which Judge Lansen appears to accept.]

> Finally, the prosecution inquired, "How many more motions are we going to have?"
>
> Tiner replied, "Since you're trying to kill me, there could be more motions!"

****

In the pretrial motions I was not able to attend there was some inquiry into the content of Karlyn's videotaped confession. But I have part of the transcript, and this I want the reader to connect with. It must be an old court tactic. I assume that "The Court" in the following transcript is no other than the presiding Judge Lansen I witnessed:

> First "The Court" says, "And I can't put my finger on it right now for the statement for the 29th of April, but I didn't mark any of those statements in that one..." [Well, why not, if it's so important?]
>
> "Specifically, what I am referring to is statements that she makes that say, 'I did'—for instance— 'the stabbing, and he was doing the shooting.' Because I didn't mark these individually line by line, I don't know that I can get more specific than that today."
>
> Why? Because this was never said. The April 29th video, the first one, is quite exculpatory. It wasn't until the May 3rd and May 5th ones that they got her to repeat what Smith had made her say over and over, what he in his wisdom knew she had to have been thinking when she took her flimsy knife into the bathroom to confront Tiner.
>
> But, this "The Court" fellow, being very precise now, goes on for three pages (pp. 10-13) stating that incriminating statements she made to the police on May 2nd, May 3rd and May 5th were highlighted. Pretty tricky, huh? It can be seen in those statements how she alternately retracts and is forced again into saying what they have coached her to say. None of those, however, are as blatant as the statement the Court alleged, that she said, "I did the stabbing, and he was doing the shooting."

I know what she said! It is transcribed and underlined in this book. This writer has had the transcripts of the interrogations for years. Reading it, you can feel the way she was pushed, and her dialogue reveals it.

I am giving you this example. But her trial documents are full of such nasty misrepresentations. It doesn't matter who is there in the courtroom. If only the defense counsel is there and is made uneasy by such forgeries, they won't try so hard.

In the transcript referred to above "The Court" then decides her statements clearly corroborate the statements "Ms. Eklof and apparently Mr. Tiner" are alleged to have made to Mr. Tiner's brother. However, we know the brother first denied their involvement and then exaggerated what "they" allegedly said.

Then, in Grand Jury on May 2, 1994, Dave Tiner, who in January quoted his brother as saying Karlyn stabbed Salmu 30 to 50 times, is backing down or at least showing he didn't believe it much in the first place. When Hugi questions him if either of them indicated how many times the guy was stabbed, he replies, "I honestly couldn't tell you."

This is the way they operate. Your revered counsel will tell you there is no going back to reverse what has been determined in a trial. But the prosecution is going back all the time, dressing it up, misrepresenting it and, if necessary, lying about it to influence a later court not prepared to challenge their lies.

Karlyn was brought in again the second day I was there at the pretrial hearing. As DA, Robert Lane began a series of questions which were all yes or no answers.

He began by saying, "This may be putting it mildly, but wouldn't you say you were shafted, railroaded?"

She said. "That doesn't even begin to describe the damage done through 80 hours of interrogation, not to mention the fact that Jerry Smith plucked pieces of other cases and plopped them right on top of this one to sensationalize it."

She asked, "Is Lane County so deprived of crime they need to drum up business?"

Robert Lane said again, "Well I said I may be putting it mildly that you were railroaded."

She said, "Yes, railroaded!"

Well, I'm sure his sympathy had only one purpose, that is, to soften her up. He looked at her as if to say: I know you didn't do this. His voice brought her right to the very moment she was standing in the kitchen that night and heard the first two gun shots.

He said, "You were in the kitchen?" Ans: "Yes."

He said, "You heard two shots?" Ans: "Yes."

He said, "Was it the defendant?" Ans: "Yes."

He said, "Did you know he had a gun?" Ans: "No."

He said, "Did you shoot Salmu?" Ans: "No."

He said, "James was your friend?" Ans: "Yes."

Then he began to ask her for a statement, and she couldn't say another word. She was on the verge of bursting into tears. Tiner's head was shaking back and forth: "No! No! No!" She could see him glaring at her out of the corner of his eye every time he shook his head.

She raised her hand and said, "That's enough. I'm through. I can't..."

But her defense attorney, Bill Kent, began to ask a few questions. His head was bent low between his shoulders. He asked, "Do you ever have memory problems?"

"After having a drink that was given to me, yes," she replied.

"Who gave you the drink?"

"Jeff Tiner," she said. He had no further questions

Bill Bishop, in his newspaper report of the trial, took the total liberty of running Jerry Smith's original version of the crime scene to fill in the area where she said, "I can't...". He didn't even record her original statements in the courtroom where she took the Fifth. Karlyn couldn't believe how he again sensationalized her alleged role in the crime where there wasn't any need for it. Did Bill Bishop ever read the coroner's report and the fact that neither he nor the anthropologist could corroborate the Hugi/Smith reenactments?

She wrote me about this tremendous hurt. She said, "Bill Bishop seems to see well past the truth and right into the political pockets of his beloved future: corruption." I think she expresses herself very well.

****

I visited Karlyn at the LC jail some time after the pretrials. My attempts to see her were at first denied although she had requested my name be on the visitors list, and I made a trip down from Dallas once to no avail. I made a phone call, however, to the DA's office and received that privilege for a later time.

It was so great to see her, in her awful orange jail clothes, the same she had to wear at the pretrial, and I spoke to her, after a long wait, through a glass and over a telephone. I still thought she looked great, and I told her what a magnificent job she had done on the stand.

While awaiting Tiner's trial Karlyn was returned to the prison in Pendleton. There on March 13, 2000 Penz wrote her that her PC trial date had been set for April 21st but that it would have to be postponed or not allowed in continuance if they were not ready. She stated that "although you have asked for certain information, you have not provided me with anything." She went on to list many things that Karlyn could not in any case provide for her, such as names of people who could verify Tiner's abuse, except for her son TJ, in whose Grand Jury testimony they had avoided this question.

She was also abusive of Karlyn because she did not know TJ's whereabouts since he was no longer staying with her mother. She also stated that she had not determined how the information recently obtained by Tiner's attorney with regard to Al Hope, Hugi and the OSP officers could be much help to her at this level.

You see, she knew! Delving into letters long since filed away, I learn that she knew all along. It was not a question of her accepting these "discoveries" from my attorney. It was a matter of ignoring them. She states, "I do not know how I can prove your attorney should have been aware of the dishonesty of the District Attorney."

She also suggested that if Karlyn did not want her to withdraw she should provide the information requested. On March 23rd Karlyn asked her to do just that, or to provide a list of the documents she already had which Karlyn had sent, plus those sent to her through my lawyer from Tiner's attorneys. This was something Penz would never do. That she had the "discoveries" she was ignoring, or at least knew about them, she could hint at, but never fully acknowledge.

Then, finally, Karlyn's Petition for Post Conviction Relief was finalized and arrived in the mail. It was not possible to quit before they'd begun. However, Penz called Karlyn's bluff and instituted an Affidavit on April 4th in

Support of Motion For Withdraw and For Motion to Continue. Penz stated on this affidavit that "Petitioner has refused to provide me with any requested information or provide me with any assistance in preparing her case." I believe her Motion For Withdraw was denied, but I find no report of it.

Thereafter, and throughout the fall, the only efforts Penz made on her case were to draft motions for payment of expenses required in obtaining documents to support her case, e. g., for copies of the pretrial hearings of Tiner (three different applications for a $25 cost). I feel rather sorry for her.

I have forgotten to mention to the reader that Mr. X, in his initial enthusiasm for aspects of Karlyn's case, had told me he was writing an approach that might be taken in order to win post conviction relief for Karlyn. When Penz was appointed to assist her, he said he would be willing to communicate it to her when the time was right.

I have never thought that this report, which he said was but a few pages, was the 42-page document I eventually found. I believe it was something he aborted when Penz proved to be so difficult to deal with.

In May I myself sent her a copy and cover letter of Karlyn's testimony at Tiner's trial in April. I took the opportunity to tell her my attorney had prepared a statement for Karlyn concerning her best line of defense if it should ever be called for. I said I hoped that she would confer with him about the list of requested items and for evidence that she, or he, felt necessary to defend her in this, her last appeal, since all of her documents were in his office.

There was some hope in there at one time. When Karlyn came back to the valley a second time for Tiner's trial, I am sure the two lawyers conferred. Suddenly my lawyer, Mr. X, was not so excited about Karlyn's chances. He started being evasive about the promised prepared statement. What was I to do? Should I have said, "Look! I want it even if she doesn't!" He was hinting at that time that I had more than used up my thousand dollar retainer.

****

At 10:25 A. M. on Tuesday, May 2nd during Tiner's trial, Karlyn was called to the stand.

After answering DA Lane's questions about her sentencing she was asked, "Do you know who killed James Salmu?"

She said, "Mr. Lane, I take the 5th on this trial."

Mr. Lane repeated, "Did the defendant, Jeffrey Tiner, kill James Salmu?"

Her answer and those which follow, as in the interrogations, indicate how easily the police officers and now the Court could wear her down:

A. I don't mean to burden the Court, and I don't mean to be impertinent or impossible. This is a very difficult position to be in. It was never represented correctly to the family or the friends or the city or the State. And until it gets correctly represented, I have nothing to say.

Q. Did the defendant, Jeffrey Tiner, shoot James Salmu, then wrap his body up in a sleeping bag or some carpet and then go dump it in the woods?

A. Yes.

Q. Did he shoot James Salmu?

A. Yes.

Q Was James Salmu your friend?

A. Yes.

Q. Did you shoot James Salmu?

A. No.

Q Why did the defendant shoot James Salmu?

A. You have to ask him.

Q. Where were you at when he shot him?

A. The kitchen.

Q. Do you remember at one point the defendant handing you a bullet?

A. I refuse to answer anymore questions.

Q. Where in the house did the defendant shoot James Salmu, which room?

A. In the bathroom.

Q. How many times did you hear gunshots come from the bathroom?

A. I heard two.

Q. Did you know that the defendant had a gun?

A. No.

Q. What did the defendant do with James' body after he shot him?

A. I'm done. I can't.

Mr. Lane: Thank you. That's all I have. Your witness.

Tiner's defense attorney Lance then CROSS-EXAMINED the witness:

Q. Ms. Eklof, you indicated you did not want to answer questions?

A. That's right.

Q. Now you have answered questions.

A. It is a very difficult position to be in.

Q. That was because you felt that if you didn't answer questions that you would be held in contempt of court?

A. I'm not scared of contempt of court. For God sakes, I've done six years on nine felonies I did not commit. I've endured humiliation, degradation, separation. I am not afraid of contempt.

Q. Doesn't seem like much of a threat then, does it?

A. It wasn't a threat.

Q. All right. And you've decided today to testify because you thought it was the best thing to do?

A. The misconception of this case has gone on long enough. And if this is where it's got to stop, let it stop here. I am done answering questions. You have your information. Everybody knows what happened. I am done.

Q. Okay. Well, unfortunately, it doesn't work that way in this system. If you start answering questions, you've got to keep answering questions.

A. No, I don't. I disagree with you. The cup -- the cup overfloweth of corruptions and injustice in the City of Lane County. And until something gets done with that, cases like this are going to be botched up for years.

Q. For years?

A. Years.

Q. You feel yours is botched up?

A. For years.

Q. And is it continuously botched up?

A. The paperwork has tripled through the system like snowflakes, just as a rolling snowball, and it isn't fair.

Q. And today you've answered some questions but you refuse to answer others. Is that correct?

A. I can't. I can't.

Q. You can't. You just feel that it's morally incorrect to answer questions?

A. I can't. It just -- I can't.

Q. Do you recall telling the police on repeated occasions that you did not kill James Salmu?

A. I didn't kill James. He was my friend.

Q. Did you tell the police that?

A. Of course.

Q. And did you tell the police that you had not—excuse me, that Jeff Tiner had not killed James Salmu?

A. I don't recall *ever* saying that.

Q. Did you tell the police that repeatedly?

A. I don't recall *ever* saying that.

Q. Has your memory changed or --

A. No, my memory never changed. It was an 80-hour interrogation that altered the facts of this case, that sensationalized every bit of people's ego in Lane County Department of Springfield/Eugene. After that this case was a wash...

Take it up with Jerry Smith. It's his interrogation. He spent over 80 hours feeding his ego, sensationalizing information that didn't need to pertain to this case. He horrified the family and friends and left me sitting here.

Now you want me to come in here and correct the damages that he did during interrogation. I'm offended. You are supposed to be professional people. Get to the facts. Stick to that and we'll get through this. Outside of that, I'm done.

Q. Are you telling me you are not going to answer anymore of my questions?

A. I'm through.

Q. If you—if I ask you more questions, are you just going to say I refuse to answer?

A. No. I'll probably pick the department apart and all of their sensational propaganda they used to misconcept [sic] this whole case. This thing could have been solved six years ago— that is the bottom line— and it wasn't.

It was taken out of context, tossed in cases -- other pieces of cases that didn't even belong, but tossed on top of this one to use as—What, you guys are hurting for crime up here? Drum up business?

Q. You indicated that your memory is good about what happened in 1993. Is that right?

A. My memory is good.

Q. Your memory is good?

A. My memory is good.

Q. You never had any memory problems?

A. The only time I ever had any memory problems is after I had a drink set in front of me and something had been put into it.

Q. When did this occur in your life?

A. Upon meeting Jeff Tiner.

Q. Something was put in your drink and that changed your memory?

A. Yep.

Mr. Lance: That's all I have.

Mr. Lane of the prosecution then conducted a REDIRECT EXAMINATION:

Q. Ms. Eklof, would it be fair to say —and I know that you'll probably think that this is an understatement— but your problem with the prosecution is that you believe that you've been falsely accused and railroaded?

A. I think that is putting it quite lightly, Mr. Lane.

Q. I said it would be an understatement.

A. It is.

Q. Okay. But that is kind of the gist of it?

A. Fred Hugi's ego is the size of a vehicle and it needs to be deflated. He needs to realize that he is human. He doesn't fear God and he doesn't respect me. And it's not fair what he does in a courtroom.

Q. He was the guy that prosecuted your case, Mr. Hugi?

A. Yes.

Q. Okay. Now, on the other hand, though, is it fair to say also that you've always been at least in your recollection-- I know you did a deposition a couple of months ago in your post-conviction case -- that you've always been consistent that it was the defendant, Jeff Tiner, who killed Mr. Salmu, not you?

A. It was. It was.

Mr. Lane: Thank you. That's all I have. May this witness be excused?

The witness: Thank you.

Mr. Lance: Yes.

THE COURT: All right. You may step down.

MS. EKLOF: Thank you... [witness then addressing the defendant Tiner] And I remember what you did to my two-year-old... [Excerpt of proceedings concluded.]

****

Again Bill Bishop, who was there and listened to the above testimony, felt obliged to fill in the horrors of what the public was supposed to remember in regard to the police version of what happened on the night of the murder. On May 3rd he wrote, "Evidence in her case showed that Eklof and Tiner wanted to be alone one night after a party at Salmu's house. When Salmu refused to leave, the pair attacked him. Evidence indicated that Eklof, a lean and strongly built woman, was proficient in martial arts.

"Salmu was beaten, stabbed and shot, and three of this fingers were cut off, according to evidence in the case. Investigators in Eklof's trial estimated that Salmu may have lingered with his wounds for 25 minutes before he died."

He also reported on two other witnesses who recalled what Tiner told them about the killing. This is very disturbing to me, the writer, because their testimony was not allowed at Karlyn's trial because it would cause the jury to realize the real treachery Tiner was capable of toward her, and therefore in his control of Eklof. The first was Linda Louise Little, the heroin addict who came to Karlyn's Grand Jury, who now tells Tiner's court one of his many tales about how the crime started: "because Eklof had attacked Salmu and he was worried that Salmu would notify police."

Bill Bishop also included the tale of Little's companion in Reno, Willis Morris, who said, "He told me that they shot the guy, put him in the bathtub, started cutting him up... To me, it was (Tiner) bragging, trying to impress me."

Bishop, you forgot the part about their planting body parts all over the hillside. That was part of the story.

You bet he was bragging. You bet this killer would want to implicate Karlyn. And these reports of his bragging, which ought to be considered hearsay, are used instead of the Tiner's testimony. At Karlyn's trial, Tiner could not be cross-examined, because Hugi took the Fifth for him. In Oregon, if an accuser's testimony is not available at a trial, hearsay can be used instead.

At this time, however, they did have Karlyn on the stand at his trial, to witness that it was Tiner, and only Tiner who did it. But it mattered to no one that she be absolved of this awful crime, because they would have to examine the whole structure of their law enforcement system.

Bishop also stated that if Tiner were convicted of aggravated murder, the same jury would reconvene to hear additional testimony about his background before deciding whether he should be executed by lethal injection.

****

Our local paper stated that a jury deliberated less than 45 minutes before giving Jeffrey Dale Tiner the death penalty. I called Karlyn's mom immediately and received a letter from Karlyn, written May 22, 2000, saying, "Mother told me that you called her with the news about Tiner's trial result. I'm numb. He'll not hurt another innocent person in this world."

During the time of Tiner's trial I wrote a three-page story entitled "What! No Media?" and sent it to Lisa Verch at KEZI, the local ABC television station in Eugene. I was listening to KEZI regularly during the trial, and I must have missed any mention of it. I remembered the media blitz they had given the "missing person" story years before and, especially, the day-by-day coverage of Karlyn's trial, which was way before I ever met her. Also, I have copies of all of newspaper coverage and remember mention of the KEZI coverage in Karlyn's journals.

Lisa made a phone call to me and expressed great sympathy, but my three-page story caused no real concern.

I also wrote a similar one to Oregon Judicial Watch, a group Karlyn wanted me to address. If you read their newsletter regularly you find that there are just a few people with their own axes to grind who report their ongoing legal procedures. They were not interested in Karlyn's story.

I'm so amazed with that girl. If I'd been on the stand, as she was, during Tiner's trial, I'd have broken down and blubbered after all she's been through. What a show of strength and integrity. No wonder Walker and Lewis have given up law enforcement and Hugi his whole career in order to avoid any more responsibility for their misuse of justice.

****

Karlyn received a status hearing from Penz' legal assistant that the court would be addressing "our motion to withdrawal" on June 23rd. Very strange wording. Karlyn picked it up and has used it ever since.

Penz continued to address the courts for payment of small fees incurred for copying documents she was procuring from the hospital in San Diego for Karlyn's medical records in regard to the beating incurred during the ritual abuse. Penz wrote on August 23rd to her to inform her that the records did not prove that "Tiner broke your leg and fractured your face." She also stated: "I understand that you were traumatized by what you and your children were subjected to following your move from Oregon. Unfortunately, it simply has no bearing on your case."

I understand the frustration of her lawyers. Without accepting that she was drawn into a ring of abuse perpetrators which led to the crime, without accepting her story, that is, they must deal with it as a crime that had no purpose except to bludgeon an individual for no reason. Did Karlyn bludgeon an individual for no reason? Is that the only question the courts can deal with?

Karlyn wrote that Penz' office was driving her crazy with their very rude behaviors, except for the young office girl who was very compassionate. She was also worried about Paya who had communicated with her during Tiner's trial, promising many things she would do, and had then ceased writing.

But she hadn't been hearing from me either. She said, "I remember when I was at OWCC back in '98 just before I was transferred here. Paya had discouraged you, and I almost lost you then. Is that what has happened again?" How well I understand how long the days, weeks, and months must be for Karlyn. It is so easy to understand how she feels abandoned.

I must have reassured her, but letters are missing throughout the remainder of the year. There were also no communications from Penz, and we were soon to find out why. Since she couldn't get Penz' office to do anything for her, so wrote to the Oregon State Bar.

She sent them a 13-page, most aptly written analysis of Hugi's character and offenses against her in the conduct of her interrogation and trial. It was modelled on "Rule 64," from the Oregon Rules of Civil Procedure regarding New Trials, that would grant her an automatic new trial because of Hugi's offenses. It was all very true, of course.

Soon she wrote me, saying, "The investigation for Ms Penz office was here three weeks ago just after they received the letter I sent them. Ed Kraft was going to talk with Steve Walker and Jeff Murdock. I tried to call last week but no answer. I just wanted to update you. Anxiously waiting for a new trial so I can put this behind me."

Frankly, as I review her confusion about the investigator's visit, I surmise that they were responding to her letter but also supervising Fenz' behavior toward her clients following her period of suspension, which will soon be explained.

It seems unfortunate that investigators would visit her—and it seems definitely in regard to her letter about Hugi—and lead her on to great hopes for some kind of relief for his misconduct.

It has been difficult at times for the writer, myself, to absorb the heartache, grief, blame, the countless untutored attempts that this girl has had to undergo. She never again heard a word about the above investigation. My feeling is that "Rule 64" was one an attorney might use if he were well paid and well placed.

Chap XXIX: Post Conviction Relief

D uring the year of Tiner's trial, Beverly Penz accomplished very little toward Karlyn's Post Conviction except for a reluctant start in accumulating relevant documents.

As we later learned, on October 19, 2000 Beverly Penz was suspended by the disciplinary board for ninety days, with sixty days of probation and supervision up to two years. The action was taken for conduct involving fraud and deceit in cashing and dispersing her clients' check for $7000 and, at the same time, a duplicate one from their insurance company, among other complaints.

It was deemed that a bipolar disorder was responsible for the actions, and treatment and supervision were mandated. Karlyn's request for a new attorney and Penz for withdrawal had been passed over in a hearing the previous year, and Penz had written Karlyn hostile letters shifting responsibility on her for not accumulating documents for the kind of defense Penz wished to present.

Karlyn finally sent me a list of required documents and transcripts from Penz, and I spent some time in Mr. X's office duplicating them for her. Although Penz' suspension was not up until February 18th, Karlyn sent me a letter of her February 12th visit. I would like to quote Karlyn's description of the visit, with some minor corrections in spelling and punctuation, which says as much about Karlyn's attitude and distrust of Penz as it does about Penz, who, I believe, was trying to build a comprehensive case:

"She 'Ms Penz' started out with a very humble smile and said, 'I like things in black and white so I'm going to be very frank with you.

"'My last client had some behavioral problems so a guard [is standing] at the door.' Then she looked at me over her eyeglasses and gave a quick sarcastic smile.

"As she pursued setting the atmosphere she accused me of 'not being honest with her' and then told me several things she's tried to confirm didn't pan out.

"I asked, like what? She gave no examples. She only suggested that [we] begin to try to work together. Yes, I was frustrated at her game and uncomfortable with [her] power.

"We talked then about where she was at with my case. She pulled out Murdock's disbarment and stated that was where she was going to head for: ineffective assistance of counsel and mostly due to the fact his opening statement kicked open the door for the prosecutor to bring in 'character bad acts'.

"I disagreed with her only because character bad acts have to be judicially determined prior to trial and Lane County failed to perform that duty. There is a six-step determination process that must be fulfilled by the judge.

"She was very surprised that I was on target and told me that I seemed very tuned in, not like before [during] our other talks.

"Then she looked away from [me] and said, under her breath, 'Well, there's the stabbing.'

"I waited till she looked... [again at me] and said, 'There was no stabbing.' The coroner's testimony was groomed for the State even though his report clearly indicated that there was no stabbing.

"Her next remark was, 'Well, you could [have] hit a bone and the State couldn't prove it [anyway].' Right, the State had burden of proof and they didn't prove it.

"Next I asked her if she noticed... my sentencing... errors. I was acquitted on the first two counts, [but the] jury proceeded to vote on lesser included (which is illegal). Once the jury acquits, that's it. The judge allowed the DA to dictate to the court when he approved of the lesser. Anyway, the judge sentenced me to the lesser and gave me life, life.

"Then on the 3rd and 4th counts of aggravated murder the jury convicted me and the judge sentenced me to 130 months on one of them and twelve months on the other.

"'Totally bizarre,' said Ms. Penz.

"Then she asked me if I had my transcripts. 'Well, no. Is now a good enough time to get them?' I said. She said she would see to it that I received them...

"I asked about prosecutorial misconduct and phony evidence submitted. She told me that DAs can and do get away with anything they want. How unfortunate for some. She stated courts do not go after prosecutors for misconduct. It's just not done anymore.

"After that she slid in with, 'I can't get a hold of your videos from Lane

County. Got any ideas?' she asked. 'What about your Mom?' I told her I do believe Mother has a copied set, but she's in between places.

"You know where she went next, Erma? 'Well, we'll go after Murdock, but I have to find an attorney who will testify against him. And nobody's really willing to do that.'

"Then she closed one eye, swayed in her chair, closed the other eye and looked at me with the one open, and swayed in her chair again. She looked as if she were drunk, though I'm confident she wasn't. It had to [have] been medication or just a dizzy spell.

"I told her don't do anything. I will get my paper work together. Just get me in front of the judge. She very cooly said, 'Don't count on him. He's not going to be much use to you.'" [End of report on interview.]

Next Karlyn said, "I can't tell you how gut wrenching her visit was— just like Thomas Evans, the first attorney Lane County gave to me. Please wait to send the transcripts you've prepared. I want to see what she does over this."

I had already sent her list of required items: copies of the Jury Instructions, the Verdict, the Sentencing, the Closing Argument at her trial, the Appellate Oral Argument, and copies of the Coroner's and Anthropologist's statements.

You can see in the above dialogue how evasive Karlyn is about where the tapes and documents are. I believe she was still laboring under the misapprehension that Mr. X might be asked to represent her. You have to realize how valiantly and consistently she was struggling to understand the available defenses open to her.

I believe that Karlyn quickly came around and gave the documents I had sent to Penz. Penz knew all along where they were, but she would not request them from someone she had determined was irrelevant as a resource to Karlyn. She more than once stated her resentment that I would dare to advise Karlyn.

Only in the above, and I hope short-lived obstruction Karlyn presented to Penz, I would agree with Mr. X, who disposed of his conscience for never writing the promised letter or presenting any hope for Karlyn by saying, when I picked up all her documents, "She is her own worst enemy."

He was, however, sufficiently interested in her case to ask if he could keep the copy of her book, which I allowed. I have no idea why he wanted it, since he never commented on it.

I will soon analyze the very good work that Penz did do in presenting a Petition for Post Conviction Relief on May 2, 2001, shortly after the above encounter. She was aware of the requirements for entering "bad act" witnesses into her trial which were not carried out. They were not carried out because Kolego did not properly object when Judge Merten allowed them in. As Penz would say in the Petition, "He did not force Judge Merten to do the appropriate analysis, thus this issue was not preserved for appeal."

Karlyn must have struggled again with the many aspects of her case which Penz had said she could not challenge. She wrote a pretty precise letter to Judge Hill on March 9, 2001, simply explaining her problems with Ms. Penz and fearing that she would not be defended properly. I don't have his response, but I recall Karlyn telling me he promised to review the evidence and the case she would present "personally" and make sure that it was to Karlyn's satisfaction.

The date set for her trial was May 4th. I suddenly got a call from Mr. X's office on April 30th requesting that I send Karlyn's four videotapes immediately to Penz in time for the trial. She had requested them through him. I sent them immediately by registered mail along with a cover letter, not taking time to duplicate them because of the urgency, and requesting that they be returned after the May 4th hearing. I also sent a copy of Jeffrey Tiner's Motion to Dismiss Interlocutory Appeal in which the validity of the videotapes was brilliantly dismissed, based upon the manner in which they were obtained and the evidence refuting them.

I believe receipt of the Tiner Motion was very important in support of prosecutorial misconduct, which she had told Karlyn couldn't be questioned in this state. She does state the fact that Karlyn's pretrial Motion to Dismiss her coerced confessions was denied, but that nonetheless they were preserved for future appeals. Kolego's blanket objection to the coerced confessions during her trial also preserved them for that purpose, but he did not inform the jury adequately of continuing objections.

Judge Merten derided him at one point for any further attempt he might make to object on that issue. But Kolego failed Karlyn if he was not aware that his objection on that one ground was not sufficient to preserve objections on other areas of gross misconduct on the part of the prosecution. Penz did make this clear in her Trial Memorandum.

She also made it very clear that Karlyn's counsel in succeeding appeals completely failed her in not revisiting the issue of her coerced testimony, which was preserved for that purpose. They also failed her completely in focusing on "bad act" witnesses and illegal "victim's impact" statements which would allow for a dismissal based on "harmless error."

Penz Trial Memorandum, May 2, 2001

Some of the issues brought forward by the Tiner team are included, except for the most egregious *Brady* issues: the Distabile and Al Hope leniency offers and evidence of Hugi's suborning of the polygraph report, coroner's report, death certificate, and the forensics analysis.

The main thrust of the Memorandum was to claim Murdock's opening argument as fatal to the petitioner's case. It charged that his effectiveness was clearly dampened by his addictions and his preoccupation with embezzlement issues, thus putting his client's character into evidence.

Numerous instances were cited of prosecutorial misconduct with no objection which would have preserved those matters for appellate review. Many statements about Eklof's alleged lying were allowed without objection, and there were unwarranted personal attacks on her which, Penz stated, "impugns the integrity of the system as a whole." Her comments on these issues, which were not subject to appeal, as well as those which follow seemed pointless.

The prosecution repeatedly vouched for the police to the jury, without objection, and improperly vouched for the truthfulness of David Tiner's testimony, again without objection. They repeatedly invited the jury to speculate about facts not in evidence. Again, defense counsel failed to properly object to this prosecutorial misconduct. They improperly drew attention to her decision not to testify, after the defense clearly stated in the opening argument that she would and that witnesses would be brought in to testify for her character. This did not happen. The defense counsel failed to produce them or to object to the attention drawn.

Thus, as the Memorandum pointed out, clearly there was reason to move for an acquittal, since one principal duty of the prosecuting attorney is to uphold a person's constitutional rights. It was brought out that in assessing ineffective counsel, PC relief need not show substantial probability that, but for the defense counsel's deficiency, the result of the criminal trial would have been different. In addition, the appellate counsel failed to challenge any reversible constitutional violation of rights and plain errors on the record.

Ineffective assistance of the appellate counsel to address the pretrial Motion to Suppress was their most egregious failure. As Penz stated, "The mere fact that a defendant has a lawyer at his side does not mean that he has the 'effective assistance of counsel' guaranteed by the Oregon and the United States constitutions. Furthermore, the fact that a particular attorney has a reputation for competence does not mean that the attorney has acted competently in a particular instance. 'Thus it is the performance, not the identity of defense lawyer which is subject to constitutional scrutiny' *Krummacher v. Gierloff, supra.* 209 Or. at 872. Petitioner's counsel performance fell below an acceptable standard."

I learned a lot and appreciated Ms. Penz work in the Memorandum. What I don't understand, however, is why the May 4th hearing was not sufficient. Isn't it unheard of that a petitioner be given two Post Conviction hearings. It is my thought that the strength of Penz' Memorandum set in motion a counter directive.

The videotapes, Tiner's Motion to Dismiss, and my letter labeled an "improper submission" are listed in the exhibits for the second hearing on June 15th, but not the first on May 4th. As I will explain later on, I believe that letter was replaced with another cover letter I wrote for Karlyn in August. These submissions, plus further evidence available about the suborned testimonies, must have alerted Judge Hill to the seriousness of the charges, charges that could not be easily dismissed. He could also plead an extra amount of time in viewing the videotapes and making a determination.

Therefore the focus changed. No longer would Penz be taking on prosecutorial misconduct. She would concentrate on Murdock's deficient performance because of substance abuse and errors in Karlyn's sentencing instead. These could be easily dismissed. She could not take on a whole corrupt system, especially when she herself had recently been suspended and was still under supervision.

****

Karlyn raised an alarm in February, 2001 while I was busy practicing for a chamber music concert at the library, that Tiner was going to "walk" in spite of his conviction because he was being held on an aggravated murder charge in violation of the Interstate Agreement on Detainers (IAD). I never believed it, but I had no time to study the issue.

When she finally sent me the legal notice on it, it appears he might have. First he sought a *writ of habeas corpus* alleging this violation which was dismissed. Then it was held that since the petitioner could raise the IAD challenge he had an adequate remedy and was not entitled to a *writ of habeas corpus*.

So Tiner filed his briefs *pro se*... The upshot is that after the trial court entered the judgment dismissing the *habeas* petition, he was convicted in the underlying criminal action of aggravated murder and sentenced to death.

Well, I'm glad. These close calls cause some trepidation. Penz explained it somewhat better in her Trial Memorandum, but I had to figure it out for myself before I had time to study it.

****

It is clear that the longer a delay is, the less likely a client is to receive an adequate response to his petition. That gives court and the defense time to get involved in other things so that they no longer remember what the issues were that were so pertinent at the time of the trial.

All summer Karlyn waited for notice of the outcome of her Post Conviction hearings. It never came. In the fall I started calling the records office in Umatilla County to learn the outcome. They finally sent me a few pages which indicated that a judgment was reached on August 14th, but it was crossed out and changed to September 14th, 2001, stating that the court had previously granted dismissal. There was no comment of any sort.

Nobody exactly told her. The records office also told me that "nothing" was recorded about the hearing. The only pages they sent were about a money judgment of $85 they had taken out of Karlyn's account. Karlyn wrote to Penz on September 1st, asking to know, among other things, "where my case is and who's doing what to assist me."

Thus Penz had the opportunity through her legal assistant to blast Karlyn shamelessly in this way: "As to your question about what this office is doing to further assist you, the response is that we have filed a Notice of Appeal on your behalf, a copy of which is enclosed. Since the appeal has now been filed, she (Penz) no longer represents you in any capacity... Within the next several weeks, your case will be assigned to an attorney who will handle your appeal. You will receive a letter from your attorney."

What a response. Here Karlyn was not even given notice that her PC was denied. And there was not one word of the judgment or the Court's response to Penz' petition Memorandum.

The Notice of Appeal was dated October 2, 2001, and Karlyn received it before she received the few copies the court sent me that her PC was dismissed. The legal assistant said it would take three hours to duplicate all her letters and documents, but the fact is, they didn't bother to inform her or send her anything.

Fortunately, or not, Karlyn had been involved in two other projects with which she requested my help. One was a continuing legal battle with Kolego over the lost journals—as if that were his only error. The other was the dispersing of a packet of appeals she wanted sent out to a considerable list of recipients on September 6th, including Judge Hill and Representative Vickie L. Walker of Eugene, who was initiating legislation to prosecute those who would use Rohyphenol or GHB as a date-rape drug. Others were the Oregon State Bar, the FBI, the Criminal Justice Commission in Salem, and attorneys Beverly Penz and Mr. X.

The packet included her latest interpretation of her unfortunate experience in this realm. Again she was drawing attention to the injustice she had suffered.

I'm glad there was someone like me out there. I could take her calls and try to gently guide her. But there were some wounds that refuse to heal. Not only did I mail out all the materials in the packet, with a cover letter, but I then helped her retrieve at least one of them because she hadn't retained any. Was she her own worst enemy? Yes, because people don't want to deal with it. But that doesn't mean her experiences of date rape and ritual abuse didn't happen.

In this case, I was doing what Karlyn wanted me to do. I was not using my own judgment or trying to advise her, as Penz had accused me.

You wouldn't believe the repercussions, however, that came about as a result of sending out this packet, especially the one sent to Judge Hill. I don't even like to think about it.

Please wait patiently until I have a chance to explain it in the right sequence!

****

Before I do, however, I will explain one last grave disappointment we experienced late in the year 2001. Karlyn had been granted an appeal for her Post Conviction and was being moved back into the Willamette Valley to the new Coffee Creek Correctional Facility at Wilsonville, which is half way between Salem and Portland. Therefore I wrote to Mr. X in some excitement that "I believe that it is time for you to act on behalf of Karlyn Eklof." I said, "Finally, it is the right time, since you have been informed all along, for you to take over and give her the help she deserves."

He wrote me a most kind letter. He said, "Thank you for your November 4, 2001. I am sorry to hear that Ms. Eklof did not win her post conviction. I am not really available to do the appointment on her appeal. I have made a commitment to indigent defense to spend more time on my duties as executive director of MCAD and have promised to not accept any more appeals for a while." Very soon thereafter I picked up all of Karlyn's documents and bid him a good-bye.

The patience of that man. I am rather mortified as I look at all the correspondence I sent him. It is even hard for me to read. It is hard but no harder for me to look at all the correspondence I sent at Karlyn's request, or her behalf. Perhaps I should have advised her not to send it. But I am not her advisor and have never felt that was my capacity. I am here on the outside trying to help with what she needs to have done. If it is only for her peace of mind, so-be-it.

I learned from the Umatilla County Court that a new attorney had been appointed for her Post Conviction appeal. It was a John Manning in Beaverton, Oregon, and I informed Karlyn through her mother. When I called him he said he couldn't file an appeal without a judgment. For him, also, the paper work was a long time in coming.

XXX: Notes for Counsel

A t the lowest point in my hopes for Karlyn, I discovered in early January 2002 the forty-two page confidential document some one prepared for mounting an adequate defense for her among her papers stored in my attic. They had been there since early fall when I had retrieved them from Mr. X and said good-bye. As I read it, I half expected the phone to ring, or a police car to drive up. For a few days I was in a panic that Mr. X would find it missing and come after me.

This document put the correct legal analysis behind every issue of misconduct that had been alleged in her indictment, the preparation for her trial, and the conduct of the prosecution during her trial. Here was corruption unveiled, with big concepts like *"Brady"* violations, complete with arrows and exclamations and, perpetually, the phrase, "this will be very important in her Post Conviction trial."

It took a couple of weeks of absorbing it before I realized that this was something I had paid for in the first place and never received. It was worth asking, why hadn't these things been discovered already? Hadn't anyone been doing anything to back up their allegations of witness tampering, gross errors of conduct during the trial, but especially, the evidence to prove the lies and false promises to Eklof? You can't just claim something without proof.

I sent a copy to Karlyn and to her newly-appointed PC appeals attorney. I also sent a cover letter explaining all I knew about its history, except that I was not naming Mr. X. I don't believe he called for quite a while. When he called he said he hadn't read my discovery document, but that he would read it one day when he got around to it.

My first call to John Manning had been on December 28, 2001, when I learned he was appointed on October 6th as Karlyn's defense. He said he knew nothing about the case except a brief report. But he warned me that nothing that had not already been brought forward in the Post Conviction hearing could be entered in Karlyn's appeal.

At the time we first talked, there were no records available of her recent PC trial, no Statement of Fact, Conclusions of Law, Order of Dismissal, or Judgment for him to consider wherein he could challenge their decisions. At the time, I did not realize that these would still be forthcoming. All I knew was that her PC Relief was denied on August 14, then crossed out to read September 14th. I did not realize the significance of that change until later.

Later, he must have received the packet from Umatilla that I did, on February 23, 2002, which finally revealed what had been the judgment issued on September 14, 2001. Karlyn never received this packet, but I duplicated it and sent it to her. Then I didn't hear from John Manning for a long time.

It took me a while to realize that the claims in the discovery document were the same as those suggested by Tiner's lawyers and Tiner himself in his letter to Karlyn. But the defense was brilliant. And that is what a good trial defense is all about. You have to be good enough that no judge, and no jury, can ignore your arguments and, especially, the evidence of prosecutorial misconduct.

****

When I finally received a copy of her Judgment on February 22, 2002, I realized why the date was changed on the original notice saying her Post Conviction Relief was denied. When I realized the significance, my heart sank. The judge had promised on April 4th he would take twenty days to review her tapes and, hopefully, Tiner's Motion that I sent with them. Then he would give his opinion. Therefore, I thought that judgment was concluded in that June 15th hearing.

Still Karlyn received no notice of it. Then on September 6th Karlyn had me send out that packet she prepared to a list of names, that repeated her unfortunate story along with numerous clippings about the prevalence of date-rape drugs in abusing, filming and killing countless women on the California and Mexican border and elsewhere.

Well, the court changed the August 14th date to September 14th so they could include it, after the fact, in the exhibits. All the time I had thought the cover letter of my "improper submission" was the one I wrote to Fenz when I sent the videotapes and Tiner's Motion to Dismiss.

Now I know the effect of that delay. Earlier Karlyn had sent me a newspaper clipping from Umatilla County describing the fact that they were hundreds of cases behind in their court calendar, which would also mean they were behind in processing their reports. I'm convinced that whatever influence we might have had in that former submission, or that Fenz might have had, as a matter of fact, in her well-presented Memorandum, was effectively wiped out by the latter. It was, indeed, an "improper submission."

I should not have cooperated in sending it. I realize now that timing is everything, and we had just blown it. The feedback I had had from more than one attorney, that she was "kind of crazy" and her own worst enemy came back to me, and I began to resent her, and Paya especially, in their efforts to publicize her case. This was something I should never have gotten into, especially since I was prone to follow their lead, and just be of service.

It was a low blow to wonder whether even Penz' carefully worded Memorandum might have been dismissed across the board because of this "Summary of Facts," Karlyn's unfortunate story, the one nobody wanted to hear.

I realized that her story creates that heartsick feeling: how could she get herself into such a mess? But now the packet we sent on September 6th was included in the exhibits as an "improper submission," and it had my name on the cover letter.

****

The reader perhaps remembers the commendable things I cited in Penz' Trial Memorandum of May 2, 2001. Now we learn, not in twenty days as he suggested, but on February 23, 2002, what decisions Judge Hill made according to her rationale on many issues and the cases she cited which had been reversed because of the same errors.

His **Conclusions of Law** are as follows:

1. Any issue that was or could have been raised on direct appeal is not a ground for postconviction relief... Therefore, Petitioner's allegations and claims of various trial court errors, which were raised upon appeal or could have been raised upon appeal, bar the assertion of the claims here... [Although there is a discussion of this issue and the one which follows, the conclusion is the same]

2. In order to state a claim for post conviction relief there must generally be an allegation of inadequate assistance of counsel... Therefore, Petitioners allegations and claims that various trial court errors deprived petitioner of petitioner's constitutional rights are not meritorious, and are not grounds for relief.

3. Petitioner's sentence was legal and proper. [Two life sentences and 202 months]

4. Petitioner received fair and impartial hearings.

5. The clearest outline of the principles by which a claim of constitutionally ineffective assistance of counsel is to be measured is that of the United States Supreme Court in *Strickland v. Washington*... [which cites two components] First, the defendant must show that counsel's performance was deficient... Second, the defendant must show that the deficient performance prejudiced the defense.

6. To prevail on a claim for post conviction relief (PCR), a petitioner must establish not only the denial of a constitutional right, but also that prejudice resulted from the denial... Petitioner failed to demonstrate that any prejudice resulted from the issues raised.

7. Petitioner presented no evidence that would clearly have a tendency to affect the result of the prosecution.

8. Trial Counsel's representation, and presentation of issues, evidence and defenses, and other matters were within the scope of tactical choice.

9. Trial counsel demonstrated reasonable professional skill and judgment.

10. Petitioner failed to present evidence of witnesses to support Petitioner's contentions.

11. Trial Counsel's investigation and preparation, including witnesses and subpoenas was proper under the circumstances then existing...

12. Trial Counsel properly objected to preserve issues for appeal.

Each issue raised by Penz was separately refuted in the Narrative and Findings of Fact preceding the above. It is interesting to me that Judge Hill states "I have looked hard to find the coercive police tactics described by petitioner and they did not appear on tape or elsewhere in the record."

He evidently did not look at the Motion for Dismissal, which was upheld in the Tiner trial and led to the state's dismissal of its own interlocutory appeal. He did not consider the two tablets telling her story which Eklof brought with her from Salt Lake City, the denial of an attorney and the gradual wearing down of her will and imposition of a police version she was forced to enact.

Judge Hill states that there was no evidence of coercion during the first part of the videotape which proves to be inculpatory. [Does that mean he discerns coercion in the last part? That is the part we're talking about.]

Just before that last tape was made, when Captain Smith made her apologize to all the officers, Detective Walker said, "You can't do that to her!" He also said in regard to his tactics of hypnotism that, "Yes!" Smith indeed was studying and using those tactics.

They also made her rehearse often that opening statement she made when the video cameras were turned on, that what she was saying was, "Absolutely! Absolutely!" of her own free will and volition and that she was telling the truth. In addition, she was always led to believe her testimony must be as they had coached her in order to convict Tiner, not herself.

I don't believe that there was any effort in this postconviction hearing to assist Karlyn in any way. In the above conclusions having to do with adequate assistance of counsel, for example, numbers 2, 4, 5, 6, 7, 8, 9, 11, and 12 all came under the rubric of number 5, which required showing that her counsel's errors were so serious as to deprive the defendant of a fair trial. These were not dealt with in any of her appeals, only the errors which led from them.

Then the burden is placed back on the shoulders of the petitioner, as in number 1, that any issue not raised on direct appeal is not a ground for postconviction relief. Therefore, any adverse of effects of Murdoch's opening statement must be denied. Those adverse effects were the only issues brought up in her oral arguments. The fact that her appeals attorneys did not bring up the well-preserved issue of Karlyn's own Motion to Dismiss in the pretrials effectively rendered them now unusable as a ground for postconviction relief.

And to challenge issue number 3, her sentence, which was not legal and proper, would open up a whole can of worms about Hugi's unethical behavior during his closing statement and his manipulation of the jury during the sentencing, and of Judge Merten's allowing it.

I am shocked that the burden of proof comes back to the defendant herself, for the errors "she allowed" her counsel to make. I am shocked that there is no redress for these errors, because her counsel cannot be deemed "ineffective" under the outlines provided in issue number 5. I am shocked that Penz herself can go through all the issues which she felt could reasonably be brought forward, only to have the judge simply pump out the same old Conclusions of Law that he had probably written for scores of other postconviction hearings.

****

It may be amusing, at least to people more versed in law than I am, to read my analyses of what I think happened in the pursuit of justice outlined above. I'm sure I miss a lot of things and misconstrue others, but I never intended to get involved in legal matters. I am totally astonished, however, to find that the corrupt ways of the legal profession are practically inapproachable.

I have a story I'd like to tell of my own, with one amusing highlight in regard to my communications with John Manning, Karlyn's subsequent PC appeals lawyer.

During the fall of 2001 I found myself unable to make my car payments when the schools cut back on hiring due to their budget cuts, which released younger music teachers into the hiring pool. Another sort of bureaucracy had kept me out of the teaching profession during my most vital years after my husband died, and I had very little pension to supplement my social security. I was feeling very used and unwanted, but I was using my extra time to begin research at the Salem Library on criminal justice for this book. I believe I learned a few things, but obviously not enough.

Not getting enough jobs was making me feel like a thing of the past. Therefore, it was quite appropriate to my mood when John Manning finally called me.

He began our conversation by saying, "I'll bet you're over 65, aren't you?" I was somewhat taken aback at his audacity and just said, "Umm,..." so he continued. He went on to tell me about all his relatives who were very elderly, etc., and the things they could or couldn't do because of age. I guess what he was saying was that such people were not to be taken seriously about anything due to their age.

I still did not respond much to him. I didn't tell him my age. I believe I went on saying, "Umm..." I'm sorry, but I believe he lost that round. I gave him no satisfaction whatsoever. I'm not about to try to make these people feel good about themselves.

So he went on to say that in Karlyn's case she had confessed to this crime on the videos. I reminded him that the "different" versions ought to have proved that she was constantly being hounded and that words were being put into her mouth. Why would she ever repeat her story, except that she didn't get it right the first time and they were going to make her tell it the way they themselves had constructed it. I went into some of the findings on the forty-two page discovery I had sent. **He said he hadn't yet seen the videos, and he hadn't looked at the discovery I sent.**

It seems he had already made up his mind there was nothing he could change. I also told him of my attempts to get Penz to look into certain things, *e. g.*, the suborned testimonies of Distabile and Al Hope, which later showed up in the discovery. We talked a little about Penz' attitude, because I wasn't at that time convinced she could not have brought these things into her Memorandum. Then he abruptly ran out of time and said he would call back.

The year ended with several long letters I wrote to Karlyn, responding to her concerns and telephone calls, and appraising her of interesting things I came across in my research. But it was a bleak midwinter.

XXXI: One Bright Light

I t was with a weary heart that I contemplated the New Year 2003. I had visited Karlyn when she first came back to the CCCF in Wilsonville in May and once again in the late summer. Almost by common agreement she stopped phoning me so often, which, however, I had welcomed, but we were both tired, I believe, of commiserating about hopes and dreams that never came true.

I had received a beautiful card she made for my birthday in December and only a letter or two through the whole spring. Her mother bought some property in a small town in Arizona after both Karlyn's grandparents had passed away, and there she continued to try to raise Karlyn's children. She had lost her husband some years before because of the problems involved in being always available to them.

I encouraged her at one time to make plans to visit Karlyn with the children and to stay with me. But when the summer arrived, she decided that there were no funds to do so.

****

In January 2003 I received a surprising call from John Manning. After a whole year of just sitting on Karlyn's case, he wanted to know where those pages of discovery had come from.

I told him the name of Mr. X, but he soon called and said Mr. X didn't know anything about it. Then I remembered Jaqua and that series of events wherein her office had tried to get in touch with me. I had given them the name of Mr. X. I wrote a letter to Manning suggesting that might have been the source. Her name as a contact was even included in the document.

No matter that we couldn't attribute it to anyone. Manning was convinced those things should be looked into and had been at least partly known by Karlyn's postconviction counsel.

Big surprise! He remanded her case back to Umatilla County, meaning he was not satisfied with the way they had handled it. This was an important breakthrough, since this objection would thus be preserved for future *habeas corpus* scrutiny.

I did not call Manning after that. I remembered his patronizing phone call. All I learned from that point on was through the Supreme Court Records office. I learned that the Remand was dismissed and that Manning had finally written a Brief. When I inquired at the records office they loaned me a copy. I copied parts of it and sent Karlyn a note about it. When I visited her again on Mother's Day I told her more.

The Brief was oversized, not even accepted until the size was approved. The issue it pursued was the known record of Jerry Smith's lying and coercion of witnesses. But this *was* the principal issue, because his treachery led to her "confessions," the only real evidence against her, except for the suborned testimonies and witnesses. This was the bright light we had been waiting for, or at least a step in the right direction.

Manning happened to call me a month or so afterward, I can't remember why, and I told him I had the Brief. I probably didn't tell him well enough my pleasure in the fact that he was finally going after the prosecution—the corrupt court that Kolego so deplored he brought forth no witnesses or objections.

The issue of her excessive sentence was also addressed in the Brief. Eventually I read the transcripts from the Boots and Proctor exoneration retrials and Judge Hargraves deposition against Smith. This was so important!—I wished I had responded more to Manning when he called, but I'm sure he couldn't care less about me.

But I must say, there were so many issues brought forward in the Notes for Counsel, which legitimately could have been raised in her appeal of the Post Conviction. And he was absolutely wrong in his first statements to me. For example, an appeals court is not bound by a trial court's ultimate holding as to voluntariness. An appeals court assesses anew whether facts suffice to meet constitutional standards; whether the historical facts as found are sufficient to sustain a finding of voluntariness. *Ball v. Gladden*, 250 Cr. 485, 487-88, 443 p. 2d 622 (1968) is one case study cited in the Notes for Counsel, and there are many others. In fact, the Notes for Counsel devotes three pages to a discussion of case law applicable to Eklof's coerced confession.

****

One aspect of Karlyn's trial, a minor one never addressed, continues to irritate me. It was the attitude of the Court toward Kolego when he did object. Judge Merten lectured him like a schoolboy, saying in effect, once is enough. If you're going to make a blanket objection just don't keep reminding us about it. And when Kolego cross-examined Dave Tiner and Dave started smart-mouthing him, Judge Merten made it Kolego's error. You keep badgering him like that, and that's what you'll get, he said in essence.

But the issue I most resent in Judge Merten's presiding over Karlyn's trial was his attitude toward the story she had to tell. Before I recount his remarks about it, I will reiterate a bit about the Springfield police department's handling of it.

Here was the testimony most critical to Karlyn's case. It had been a factor all through her pretrials, because all Karlyn had to offer in evidence of her coerced testimony was her own damaged self. That was why she was fair game to the police team who preyed upon her confidence while neglecting her own story. She probably was not mentally fit to be interrogated when she came from Salt Lake.

She begged to have them accept her small tablets they had coached her to write while there which told the truth about what happened. Then they took them and hid them. They did not allow them to be entered as her testimony, because they did not want evidence that they had greatly revised her story.

She tried desperately to fill the role they seemed to be expecting of her. And she really thought they were her friends, guiding her. Soon she began to have grave doubts about that, but she was under their complete control and continuous supervision, and she didn't know what else to do.

Even in the last desperate attempt to tell her story, she was told that she had lied on her polygraph—reacting to the question about the gun because Tiner dropped the hot bullet casings in her hand—and that they would keep having her modify it until it matched the polygraph.

Now the reason I am going into this is that in the first dozen pages of her trial transcript Judge Merten has an attitude which he finally expresses. He says, "This is a can of worms we are not willing to open!"

Why, in heaven's name, not? This is a human being you're dealing with. You've got to look at what happened to her that caused her to bend, first to those criminals, and then to police brutality.

In not allowing "her" story of what happened to her, by his attitude, Judge Merten thereby colored everything Kolego said with doubt and innuendo and actually trumpeted for details concerning every aspect of the prosecution's scenario.

His attitude probably inspired Murdock's knee-jerk defense of her character which led to an opposite effect as a result of "bad acts" allowed in. All of this was Judge Merten's responsibility. He wasn't even legally allowed to do this without some sort of review elements, as cited by Penz in her Memorandum.

He also allowed the prosecution, i. e., Hugi, to slander her. When Hugi called her a "biker bitch" Kolego objected. Merten denied the objection say-

ing, "It's in the record." I can't believe this. That any slander the police intro-
duces against a defendant can then be used as an absolute fact.

Hugi alluded to evidence of her lying which would never be forthcoming. The Court is obliged to monitor and object to such remarks, even if the
defense does not. They are obliged to see that the defendant receives a fair
trial.

Hugi's egregious remarks are clearly cited in **Penz' Trial Memorandum**, which Judge Hill in Umatilla dismissed without a word. Penz clearly
saw that slander was involved in Karlyn's trial and stated:

The Prosecutor repeatedly and improperly commented on the veracity of the statements
made by Eklof, which the State presented, absent any objections by Defense Counsels Kolego
and Murdock.

° Is Eklof a liar? You bet she is. Did she lie on those all the way through from the
beginning to end? Yes, she does. Do we catch her at it? Absolutely. (TR 608, L13-15).

° She [Eklof] told him [police officer Mike McCarthy] flat out lied, said James was seen
leaving a party with a lady.

° She [Eklof] was just a victim. Which is, you know, it's a nice story, if you like to hear
stories (TR p. 651, L 17-19).

° She says she did it out of self-preservation to save her own life and the lives of her
children. Well, that's baloney. (TR 654, L. 14-16).

° [Eklof] lies to cops when they come around, flees with Jethro to Fresno, back to San
Diego and continues to lie about it. (TR 571, L 14-16).

° Eklof has not told the truth. (TR 609, L 19).

It was unethical and improper for the prosecution to make assertions to
the jury in closing arguments. The State cannot comment on nor address the
truthfulness or the untruthfulness of a witness... What the prosecutor did was
wrong under the law, but more importantly, the defense counsels did not object. Nothing was preserved for appeal.

Another remark Penz made in her Memorandum, in regard to Kolego's
repeated failures to object, was that: "An objection on one ground is insufficient to preserve another objection." It is doubtful that Kolego was laboring
under any such misconception, however. With both Hugi and Merten ready to
pounce on him, he probably decided that bringing forth witnesses in her favor
would be counterproductive. They would be cross-examined with the same
kind of slurs and innuendos. He really believed, and Hugi half believed at one
point, that the jury would see through this farce, this complete lack of evidence, and not convict her.

His failure to defend her by stating, "No defense... I cannot move a
corrupt court," did not absolve him from trying, however. His failure was then
chiseled in stone. Gartlan, in the oral arguments, didn't even bother with it but
focused only on Murdock's opening argument which allowed Hugi, and Merten,
to bring in the "bad acts" and "victim's impact" statements before the verdict.
And, as indicated above, Penz cited Kolego's failures, but they were dismissed

without comment by Judge Hill on the basis of the laws protecting "ineffective" counsel.

The failure of her counsel to defend her by bringing in promised witnesses is apparent. He had just delivered a fair summary of the mistreatment against her in his closing remarks. The gross prejudice against her by the prosecution and the Court for allowing it demonstrates that integrity is not a factor in controlling such abuse and corruption. If they truly wanted to conduct a fair trial, the Court should have known what deceit this prosecution team was capable of and taken steps to look into it. The fault is as much with the Court as with the inadequacy of her counsel, John Kolego. Yet his sudden decision to rest his case surprised everyone.

If her story were made into a film there would be no need for a script. Just a virtual reenactment of the dialogue in the police and Grand Jury records— those that haven't been destroyed—and the trial itself, along with a reenactment of the deals made, would be a vindication, without Karlyn's journals and stories of what happened to her.

As Albert Camus has said, "Integrity has no need of rules." Our court system, for indigents at least, abides by certain rules while ignoring many others in order to accomplish their goals, which are convictions. Then the public is satisfied, because of the numbers of crimes solved and the numbers of convictions.

What can of worms didn't Judge Merten want to open? Well, of course, Karlyn's. What can of worms does he indeed want to open?

Tiner's. Yes. The prosecution takes the Fifth for him so he won't be allowed to deconstruct the "evidence" they have used to build the police version of the crime scene. She said not a word, at the crime scene, while the police forced her to verbalize in the videos what they told her she must have been thinking. And she said not a word, at Dave Tiner's, while Jethro concocted a bloody scene and a stabbing for his brother's benefit.

Therefore, because Tiner wouldn't testify, that entitles the prosecution, *i. e.* Jerry Smith, to state, even though Dave Tiner's testimony keeps changing, that "she said she stabbed him 30 to 50 times," which is a lie. The law has decided that it is not hearsay, because of a rule that if a codefendant won't testify, his words at a prior time can be used as evidence.

Judge Hargreaves, in a deposition against Jerry Smith barring him from his courtroom, said he lied but that the judge could not put his finger on exactly when. Well, I can. It is right there, above. And a corrupt court allowed him to present this, without qualification, to a jury that was not even informed that this gross misinterpretation was not even in the coerced testimony she objected to.

Then the prosecution brought in the clinchers, the suborned testimony of Al Hope, who said she procured the weapon before she went to San Diego, before she met Tiner, and of John Distabile, who said she had told him she had to stab Salmu to put him out of his misery. They were both gross lies, purchased from Hope in exchange for leniency in a child pornography charge, and from Distabile, granting him immunity from further questioning in an agreement with his lawyer. But they convinced the jury.

****

The papers to back up the "discovery" document, Notes to Counsel, which no one would admit writing, I discovered in my attic, a huge stack of documents to which the Notes referred. For a year and a half I thought those were some of the trial transcripts from my own returned documents.

The significance of my discovery was that these documents would not have to be retrieved in order for the Notes to be used. No one could refuse to produce them for me or for anyone else. I had them. I could write about them, not because they existed somewhere, but because I possessed them myself. There in the attic was a large pack, four inches thick, with Document A: Letter from Distabile's attorney, Robert Cole Tozer to Fred Hugi, 6/14/94 on top.

Therefore, I could go on, as I always intended, telling precisely how Hugi orchestrated the lies that led to Karlyn's conviction, but now knowing that the proof was right here. I want to say, however, that time has put the Notes and documents in perspective for me, and I realize that anyone in contact with Tiner's lawyers during the time they were building his case could have written and collected them. Since I could not have known about the violations, except through finding them, they were a revelation to me.

Since no one will acknowledge having written them, I will now use them, in exact quotation, in order to uncover further violations in detail:

A. Document: ...Hugi had a transactional immunity deal with Distabile. Absolute *Brady* material as key impeachment evidence which should have been produced to Eklof's counsel prior to trial. This letter was hidden from Eklof and her counsel. Hugi never revealed the deal, to the jury.

B. Documents: Numerous, relevant to Alven Hope. Hope is the witness who claimed to have sold a gun, variously to Tiner and/or Eklof. Hope's indictment for child molestation delayed 2 yrs, by Hugi.

[1] Patricia Jaqua interview of John Perdue. 5/2/97. Perdue reveals Hope allowing that prosecutor Hugi suborned Hope's perjury against Eklof.

[2] SEVEN STAPLED PAGES:

(a) Tiner Discovery pp 1536-1538. Second Alven Hope arrest, after Hugi delayed Hope's indictment on molestation charges until after he had testified against Eklof. Hugi concealed the pending Hope charges from Eklof's attorney, thus concealing/withholding crucial impeachment evidence, Not @ Disc. p 1537, "NARRATIVE"—"Hope was indicted as having participated in a homicide" in Lane County. it says: "(See attachment)

(b) The "attachment" referred to above was not produced. Tiner had to file a separate motion to hold the current prosecutor, Bob Lane, in contempt for withholding *Brady* material which the Tiner Trial Court ordered to be produced. ***CRUCIAL NOTE*** See bottom right-hand corner, in Hugi's handwriting: "Not for discovery"** This is Oregon State Police dispatch notification re second arrest of Alven Hope at Portland V. A. Hospital, see p 2242: "Hope is also said to have AIDS. Hope can be unpredictable and violent. He was recently involved in a homicide in Springfield, for which he was not charged, but acted as a participant." All of this key impeachment evidence was deliberately concealed from Eklof's counsel.

(c) Hope was such a suspect, that a handgun was recovered from Hope and ballistic tests were run. Tiner Disc. p 2235. This evidence was concealed from Eklof, and from Tiner until recently. No comparisons have ever been produced. Second arrest report, Tiner Disc. pp 1539-1540 Concealed from Eklof. ***CRUCIAL NOTE P 1540, "action taken" identifies 2 CSD videos. Tiner's investigator, Patricia Jaqua, has copies of those videos. The second video has Hope's daughter Merrilea describing multiple vaginal and anal rapes with foreign objects, specifically identifying objects. KEY: the tape has the shell-shocked social worker specifically saying "Be sure to give a copy of this tape to Fred {Hugi}. Hugi personally dismissed the foreign object charges against Hope as part of the deal to testify against Eklof.

(d) 10 Count indictment against Hope dope was initially arrested April 29, 1994. Hugi parlayed indictment until January 18, 1996, in order to avoid Hope's impeachment. ***CRUCIAL NOTE*** Hugi then lied to Eklof jury about Hope's status: (A) Gamesmanship by Hugi where he fails to inform of Hope's pending charges [see Eklof trial trans p 145 L 9-18] and (B) directly on closing argument to Eklof jury when Hugi says "He [Hope] admits to his guilt in a crime [possession of a gun allegedly sold to Eklof]. He got a deal or something "No." [see Eklof trial trans. p 606 L 13-14]. At no time did Hugi inform the Eklof trial jury, trial court, or defense counsel of pending prosecution of Hope which Hugi was personally delaying at the time of Eklof's trial...

(e) Transcript of proceedings in *State v. Hope*, Lane Co. Cir. Ct. #10-96-00522. "Stipulated Facts" trial. Hugi waltzed Hope through sweetheart deal, then even argued for Hope to remain free pending sentencing hearing.

(f) Judgment of conviction against Hope NOTE** Counts 4 and 5, vaginal and anal penetration with a foreign object counts specifically dismissed on motion by Fred Hugi.

(g) Search warrant, affidavit, return of warrant. This all came down on April 29, 1994, 2 weeks prior to Hope testifying against Eklof at her Grand Jury. ***KEY NOTE*** Hugi had Hope secreted into the Douglas County Jail, rather than Lane County, where Hope was arrested. NOTE** Tiner's defense team is currently pinning down further details, which will be provided as they become available ** Hugi then withheld Hope's indictment, had Hope's armed robbery parole reinstated, used Hope to testify about "gun sales" at Eklof's trial, waited until Tiner was indicted on Salmu murder charges in December of 1995, then rearrested Hope on the molester charges 3 weeks later.

(h) Attaching documents from search warrant, shows Hope as police sting target, selling his child, etc. sick puppy [etc.]

C. Document: Tiner's MOTION TO COMPEL PRODUCTION OF EVIDENCE RELATING TO ALVEN HOPE.

Status: Granted in full.

Facts: This is key motion which led to Order to Produce, in Tiner case.

**** ALL OF THE ALVEN HOPE EVIDENCE (above) IS NEWLY DISCOVERED for EKLOF'S POST CONVICTION APPEAL PURPOSES.**

One has to smile, here, and realize that whoever researched and wrote the above had an excess of enthusiasm about what could feasibly be accomplished in a Post Conviction review. As if a Post Conviction defense were only so easy!

Some of these are extraordinary conclusions. Though all details of the research are precise, it would be too much to hope they could be addressed in the present legal system by underpaid post conviction defense attorneys and overworked judges due to the "procedural default" rule. This is material for *habeas corpus*.

It occurs to me that, with the thirty or so motions to suppress Tiner constructed with his attorneys and the 18-month delay he caused in his own trial, he would have been privy to all these findings and their legal implications. He could have written this.

There is another whole page in the Notes on this issue, stating: Excellent source of constitutional case law... Much of this will transfer directly to Eklof post. conv. app. brief.

Well, it didn't, did it? There are five more pages citing constitutional law that would apply to the suborning of the testimonies of Al Hope and John Distabile.

Next in the Notes for Counsel are errors in the conduct of Eklof's Grand Jury, the playing of selected videotapes while she was available as a witness and the erasing of Walker's and Lewis' testimonies. In addition there was an audiotape played which was gained illegally, which though exculpatory to her in general, established that as early as April 1, 1993, before she even left Oregon and within days of the alleged crime she was considered a primary homicide suspect. The police repeatedly claimed she wasn't initially a suspect in order to clean up lack of *Miranda* warning in all of the initial conversations with Eklof. Hugi and the cops made that claim in Eklof's pretrial admittance hearings. As the Notes explain, "They are cold busted for lying to gain admittance of the *un-Mirandized* Eklof statements from April '93 to May '94 which is: EVERY TAPE THE STATE USED AT EKLOF'S TRIAL!!!"

Hugi deliberately, willfully, and knowingly concealed this evidence at the time of Eklof's pretrial proceedings which were meant to suppress her coerced testimony.

The Notes also state that there was no medical examiner listed as ever testifying at her Grand Jury, and no death certificate or vital statistics illustrating death are listed at the foot of Eklof's indictments. Salmu's body was not discovered, however, until six months later, but perjury concerning those documents was orchestrated and prompted by Hugi at the trial.

John Manning had the Notes for Counsel which I submitted to him in January 2002. After a year-and-a-half, however, citing Jerry Smith's known lying was as far as he would go in charging prosecutorial misconduct.

Manning did call me recently. He did ascertain that I was aware of the Remand and of the Brief he wrote.

Then he said that what was in the Confidential Notes for Council would be very important in Karlyn's *federal habeas corpus*. That is the one bright light at the end of the tunnel, if I can believe his words. I must trust that someone, somewhere will do the right thing.

Chap XXXII: Ritual Abuse Reexamined

The abuse that Karlyn alleges she and her children suffered at this time deserves some analysis. Not everyone reading her story is prepared to believe these things. Rather it is easier for them to surmise that her experiences were imaginary, drug-induced or both.

Certainly the detectives who kept track of her during the year following the disappearance of James Salmu did not believe her or investigate. When they first visited her after the ritual abuse, there was no evidence to back up her story except her broken bones and smashed face.

Once the police have named a suspect, according to their usual procedures, they do not investigate any other criminal activity. They would later say that she was not a suspect in his disappearance at that time, which is false. But taking her into custody for her protection was the farthest thing from their minds. Neither was looking into who might have beaten her so brutally any consideration of theirs. Lying to her tormentor to cause him to torment her further, thereby bringing them both to justice, was their goal. An attempt on her part to seek protection or to testify against Tiner would only have hastened her interrogation by the prosecution team in Springfield.

Her claim of ritual abuse, when she finally could extract herself from its recurrence, they found quite laughable. They tormented her with sarcasm, and Jerry Smith even tried to induce hypnosis himself in order to have her recall the details of Salmu's murder. If it worked in Imperial Beach, it would work for them.

Satanic ritual abuse, using enslaved persons, children, babies, or animals, for cult purposes has existed since the beginnings of human life on earth. It is startling to contemplate that what seems so unbelievable, so ghastly, and so inhuman to us now was a fact of life for worship in ancient cultures. It has even been encountered in modern times among aborigines. What could it be in the human spirit to allow such ultimate betrayal of existence itself? Even Abraham was prepared to sacrifice his own son, Isaac, in the Bible.

It is difficult for us to associate it with religious worship or any laudable motive, even a bargain with the gods for stability, victory over enemies, or a successful harvest. In civilized countries of today, one could almost say it is unheard of.

Yet satanic ritual abuse (SRA) is more prevalent than almost anyone can imagine. Some even allege that there are hundreds of thousands of persons involved in such abuse, involving many, many cults, families, and communities. But there is not much proof of this. One wonders why, if there is so much of it reported by persons who have experienced it, why is there so little evidence?

There is a preponderance of SRA in fiction and movies, even extending to elements of it in children's literature. The closest reality, however, exists only in the report of random cases of child abuse, serial killing animal torture, etc. SRA, if it exists as alleged, simply hasn't been discovered yet.

The reason its existence, or nonexistence, has not been investigated is the prevailing climate of the judicial system. We simply don't know because those who might seek to prosecute its perpetrators are not interested. Decades went by before child sexual abuse was finally taken seriously. Now, immediate action is taken when it is established that a child has disappeared or that one is being abused. Professionals who deal with children are trained to spot physical and other evidences of it. At one time, however, doubt was the public's reaction and proof difficult to establish. The same can be said for the now-established sexual abuse by priests. Who could have dreamed at a time not so long ago that this would be revealed?

This is still not to prove the existence of SRA to any great extent. It may exist at two different levels: that which Karlyn experienced primarily, which would be associated with the production of pornography or prostitution in support of the drug trade, and that which is alleged to exist in a highly ritualized way, which she experienced at least once when she awakened during the ceremony and probably many more times that she would never recall.

There are many organizations around the country, including the FBI, that are gathering statistics about the highly organized kind and alleging the existence of many such cults, families and secret organizations. Often the damage of SRA is learned long afterward when individuals are finally able to break free and seek therapy. Again, there is little evidence and much guesswork. Hard facts are elusive, since the perpetrators are often accepted members in a community: doctors, health workers, teachers, etc., whom Karlyn alleged preyed upon her and her children.

It has also been said that certain biker groups have produced the most evidence of the existence of SRA. The police exploited Karlyn's brief search for her father among the Hell's Angels as a means to degrade her, knowing what the jury's reaction would be.

Returning, however, to the level of SRA when it occurs as part of a drug culture, it would seem that the purpose of the arrests, when they are made, are for drug possession, prostitution, or for the selling of pornography, if these physical evidences can be discovered. But there is little, if any, concern for the victims of this crime, unless they, also, can be arrested for possession or prostitution. What ought to be obvious, however, is that the purchase of drugs and the production of pornography are in many cases supported by the abuse of victims.

Why do police not go after the abusers? Because drugs, pornography, and solicitation for prostitution are concrete evidences. Victims of SRA are watched assiduously by its perpetrators, and if they are ever able to report their abuse, proof would be hard to find.

Karlyn was always told by her interrogators that she was kind of crazy. Even her trial lawyers and those who perused her story remarked to this writer that they thought so. Is it a kind of brotherhood, that refuses to look into this kind of crime? When eventually her defense sent investigators to Imperial Beach, with names from her by this time, they went, stupidly, and questioned those named, and it's not difficult to imagine what they were told. The fox guarding the henhouse is sure to implicate the hens!

One of the detectives told this writer at a break in Tiner's trial—when questioned how he could so lie to Karlyn about testifying for Grand Jury—that she had known Tiner for years and was not just a victim in what was going on down there. I had never heard anyone seriously question that she had known Tiner only a few weeks, however. Patrick Walsh could have been cross-examined to verify this, but he could probably have been suborned to say otherwise. Rick Lewis's tack was a new one to me, and I believe it was said just to frighten me away.

It would not take much imagination to perceive that those named do not get all of their money for drugs from petty thievery or from dealing with used cars and motorcycles. Most of them have been busted for one crime or another. But they gravitate right back to the Tecate area where they serve a function that allows them to maintain a public presence while conducting shady deals undercover. Their surface network would be hard to penetrate.

The fact that Karlyn did indeed know some of them and consider them her friends is no great discredit to her or proof of her involvement in any of their illegal activity. It seems she was always approached by that kind of person because of her basic trust. She is the kind of person who attracts attention, because of her loveliness, but she is also unaware. In all the serious encounters of her life she has been accepting, unquestioning, and unsuspecting of the deals that were made around her and of the traps that were being set for her. She could always remove herself from a situation if it didn't suit her, unless she didn't know she was in danger.

Then she became a victim, perhaps unknowingly at first, but then irretrievably. First she was a victim of her own stupidity, to allow first Distabile and Walsh and then Tiner to encroach upon her susceptibility to certain mind-altering drugs and hypnosis. She knew "something" was going on, but she allowed it. It says much about the self image she had as a result of her father's abuse that she would allow something improper to happen to her, if she were unaware of it, or could not be expected to be responsible for it.

It was when she knew too much and could, perhaps, *tell* about it that she became a target. She became a victim from the very hour of the murder. The frantic phone call she made to the Keiths after the chaos started would alone prove her lack of knowledge, lack of intent for the crime which followed. That John Distabile was there attempting to control James by ordering him to leave his own house, makes the teamwork all the more obvious. Then as he left the house she was made to feel as though she had overreacted by calling Keith's. John might not have known what would happen to James, but he knew what they were planning for her. Karlyn didn't.

It is apparent in the testimonies that were heard during Karlyn's trial how terribly Tiner used women who copped drugs for him. Karlyn was not in that category. She didn't even know for sure about his cocaine habit for a long time. She was preyed upon and victimized as a desirable sex object, to be drugged and violated, and not to know about it. Tiner prized her naivete. He kept her as a sex slave and she allowed herself that role because of the intense fear she had of him.

It can't be supposed that she didn't cooperate. Try to imagine her fear, however. The episode in Fresno, while at his brother's apartment, which described Tiner's meeting and "selling" her to an unknown individual in an alley, could not have happened without her cooperation. She was certainly not dragged, kicking and screaming, to that encounter. She remembered it well enough to tell about it. Therefore, out of fear, she at times "allowed" herself to be drugged, one has to believe. But she was deathly afraid of him. What else could she have done?

We return to the original statement alluded to in this chapter, that the

reason its existence (SRA), or nonexistence, has not caught the public's imagination yet is the prevailing climate of the judicial system. We simply don't
know because those who might seek to prosecute its perpetrators are not interested. They are not interested because there is no public outrage concerning
some hundreds of missing women who simply disappear. For every drug deal
that is made there is probably some woman who is violated for profit, either
willingly or unwillingly.

Law enforcement, including municipal forces and narcotics squads, are
not interested in the ways women are kept in control by mind-altering drugs
such as Rohyphenol and GHB where it pertains to pornography and supporting the drug traffic. Investigating such claims are about as popular with law
enforcement as rape in the military. The only time you hear about their use is
in connection with "date rape" in colleges and universities, where coeds seek
the right to come and go freely, without fear of being slipped a narcotic in
their cocktail and taken against their will. The fact that it happens more and
more, however, has led to the introduction in Oregon of House Bill 2353 out-
lawing the use of these drugs, promoted by Representative Vickie Walker, to
whom Karlyn sent the packet which ended up in her Post Conviction exhibits.

There is not a thought in the minds of those pursuing the drug traffic
that these mind-altering drugs might be connected to white slavery, coerced
prostitution, rape and murder. To them, possession of drugs and/or sale of
pornography are the crimes, not the satanic abuse of women whose bodies are
used to produce and support the crime. When they discover bodies, the killers
are long gone and in most cases the identities of the victims are unknown, so
how can they explain what happened? They never admit that it is a problem,
because there is no public outcry.

The level of satanic ritual abuse the thugs Karlyn knew were able to
stage was at best sporadic and disorganized. What she awoke to encounter
was so sadistic and amateurish that it seemed more to impress each other than
to carry out a committed ritual. However, the fact they knew so well how to do
it, and that some were so surprised that Karlyn, their friend, had been drawn
into it indicates they were no strangers to it.

It should not be hard to imagine that there are many takers for observing
such rituals, many going to place "football bets" for sports games, which is
the code, and many who will pay money to see women brutalized in some out-
of-the-way shanty. Certainly the films produced of the events have a market
and are probably the principal product.

In the case of Karlyn's abuse one should look well at the known character and criminal record of Tiner. His initial petty crimes were almost banal:
stealing six packages of meat stashed under his pants at the supermarket and

attacking the owner with a knife, possessing firearms and counterfeit money, and assault with a deadly weapon with great bodily injury, which occurred in 1987 for which he served time. He was in and out of prison on these lesser crimes, but he also allegedly killed a man while in Folsom whom he considered a child molester, which was the pattern of his crime in Oregon.

It is evident he had, in addition to the kinds of criminal propensity he displayed to support his cocaine habit, an insane preoccupation with the god Odin and the murder of child molesters. This was just the beginning. Karlyn's experiences of forced abuse with him were civil compared with the bestiality he described to the women he used to support his habit thereafter. Even in prison, when he was finally convicted, he would cause a social worker to burst into tears at the trap he had set for her to sell his "art" works.

Karlyn's only arrest record, in May 1990, was for assault, but it was determined both participants were to blame, that elements of a crime were not present, and she was released.

Unfortunately, it was her defense counsel itself which set her up for bringing in these "bad acts," by trying to characterize her as a somewhat hard, but naive woman in the opening argument. Of course, this was all deemed "harmless error" in the oral arguments of her appeals. For the prosecution it was an opening they had been looking for. It was essential to try to establish the allegation that, since there was no motive for her to murder her friend Salmu, she was the kind of woman who didn't need a motive for killing.

We know of her behavior in Eugene and Springfield when she was on her own turf. She did not allow drugs in her house, either from her son's friends when she discovered it, nor even from Jethro, except for the one "meth" celebration in her bedroom between James and Jethro the night the latter arrived.

It is also evident how quickly Jethro could tap into a network of big time drug dealers there in Eugene away from Karlyn's house, where she thought he was starting a tow business. In addition, his connections must have immediately converged with those of Al Hope, who turned out to be a child pornographer *par excellence*. Discovery now has it that he was considered a "participant" in the murder of Salmu as well as the suborned witness of the State in Karlyn's trial. This was not allowed into the appeals courts, because it was not known to her defense team at her trial.

Her defense team failed to raise objections to countless errors, innuendos and lies that were obvious, it is true. But how could they have known that the primary witnesses and reports of experts were rigged?

****

In Karlyn's descriptions of her ordeal in the netherworld of ritual abuse and white slavery, one is aware how few were her memories of scenes of debauchery she could actually describe. Because of her drug-induced state of mind, her memories of that period could not be revived with the same clarity that she revisited upon her experiences before the murder. Her memories are still sparse.

It was an ordeal wherein she was only sporadically in control of her situation. Even in her contacts with her family, there was much blame heaped upon her, because she couldn't seem to get herself together or explain lost episodes in her life. There were two very numbing experiences, the first, a six-week period when she tried to live with Jethro, subjecting herself to his using, selling and three times beating her, the last being the ritual abuse scene; and secondly, another six-week period almost lost to her ability to recall.

Her memories are still very spotty, and she concentrates on the general ways that she was kept in control. The specifics have all but vanished.

Jethro went out of his way to avoid any further complication following the murder, putting distance between himself and Springfield, Oregon, dragging her and her children through hell. He connected with associates all the way down the I-5 who specialized in pornography and white slavery.

More specifics have emerged about an episode on that trip previously referred to but briefly. Recalling it again adds to our understanding of how it was accomplished:

Somewhere down the I-5 freeway Tiner stopped the vehicle. A man standing outside the vehicle passed Tiner a Red 7/11 cup of Coke. It was passed around to all of us. We were thirsty from the drive.

Drugged and slipping into a sleepy state, I heard Tiner say to the man, "You will bring her back, won't you?"

The man said, "Well, if I don't, you know what to do with the children, don't you? You are a professional, aren't you?" Yeah man! Professional!

****

As indicated in a previous chapter, Karlyn would remember more details of the ritual abuse scene after she began to meet more and more characters who were involved in it. It was her most ghastly nightmare, except that it had been real. At one point, before her recent letter identifying additional elements, she wrote:

It was in October that I began to remember the details, the vague, fleeting bits of recollection, of the agony I went through during that session of ritual abuse, which happened June 12th, before the detectives finally arrived. When I was finally able to stop being moved around and to get my own apartment, I only stayed in the apartment six weeks before I just couldn't take the ongoing weird dangers that my children and I were still being subjected to. But I did finally meet some of those people who had been involved, and remembering their faces, I could finally put together more pictures of their ghastly ritual...

I have found a pattern that describes their awful mischief. These demented people tried to surround us in a disguise of friendship, while limiting our boundaries and suffocating our freedom. With their deceitfulness, they falsely represented themselves as friends, guardians and honorable characters...

They moved us around so ones that did know us wouldn't get close enough to see the ongoing horror we were unconsciously being put through. As it became easier to abuse my family, they came at a more constant rate. They filmed their cruel and unusual punishments done to us and to others.

As Karlyn summed up her position during the period just recounted above, she really wondered why she was so abandoned by the police and left to the devices of Jethro. In response to the police reports of their contacts with her at that time she wrote:

There should have been attempts to try to locate me and help me after those first months of being knocked around. After the ghastly beating and the police interviews with TJ and Sparky, you'd have thought the police might say something's not right here. She's afraid. She's abused. How can she come forward unless we can offer her some protection?

But that never occurred to them. They were relentlessly pursuing the wildest figment of Jethro's imagination as he bragged to his brother, his cousin, and all his companions in his relentless pursuit of heroin and the abuse of the women he used to get it for him. If he let up on me a little, it was because I was broken, controlled, and abused in turn by his cohorts. It was hard enough for him to collect a little from them now and then, and he had his other women to control who weren't obsessed with keeping three children safe and fed.

As long as he could use his network to inform him if I was starting to talk about the crime in Oregon , he'd leave me pretty much alone. He knew where my mind was at that time. He knew there wasn't much left up there to worry about. Besides, I couldn't cop heroin for him. I didn't even know about it for sure.

I had been his "angel baby" at one time, but he couldn't afford to have one. I was too smart now. If he couldn't use me in his operations and had to have me worry about my kids all the time, he'd have to find some less classy dames to run with. It wasn't hard. They just weren't as saleable for making porn or abuse films. What he liked though was one to run with and maybe a few more who would cop for him, so he could control all of them and whoever they were living with. Then he'd have plenty of places to stay, and plenty of deals to make that involved abusing women.

The police reports at this time were sparce. Some were held back and not submitted to public record, so that the detectives could plot how they might lure me in and fulfill Jethro's wildest imaginings about what the crime might have been at its bloodiest, goriest best, perhaps with me running all over the hillside planting arms and legs which had been hacked off the body of the missing deceased, in little graves, which is what Jethro told his friends in Reno he had done.

Hugi did not want to have it in the record that she was a suspect. He intended to have his team continue reeling her in, without the obligation to respect her rights to counsel.

When she tried to explain happenings she experienced in her apartment in La Mesa, however, there was still a lot of confusion in her thinking:

Can you imagine such things happening in today's world, destroying and damaging precious human lives? During our ordeal my children and I experienced many deceitful people, probing around every nook-and-cranny of our lives, eventually collecting enough history or involvement in our daily activities to gain control. I think back on people we came to rely upon, in our beaten and desperate condition, who seemed to befriend us but were actually delivering us over to the highest bidder.

Once again I will try to explain what happens to the mind of a victim who is subjected to this kind of enslavement.... If I could put a rational mind toward identifying my attackers and describing what was happening when I lost control, I would! But it is something that one isn't aware of after it starts to happen. The mind is lulled. If and when you recover from the experience, when you somehow come out the other end, you have no memory of the events that led to it...

So why didn't I walk away from it? Wouldn't my family even help? No they wouldn't. They still don't know! They'd have been furious if they had suspected, and I couldn't involve them without jeopardizing their safety. Even my own brother used these people against me!

A victim doesn't know who to trust, but can't afford not to act trusting. Chaos is usually stirred up around the victim in order to distract them so that they have no particular knowledge of what occurred. The nervous system and the mind are very fragile. Associates can break down a person to irreparable confusion, closing a mind permanently.

I unfortunately fell prey to this. My children and I needed help. All because I witnessed my friend and roommate's murder. Jethro, who has now been tried and convicted, tossed us into this!

In the above description that "chaos is usually stirred up" one is re-minded of the fight and police intervention at the home of Karlyn's new friends, Michael and Michelle, when the car she had arrived in was taken to retrieve someone from the police station. She was twelve hours without seeing her children or finding someone to help her get home. She found them with red blotches, covered with white salve, and crying out over the nameless fears that were induced in them.

Karlyn has sent me many clippings which suggest that scores of women are victims of ritual abuse and torture in the area where she was at that time. The families of these victims have no resources to investigate their disappear-ances, and the border police try to explain it as the result of drug wars, which doesn't explain anything.

The *Oregonian* reported on July 24, 2003 that Mexico was sending "300 federal agents to Ciudad Juarez to bolster a local police force that has proved incapable of halting a decade-old string of rapes and slayings of women in the border city... Some parents in the city of 1.4 million people, across the Rio Grande from El Paso, Texas, have stopped sending their daughters to school or work for fear of never seeing them again." Similarly, bodies are found, sometimes in mass graves, in the Tecate and Tijuana area and all along the border between.

One has to wonder why federal agents of the United States have not responded with a similar concern. Women disappear, and their bodies are found, but there appears to be little curiosity about the techniques of abduction that have allowed this to happen. These women were not dragged, kicking and screaming, for all the world to see either.

They were lured and enticed by friendly, ordinary-looking guys who asked them out for a drink. The pleasure of a few hours companionship, per-haps stolen from their ordinary lives, they never expected would be their last.

Chap XXXIII: She Came Forward

The first version of this book was ghostwritten for Karlyn, because I did not have the courage to sign my name to it. Kartlyn rejected it because it included so much of the early history her mother objected to. She also felt her confused narrative played right into the police version. The revisions have not avoided the truth as she presented it, but her story has paled in comparison to the corruption visited upon her by the prosecution.

When I went to a printer to have the first version of her book put into galley form, the printer's assistant, who handled the five copies for me, read it, or at least large parts of it. When he came to the chapter about her gradual victimization into white slavery and ritual abuse, he scribbled an editor's note for me.

He said: "Sometimes her narrative is confused or incoherent, but you've left it that way to accurately reflect her thinking at the time. So, it shall be clear to the reader by the time Karlyn is subjected to ten days of interrogation that due to whatever combination of abuse, drugs, coercion, and control, lack of education, she was clearly not mentally capable of giving a statement."

The prosecution never wanted to give anyone an inkling that such was the case. The investigator they sent to California to learn of any such activity, Debra Martin, came back ready to give testimony that there was indeed such activity in the locale she described and that Tiner had definitely been involved in it.

Kolego never called this investigator to the stand. He never questioned

Karlyn's son about Tiner's abuse, or brought forward the young woman who broke into tears at Grand Jury telling about her terror of him. Kolego presented no defense, even to counter the "bad act" witnesses against Karlyn. No one, it seems, wanted to let the jury know that Karlyn had called Walker and Lewis for help two weeks before they finally came, or that they witnessed her condition after the ritual beating and then left without looking into it.

The jury had no word of the ritual abuse or its possible effects until she was allowed seventeen and a half minutes to tell it, after they had already convicted her. Half of the jury wanted to change their vote, but Hugi reminded them they had already convicted her. The record of their change of heart is somewhere in a sealed envelope.

Through the years, Karlyn's way of telling her story does indeed change. Her background had been a lot gentler than her interrogators ever gave her credit for, notwithstanding her brother's unworthy behavior, and in certain ways she had not been able to stand up for herself. She never questioned her father's discipline and brutality, and when bad things happened to her she was remarkably vulnerable, malleable, and cooperative.

Each telling of her story, however, yields new truths. She is able to stand up for herself now and has gained many insights about things that happened to her. As her editor, I want to give a synopsis, to sum up the months following the murder, of her control by Tiner and his abuse ring before she first attempted to come back to Eugene to tell her story to the police.

Then I will let her tell again what happened in the San Francisco airport, a story expanded here, which gives some idea of her personal debasement and struggle. I also want to emphasize how difficult it was for her. Then she will tell in more detail the reactions of her friends when she showed up in Eugene.

****

After the missing person's report, in April 1993, the detectives walked through her house with the landlord and then took Eklof to the police station. She couldn't say anything. Tiner was holding her children. Then they returned her to the house and evicted her.

Tiner forced her to leave in the vehicle. If she didn't get in he would pull away with the children. Tiner drove down the I-5, making several stops trying to get rid of her, drugging her and the children with soda drinks, and selling her.

He pulled into his brother's apartment in Fresno, California. He told his brother Dave an exaggerated version of the murder designed to horrify and impress, also to implicate her so she would be dependent on him. Dave told Eklof she was in danger and that he would try to help them. They looked for an apartment for rent. Dave tried to encourage his brother to leave the Eklofs behind. But Tiner became angry and told everybody to get into the car. He drove them to Imperial Beach near the Tijuana border.

Salmu's family used Karlyn's phone bill in Springfield to lodge a witch hunt against her, accusing her of being a murderer. The police in their search for the missing person encountered a woman named Francis at the White Horse Tavern who called Karlyn a "biker bitch." It has been alleged by this woman's daughter that they paid her a large sum to arrange for her employer to tell an exaggerated story of Karlyn's bouncing customers while working there. The police then gave the story to the newspapers, starting a media blitz.

Tiner checked in with his parole officers in Imperial Beach, who cuffed him immediately and called Lane County. Tiner denied that he had even seen Eklof since his departure and had no idea of her whereabouts. But the police told Tiner that Eklof had been in contact with them and had told them what she had witnessed. This was an impossibility since she had been totally under his control.

He was released and returned to her and the three children. He was enraged by his dilemma and slapped her several times. Aware, however, of his next possible encounter with police, he wanted Karlyn's family to see her and her children alive. Therefore he drove them to her grandparents, borrowing $714 from them and stating that he planned to place the family into a rental and turn himself in... The story of his beating her and raping her baby has been told...

While at her grandparents, she had had a chance for the first time to call the Springfield P.D. for help. They told her they would be down right away...

There was a short while during this period that Tiner tried to make things up to her, posing as a doting boyfriend to her family and friends, telling them of his loving plans for the future. Knowing of the missing person's report, they said nothing so as not to arouse his anger. Karlyn went along, hoping the abuse would stop. But this was very short-lived. On the way back from a trip to Vegas with Val and Tony he began abusing her again. Loyalty was not a role he could long tolerate.

Soon he abandoned her and the children and was flaunting his relationship with another woman. This is when Jerry Smith called, taunting her about Tiner leaving her. When she finally acquired a car and began showing some independence, Tiner panicked, considering what she might do. It was soon thereafter that the ritual abuse scene occurred.

Two weeks from the time she called for help, the detectives came as she was arriving back from the hospital for injuries sustained in that beating. They began to interrogate her, but she was too battered, broken, and disoriented to say much.

The story has been told of Karlyn's struggle, between June and September, through three battered women's shelters and three friend's homes. When she finally got public assistance, an apartment, and the cast off her leg, she was still wearing bruises under each eye.

The attacks on herself and her children, however, using various types of ritual abuse from Tiner's ring, continued even in her secure apartment. Eklof thought she would lose her mind, from the anxiety, but also from the effects of the mind-control and drugging. Her children also were in danger. She was in La Mesa for another six weeks, and there are large blocks of time that she could never recall. After a particularly brutal assault on her children, she placed her personal belongings in the back of Bruce Lambert's vehicle, and after some visits with her mother and sister, was taken to the airport.

She was heading back to Eugene to get help, still imagining that Spider might be the one to protect her and vouch for her if she should come forward with the truth, but she had just enough money to get a flight to San Francisco. No matter, she would risk anything just to get out of the danger they were in. She arrived in San Francisco Friday the 13th of November, 1993 at 5:25 P. M.

When she first wrote of this episode in the small tablets she brought with her from Salt Lake City, she provided but a skeleton of the true scenario. Here is where the writer is glad to have Karlyn's help later in recalling exactly what happened. In third person, but in her own words the story unfolds:

She informed the security that she needed shelter for herself and her two children. He called around and found nothing for them and thereby escorted them to the upstairs nursery. It was the week before the Thanksgiving holidays and every shelter was full. Three very tired and frightened people slept on the floor of the San Francisco Airport nursery for the entire weekend.

Saturday Eklof called on the in-house phone to another agency asking the airlines if her original ticket could be used to forward her to Eugene, Oregon. No help was available, and no one brought her blankets. Saturday came and went. Some other flyers came in to change their children, and she told them that they were stuck there. Nobody had any suggestions.

On Sunday morning Eklof woke up on the cold hard floor with a bloody urine infection. She doubled over in pain, gathered up the property they had brought and started for the down stairs, unable to understand why she was ill. She called her grandparents who tried to comfort her. She also called a military commanding officer who told her that he couldn't help her because she was not of the military.

Eklof noticed that her daughter had on silver and purple hair ties she had never seen before. When asked what happened, where did she get them, the daughter said, the "black broom man" gave them to her when two men took her mother sleep walking into the other room.

On Monday Eklof sat in the airport restaurant, and a couple overheard her complaining of the pain she was in. They told her to get ahold of the San Francisco Police, not the airport security, because that is where her problem started.

She called in an alarm but also told an airport security person, a woman with a birthmark on her neck, that she had encountered an unusual situation that needed immediate attention. Understanding the situation completely, the woman said to two men standing by that this would be the last time she would cover for them. She handed Eklof a small pink pill to take.

Suddenly a call went out over the intercom that a woman and her children were found on the grounds, and several airport personnel officers came running. As they approached, the female officer turned them away, stating that the woman, meaning Eklof, had found some money on her and would be on her way.

One of her fellow officers standing by, apparently one of the culprits, prepared to escort Eklof and her very distraught children across the San Francisco airport to the Greyhound bus station. But Karlyn was not satisfied. She requested to speak to the administration, but was told no, that the administration would be furious. He said, "With 23 years being married and 17 years on the job, wouldn't you expect a guy to have a little fun?"

"No! I wouldn't," said Eklof. Then the airport escort bought breakfast for the Eklof family to carry on the bus and made sure they had enough for their tickets.

I don't know which hurts the most, the long version or the short version. There's no way to mask the degradation, the weary desperation, or the pain of her flight from her tormenters.

There is at least a certainty, corroborated by John Distabile and others, that she arrived with her two children in Eugene at 4:30 A. M. and was picked up by Dave Wilson who, I believe, allowed her to rest with them before taking them over to Distabiles. There she surprised both John and Patrick, who himself had just arrived back in Eugene by way of Greyhound.

Their shock and dismay, since they were the only ones she could think of in La Mesa to call for help, got her thinking. She really had no value to them or to anyone. All those pleasant but fleeting hours she had spent with them a year or so before meant something else to them. They were deathly afraid of her and what her awareness might mean. Until then they had all been victims of Jethro's crime to which their folly had led. But now? As she summarized that event:

Patrick was standing in the driveway of the garage, and his mouth fell open when he saw me getting out of the truck. Yeah, we were alive! This is the first time he had returned to Springfield since leaving on a plane with Dennis and me, clear back in March; he's the one who initiated the Imperial Beach setup, and the one Tiner thanked immensely for connecting him to me.

Fear consumed me as I came to the realization that it was these two men who had originally encroached on my family, with dishonest intentions.

What I couldn't figure out was whether these two guys actually ran parallel to the assortment of incidents that were performed against me and my children down there recently.

How could it all be connected, or was it just an unending set of unrelated incidents, like falling into a vortex? I could not get out from under the voluminous chain of events. People truly cannot be this careless with other peoples' lives. Or could they?

She began to get a different picture. Jethro was no longer an immediate threat, but they wanted no part of her. There was no sympathy for what she had suffered. The phones were unplugged. They monitored her every move. They warned her not to draw attention to the crime or to alert anyone to her whereabouts.

Distabile saw that Eklof was beginning to get close to the truth and decided to scoot them along. He and Walsh purchased more Greyhound tickets for them and persuaded her she should get as far away as possible for a while.

The tickets were all the way to Denver, but she and the children stepped off in Salt Lake City. She was too sick to travel further...

The detectives, after a full year, couldn't solve the missing person report and suspected murder. So they encouraged her to come forward as a witness. She solved the case in the first two hours of an interview which then became an interrogation, altering between harsh and friendly tactics, for ten hours a day and ultimately went on and on for nine more days.

Captain Jerry Smith said he couldn't allow a woman to just walk in and solve the case. It would be politically embarrassing. So they used tactics which deleted the truth.

At the end of the third day during interrogation, a video was used to capture the coerced confessions. Video was used again at the end of the sixth day, after eight or more hours of forcing Dave Tiner's version of the story on her, again after the seventh day, and also after the ninth day. The four videos were illegally produced, never with the consent of the witness, all to convict a woman who in good faith trusted the police officers. She was made to say only that she was "aware" that she was being photographed.

The petitioner asked if the captain knew hypnotics. The reason she asked this was because she noticed he used a tactic, that of doing to her exactly what the perpetrator of the crime had done to her. One officer answered that the captain did not know hypnotics. At that same moment the other officer standing by said, "Yes, he does. He just gave a seminar on it last Friday," confirming her suspicion.

Later, while they were alone, the police captain told Karlyn to lay back her head and close her eyes and repeat after him. The captain repeatedly told petitioner, "Just say you did it and we can take you back to your children. Come on, just cooperate, and we can both get out of here." Then he told her she would get a good night's sleep after this was over.

This is when she opened her eyes and saw the captain touching himself. Seeing that she saw him, he jumped up stating you'll not embarrass this department. You'll apologize to my officers for believing in you. Thereby she was made to submit an apology to the officer who was brought in. Again the officer told her everything would be all right...

She describes the phone call put through to Tiner at the Nevada State Prison the day she was indicted. He had been in a high speed chase and wrecked a vehicle, leaving behind a woman named Jamie whom he had just married, he said. Left with a broken neck, Jamie was taken to the hospital, and Tiner just ran off and left her there to die. He was taken into custody a day or so later.

Tiner, of all people, assured her that "she had done nothing wrong." **It was very clear on the tape that she had not been a coconspirator.** But just as important: he was the only one to tell her that these people questioning her were not her friends...

When I first knew her and until he was finally given the death penalty, she lived in fear that he would somehow walk and she alone would serve his sentence. And that is what almost happened.

Tiner's trial was stopped by the state on the day of jury selection, June 10, 1997. Tiner had the vast majority of Eklof statements excluded. Tiner kept discovering new evidence of State coercion of Eklof, plus prosecutorial and police misconduct. State kept fighting against supplementation of record with newly discovered evidence. Tiner then outright accused them of fraud upon the courts, after he filed this motion. Then the State voluntarily dismissed its own interlocutory appeal, never having filed an Opening Brief, rather than to answer to the allegations of misconduct raised in the dismissal motion.

The appellate court only denied this motion because it simply went to the merits, which would properly be argued on the defense Response Brief. The state took a 25 month delay, then dropped its appeal rather than deal with the issues raised in this motion. Documentation for the previous statements is given in the Notes For Counsel...

It is interesting that she says that Mr. Evans brought in the videos for her to view and to show her all that she had said. This was some nine months after they had been made, and she was many times made to say that she told the "truth" in them. Upon viewing them Eklof's head dropped to the table. She had no memory of saying the things that were there on the videotapes. Evans said he knew he could get her out of the bind she was in, but he refused to go against the good ol' boys.

There is an interesting statement she wrote recently in this regard which tallies with the "discoveries" of Tiner's defense team: Mr. Evans told her that Lane County refused to clear her because they had already taken it (the videos) to the Grand Jury. This, she states in the year 2000, was a *reversible error*, only revealed to her after years of sitting in prison. Information of this sort which Karlyn found in the prison library was what kept her going.

Aspects of the above were new to me. It was incredible, if true, and why wasn't it spotted by her appeals counsel? Even without that reversible error, however, her Motion to Dismiss was always available for her appeals.

As it is revealed in the "Notes for Counsel," there is a step-by-step delineation of highlights in the S.P.D. deception of Karlyn Eklof, 1) physical evidence debunks Eklof's statements after Salmu's body is found, 2) her involuntary confession is a goldmine of applicable case law, 3) the Grand Jury "witness" scam employed on Eklof is a clear demonstration of the kind of scam Smith has been known to employ, 4) a step-by-step of leniency offers to Eklof mirrors Eklof's situation at the time the videotapes were made, 5) the error of using Eklof's kids as pawns, 6) prior inconsistent statements of Eklof [in the videos] may have limited use on a post conviction appeal. However, Hugi may have played only the inculpatory tapes to the Grand Jury while withholding the prior exculpatory tapes, in which case he was concealing evidence of police coercion, effectively forcing Eklof to testify against herself, and 7) Hugi admits, as has been previously cited in this book, that Eklof's statements are "lies from beginning to end," yet, why did he knowingly present "evidence" he knew to be false? And, as previously noted, he brought in all the evidence to overwhelm the jury, then waited for the closing arguments to discount their validity. Well, Kolego was not up to it and agreed all along not to bring in witnesses or to lend any validity to Karlyn's story of abuse except to make a blanket objection.

"I cannot move a corrupt court," Kolego said. Contrary to the above analysis contained in the Notes for Counsel, Hugi expected this to happen and knew that, with a huge bit of smoke and mirrors, he had indeed overwhelmed the jury. They had no mind of their own. He was the educated, the sly, the corrupt destroyer of truth… they, the uneducated, the meek, the dutiful, the foolish.

The *reversible error* that Karlyn is referring to was one of the errors included in Tiner's Motion to Compel Production of Grand Jury-related Evidence. At the time the "Notes for Counsel" were written, the State had refused to respond. I believe that when I was there at the pretrial hearings I was witness to Jerry Smith on the stand being queried about Grand Jury transcripts and mysteriously missing police testimony. I remember his stating that he didn't think they were important. He was tall, dark, and repulsively devastating.

Hugi was there, also being queried. As previously indicated, he was asked to leave the stand for a short break and he went off to play basketball. The Court, therefore, had to adjourn until after the noon hour. When he came back he was all sweaty in his grey teeshirt, a smaller, tired-looking man. He crossed his legs and turned his side to the court, displaying as much contempt as he could show without being called for it. At the time I did not know he had stepped down from his position as DA and was being cited for prosecutorial misconduct.

A key *reversible error* in Karlyn's trial, according to the Notes for Counsel is whether the cops played the four videotapes to the Grand Jury? If so, they were not listed on the foot of her indictments, and were therefore not admissible at her trial ORS 132.580 (1) (2). As I believe I have stated elsewhere, In order to satisfy *due process* during Grand Jury proceedings, the State is required to present any evidence which objectively refutes facts as they appear from the State's evidence which is presented to the Grand Jury.

We know that Eklof's counsel was not willing to look at anything for her Post Conviction relief except Murdock's "ineffectiveness." We know that Beverly Penz was not open to input of any sort, but it becomes more and more evident that she was aware of all of the areas that could have been contested. My "improper submissions" were included as Exhibit 9, and the Exhibits are here described and abridged:

Petitioner's exhibits 1-8 were offered. Defendant objected to 1,2,3, & 4 on relevance, OEC 401. Exhibit 5, is in effect a Balfour brief (allowed as such and not as evidence), and exhibit 5 is defense 102 the transcripts. Exhibits 7 are video tapes [which I sent], and Exhibit 8 is a motion to dismiss re CA A 98343 . I allow exhibits 1-4, and take them to their weight. Separately, or as a whole, however, they fail to prove that any substance abuse problems that Mr. Murdock had affected the outcome of Petitioner•'s case, especially in light of the substantial evidence against her. Defense stated in its supplemental trial memorandum that exhibit 7 does not show any evidence of coercion and further states that defense counsel did object to the tapes on *Miranda* grounds (supported by petitioner's deposition). Defense also argues that exhibit 8 should be given no weight. [I believe this is Tiner's Motion to Dismiss which I sent which proves to the ultimate degree the coercion used in obtaining Karlyn's videotapes.] I allow exhibit 7 and 8 as to their weight which is little to benefit petitioner.

Subsequently by mail postmarked August 6, 2001, through the petitioner, petitioner submitted directly materials prepared by her, with a cover letter from an Erma Armstrong. I have marked them as Exhibit 9. I include them in the case file and give them no weight as they are not evidence and were not properly submitted.

My original submission, a letter to Judge Hill and a copy of one submitted to Beverly Penz urging an investigation into Hugi's suborned witnesses, was replaced by the cover letter for Karlyn's clippings on ritual abuse and the story she had written of her experience. They wanted no record that Ms. Penz was made aware of the suborned witnesses.

Her Post Conviction was, of course, denied. Her PC Appeals attorney, on reading the "Notes for Counsel" I provided, remanded her case back to Umatilla County. His Remand was denied, but nonetheless preserved for *habeas corpus*. His subsequent brief concentrates on the known Smith scams and the inordinate length of her sentence.

I was not allowed to make any sort of legitimate "submission." My attempts to affect her case, through her lawyers, were denied throughout.

****

I am backtracking here a bit, trying to connect the past with the present. Throughout the spring of 1999 I worked on her ghost-written book, organizing all the journals and documents so that everything would be taken into account. The accounts of her ordeal and trauma in the early chapters of this book, rewritten in third person, are based on that book, except for asides referring to the information I have now.

The events of the last several years have augmented her tale considerably, because of her appeals and the decision to make myself an active participant in her story. Every day I find new discoveries. I am able to bring together errors and lost opportunities of her defense and the neglect of her civil rights.

If only, "You'll get your appeals!" had any meaning when it was promised to her. I wonder if Walker and Lewis had any idea what they had done to her when they said that. It was like being headed toward a brick wall.

While writing this book, I called the Lane County Records in the citadel to ask once again if there were any on John Distabile, knowing that he was granted leniency from further investigation by testifying at Grand Jury and at Karlyn's trial. His perjury in quoting her as saying she had to "put him out of his misery," referring to Salmu, was critical in building up a picture of guilt for the jury.

The clerk there agreed that his name did appear in the files and that he was given a mug shot, but that he was never charged with anything. We concurred that evidently the leniency granted was that he would not be investigated for being at the scene of the crime, ever. Neither was he investigated for assisting in its cover-up.

Then this clerk volunteered that Karlyn was at the scene of the crime and that "they stabbed him." She said, "She confessed to that. There was never any question about it." It is as though it were chiselled in stone, the lies, the scenario that Hugi concocted and forced her to enact. The picture that sticks in the public mind, of justice-well-served, takes my breath away.

It destroys my confidence. As my book comes together I am aware of the irreversible aspect of what the clerk was feeling. Can there be any truth in the proverb: *The laws sometimes sleep, but never die?*

****

If, as it must seem, I have repeated too many times the actual dialogue from her interrogations, it is in response to the transpositions that Fred Hugi, Jerry Smith, and Tiner's "Court" subsequently made of it. Smith told the jury, "She said she stabbed him 30 to 50 times," and everyone, including her own counsel, Peter Gartlan, repeated it. Beverly Penz said that Eklof "repeatedly stabbed the victim," and Manning also repeated it, saying that it was her "buckknife," which she had used to clean her nails, instead of the flimsy, plastic-handled steak knife, she allegedly used to do the job.

Fred Hugi, summing up her trial for the Lane County records archives, filed a motion stating that "the ultimate outcome of Salmu's death was by the stabbing of Eklof, attempting to put him out of his misery."

And the judge in Tiner's "Court" deliberately misquoted from her transcript that she said, "I did the stabbing. He was doing the shooting."

If the lies of these public officials can be repeated with impunity, so can the actual dialogue of a sick and tormented girl, along with the goading solicitations of her tormenters.

Yes, the *laws sometimes sleep, but never die.* I believe in this Chinese proverb. When the agents for *federal habeas corpus* contact me, I will be ready, with boxes of documents neatly arranged to support her story, including those which sustain the Documents for Counsel. And they will! The manuscript for this book will serve as a guide to the treachery and tragedy of the injustice against her.

Karlyn came forward to tell her story. Through some miracle I have been there to help her. It has been a privilege, not a burden, since I have my health and all the gifts that God has bestowed on me. It is Karlyn who suffers.

Do I fear retribution? Not really. It is Karlyn's story. Let Hugi sue her for the culprits he shielded from inquiry in order to suborn their testimony against her.

Again I will quote Dietrich Bonhoeffer:

Civil courage can grow only out of the free responsibility of free men. It depends on a God who demands responsible action in a bold venture of faith, and who promises forgiveness and consolation to the man who becomes a sinner in that venture.

Epilogue

Two years ago, in August 2003, I took a manuscript copy of this book to the Willamette Writers Conference in Portland and gave my pitch to several publishing agents. The consensus of each was the same: it had no positive outcome, which was a liability; and it was a local story that required a regional small publisher. I had published several books under my own logo and could handle the latter aspect, but the positive outcome was beyond my control.

The encouragement that lifted my spirits and kept me going, however, came from Elizabeth Lyons, a major editor in the Northwest and a presenter at the Conference, who took my manuscript, edited part of it, and wrote the blurb which appears on the back of this now published book. Recently, also, I solicited and hoped for one from Gerry Spence, whose NYT best seller *Smoking Gun* mentioned the involvement in another case here in Oregon of the same state medical expert who had skewed forensic evidence in Karlyn's case. His kind response commending my commitment and yearning to get the truth out was a huge plus, though I quite understand his being too busy to accept and otherwise respond to my manuscript.

Patience is rewarded, however, I am happy to say. On January 19, 2005 I received a request from Tony Bornstein, *federal habeas corpus* investigator, requesting the input I had been volunteering in correspondence with Stephen T. Wax, head of the Federal Public Defenders Office in Portland.

On January 28, 2005, a rainy Friday, my husband and I negotiated parking in that city now so congested and unfamiliar to me, and I entered the federal building occupying a full city block off First Avenue near the river. In my one-hour appointment with Mr. Bornstein I was given the reassurance that my many years of effort, culminating in the Notes for Counsel and supporting documents, would be very valuable in reviewing Karlyn's case.

I left the packet of documents with him, with the promise that, although he could not duplicate them at that time as he had indicated he would in his e-mail, they would be safely guarded and returned to me. I also left a copy of my manuscript in two three-hole notebooks and assured him that I possessed all the other supporting documents and would turn them over to him and the other investigator who would be working with him on the case on request. I followed up with an e-mail affirming the offer, requesting a time the transfer might be accomplished. I have not heard from them since.

Now comes, however, the great light at the end of the tunnel: On May 8th, 2005 Tony Bornstein and the other federal investigator he told me I would be meeting spent the entire day with Karlyn at the prison in Wilsonville, questioning her about all aspects of the case and especially about the murder scene and her state of mind moment by moment.

They told her, emphatically, throughout the day, the message we have been waiting to hear: "We're going to get you home!"

"We're going to get you home!" This is our reward, the lovely answer to our prayers. This is the protection we have as Americans, the promise of our constitutional system, finally, at its fruition, that each case will be subject to an impartial review.

The investigators don't know how long it will take. Mr. Bornstein in January had told me perhaps six months. But they held out no time schedule for Karlyn except to review other cases which had taken as long as two to six years. They must carefully, legally, make their case. It is gratifying to me that I was of help, without any legal expertise at all, but only because I was persistent and believed in her.

Smile with me, reader, and wonder, as I do, why the federal investigators asked Karlyn that day, three months after my visit with Mr. Bornstein, how they could retrieve more documents supporting her case. How about her mother? How about locating Paya?

What about me? How many ways can I be available? Perhaps they didn't like my book. Perhaps they believe any further acknowledgment of my help would be seen as support for it. I don't have any answers and, again, it is a lonely world. Certainly a "legal read" as an editing tool would be too expensive for me. I haven't asked them to endorse what I have written, only that I be allowed to help in her defense as much as possible. It has been a lonely business, and I may have blundered. Again my "improper submissions" are not wanted.

I hope, I pray, that Karlyn will soon be safely home where she is badly needed to help her children, especially her daughter Caroline, who finally was able to visit Karlyn with my help in January this year, after more than ten years.

But will I be safe? Put all the truths together in one place, between the covers of a book, and they are explosive. The federal investigators will pick and choose what is required to free Karlyn, but they are not here to take on unnecessary elements of the whole corrupt justice system. They may not be prepared to acknowledge the totality of her story.

Well, now I'm telling it. I only hope the documents I left with the investigators are safe, and also the videotapes, which they were astonished to learn also belonged to me. I learned after Karlyn's visit with them that two of her former counselors are presently disbarred, Jeffrey Murdock, who gave the provocative summary of her life at her trial, and Beverly Penz, to whom I sent the videotapes.

Here is a young woman, who unknowingly submitted herself to a band of porn and ritual abuse traffickers, inappropriately and then irretrievably, who suffered greatly to come forward to describe that error and its consequences. She has shown remarkable resilience and devotion to the accuracy of her story, with all its horrors, which she has never allowed to be corrupted and modified to suit those who would reconstruct it to her disadvantage. But she is no criminal! In addition, she is beautiful, talented, and much loved by her family and those who know her.

I hope that with this book I can at least influence public opinion—and answer to the media blitz which cooperated with the prosecution—in preparation for the *federal habeas corpus* announcement. If I have erred, there is no help for it. The truth is here, but the whole truth may not be wanted.. If I am in trouble, perhaps you, the reader, will come to my rescue.

Quick Order Form

Fax orders: 503-623-0097. Send this form.
Telephone orders: Call 503-623-2466, leave message.
      Have your credit card ready.
e-mail orders: earmstrong@navicom.com
Postal orders: **Tanglewood Hill Press**, PMB 410,
      170 W. Ellendale, Suite 103, Dallas, OR 97338

****

Please send: I understand that I may return my order for a full refund—for any reason, no questions asked.
      Improper Submission: Records of a Wrongful Conviction
          by Erma Armstrong
No. of copies ___   Cost per copy $24.95   Total $ _____

Please send information on:
Other books _____   Speaking/Seminars _____

Name _____
Address _____
City _____ State ___ Zip _____
Telephone _____ e-mail _____

Sales tax: please add 7.75% for products shipped to California addresses.
Shipping by air:
U.S.: $3.00 for first book, $1.00 for each additional book

                                  $_____

Payment: Cheque _____ Credit card _____
           Visa _____ MasterCard _____